D0876445

# RAMAKRISHNA THE MAN-GODS AND THE UNIVERSAL GOSPEL OF VIVEKANANDA

## (A STUDY OF MYSTICISM AND ACTION IN LIVING INDIA)

## VOLUME II

# THE LIFE OF
# VIVEKANANDA
## AND THE
## UNIVERSAL GOSPEL

BY

## ROMAIN ROLLAND

Translated from the original French by

E. F. MALCOLM-SMITH, M.A., PH.D. (Cantab.)
*Late Research Fellow, Newnham College, Cambridge*

## ADVAITA ASHRAMA
5 DEHI ENTALLY ROAD
CALCUTTA 14

PUBLISHED BY
SWAMI CHIDATMANANDA
PRESIDENT, ADVAITA ASHRAMA
MAYAVATI, ALMORA, HIMALAYAS

*Sixth impression, February, 1965*
6M3C

SET AND PRINTED IN INDIA
IN 11 ON 12 PT. BASKERVILLE TYPE
BY P. K. GHOSH AT THE EASTEND PRINTERS
3 DR SURESH SARKAR ROAD, CALCUTTA 14

## PUBLISHER'S NOTE

We would like to remind the readers of the present volume that it was, like its predecessor (*The Life of Ramakrishna*), primarily written for the Western readers, and that the views and interpretations given in it are not all of them necessarily those of the Ramakrishna Order. We should also mention that we have omitted a few footnotes as unnecessary, and also a chapter ("The Awakening of India after Vivekananda") which was written specially for the Western readers, and have added a few footnotes of our own—all at the wish and with the approval of M. Romain Rolland.

15th April, 1931                                    PUBLISHER

## PUBLISHER'S NOTE TO THE
## FOURTH IMPRESSION

It is over twenty-two years since the first edition of this volume was published. During these years the activities of the Ramakrishna Math and Mission have considerably expanded, and some new centres have come into existence, both in and outside India. As such, some of the facts mentioned in Note I, entitled "The Ramakrishna Math and Mission", appended to this volume by the learned author will have to be altered in the light of the latest General Report of the Organisation published from its Headquarters, Belur Math,

Dist. Howrah. Of the magazines referred to in our note on page 324 (322 of fifth edition), *The Morning Star* has ceased to exist and *The Message of the East* does not belong to the Organisation, since the Ananda Ashrama. is no longer part of it.

15th November, 1953                          PUBLISHER

# CONTENTS

## PART I

## THE LIFE OF VIVEKANANDA

viii

# PART I

# THE LIFE OF VIVEKANANDA

"NEVER FORGET THE GLORY OF HUMAN NATURE ! WE ARE THE GREATEST GOD.... CHRISTS AND BUDDHAS ARE BUT WAVES ON THE BOUNDLESS OCEAN WHICH *I AM*."

*Vivekananda in America*, 1895.

Colombo, January 1897

# PRELUDE

THE great disciple whose task it was to take up the spiritual heritage of Ramakrishna and disseminate the grain of his thought throughout the world, was both physically and morally his direct antithesis.

The Seraphic Master had spent his whole life at the feet of the Divine Beloved, the Mother—the Living God. He had been dedicated to Her from infancy; before he had attained self-consciousness he had the consciousness that he loved Her. And although, in order to rejoin Her, he had been condemned to years of torment, that was only after the manner of a knight-errant, the sole object of whose trials was to make him worthy of the object of his chaste and religious love. She alone was at the end of all the interlacing paths in the forest —She alone, the multiple God, among the thousands of faces. And when he had reached Her, he found that he had learnt to recognise all those other faces and to love them in Her, so that with Her he embraced the whole world. The rest of his life had been spent in the serene fullness of this cosmic Joy, whose revelation Beethoven and Schiller have sung for the West.[1]

But he had realised it more fully than our tragic heroes. Joy appeared to Beethoven only as a gleam of blue through the chaos of conflicting clouds, while the Paramahamsa—the Indian swan—rested his great white wings on the sapphire lake of eternity beyond the veil of tumultuous days.

[1] Reference to Beethoven's Ninth (Choral) Symphony, which ends with a setting of Schiller's Ode to Joy.—*Translator*.

It was not given to his proudest disciples to emulate him. The greatest of them, the spirit with the widest wings—Vivekananda—could only attain his heights by sudden flights amid tempests, which remind me over and over again of Beethoven. Even in moments of rest upon its bosom the sails of his ship were filled with every wind that blew. Earthly cries, the sufferings of the ages, fluttered round him like a flight of famished gulls. The passions of strength (never of weakness) were striving within his lion's heart. He was energy personified, and action was his message to men. For him, as for Beethoven, it was the root of all the virtues. He went so far in his aversion to passivity, whose secular yoke weighs so heavily on the patient bovine brow of the East, as to say, "Above all, be strong, be manly! I have a respect even for one who is wicked, so long as he is manly and strong; for his strength will make him some day give up his wickedness, or even give up all work for selfish ends, and will then eventually bring him into the Truth."[1]

His athletic form was the opposite of the fragile and tender, yet wiry body of Ramakrishna. He was tall (five feet, eight and a half inches),[2] square-shouldered, broad-chested, stout, rather heavily built; his arms were muscular and trained to all kinds of sports. He had an olive complexion, a full face, vast forehead, strong jaw,[3] a pair of magnificent eyes, large, dark, and rather

[1] 1891, to his Alwar disciples in Rajputana.
[2] He weighed 170 pounds. In the *Phrenological Journal of New York* (reproduced in Volume II of *The Life of the Swami Vivekananda*) the exact measurements may be found that were taken at the time of his first journey to America.
[3] His jaw was more Tartar than Hindu. Vivekananda, boasted of his Tartar ancestors, and he loved to say that "the Tartar is the wine of the race."

prominent, with heavy lids, whose shape recalled the classic comparison to a lotus petal. Nothing escaped the magic of his glance, capable equally of embracing in its irresistible charm, or of sparkling with wit, irony, or kindness, of losing itself in ecstasy, or of plunging imperiously to the very depths of consciousness and of withering with its fury. But his pre-eminent characteristic was kingliness. He was a born king and nobody ever came near him either in India or America without paying homage to his majesty.

When this quite unknown young man of thirty appeared in Chicago at the inaugural meeting of the Parliament of Religions, opened in September 1893, by Cardinal Gibbons, all his fellow-members were forgotten in his commanding presence. His strength and beauty, the grace and dignity of his bearing, the dark light of his eyes, his imposing appearance, and from the moment he began to speak, the splendid music of his rich deep[1] voice enthralled the vast audience of American Anglo-Saxons, previously prejudiced against him on account of his colour. The thought of this warrior prophet[2] of India left a deep mark upon the United States.[3]

It was impossible to imagine him in the second place. Wherever he went he was the first. Even his master

---

[1] He had a beautiful voice like a violoncello (so Miss Josephine MacLeod told me), grave without violent contrasts, but with deep vibrations that filled both hall and hearts. Once his audience was held, he could make it sink to an intense *piano* piercing his hearers to the soul. Emma Calvé, who knew him, described it as "an admirable baritone, having the vibrations of a Chinese gong."

[2] He belonged to the Kayastha class, a sub-caste of warriors.

[3] The Ramakrishna Mission, after its introduction by him, spread rapidly, and he found among Americans several of his most devoted disciples.

Ramakrishna, in a vision which I have related,[1] represented himself with regard to his beloved disciple as a
child beside a great Rishi. It was in vain that Vivekananda refused to accept such homage, judging himself
severely and humiliating himself—everybody recognised in him at sight the leader, the anointed of God,
the man marked with the stamp of the power to
command. A traveller who crossed his path in the
Himalayas without knowing who he was, stopped in
amazement, and cried, "Shiva!..."[2]

It was as if his chosen God had imprinted His name
upon his forehead.

But this same forehead was weather-beaten like a
crag by the four winds of the spirit. He very rarely
realised the calm air, the limpid spaces of thought
whereupon Ramakrishna's smile hovered. His super-
powerful body[3] and too vast brain were the predestined
battlefield for all the shocks of his storm-tossed soul.
The present and the past, the East and the West, dream
and action, struggled for supremacy. He knew and
could achieve too much to be able to establish harmony
by renouncing one part of his nature or one part of
the truth. The synthesis of his great opposing forces
took years of struggle, consuming his courage and his
very life. Battle and life for him were synonymous.[4]
And his days were numbered. Sixteen years passed
between Ramakrishna's death and that of his great

[1] *Cf.* Vol. I, pp. 250-251.

[2] Related by Dhan Gopal Mukerji.

[3] Although marred very early by the first attacks of diabetes, the
poison from which he died. This Hercules had death always sitting
by his side.

[4] Did he not define life as "the tendency of the unfolding and development of a being under circumstances tending to press it down"?
(April, 1891: Interview with the Maharaja of Khetri.)

disciple...years of conflagration....He was less than forty years of age when the athlete lay stretched upon the pyre....

But the flame of that pyre is still alight today. From his ashes, like those of the Phoenix of old, has sprung anew the conscience of India—the magic bird—faith in her unity and in the Great Message, brooded over from Vedic times by the dreaming spirit of his ancient race—the message for which it must render account to the rest of mankind.

# I

## THE PARIVRAJAKA

### The Call of the Earth to the Wandering Soul

AFTER Christmas Night, 1886, described in my preceding volume—the mystic vigil of Antpore where the New Communion of Apostles was founded amid tears of love in memory of the lost Master—many months and years elapsed before the work was begun that translated Ramakrishna's thought into living action.

There was the bridge to be built, and they could not at first make up their minds to build it. The only one with the necessary energy and constructive genius—Naren[1]—hesitated himself. He, even more uncertain

[1] I would remind the reader that his real name was Narendranath Dutt. He did not adopt the name of Vivekananda until the moment of his departure for America in 1893.

I have consulted the Ramakrishna Mission on this subject. Swami Ashokananda has been good enough to put at my disposal all the results of a profound research. According to the decisive witness of one of Vivekananda's most important monastic disciples, the Swami Shuddhananda, the present Secretary of the Ramakrishna Mission, Ramakrishna always used his name Narendra, or more shortly, Naren. Although he had made Sannyasins of certain of his disciples, it was never according to the usual forms and he never gave them monastic names. He had indeed given Naren the cognomen of *Kamalâksha* (lotus-eyed), but Naren dropped it immediately. During his first journeys in India he appeared under different names, in order to conceal his identity. Sometimes he was the Swami Vividishananda, sometimes Satchidananda. Again on the eve of his departure for America, when he went to ask Colonel Olcott, then President of the Theosophical Society, for letters of introduction to America, it was under the name of Satchidananda that Colonel Olcott knew him, and, instead of recommending him to his friends in America, warned them against him. It was his great friend, the Maharaja of Khetri, who suggested the name Vivekananda to him when he was about to go to America. The choice of the name was inspired by an allusion to the "power

than them all, was torn between dream and action.
Before he raised the arch that was to span the two
banks, it was necessary for him to know and to explore
the *other bank*—the real world of India and the present
day. But nothing as yet was clear: his coming mission
burnt dimly in the feverish heart of this young man of
destiny, whose years only numbered twenty-three. The
task was so heavy, so vast, so complex! How could it
be accomplished even in spirit? And when and where
was it to be begun? In anguish he put off the decisive
movement. But was he able to prevent its impassioned
discussion in the secret depths of his mind? It pursued
him every night from his adolescence, not consciously
but subconsciously, through the ardent and conflicting
instincts of his nature, with its conflicting Desires—
the Desire to have, to conquer, to dominate the earth,
the Desire to renounce all earthly things in order to
possess God.[1]

The struggle was constantly renewed throughout his
life. This warrior and conqueror wanted to have everything, both God and the world—to dominate everything—to renounce everything. The superfluity of
powers striving within his Roman athlete body and
*imperator* brain contended for mastery. But this very
excess of force made it impossible for him to confine his
torrential water within any bed save that of the river
of God—and complete self-surrender to the Unity. How
was this contest between pride and imperious love,

of discrimination" possessed by the Swami. Naren accepted it, perhaps
provisionally, but he could never have changed it, even if he had
wanted to; for within a few months it had acquired an Indo-American
celebrity.

[1] *Cf.* the story told by Naren of his spiritual conflicts in our first
volume, p. 260.

between his two great Desires, rival and sovereign brothers, to be decided?

There was a third element, which Naren himself had not foreseen, but which the prophetic eye of Rama- krishna had discerned from afar. At the time when the others were showing anxiety of mistrust with regard to this young man, in whom such tumultuous forces were at work, the Master had declared:

"The day when Naren comes in contact with suffer- ing and misery the pride of his character will melt into a mood of infinite compassion. His strong faith in him- self will be an instrument to re-establish in discouraged souls the confidence and faith they have lost. And the freedom of his conduct, based on mighty self-mastery, will shine brightly in the eyes of others, as a manifesta- tion of the true liberty of the Ego."[1]

This meeting with suffering and human misery—not only vague and general—but definite misery, misery close at hand, the misery of his people, the misery of India—was to be the flint upon the steel, whence a spark would fly to set the whole soul on fire. And with this as its foundation-stone, pride, ambition, and love, faith, science, and action, all his powers and all his desires were thrown into the mission of human service and united into one single flame: "A religion which will give us faith in ourselves, a national self-respect, and the power to feed and educate the poor and relieve the misery around me....If you want to find God serve man!"[2]

But this consciousness of his mission only came and

[1] That is to say the one Divine Being. (Quoted from the work of Saradananda: *Divya Bhâva*).

[2] *The Life of the Swami Vivekananda*, Vol. II, Chapter LXXIII. Conversations before 1893.

took possession of him after years of direct experience,
wherein he saw with his own eyes and touched with his
own hands the miserable and glorious body of humanity
—his mother India in all her tragic nakedness.

We shall accompany him throughout the pilgrimage
of his *Wanderjahre*.[1]

*

The first months, the first year at Baranagore, were
devoted to the mutual edification of the disciples. As
yet not one of them was prepared to preach to men.
They desired to concentrate on the search for mystic
realisation; and the delights of the inner life made them
turn away their eyes from outside. Naren, who shared
their longing for the Infinite, but who realised how
dangerous for the passive soul was this elementary
attraction, which acts like gravity on a falling stone—
Naren, with whom dream itself was action—would not
allow them to be torpidly engulfed in meditation. He
made this period of conventual seclusion a hive of laborious education, a High School of the spirit. The superiority of his genius and his knowledge had from the
first given him a tacit but definite guidance over his
companions, although many of them were older than
he. Had not the last words of the Master, when he took
leave of them, been to Naren: "Take care of these
boys!"[2]

*N. B.* The Life of Vivekananda, to which I shall constantly refer
in the course of this book, is the classic work in India in four volumes
published by the Advaita Ashrama of Mayavati, under the title of
*The Life of the Swami Vivekananda, by his Eastern and Western Disciples*,
1914-1918. (Now compressed into one volume—*Publisher*.)
[1] This, as is well known, is the title of a book by Goethe, *The Wander-
years of Wilhelm Meister*...(*Wanderjahre* literally means *Wander-years*.
—*Translator*.)
[2] Memoirs of the Disciple Ramakrishnananda of the last moments

Naren resolutely undertook the conduct of the young seminary, and did not permit it to indulge in the idleness of God. He kept its members ever on the alert, he harried their minds without pity; he read them the great books of human thought, he explained to them the evolution of the universal mind, he forced them to dry and impassioned discussion of all the great philosophical and religious problems, he led them indefatigably towards the wide horizons of boundless Truth, which surpass all the limits of schools and races, and embrace and unify all particular truths.[1] This synthesis of spirit achieved the promise of Ramakrishna's message of love. The unseen Master presided over their meetings. They were able to place their intellectual labours at the service of his universal heart.

But it is not in the nature of the religious Indian, notwithstanding Europe's belief in Asiatic immobility, to remain, like a French bourgeois, shut up in one place. Even those who practise contemplation, have in their

of Ramakrishna, published in *The Message of the East* in the United States. (See the last chapter of the preceding volume.)

[1] In this panorama of all the heroic and divine thoughts of humanity, we must again notice the place of honour which seems to have been given to Christ and the Gospels. These Hindu monks kept Good Friday, and they sang the Canticles of St. Francis. Naren spoke to them of the Christian saints, the founders of the Western Orders. *The Imitation of Jesus Christ* was their bedside book together with the Bhagavad-Gita.    Nevertheless there was never for a moment any question of enrolling themselves with the Church of Christ. They were and remained complete and uncompromising Vedantic Advaitists. But they incorporated in their faith all the faiths of the world. The waters of Jordan mingled with their Ganga. If any Westerner waxes indignant at the abuse he sees in this connection, we would ask him whether the mingling of the waters of the Tibur with the river of Palestine is any better. [It must be clearly understood that though the disciples of the Master had a great veneration for the Christ, he for them was always *one* of the many prophets and Incarnations, and at no time did he predominate in their thought over the great Hindu Incarnations.—*Publisher.*]

blood the secular instinct of wandering through the universe without fixed abode, without ties, independent and strangers wherever they go. This tendency to become a wandering monk, known in Hindu religious life by the special name of Parivrajaka, soon spurred some of the brethren of Baranagore. From the moment of union the whole group had never assembled in its entirety. Two of its chiefs, Yogananda and Latu,* were not present at the Christmas consecration of 1886. Others followed Ramakrishna's widow to Vrindaban. Others, like the young Sarada, suddenly disappeared, without saying where they were going. Naren, in spite of his anxiety to maintain the ties uniting the brotherhood, was himself tormented with the same desire to escape. How could this migratory need of the soul, this longing to lose itself in the Ocean of the air, like a carrier-pigeon that stifles beneath the roof of the dovecote, be reconciled to the necessary fixity of a nascent Order? It was arranged that a portion at least of the group should always remain at Baranagore, while the other brethren followed the "Call of the Forest". And one of them—one only, Shashi, never quitted the hearth. He was the faithful guardian of the Math, the immobile axis, the coping-stone of the dovecote, whereto the vagabond wings returned.[1]

Naren resisted the call to flight for two years. Apart

---

* Rakhal, Hari, and some others also were absent.—*Publisher*.

[1] I have said above that Ramakrishna the free, differing in this respect from other Gurus, had not in the case of his disciples carried out the ceremony of initiation in its usual forms. (This was later a subject of reproach to Vivekananda.) Naren and his companions supplemented it themselves about 1888 or 1889 by proceeding to the Viraja Homa, the traditional ceremony of Sannyasa, at the monastery of Baranagore. Swami Ashokananda has also told me that another kind of Sannyasa is recognised in India, as superior to the formal Sannyasa consecrated

from short visits he remained at Baranagore until 1888. Then he left suddenly, not at first alone, but with one companion, and intense though his desire to escape, for two and a half years he always returned if he was recalled by his brethren or by some unforeseen event. Then he was seized by the sacred madness to escape; the longing suppressed for five years burst all bounds. In 1891, alone, without a companion, without a name, staff and bowl in hand, as an unknown beggar, he was swallowed up for years in the immensity of India.

But a hidden logic directed his distracted course. The immortal words: "Thou wouldst not have looked for Me, if thou hadst not found Me"[1] were never so true as for those souls possessed by the hidden God, who struggle with Him in order to drag from Him the secret of the mission with which they are charged.

Naren had no doubt that a mission awaited him: his power, his genius spoke within him; and the fever of the age, the misery of the time, and the mute appeal rising all around him from oppressed India, the tragic contrast between the august grandeur of her ancient might and her unfulfilled destiny and the degradation of the country betrayed by her children, an anguish of death and resurrection, of despair and love, devoured his heart. But what was his mission to be? Who was to dictate it to him? The holy Master was dead without having defined it for him. And among the living was any[2] capable of enlightening his path? God alone. Let

in the usual way. He who feels a strong detachment from life and an intense thirst for God, can take the Sannyasa alone, even without any formal initiation. This was doubtless the case with the free monks of Baranagore.

[1] Pascal.

[2] There was only one—a holy man, revered by the wisest in India,

Him then speak. Why was He silent? Why did He refuse to answer?

Naren went to find Him.

He suddenly left Calcutta in 1888 and went through Varanasi, Ayodhya, Lucknow, Agra, Vrindaban, Hathras, and the Himalayas. Nothing is known of this journey or of the subsequent ones—Naren kept the secret of his religious experiences—except from the memoirs of the brethren who met him or accompanied him.[1] In 1888, during the first of these pilgrimages after he had left Vrindaban, at Hathras, a small

Pavhari Baba of Ghazipur. This great hermit, born of Brahmin parents near Varanasi, and very learned, knowing many Indian religions and philosophies, the Dravidian languages and ancient Bengali, who had travelled in many provinces, had retired into solitude and prac- tised the strictest asceticism. The tranquillity of his intrepid soul, his heroic humility, which had taught him to look the most terrible real- ities in the face with a calm smile, and which made him say in the midst of cruel sufferings caused by the bite of a cobra that "it (cobra) was a messenger from his Beloved"—fascinated the highest minds of India. He had been visited by Keshab Chandra Sen; and even dur- ing the lifetime of Ramakrishna, Vivekananda had been to him.* (Pavhari recognised Ramakrishna's sanctity.) Naren saw him again during the period of uncertainty following Ramakrishna's death; he visited him daily and was on the verge of becoming his follower and demanding initiation of him. This torment of soul lasted several weeks; he was torn between the two mystic appeals of Ramakrishna and Pavhari Baba. The latter would have satisfied his passion for the Divine gulf, wherein the individual soul renounces itself and is entirely absorbed without any thought of return. And he would have appeased the remorse, always gnawing at Naren's heart, for turning from the world and social service: for he professed the faith that the spirit can help others even without the help of the body, and that the most intense action is that of the most intense concentration. What religious spirit has not heard this voice with its deadly attraction? Naren was for twenty-one days within an ace of yielding. But for twenty-one nights the vision of Ramakrishna came to draw him back. Finally after an inner struggle of the utmost intensity, whose vicissi- tudes he always consistently refused to reveal, he made his choice for ever. He chose the service of God in man.

* This is not confirmed by any other biography.—*Publisher*.

[1] Saradananda, Brahmananda, Premananda, Yogananda, Turiya- nanda, especially Akhandananda, who was with him the longest.

railway station he quite unintentionally made his first*
disciple—a man one minute a complete stranger, the
next impelled by the attraction of his glance to leave
all and follow him, and who remained faithful unto
death: Sharat Chandra Gupta (who took the name of
Sadananda).[1] They went about in the guise of beggars,
often repulsed, at times almost dying of hunger and

* Subsequent research reveals that he was not the first but one of
the earliest disciples.—*Publisher.*

[1] In her unpublished Memoirs which have been shown to me, Sister
Christine, Vivekananda's great American disciple, has left a precious
account of this episode and the attractive personality of Sadananda,
gleaned from Vivekananda's confidences to her.

Sadananda was the young station-master of Hathras. He saw Naren
arrive at the station dying of hunger. He was captivated by his glance.
"I followed two diabolical eyes," he said later. He made him come
into his house, and when his guest departed, he followed him—for life.

Both young men were artists and poets. But, unlike his master,
with Sadananda the intellect held a secondary place, although he was
well educated (he had studied Persian and been influenced by Sufism).
Like him he had a very vivid sense of beauty and enjoyed the delights
of Nature and of the countryside. None remained more devoted to
Vivekananda. He was impregnated with the being of the Master;
he had only to close his eyes, to meditate on his features and gestures,
to be immediately filled with the profundities of his thought. Vivekananda described him as "the child of my spirit."...He cared
for the lepers; worshipping them as God; for the whole of one night
he held a man burning with smallpox against his body to refresh his
fever. He was one of the first of the Mission to organise a corps of
scavengers during the plague. He loved the untouchables and shared
their life. He was adored by young people. During his last illness
a devoted band who called themselves Sadananda's dogs, watched
over him with passionate devotion. He did not allow the usual relations of disciples and Guru to be established between them; he was
their companion. "I can only do one thing for you," he said to them,
"That is to take you to the Swamiji." Although he could at times
be severe, he was always bubbling over with joy—as his chosen name
shows—and he transmitted this joy to them. They ever held him in
loving memory.

My readers will pardon this long note, which breaks the thread of
the narrative to a certain extent. The preservation for pious hearts
of the West of this "little flower" of India, whose culling we owe to
Sister Christine, full as it is of Franciscan grace, seemed to me more
important than the exigencies of literary composition.

thirst, with no regard for caste and willing to smoke even the pipe of the pariah. Sadananda fell ill, and Naren carried him on his shoulders through dangerous jungles. Then he in turn fell ill and they were obliged to return to Calcutta.

This very first journey had brought ancient India vividly before his eyes, eternal India, the India of the Vedas, with its race of heroes and gods, clothed in the glory of legend and history, Aryans, Moguls and Dravidians—all one.[1] At the first impact he realised the spiritual unity of India and Asia, and he communicated this discovery to the brethren of Baranagore.

From his second journey in 1889 to Ghazipur, he seems to have brought back some intuition of the Gospel of Humanity, which the new democracies of the West were writing unconsciously and blindly. He told his brethren how in the West the ancient ideal of divine right, which had formerly been the appanage of one single being, had gradually been recognised as the property of all without distinction of class, and that the human spirit had thus come to a perception of the divinity of Nature and of Unity. He saw and immediately proclaimed the necessity of introducing into India the same ideas which had been tried by America and Europe with such happy results. Thus from the first he exhibited that freedom and greatness of spirit, that seeks and desires the common good, the spiritual progress of all men by the united efforts of all men.

The short journeys that followed in 1889 and 1890 to Allahabad and Ghazipur still further enlightened this

[1] The revelation of Mogul grandeur at Agra reduced him to tears. At Ayodhya he re-lived the story of the Ramayana, and at Vrindaban the childhood of Krishna. In the retreats of the Himalayas he meditated on the Vedas.

2

universal conception. During his interviews at Ghazipur he can be seen travelling towards the synthesis of Hindu faith and modern science, of the ideas of the Vedanta and the social realisations of the present day, of the pure Spirit and the innumerable gods which are the "lower ideas" of all religions, and which are necessary for human weakness—for they are all true in their quality of phantoms of knowledge—of the various methods and diverse stages in the development of the human spirit, which climbs slowly towards the summit of its being.

These were as yet nothing but flashes, rough sketches of his future. But they were all being stored up and fermenting in his brain. A prodigious force was rising in this young man within the narrow bounds of his monastery at Baranagore, of the daily round prescribed by duty and even of communion with his friends. It could no longer be contained! He was driven to break the ties that bound him, to cast off his chains, his way of life, his name, his body—all that was Naren—and to remake with the help of different ones another self wherein the giant which had grown up could breathe freely—to be born again. This rebirth was to be Vivekananda. He was like a Gargantua rending asunder the swathing bands that were throttling him . . . . It can no longer be described as the religious Call of the pilgrim, who bids farewell to his brother-men in order to follow God! This young athlete, reduced to death's door by his unused powers, was driven forth by a vital instinct and betrayed into the brutal speech over which his pious desciples have drawn a veil. He said at Varanasi, "I am going away; but I shall never come back until I can burst on society like a bomb, and make it follow me like a dog."

We know how he himself vanquished these redoubtable demons, and turned them to the service of the
humble in supreme humility, but we nevertheless rejoice at the contemplation of the savage forces of pride
and ambition which suffocated him. For he suffered
from that excess of power which insists on domination
and within him there was a Napoleon.

He accordingly broke loose at the beginning of July,
1890, this time for years, from the dear home of Baranagore, which he had founded, from the spiritual nest
whereon Ramakrishna himself was brooding. His wings
swept him away. He went first to ask for the blessing
of the "Holy Mother" (Ramakrishna's widow) for his
long journey. He desired to cut himself free from all
ties and to go into retreat in the Himalayas. But of
all good things solitude (the treasure! and terror of
gregarious souls!) is the most difficult to achieve.
Parents, friends, all would deny it. (Tolstoy knew this
and could never attain it until the deathbed of Asta-
povo ....) Social life makes a thousand claims on
those who flee it. And how much more when the fugi-
tive is still a young prisoner! Naren discovered this to
his cost. And also at the cost of those who loved him!
His brother-monks were bent upon following him. He
was obliged to break with them almost brutally.[1] Even
so the tragic world would not allow him to forget it.
The death of a sister found him in his solitude. The
pitiful victim of a cruel society, she reminded him of

[1]Akhandananda accompanied him to the Himalayas; there he fell
ill. At Almora Naren found Saradananda and Kripananda. A little
later Turiyananda. They attached themselves to him. He left them
at Meerut near the end of January, 1891; their anxious affection
followed him to Delhi. His anger was kindled and he ordered them
to leave him.

the sacrificial fate of the Hindu woman and the sad
problems of the life of his people, which made it crimi-
nal for him to remain a disinterested spectator. By a
chain of circumstances, which might be accounted fore-
ordained, he was constantly torn from his *"Beata Soli-
tudo, Sola Beatitudo"*[1] at the very moment when he
thought that he had at last attained it, and thrown
back from the silent Himalayas to the plains filled with
the noise and dust of mankind. As a result of these
mental agitations, added to fatigue and privation, he
had two serious illnesses at Rudraprayag and at Hrishi-
kesh at the foot of the Himalayas on the Ganga; he
almost died of diphtheria. The extreme weakness which
resulted made it still more difficult for him to achieve
his great solitary journey.

Nevertheless that journey was accomplished. If he
was to die it should be on the way, and his own way—
the way revealed to him by his God! In February, 1891,
in spite of his friends, he left Delhi alone. This was
the great departure. Like a diver he plunged into the
Ocean of India, and the Ocean of India covered his
tracks. Among its flotsam and jetsam he was nothing
more than one nameless Sannyasin in saffron robe
among a thousand others. But the fires of genius burned
in his eyes. He was a prince despite all disguise.

---

[1] "Blessed Solitude, the only Blessedness."—*Translator.*

# THE PILGRIM OF INDIA

His great *Periplus* of two years through India and then
of three years round the world (was this part of his
original intention?) was the adequate reply of his
instinct to the double exigencies of his nature: independence and service. He wandered, free from plan,
caste, home, constantly alone with God. And there was
no single hour of his life when he was not brought into
contact with the sorrows, the desires, the abuses, the
misery, and the feverishness of living men, rich and
poor, in town and field; he became one with their
lives; the great Book of Life revealed to him what all
the books in the libraries could not have done (for after
all they are only collections), which even Ramakrishna's
ardent love had only been able to see dimly as in a
dream—the tragic face of the present day, the God
struggling in humanity, the cry of the peoples of India
and of the world for help, and the heroic duty of the
new Oedipus, whose task it was to deliver Thebes from
the talons of the Sphinx or to perish with Thebes.

*Wanderjahre. Lehrjahre.*[1] What a unique education!
...He was not only the humble little brother, who
slept in stables or on the pallets of beggars, but he was
on a footing of equality with every man, today a despised beggar sheltered by pariahs, tomorrow the guest
of princes, conversing on equal terms with Prime
Ministers and Maharajas, the brother of the oppressed

---

[1] "Years of travel. Years of apprenticeship" (Goethe).

bending over their misery, then probing the luxury of
the great, awakening care for the public weal in their
torpid hearts. He was as conversant with the knowledge
of the pandits as with the problems of industrial and
rural economy, whereby the life of the people is controlled, ever teaching, ever learning, gradually making
himself the Conscience of India, its Unity and its
Destiny. All of them were incarnate in him, and the
world saw them in Vivekananda.

His itinerary led him through Rajputana, Alwar
(February to March, 1891), Jaipur, Ajmere, Khetri,
Ahmedabad, and Kathiawar (end of September),
Junagad and Gujarat, Porebander (a stay of between
eight and nine months), Dwaraka, Palitana—the city
of temples close to the gulf of Cambay, the State of
Baroda, Khandwa, Bombay, Poona, Belgaum (October,
1892), Bangalore in the State of Mysore, Cochin,
Malabar, the State of Travancore, Trivandrum,
Madura....He travelled to the extreme point of the
immense pyramid, where is the Varanasi of Southern
India, Rameswaram, the Rome of the Ramayana,
and beyond to Kanyakumari, the sanctuary of the
Great Goddess (end of 1892).

From North to South the ancient land of India was
full of gods; yet the unbroken chain of their countless
arms formed only one God. He realised their unity of
flesh and spirit. He realised it also in communion with
the living of all castes and all outside caste. And he
taught them to realise it. He took mutual understanding from the one to the other—to strong spirits, to the
intellectuals obsessed with the abstract, he preached
respect for images and idol Gods; to young men the
duty of studying the grand old books of the past: the

Vedas, the Puranas, the ancient annals, and still more the people of today—to all a religious love for mother India and a passion to dedicate themselves to her redemption.

He received no less than he gave. His vast spirit never for a single day failed to widen its knowledge[1] and its experience, and it assimilated all the rivers of thought scattered and buried in the soil of India, for their source seemed to him identical. As far removed from the blind devotion of the orthodox, who were engulfed in the muddy stench of stagnant waters, as from the misguided rationalism of the reformers of the Brahmo Samaj, who with the best intentions were busied in drying up the mystic fountains of hidden energy, Vivekananda wished to preserve and to harmonise them all by draining the whole entangled reservoir of the waters of a whole continent possessed by a deeply religious soul.

He desired more than this: (nobody can be with impunity the contemporary of the great engineers who cut a passage between oceans, and willy-nilly rejoin the hands of continents!)—everywhere he carried with him *The Imitation of Christ*, and side by side with the Bhagavad-Gita he spread the thought of Jesus;[2] and he urged young people to study the science of the West.[3]

[1] At Khetri he became the pupil of the foremost Sanskrit grammarian of the time. At Ahmedabad he completed his knowledge of Mohammedan and Jain culture. At Porebander he stayed three quarters of a year, in spite of his vow as a wandering monk, to perfect his philosophical and Sanskrit studies with learned pandits; he worked with a court pandit who translated the Vedas.

[2] But he was merciless towards the intolerance of the missionaries, and never forgave them for it. The Christ whom he preached opened his arms to all.

[3] During the beginning of his great journey at Alwar in Rajputana (February to March, 1891), when he was hurt by the lack of the spirit

But the widening of his mind was not only in the realm of ideas. A revolution took place in his moral vision with regard to other men and his relations to them. If ever there was pride in a young man, coupled with intellectual intolerance, the contempt of the aristocrat for everything that fell below his high ideal of purity, it was present in young Narendra:

"At twenty years of age (*it is he himself speaking*) I was the most unsympathetic, uncompromising fanatic; I would not walk on the footpath on the theatre side of the street in Calcutta."[1]

During the first months of his pilgrimage when he was with the Maharaja of Khetri near Jaipur (April, 1891), a little dancer gave him all unwittingly a lesson in humility. When she appeared, the scornful monk rose to go out. The prince begged him to remain. The little dancer sang:

"O Lord, look not upon 'my evil qualities! Thy name, O Lord, is Same-sightedness. Make of us both the same Brahman! One piece of iron is in the image in the temple, and another is the knife in the hand of the butcher. But when they touch the philosophers' stone both alike turn into gold. So, Lord, look not upon my evil qualities! Thy name, Lord, is Same-sightedness . . . .

"One drop of water is in the sacred Jamuna and another is foul in the ditch by the roadside. But when

of precision, of exactitude, and of scientific criticism in Indian history. He set up the example of the West in opposition to it. He wished India to be inspired by its methods, so that a young school of Hindu historians might arise to devote themselves to resuscitating India's past. "That would be real national education; and thus a true national spirit would be awakened."

[1] Letter of July 6, 1896. He added, "At thirty-three I can live in the same house with prostitutes."

they fall into the Ganga both alike become holy. So, Lord, do not look upon my evil qualities. Thy name, Lord, is Same-sightedness...."[1]

Naren was completely overwhelmed. The confident faith expressed in the humble song affected him for life. Many years later he recalled it with emotion.

One by one his prejudices disappeared—even those which he had thought most deeply rooted. In the Himalayas he lived among Tibetan races, who practise polyandry. He was the guest of a family of six brothers, who shared the same wife; and in his neophytic zeal he tried to show them their immorality. But it was they who were scandalised by his lessons. "What selfishness!" they said. "To wish to keep one woman all to oneself!..." Truth at the bottom of the mountain and error at the top....He realised the relativity of virtue—at least of those virtues having the greatest traditional sanction. Moreover a transcendental irony, as in the case of Pascal, taught him to broaden his moral conception when he judged of good and evil in a race or in an age, according to the standards of that race or that age.

Again he kept company with thieves of the most degraded caste, and came to recognise even in highway robbers "sinners who were potential saints."[2] Everywhere he shared the privations and the insults of the oppressed classes. In Central India he lived with a family of outcast sweepers. Amid such lowly people who cower at the feet of society, he found spiritual

[1] The poem of a Vaishnavite saint: Suradas.
[2] He met a thief who had plundered Pavhari Baba, and then touched with repentance had become a monk.

treasures, while their misery choked him. He could not bear it. He sobbed, "O my country! O my country!..." when he learnt from the papers that a man had died of .hunger at Calcutta. He asked himself as he beat his breast, "What have we done, we so-called men of God, the Sannyasins, what have we done for the masses?"

He recalled Ramakrishna's rough words: "Religion is not for empty bellies." And waxing impatient with the intellectual speculations of an egoistic faith, he made it the first duty of religion "to care for the poor and to raise them."[1] He imposed this duty on the rich, on officials and on princes: "Is there none among you who can give a life for the service of others? Let the study of the Vedanta and the practice of meditation be left over to the future life! Let this body be dedicated to the service of others! And then I shall know that you have not come to me in vain."[2]

On a future day his pathetic accents were to sound this sublime utterance: "May I be born and reborn again and suffer a thousand miseries if only I am able to worship the only God in whom I believe, the sum total of all souls, and above all my God the wicked, my God the afflicted, my God the poor of all races!..."

At this date, 1892, it was the misery under his eyes, the misery of India, that filled his mind to the exclusion of every other thought. It pursued him, like a tiger following his prey, from the North to the South in his flight across India. It consumed him during sleepless nights. At Cape Comorin it caught and held him in

---

[1] See above, page 11.
[2] The utterance of these words belongs to a later date. But the sentiment that inspired them belongs to this time.

its jaws. On that occasion he abandoned body and soul to it. He dedicated his life to the unhappy masses.

But how could he help them? He had no money, and time was pressing, and the princely gifts of one or two Maharajas or the offerings of several groups of well-wishers could only nourish a thousandth part of the most urgent needs. Before India woke up from her ataraxy and organised herself for the common good, the ruin of India would be consummated. He lifted up his eyes to the ocean, to the land beyond the seas. He must appeal to the whole world. The whole world had need of India. The health of India, the death of India, was its concern as well. Could her immense spiritual reserves be allowed to be destroyed as so many others had been—Egypt and Chaldea—which long afterwards men struggled to exhume, when nothing was left but debris, their soul being dead for ever?....An appeal from India to Europe and America began to take shape in the mind of the solitary thinker.

It was at the end of 1891 between Junagad and Porebander that he appears to have thought of it for the first time. At Porebander, where he began to learn French, a pandit advised him to go to the West, where his thought would be better understood than in his own country: "Go and take it by storm and then return!" At Khandwa in the early autumn of 1892 he heard of a Parliament of Religions to be held during the following year at Chicago, and his first thought was how he might take part in it. At the same time he would not allow himself to take any steps towards the realisation of this project, and he refused to accept subscriptions for the purpose, until he had achieved the vow of his great pilgrimage round India. At Bangalore

towards the end of October he specifically declared
to the Maharaja his intention of going to ask the West
"for the means to ameliorate the material condition
of India", and to take to it in exchange the Gospel of
the Vedanta. At the end of 1892 his mind was made up.

At that moment he found himself at the "Land's
End" of India, at the extreme southern point where
Hanuman, the Monkey-god, made his fabulous leap.
But Vivekananda was a man, as we are, and could not
follow the ways of demigods. He had traversed the
vast land of India upon the soles of his feet. For two
years his body had been in constant contact with its
great body; he had suffered from hunger, from thirst,
from murderous nature and insulting man. When he
arrived at Cape Comorin, he was exhausted, but, having no money to pay for a boat to take him to the end
of his pilgrimage he flung himself into the sea, and swam
across the shark-infested strait. At last his task was
at an end, and then, looking back as from a mountain
he embraced the whole of the India he had just traversed, and the world of thought that had beset him
during his wanderings. For two years he had lived
in a seething cauldron, consumed with a fever; he
had carried "a soul on fire", he was a "storm and
a hurricane".[1] Like criminals of old who suffered the
torture of water, he felt himself submerged by the
torrents of energy he had accumulated, the walls of his
being were crumbling beneath their flood....[2] And
when he stepped on to the terrace of the tower he had

---

[1] It was Abhedananda, who, meeting him in October, 1892, in the
State of Baroda, described him thus.

[2] "I feel a mighty power! It is as if I were about to blaze forth.
There are so many powers in me! It seems to me as if I could revolutionise the world."

just climbed at the very edge of the earth with the panorama of the world spread before his eyes, the blood pounded in his ears like the sea at his feet; he almost fell. It was the supreme assault of the Gods striving within him. When the struggle was over, his first battle had been won. He had seen the path he was to follow. His mission was chosen.

He swam back to the continent of India. From the opposite coast he went northwards. On foot, by Ramnad and Pondicherry, he came to Madras. And there in the first weeks of 1893, he publicly proclaimed his wish to conduct a Mission in the West.[1] His fame, contrary to his own desire, had already spread abroad; he was besieged by visitors in this intellectual and vital city where he stayed on two occasions, and it was in Madras that he founded his first group of devoted disciples, who dedicated themselves to him, and who never left him: after his departure they continued to support him with their letters and their faith; and he from countries far away kept his direction over them. His burning love for India awakened passionate echoes in their hearts, and by their enthusiasm, the strength of his own conviction was increased tenfold. He preached against all search for personal salvation. It was rather public salvation that should be sought, the regeneration of the mother country, the resurrection of the spiritual powers of India, and their diffusion throughout the universe....

"The time is ripe. The faith of the Rishis must become dynamic. It must come out of itself."

Nabobs and bankers offered him money for his

[1] This was the title of a lecture he delivered at Hyderabad in February, 1893: *My Mission to the West*.

journey overseas, but he refused it. He asked the disciples, who were collecting subscriptions, to appeal
rather to the middle classes: for "I am going on behalf
of the people and the poor."

As he had done at the beginning of his pilgrimage,
he asked the blessing of the "Holy Mother" (the wife
of Ramakrishna) for the more distant journey. And
she sent him Ramakrishna's as well, for he had delivered it to her for the beloved disciple in a dream.

It does not appear that he wrote to his spiritual
brethren of Baranagore: (doubtless he thought that
their contemplative souls, used to the warmth of the
nest, would be terrified at the thought of social service
and evangelising journeys in the countries of the
Gentiles; such ideas disturbed the pious calm of souls
who were preoccupied with their own salvation without troubling about that of others). But chance decreed
that almost on the eve of his departure, at the Abu
Road Station, near Bombay, he met two of them,
Brahmananda and Turiyananda; and he told them with
pathetic passion, whose repercussions reached Baranagore,[1] of the imperious call of suffering India that
forced him to go:

"I have now travelled all over India....But alas,
it was agony to me, my brothers, to see with my own
eyes the terrible poverty and misery of the masses, and
I could not restrain my tears! It is now my firm con-

[1] It does not seem, however, that the monks of Baranagore were
tempted to follow his example. Even on his triumphal return from
America, they found it difficult to yield to his arguments for sub-
ordinating and even sacrificing, if need arose, the contemplative life
to social service. Only one Akhandananda (Gangadhar), moved by
the words Brahmananda and Turiyananda had brought back, went
during 1894 to open schools at Khetri and to work at the education
of the masses.

viction that it is futile to preach religion amongst them
without first trying to remove their poverty and their
sufferings. It is for this reason—to find more means
for the salvation of the poor of India—that I am now
going to America."[1]

[1] These words, quoted in the great *Life of the Swami Vivekananda*,
are completed by Turiyananda's reminiscences, which Swami Jnanes-
warananda took down and published in *The Morning Star* on January
31, 1926:

Brahmananda and Turiyananda were in retreat on Mt. Abu, where
they were practising a very strict Tapasya (practice of meditation and
asceticism). They did not expect to meet Naren. They saw him at
Abu Road Station several weeks before his departure. Naren told
them his plans, his hesitations, and his conviction that the Parliament
of Religions was willed by God to prepare his success. Turiyananda
recalled each one of his words and the tone of his voice: "Hari Bhai,"
Naren cried, his face red with his rising blood, "I cannot understand
your so-called religion!...." With a profound expression of sadness
and intense emotion through all his being, he pressed a trembling hand
upon his heart and added: "But my heart has grown much, much
larger, and I have learnt to feel (the sufferings of others). Believe me,
I feel it very sadly!"

His voice was choked with emotion. He was silent. Tears streamed
down his cheeks.

Turiyananda, in giving this account, was himself deeply moved,
and his eyes filled with tears. "You can imagine," he said, "what went
through my spirit when I heard these pathetic words and saw the majestic sadness of the Swamiji. 'Are these not,' I thought, 'the very words
and feelings of the Buddha?' And I remembered that a long time before,
when he had gone to Bodh Gaya to meditate under the Bodhi tree,
he had had a vision of the Lord Buddha, who entered into his body....
I could clearly see that the whole suffering of humanity had penetrated his palpitating heart." "Nobody," continued Turiyananda
with passion, "nobody could understand Vivekananda unless he saw
at least a fraction of the volcanic feelings which were in him."

Turiyananda told of another scene of the same kind, at which he
was present, after Vivekananda had come back from America—
probably in the house of Balaram at Baghbazar (Calcutta):

"I had gone to see him and I found him pacing the verandah like
a caged lion. He was deep in thought and did not notice my presence.
...He began to hum under his breath a celebrated song of Mirabai.
And the tears welled up in his eyes. He stopped and leaned against
the balustrade, and hid his face in his two palms. His voice became
more distinct and he sang, repeating several times:

'Oh, nobody understands my sorrow!'

He went to Khetri, where his friend the Maharaja gave him his Dewan (Prime Minister) to escort him to Bombay, where he embarked. At the moment of departure he put on, with the robe of red silk and ochre turban, the name of Vivekananda, which he was about to impose upon the world.[1]

And again:
'Only he who suffers knows the anguish of sorrow....'
His voice pierced me through and through like an arrow. I could not understand the cause of his affliction....Then suddenly I understood. It was his rending sympathy which made him often shed tears of burning blood. And the world would never have known it...."
But addressing his listeners, Turiyananda said, "Do you think that these tears of blood were shed in vain? No! Each one of those tears, shed for his country, every inflamed whisper of his mighty heart will give birth to troops of heroes, who will shake the world with their thoughts and their deeds."

[1] I have noted on page 8 the origin of this name. which was suggested to him by the Maharaja. During his journey in India, he bore so many different names that, just as he desired, he usually passed by unobserved. Many of those who met him had no suspicion of his identity. It was so at Poona in October, 1892; Tilak, the famous savant and Hindu political leader, took him at first for a wandering monk of no importance and began by being ironical; then, struck by his replies revealing his great mind and knowledge, he received him into his house for ten days without ever knowing his real name. It was only later, when the newspapers brought him from America the echoes of Vivekananda's triumph and a description of the conqueror, that he recognised the anonymous guest who had dwelt beneath his roof.

# III

## THE GREAT JOURNEY TO THE WEST AND THE PARLIAMENT OF RELIGIONS

THIS journey was indeed an astonishing adventure. The young Swami went into it at random with his eyes shut. He had heard vaguely of a Parliament of Religions to be opened some day somewhere in America; and he had decided to go to it, although neither he, nor his disciples, nor his Indian friends, students, pandits, ministers, or Maharajas, had taken any trouble to find out about it. He knew nothing, neither the exact date nor the conditions of admission. He did not take a single credential with him. He went straight ahead with complete assurance, as if it was enough for him to present himself at the right time— God's time. And although the Maharaja of Khetri had taken his ticket on the boat for him, and despite his protests had provided him with a beautiful robe that was to fascinate American idlers no less than his eloquence, neither he nor anybody else had considered the climatic conditions and customs; he froze on the boat when he arrived in Canada in his costume of Indian pomp and ceremony.

He left Bombay on May 31, 1893, and went by way of Ceylon, Penang, Singapore, Hongkong, and then visited Canton and Nagasaki. Thence he went by land to Yokohama, seeing Osaka, Kyoto, and Tokyo. Everywhere both in China and Japan his attention was attracted by all that might confirm his hypothesis—his

3

conviction—alike of the religious influence of ancient India over the Empires of the Far East, and of the spiritual unity of Asia.[1] At the same time the thought of the ills from which his country was suffering, never left him; and the sight of the progress achieved by Japan reopened the wound.

He went from Yokohama to Vancouver; thence by train he found himself towards the middle of July in a state of bewilderment at Chicago. The whole way was strewn with his feathers, for he was a marked prey for the fleecer: he could be seen from afar! At first like a great child he wandered, gazing, mouth agape, in the world's fair, the Universal Exposition of Chicago. Everything was new to him and both surprised and stupefied him. He had never imagined the power, the riches, the inventive genius of this Western world. Being of a stronger vitality and more sensitive to the appeal of force than a Tagore or a Gandhi, who were oppressed by the frenzy of movement and noise, by the whole European-American (especially American) mechanism, Vivekananda was at his ease in it at least at first; he succumbed to its exciting intoxication, and his first feeling was of juvenile acceptance; his admiration knew no bounds. For twelve days he filled his eager eyes with this new world. A few days after his arrival in Chicago he bethought himself to go to the Information Bureau of the Exposition....What a shock! He discovered that the Parliament did not open until after the first week of September—and that it

[1] He was struck when he visited the Chinese temples, consecrated to the first Buddhist Emperor, to find Sanskrit manuscripts written in old Bengali characters. He noticed the same in Japan in the temples —inscriptions of Sanskrit Mantras (sacred texts) in ancient Bengali characters.

was too late for the registration of delegates—moreover, that no registration would be accepted without official references. He had none, he was unknown, without credentials from any recognised group; and his purse was nearly empty; it would not allow him to wait until the opening of the Congress. . . . He was overwhelmed. He cabled to his friends in Madras for help and applied to an official religious society that it might make him a grant. But official societies do not forgive independence. The chief of the society sent this reply:

"Let the devil die of cold!"

The devil neither died nor gave up! He threw himself upon fate, and instead of hoarding in inaction the few dollars remaining to him, he spent them in visiting Boston. Fate helped him. Fate always helps those who know how to help themselves. A Vivekananda never passed anywhere unnoticed, but fascinated even while he was unknown. In the Boston train his appearance and conversation struck a fellow traveller, a rich Massachusetts lady, who questioned him and then interested herself in him, invited him to her house, and introduced him to the Hellenist, J. H. Wright, a professor at Harvard; the latter was at once struck by the genius of this young Hindu and put himself entirely at his disposal; he insisted that Vivekananda should represent Hinduism at the Parliament of Religions, and wrote to the President of the Committee. He offered the penniless pilgrim a railway ticket to Chicago, and letters of recommendation to the Committee for finding lodgings. In short all his difficulties were removed.

Vivekananda returned to Chicago. The train arrived late; and the dazed young man, who had lost the address of the Committee, did not know where to go.

Nobody would deign to inform a coloured man. He saw a big empty box in a corner of the station, and slept in it. In the morning he went to discover the way, begging from door to door as a Sannyasin. But he was in a city that knows, Panurges-like, a thousand and one ways of making money—except one, the way of St. Francis, the vagrancy of God. He was rudely dismissed from some of the houses. At others he was insulted by the servants. At still others, the door was slammed in his face. After having wandered for a long time, he sat down exhausted in the street. He was remarked from a window opposite and asked whether he were not a delegate to the Parliament of Religions. He was invited in; and once more fate found for him one who was later numbered among his most faithful American followers.[1] When he had rested he was taken to the Parliament. There he was gladly accepted as a delegate and found himself lodged with the other Oriental delegates to the Parliament.

His adventurous journey, which had almost ended disastrously, brought him on this occasion into port, but not for rest. Action called him, for now that fate had done its worst, it had to give place to resolution! The unknown of yesterday, the beggar, the man despised for his colour by a mob, wherein the dregs of more than half a dozen of the peoples of the world meet—at the first glance was to impose his sovereign genius.

*

On Monday, September 11, 1893, the first session of the Parliament was opened. In the centre sat Cardinal Gibbons. Round him to left and right were grouped

[1] Mrs. G. W. Hale.

the Oriental delegates Protap Chunder Mozoomdar,[1] the chief of the Brahmo Samaj, an old friend of Vivekananda, representing the Indian theists together with Nagarkar of Bombay; Dharmapala, representing the Buddhists of Ceylon; Gandhi[2] representing the Jains; Chakravarti, representing with Annie Besant the Theosophical Society. But amongst them all it was the young man who represented nothing—and everything —the man belonging to no sect, but rather to India as a whole, who drew the glance of the assembled thousands.[3] His fascinating face, his noble stature, and the gorgeous apparel,[4] which heightened the effect of this apparition from a legendary world, hid his own emotion. He made no secret of it. It was the first time that he had had to speak before such an assembly; and as the delegates, presented one by one, had to announce themselves in public in a brief harangue, Vivekananda let his turn go by hour after hour until the end of the day.[5]

But then his speech was like a tongue of flame. Among the grey wastes of cold dissertation it fired the souls of the listening throng. Hardly had he pronounced the very simple opening words "Sisters and brothers of America!" than hundreds arose in their seats and

[1] See our Volume 1: *The Life of Ramakrishna*, the Chapter on the Builders of Unity.

[2] Naturally this was not the same as our M. K. Gandhi, who about this time was landing in South Africa. But his family had intimate relations with the Jains, and it may well have been that the Gandhi of the Parliament of Religions was a distant connection.

[3] The American Press testified to the truth of this.

[4] His red robe, drawn in at the waist by an orange cord, his great yellow turban, accentuated the raven black of his hair, his olive complexion, his dark eyes, his red lips. (Description from the papers).

[5] Let us add that the improvident one had prepared nothing, while the others all read from a written text.

applauded. He wondered whether it could really be he they were applauding. He was certainly the first to cast off the formalism of the Congress and to speak to the masses in the language for which they were waiting. Silence fell again. He greeted the youngest of the nations in the name of the most ancient monastic order in the world—the Vedic order of Sannyasins. He presented Hinduism as the mother of religions, who had taught them the double precept: "Accept and understand one another!" He quoted two beautiful passages from the sacred books:

"Whoever comes to Me, through whatsoever form, I reach him."

"All men are struggling through paths which in the end lead to Me."

Each of the other orators had spoken of his God, of the God of his sect. He—he alone—spoke of all their Gods, and embraced them all in the Universal Being. It was the breath of Ramakrishna, breaking down the barriers through the mouth of his great disciple. The Parliament of Religions gave the young orator an ovation.

During the ensuing days he spoke again ten or twelve times.[1] Each time he repeated with new arguments but

[1] Both at the plenary sessions of the Parliament and at the scientific sections which were affiliated to it. His principal dissertations were on the following subjects:

I. September 15: Why We Disagree. (He there denounced the insularity of different religious points of view, which is the source of fanaticism.)

II. September 20: Religion Not the Crying Need of India. (But bread. An appeal for help for all his people who were dying.)

III & IV. September 22: Orthodox Hinduism and Vedantic Philosophy. The Modern Religions of India.

V. September 25: The Essence of the Hindu Religion.

VI. September 26: Buddhism, the Fulfilment of Hinduism.

And four other lectures.

with the same force of conviction his thesis of a universal religion without limit of time or space, uniting the whole *Credo* of the human spirit, from the enslaved fetishism of the savage to the most liberal creative affirmations of modern science. He harmonised them into a magnificent synthesis, which, far from extinguishing the hope of a single one, helped all hopes to grow and flourish according to their own proper nature.[1] There was to be no other dogma but the divinity inherent in man and his capacity for indefinite evolution.

"Offer such a religion and all the nations will follow you. Asoka's council[2] was a council of the Buddhist faith. Akbar's[3], though more to the purpose, was only a parlour meeting. It was reserved for America to proclaim to all quarters of the globe that the Lord is in every religion.

"May He who is the Brahman of the Hindus, the Ahura Mazda of the Zoroastrians, the Buddha of the Buddhists, the Jehovah of the Jews, the Father in Heaven of the Christians, give strength to you. . . .[4] The Christian is not to become a Hindu or a Buddhist,

But the most famous discourses were:

XI. September 19: The most famous Paper on Hinduism, although he was its sole universal representative without distinction of sect at the Congress. We shall return to it later, when we examine Vivekananda's thought.

XII. September 27: Address at the Final Session of the Congress.

[1] But the young Hinduist, convinced in spite of himself of the superiority of his own ideal, presented Hinduism in its essentials, rejuvenated and purified of its degenerate parts, as the universal religion of which he spoke.

[2] The Council of Pataliputra, to which the Emperor Asoka convoked the Buddhists about 253 B.C.

[3] The great Mogul Emperor of the sixteenth century (1556-1605), who, abjuring Islam, tried to found eclectic rationalism, which was to become an imperial religion, with the agreement of the Hindus, Jains, Mussulmans, Parsees, and even Christians.

[4] Paper on Hinduism (September 19).

nor a Hindu or a Buddhist to become a Christian. But each must assimilate the spirit of the others and yet preserve his individuality and grow according to his own law of growth.... The Parliament of Religions... has proved...that holiness, purity, and charity are not the exclusive possessions of any church in the world, and that every system has produced men and women of the most exalted character....Upon the banner of every religion will soon be written in spite of... resistance: 'Help and not Fight,' 'Assimilation and not Destruction,' 'Harmony and Peace and not Dissension.' "[1]

The effect of these mighty words was immense. Over the heads of the official representatives of the Parliament they were addressed to all and appealed to outside thought. Vivekananda's fame at once spread abroad, and India as a whole benefited. The American Press recognised him as "Undoubtedly the greatest figure in the Parliament of Religions. After hearing him we feel how foolish it is to send missionaries to this learned nation."[2]

It may be imagined that such an avowal did not sound sweetly in the ears of Christian missionaries, and Vivekananda's success roused bitter rancour among them, which did not stop short of the use of the most dishonourable weapons. It sharpened no less the jealousy of certain Hindu representatives, who saw

---

[1] Address at the Final Session (September 27).
[2] *The New York Herald. The Boston Evening Transcript* stated that he was "a great favourite of the Parliament." It was only necessary for him to cross the platform to be greeted with acclamations. And the only way of keeping the public at the meetings, for their attention often flagged, was to announce that Vivekananda would speak at the end.

themselves put in the shade by this "wandering monk", without title or ties. Theosophy in particular, a religion Vivekananda did not spare, never forgave him.[1]

But in this first hour of dawning glory—of the rising sun—the brightness of its light extinguished the shadows. Vivekananda became the man of the hour.

What did he think of his victory? He wept over it. The wandering monk saw that his free solitary life with God was at an end. Is there any truly religious soul who does not sympathise with his regrets? He had himself willed it...or rather he had been *willed* by the unknown force that had dictated his mission....But there was always the other inner voice, which said to him, "Renounce! Live in God!" He never could satisfy the one without partially denying the other. Hence the periodic crises traversed by this stormy genius and the torments which, apparently contradictory but really logical, can never be understood by single-minded spirits, by those who, having only one thought in their heads, make of their poverty an obligatory virtue, and who call the mighty and pathetic struggling towards harmony of souls, too richly endowed, either confusion or duplicity. Vivekananda was and will always be the butt of such malevolent interpretations, which his high pride made no attempt to excuse.

But his complexities at this time were not only of the spirit. They were inherent in the situation itself.

---

[1] In an address at Madras on his return from America, *My Plan of Campaign*, Vivekananda unmasked all those who had attacked him, and told the Theosophical Society sharply what he thought of it. The reader may also consult *The Travel Diary of a Philosopher* by Count Keyserling, the chapter on Adyar, the Headquarters in India of the Theosophical Society, where the spirit of the Society is unmasked with singular penetration.

After, as before, success (and perhaps even more so) his task was a difficult one. Having nearly succumbed to poverty, he was now in danger of being overwhelmed by riches. American snobbery threw itself upon him, and, in its first flush, threatened to smother him with luxury and vanities. Vivekananda grew almost physically sick from this excess of money. At night in his bedroom he gave vent to cries of despair and rolled on the ground when he thought of the people who were dying of hunger. "Oh Mother," he groaned, "what have I to do with fame when my people are lying in misery!..."

In order to serve the cause of his unfortunate India and to free himself from the tutelage of his rich protectors, he accepted the offer of a Lecture Bureau for a tour of the United States: the East and the Middle West, Chicago, Iowa, Des Moines, St. Louis;* Minneapolis, Detroit, Boston, Cambridge, Baltimore, Washington, New York, etc. But this proved a risky method: for it was a mistake to imagine that he, like so many other lecturers, was going to buy applause and dollars by burning incense under the nose of the American public!...

His first feeling of attraction and admiration for the formidable power of the young republic had faded. Vivekananda almost at once fell foul of the brutality, the inhumanity, the littleness of spirit, the narrow fanaticism, the monumental ignorance, the crushing incomprehension, so frank and sure of itself with regard to all who thought, who believed, who regarded life differently from the paragon nation of the human race....

---

*Later research shows that he did not visit St. Louis (*Swami Vivekananda in America: New Discoveries*, p. 134).—*Publisher*.

And so he had no patience. He hid nothing. He stigmatised the vices and crimes of the Western civilisation with its characteristics of violence, pillage, and destruction. Once when he was to speak at Boston on a beautiful religious subject particularly dear to him,[1] he felt such repulsion at the sight of his audience, the artificial and cruel crowd of men of affairs and of the world, that he refused to yield them the key of his sanctuary, and brusquely changing the subject, he inveighed furiously against a civilisation represented by such foxes and wolves.[2] The scandal was terrific. Hundreds noisily left the hall and the Press was furious.

He was especially bitter against false Christianity and religious hypocrisy: "With all your brag and boasting, where has your Christianity succeeded without the sword? Yours is a religion preached in the name of luxury. It is all hypocrisy that I have heard in this country. All this prosperity, all this from Christ! Those who call upon Christ care for nothing but to amass riches! Christ would not find a stone on which to lay his head among you.... You are not Christians. Return to Christ!"

An explosion of anger was the answer to this scornful lesson, and from that moment he had always at his heels a band of clergymen, who followed him with invective and accusation, even going so far as to spread infamous calumnies of his life and behaviour in America

[1] Ramakrishna.
[2] I have heard a similar scene related about a great Hindu poet, whom we all revere. He was invited to the United States to address a meeting on the subject of a work very near to his heart. But when he saw the audience, who were prepared to subscribe to it, he was so revolted at the sight that he attacked them and their stifling material civilisation. Hence he himself destroyed the work whose success seemed assured.

and India.[1] No less shameful was the action of certain Hindu representatives of rival societies, who were offended by Vivekananda's glory, and did not scruple to spread the base charges started by malevolent missionaries. And in their turn the Christian missionaries used the weapons provided by the jealous Hindus,[2] and denounced the free Sannyasin in India with almost comic zeal, because in America he no longer kept to the strict regime prescribed by orthodox Hinduism.[3] Vivekananda with disgust saw the scum of the rancorous wave, raised by the devotees, returning to him from India in the frightened letters of his disciples. And with what scorn he flung it back in the faces of those who had bespattered him with it![4]

[1] It goes without saying that they produced the classic accusation of Anglo-Saxon countries, seduction! In order to stop the false rumour spread by a vulgar-minded clergyman that he had wronged a servant dismissed by the Governor of Michigan, letters of public denial (March, 1895) were necessary from the Governor's wife, testifying to the moral dignity of Vivekananda. But no denials ever repair the damage done by unscrupulous lies.

[2] Some of the Brahmos treated as blasphemy certain of Vivekananda's expositions of Vedantism in America: his "pretensions to divinity" (that is to say, to the divinity of the human soul), his "denial of sin", (which came to him from Ramakrishna), his "evolutionism", his "Western ideas introduced into Hinduism", etc. (*Cf.* B. Mozoomdar in a pamphlet on *Vivekananda, the Informer of Max Müller.*) He had against him a curious alliance of Protestant missionaries, Theosophists, and some members of the Brahmo Samaj.

[3] The chief charge was that he had eaten beef. He hated the bigotry which believes that it is acquitted in respect of morality and God, when it has observed certain practices, holding their non-observance as a cardinal sin. He held nothing inviolable save his two vows of poverty and chastity. For the rest with much common sense he held that a man should follow as far as possible the customs of the country in which he was living.

[4] To the scandalised remonstrances of Indian devotees, horrified to hear that their Swami ate impure food at the table of infidels, he retorted: "Do you mean to say I am born to live and die one of those caste-ridden, superstitious, merciless, hypocritical, atheistic cowards that you only find among the educated Hindus? I hate cowardice. I will

A letter from one of his American disciples, Swami Kripananda,[1] depicts in retrospect his tribulations in the United States: "This hotbed of pseudo-religious monstrosities, devoured by a morbid thirst for the abnormal, for the occult, for the exceptional—whence a senseless credulity leads to the dissemination of hundreds of societies: goblins, ghosts, mahâtmâs, false prophets—this refuge for aliens of all colours was an abominable place to Vivekananda. He felt himself obliged to cleanse this Augean stable at the outset."

He committed to the devil the idlers, buffoons, fishers in troubled waters, gulls, who thronged to his first lectures. He was immediately the recipient of offers of association, promises, threats, and blackmailing letters from intriguers, busy-bodies, and religious charlatans. It is needless to state their effect on a character such as his. He would not tolerate the slightest domination. He rejected every alliance of one sect against another. And more than once he embraced the opportunity to engage in a public struggle without quarter against "combinations" wishing to use him for their own ends.

For the honour of America it must be said here and now that his moral intransigence, his virile idealism, his

have nothing to do with cowards.... I belong to India just as much as to the world, no humbug about that.... What country has any special claim upon me? Am I any nation's slave?.... I see a greater Power than man or God or devil at my back. I require nobody's help. I have been all my life helping others...." (Letter written from Paris, September 9, 1895, to his Indian disciples.)

[1] Kripananda was the name taken by Leon Landsberg, at his initiation. He was a Russian Jew by birth, a naturalised American citizen, and part-owner of a big New York journal, and was one of the first Western disciples accepted by Vivekananda. I shall speak of him later.

The letter of which I give a summary was written in 1895 in the Madras journal, *The Brahmavadin*.

dauntless loyalty attracted to him from all sides a chosen band of defenders and admirers, a group of whom were to form his first Western disciples and the most active agents in his work for human regeneration.

# IV

## AMERICA AT THE TIME
## OF VIVEKANANDA'S FIRST VISIT

### The Anglo-Saxon Forerunners of the Spirit of Asia: Emerson, Thoreau, Walt Whitman

It would be a matter of deep interest to know exactly how far the American spirit had been impregnated, directly or indirectly, by the infiltration of Hindu thought during the nineteenth century: for there can be no doubt that it has contributed to the strange moral and religious mentality of the modern United States—which Europe has so much difficulty in understanding—with its astonishing mixture of Anglo-Saxon Puritanism, Yankee optimism of action, pragmatism, "scientism", and pseudo-Vedantism. I do not know whether any historian will be found to occupy himself seriously with the question. It is nevertheless a psychological problem of the first order, intimately connected with the history of our civilisation. I do not possess the means for its solution, but at least I can indicate certain elements in it.

It would seem that one of the chief people to introduce Hindu thought into the United States was Emerson,[1] and that Emerson in so doing had been deeply influenced by Thoreau.

[1] The article of a Hindu, Herambachandra Maitra, entitled *Emerson from an Indian Point of View*, in the *Harvard Theological Review* of 1911, was mentioned to me in this connection. But I have not been able to study it.

He was predisposed to such influences; from 1830 onwards they began to appear in his *Journal*, wherein he noted references to Hindu religious texts. His famous lecture, which created a scandal at the time, given in 1838 at the University of Harvard, expressed belief in the divine in man akin to the concept of the Soul, Atman-Brahman. It is true that he attached a strictly moral or moralist interpretation to it, his own stamp and that of his race. But its fulfilment was the ecstatic realisation of a veritable Yoga of "justice", conceived in the double sense of moral good and cosmic equilibrium, and uniting at one and the same time Karma (action), Bhakti (love), and Jnana (wisdom).[1] Emerson exercised little method either in his reading or writing; and Cabot in his Memoir of him, tells us that he was easily satisfied with extracts and quotations, and did not consult the authorities as a whole. But Thoreau was a great reader; and between 1837 and 1862, he was Emerson's neighbour. In July 1846 Emerson notes that Thoreau had been reading to him extracts from his *A Week on the Concord and Merrimack Rivers*. Now this work (section, Monday) is an enthusiastic eulogy of the Gita, and of the great poems and philosophies of India. Thoreau suggested a "joint

[1] "If a man is at heart just, then in so far is he God: the safety of God, the immortality of God, the majesty of God, do enter into that man with justice....For all beings proceed out of this same spirit, which is differently named love, justice, temperance, in its different applications, just as the ocean receives different names on the several shores which it washes....The perception of this law of laws awakens in the mind a sentiment which we call the religious sentiment, and which makes our highest happiness. Wonderful is its power to charm and to command. It is a mountain air....It makes the sky and the hills sublime, and the silent song of the stars is it...."
[Address to the Senior Class in Divinity College, Cambridge (U.S.A.), July 15, 1838].

Bible" of the Asiatic Scriptures, Chinese, Hindus, Persians, Hebrews, "to carry to the ends of the earth." And he took for his motto, *Ex Oriente lux*.[1]

It may be imagined that such suggestions were not thrown away upon Emerson, and that the ardent *Asiatism* of Thoreau was extended to him.

It was at the same time that the "Transcendental Club" he had founded was in full swing; and after 1840, *The Dial*, its quarterly, which he edited with the American Hypatia, Margaret Fuller, published translations from the Oriental languages. The emotion produced in him by Indian thought must have been very strong for him to write in 1856 such a deeply Vedantic poem as his beautiful *Brahma*.[2]

It must be taken into consideration that New England

---

[1] Thoreau gives his sources: a French translation of the Gita, whose author must be Burnouf, although he does not mention him, published in 1840, and more important, the English translation of Charles Wilkins, of which an edition had just appeared in 1846 with a preface of Warren Hastings. This great man (Hastings), the conqueror, although he governed India, submitted to and publicly avowed the spiritual domination of the land of the Vedas. In 1786 he "recommended" a translation of the Bhagavad-Gita to the President of the East India Company, and wrote a preface to it, where he declares that "the writers of the Indian philosophies will survive, when the British dominion in India shall long have ceased to exist, and when the sources which it yielded of wealth and power are lost to remembrance." Thoreau also mentions other Hindu works, such as the *Shakuntala* of Kalidasa, and speaks enthusiastically of Manu, whom he knew through the translations of William Jones. His *Wheel's Journey*, written from 1839 onwards, was published in 1849.

I owe these details to Miss Ethel Sidgwick, who was kind enough to look them up for me with the learned help of the Master of Balliol College and of Prof. Goddard of Swarthmore College (Pennsylvania). I here make grateful acknowledgment to them for their valuable help.

[*Ex* etc. = Light from the East.—*Translator*.]

[2] If the red slayer think he slays,
Or if the slain think he is slain,
They know not well the subtle ways
I keep, and pass, and turn again.

at that time was going through a crisis of spiritual renaissance and intoxicating idealism, corresponding (though composed of very different elements, less cultivated, more robust, and infinitely nearer to nature) to the idealistic flame of Europe before 1848.[1] The anarchic Brookfarm of George Ripley (between 1840 and 1847), the feverish assembly of the *Friends of Universal Progress* at Boston in 1840, brought together in one group men and women of all opinions and professions, all fired with primitive energy, and aspiring to shake off the shackles of past lies without knowing what

> Far or forgot to me is near;
> Shadow and sunlight are the same;
> The vanish'd gods to me appear;
> And one to me are shame and fame.
>
> They reckon ill who leave me out;
> When me they fly, I am the wings;
> I am the doubter and the doubt,
> And I the hymn the Brahmin sings.
>
> The strong gods pine for my abode,
> And pine in vain the sacred Seven;
> But thou, meek lover of the good!
> Find me and turn thy back on heaven.

My friends, Waldo Frank and Van Wyck Brooks, have given me some important details. In 1854 the Englishman, Thomas Cholmondeley, the nephew of the great Bishop, Reginald Heber, visited Concord and became the friend of the whole intellectual colony. On his return to England he sent Thoreau a collection of Oriental classics in 44 volumes. Thoreau said that it was practically impossible to find any of these works in America. It may justly be thought that Emerson's poem, *Brahma*, was the flower of the tree which had just drunk greedily of this flood of Indian thought.

[1] This is only one example among a thousand others of the synchronism of the human Soul in its most diverse ethnic expressions—which has often led me to think, as I have studied history, of the different branches of the same tree, mutually sharing the same changing seasons. The conviction has slowly ripened in my mind until it is now firmly established that all the laws governing the particular evolution of peoples, nations, classes, and their struggles, are subordinate to greater cosmic laws controlling the greater evolution of humanity.

truth to adopt; for no human society can live unless it has persuaded itself that it possesses *The* Truth![1] Alas, the Truth espoused by America during the subsequent half century bears no resemblance to the generous expectation of the honeymoon! Truth was not ripe, still less those who wished to pluck it. Its failure, however, was by no means due to lack of noble ideals and great ideas, but they were all too mixed and too hastily digested, without time for them to be healthily assimilated. The nervous shocks produced by the grave political and social upheavals after the War of Secession, the morbid haste which has developed into the frantic rhythm of modern civilisation, have thrown the American spirit off its balance for a long time. It is, however, not difficult to trace during the second half of the century the seeds sown by the free pioneers of Concord—Emerson and Thoreau. But from their grain what strange bread has been kneaded by the followers of the "Mind-cure", and of Mrs. Mary Baker Eddy!

Both of them have used, more or less wittingly, Indian elements strained through the idealism of

[1] John Morley, in his critical Essay on Emerson, has painted a charming picture of this hour of intellectual intoxication—of this "madness of enthusiasm", as Shaftesbury called it, which from 1820 to 1848 turned the heads of New England.

Harold D. Carey, in a recent article in *The Bookman* (February, 1929) devoted mainly to this strange Brookfarm, has shown the revolutionary character of its spiritual and social movement and the impression of "Bolshevism", which it produced on the minds of the governing classes and on middle class opinion. It was an unchaining of terrifying and troublous furies. Especially did they turn against Emerson, and accuse him of being chiefly responsible for the spirit of revolt. Our generation has forgotten all too soon the very brave part played by Emerson and his friends. Thoreau and Theodore Parker at the same time flagellated legal lies, and protested against the nascent monster of imperialism in affairs (on the occasion of the war engineered by the American Government against Mexico in 1847).

Emerson.[1] But they have reduced them to the dead level of a utilitarianism that looks only to the immediate profit, of a kind of mystic hygiene, resting on a prodigious

[1] William James said of the "Mind-cure": "It is made up of the following elements: the four Gospels, the idealism of Berkeley and Emerson, spiritism with its law of the radical evolution of souls through their successive lives, optimistic and vulgar evolutionism, and the religions of India."

Charles Boudouin adds that after 1875 the influence of the French hypnotic schools was superimposed. He notes that in return Coué profited by it, for he learnt English especially to make the acquaintance of the vulgarised mysticism of America, and has developed from it its simplest, most rational, and positivist expression.

But it is necessary to go back to the magnetism of Mesmer at the beginning of the eighteenth century for the common source, and further to the elements making up this powerful and enigmatic personality (*cf.* Pierre Janet: *Médications psychologiques*, Vol. I, Alcan, 1919).

As for Christian Science, it is enough to mention the little lexicon of philosophic and religious terms added by Mrs. Eddy to her Bible: *Science and Health*, in order to see the likeness of certain of its fundamental ideas to those of Hindu Vedantism:..

Me or I. The Divine Principle, the Spirit, the Soul....Eternal Mind. There is only one ME or US, only one Principle or Mind, which governs all things....Everything reflects or refracts in God's Creation one unique Mind; and everything which does not reflect this unique Mind is false and a cheat...."

"God—the great I AM....Principle, Spirit, Soul, Life, Truth, Love, all substance, intelligence."

It would appear that Mrs. Eddy did not wish to acknowledge their origin. She has been silent on that point in the new editions of her book. But in the first she quoted from Vedantic philosophy. The Swami Abhedananda, a disciple of Ramakrishna, has related that the 24th edition of *Science and Health* contained a chapter, since suppressed, which began with four Vedantic quotations. In the same chapter Mrs. Eddy quoted the Bhagavad-Gita, from the translation of Charles Wilkins, published in London in 1785 and in New York in 1867. These quotations were afterwards omitted from the book: only one or two veiled allusions to Indian thought can be found. This attempt at dissimulation for the sake of the unwarned reader is a clumsy confession of its importance. (*Cf.* an article by Madeline R. Harding in *Prabuddha Bharata*, March, 1928).

Lastly, analogies to Indian thought are still more striking in the most important treatises on the Mind-cure by Horatio W. Dresser, Henry Good, and R. W. Trine. But as they date from the end of the century, that is to say, after the death of Vivekananda, they may well have owed a great deal to the teachings of the latter. They agree on all points with the rules of Yogic concentration and with the faith

credulity which gives to Christian Science[1] its proud pseudo-scientific aspect and its pseudo-Christianity.

One trait common to these doctrines is the vulgar optimism, which resolves the problem of evil by a simple denial, or rather by its omission. "Evil does not exist. Then let us turn away our eyes!"...Such an intellectual attitude in all its naïve simplicity was too often that of Emerson. He omitted as often as possible from his subjects those of illness and death. He hated the shades: "Respect the light!" But it was the respect of fear. His eyes were feeble and so he began by putting the sun under a shade. In this he was only too closely followed by his fellow countrymen. Perhaps it is not too much to say that such optimism was necessary for action, but I have no great faith in the energy of a man or of a people, which rests on conditions contrary to the *Natura Rerum*. I prefer Margaret Fuller's saying: "I accept the universe." But whether one accepts it or not, the first essential is to see it and to see it as a whole! We shall soon hear Vivekananda saying to his English disciples, "Learn to recognise the Mother in Evil, Terror, Sorrow, Denial, as well as in Sweetness and in Joy." Similarly the smiling Ramakrishna from the depths of his dream of love and bliss could see and remind the complaisant preachers of a "good God" that Goodness was not enough to define the Force which daily

behind it. The French reader will find some characteristic extracts in the *Varieties of Religious Experience* of William James (French translation of Frank Abauzit, 1906, pp. 80-102).

[1] It is to be remarked that this name, *Christian Science*, had already been used by a precursor of Mrs. Eddy, Dr. Quimby, who several years before her (about 1863) had laid down a similar doctrine under the name of Christ Science, Christian Science, Divine Science, the Science of Health. Quimby's manuscripts, recently published, establish his influence over Mrs. Eddy.

sacrificed thousands of innocents.[1] Therein lies the capital difference separating India and heroic Greece from Anglo-Saxon optimism. They look Reality in the face, whether they embrace it, as in India, or struggle against it and try to subdue it, as in Greece. But with them action never impinges on the domain of knowledge as in America, where knowledge has been domesticated in the service of action and wears a livery with gold-braided cap bearing the name: Pragmatism.[2] It can easily be understood that a Vivekananda would not like such trappings, concealing, as they did, puny and degraded bastards of his glorious, free, and sovereign Vedantism of India.[3]

*

But overtopping this herd of living men there was a dead giant,[4] whose shade was a thousand times warmer

[1] See later, p. 142, Note 2.

[2] In weakened post-war Europe these same moral characteristics have unfortunately a tendency to be established; and the worst feature of this moral slackness is that it is accompanied with false bragging which flatters itself on its realism and virility.

[3] At the time of his first stay in the United States, the Metaphysical College of Massachusetts, opened by Mrs. Eddy at Boston, where she taught in seven years more than four thousand pupils, was temporarily closed (in October, 1889) in order to allow the foundress, "Pastor Emeritus of the First Church of Christ Scientist," to write her new *Science and Health*, published in 1891. The College re-opened under her presidency in 1899.

The Mind-cure was flourishing and produced the New Thought, which is to Christian Science what rationalistic Protestantism is to orthodox Catholicism.

The Theosophical Society, of which one of the two founders (in 1875), Colonel Olcott, was an American, worked vigorously in India and elsewhere. His action, as I have said, now and then came up against that of Vivekananda.

I have only mentioned here the three chief currents then stirring the religious subconsciousness of America, together with Revivalism (the religion of revivals) also leading to abandonment to subconscious forces, while Myers was evolving (between 1886 and 1905) the scientifico-spirit theory of knowledge and the subconscious life.

A crater in eruption. Mud and fire.

[4] Besides Whitman, who was already dead, there was another, no

than such pale reflections of the Sun of Being, seen through their cold methodist window-panes. He stood before Vivekananda and held out his great hand to him.... How was it that he did not take it?... Or rather (for we know that later in India Vivekananda read his *Leaves of Grass*) how is it that Vivekananda's chroniclers, however careless and ill-informed, have managed to leave this capital event out of their story: the meeting of the Indian Ambassador of the Atman-Brahman with the epic singer of *Myself*—Walt Whitman?

He had just died on March 26, 1892, the previous year, near Camden, the workman's suburb of Philadelphia. The triumphant memory of his obsequies—not pagan as they have been described, but exactly in the spirit of Indian universalism[1]—was still reverberating. Vivekananda saw more than one of Whitman's intimates coming to him; he was even joined in friendship to the man, who had bidden the last farewell to the poet, the famous agnostic and materialist author, Robert Ingersoll.[2] He more than once argued with

less great, who had an equal affinity to the spirit of India: Edgar Allan Poe. His *Eureka*, published in 1848, showed thought closely akin to that of the Upanishads. Some people, such as Waldo Frank, believe that he must in the course of his wanderings (it is practically certain that he visited Russia in his early youth) have come in contact with Indian mysticism. But *Eureka* did not affect contemporary thought. Even though Whitman for a time collaborated with Poe (in the *Broadway Journal* and in the *Democratic Review*), it is certain that he never made an intimate of Poe, that he never fathomed his thought, that he in fact felt an instinctive antipathy to him, and that it was only with an effort that he made a tardy recognition of his greatness. (In 1875, at the age of 56, he went to Baltimore for the inauguration of a monument to Poe.) Poe remained an isolated figure in his age.

[1] Between each discourse some great saying was read from the Bible of Humanity: "Here are the words of Confucius, of Gautama Buddha, of Jesus Christ, of the Koran, of Isaiah, of John, of the Zend Avesta, of Plato."

[2] In this funeral speech Ingersoll celebrated the poet, who had sung the splendid "Psalm of Life" and a tribute of thanks "to the Mother

him in friendly fashion,[1] so it is impossible that he had not heard of Whitman.

However famous this great man may be through the many works that have been devoted to him in all lands, it is necessary for me to give here a short account of his religious thought; for that is the side of his work that has come least into the limelight—and at the same time it is the kernel.

There is nothing hidden in its meaning. The good Whitman does not try to veil his nakedness. His faith appears best of all in *Leaves of Grass*, and is especially concentrated in one great poem, which has been thrown too much into the shade by his *Song of Myself*, but which must be replaced in the front rank, where Whitman himself placed it at the head of his own definitive edition, immediately following the *Inscriptions*, namely *Starting from Paumanok*.[2]

in response to Her kiss and Her embrace." Ingersoll thought of Nature as "the Mother". Whitman's poems are full of Her, and there She is sometimes Nature, "the great, savage, silent Mother, accepting all," sometimes America, "the redoubtable Mother, the great Mother, Thou Mother with equal children." But whatever may be the mighty entity to which the word is attached, it always represents a conception of a sovereign being, and its deep tones recall the conception of India; they are always attached to the visible God, on whom all living beings depend.

[1] The great *Life of the Swami Vivekananda*, published by his disciples, has very briefly noticed several of these interviews, merely remarking that they show that Vivekananda has the *entrée* into the freest and most advanced circles of American thought. Ingersoll in the course of one discussion warned Vivekananda in a friendly way to be prudent. He revealed to him the hidden fanaticism of America, not yet stamped out. Forty years before, he said, an Indian Vedantist would have run the risk of being burnt alive, and still more recently of being stoned.

[2] *Paumanok* does not appear in the first three editions (1855, 1856, and 1860-1). It is not included until the fourth (1867), where it is placed at the beginning of the volume. But in the first edition of the *Leaves of Grass*, as my friend Lucien Price pointed out to me, the *Song of Myself* opens on page 2; and in its original, much starker

What does he say in it?

"I inaugurate a religion....

... I say the whole earth and all the stars in the
sky are for religion's sake....

Know you, solely to drop in the earth the germs of
a greater religion....

I sing....

For you to share with me two greatnesses, and a
third one arising inclusive and more resplendent.

The greatness of Love and Democracy, and the
greatness of Religion...."

(Why then have the first two "greatnesses", which
are of an inferior order, generally eclipsed the third,
which embraces and dominates them, in the minds of
Whitman's commentators?)

What was this religion that so filled his heart that
he meditated spreading it abroad throughout all
lands by means of lectures, in spite of the little taste
he had for speaking in public?[1] It is summed up and
contained in one word, which rings in the ears wonderfully like Indian music: the word *Identity*. It fills
the whole work. It is to be found in almost all his
poems.[2]

Identity with all forms of life at every instant. The
immediateness of realised Unity. And the certainty of

and more virile form, it produces a striking impression: everything
that is vital and heroic in the Great Message is to be found condensed
with flaming clarity in it. (*Cf.* William Sloane Kennedy: *The Fight
of a Book in the World.*)

[1] Ibid, pp. 140-171. He thought of it before and after the publication
of his poem.

[2] *Starting from Paumanok, Song of Myself, Calamus, Crossing Brooklyn
Ferry, A Song of Joys, Drum-Taps, To Think of Time,* etc.

The word can be used to mean two rather different things: (1) the
more usual: an immediate perception of Unity; (2) the permanence
of the Ego throughout the eternal journey and its metamorphoses.

Eternity for every second, for every atom of existence.
How had Whitman come by this faith?

Certainly by enlightenment, by some blow he had
experienced, by illumination, probably arising from
some spiritual crisis, a short time after he had reached
his thirtieth year and experienced the emotions
aroused by his journey to New Orleans,[1] of which little
is known.

It is improbable that it was any reading of Indian
thought that touched him. When Thoreau, in November,
1856, came to tell him that his *Leaves of Grass* (first
appeared in July, 1855, then a second edition in the
summer of 1856) recalled to his mind the great Oriental
poems and to ask if he knew them, Whitman replied
with a categorical "No!" and there is no reason to
doubt his word.* He read little, certainly very few

It seems to me that it is this latter meaning that predominated in his
years of illness and old age.

If I was going to make a complete study of Whitman here, it
would be necessary to trace the evolution of his thought (without,
however, losing sight of its essential unity) under the blows of life,
from which he suffered much more than his publicly confessed
optimism would lead one to suspect. *Cf.* in the collection: *Whispers
of Heavenly Death*, his *Hours of Despair*. Then the invincible spirit,
insufficiently nourished by life, is restored by death. Then the
"known" life is completed by the "unknown". Then "day"
brings new light to "non-day". (*Cf. To Think of Time: Night on
the Prairies*). And his ear is opened to other "music" that his
ignorance had not previously recognised. Finally, the dead are more
alive than the living, "haply the only living, only real". (*Pensive
and Faltering*).

"I do not think that Life provides for all....But I believe Heavenly
Death provides for all." (*Assurances*).

"I was thinking the day most splendid till I saw what the not-day
exhibited....Oh! I see how Life cannot exhibit all to me as the
day cannot—I see that I am to wait for what will be exhibited by
death." (*Night on the Prairies*, etc.).

But the foundation of the faith, *Identity*, the solely existent eternity,
never varied.

[1] *Cf.* Bucke: *Walt Whitman.*

* But he had read "the ancient Hindoo poems" before writing his

books; he did not like libraries and men brought upon them. To the very end of his life he does not seem to have had any curiosity to verify the similarity between his thought and that of Asia, so obvious to the little circle of Concord. The extreme vagueness of the expressions used every time that he introduces a glimpse of India into his Homeric enumerations is the best guarantee of his ignorance.[1]

It is then all the more interesting to discover how without going beyond himself—a hundred per cent American self—he could all unwittingly link up with Vedantic thought. (For its kinship did not escape any of the Emerson group, beginning with Emerson himself, whose genial quip is not sufficiently well known: "*Leaves of Grass* seems to be a mixture of the Bhagavad-Gita and *The New York Herald*.")

The starting point with Whitman was in the profundities of his own race, of his own religious life—paradoxical though it may seem. His paternal family belonged to the Quaker Left, grouped round a free

*Leaves of Grass.* See his own admission in his *A Backward Glance o'er Travel'd Roads.* Also see pp. 513-14 of *Prabuddha Bharata*, October, 1930.—*Publisher.*

[1] Once or twice he mentions *Maya* (*Calamus:* "The basis of all metaphysics"), *avatar* (*Song of Farewell*) and *nirvana* (*Sands at Seventy:* "Twilight"), but in the way of an illiterate: "mist, nirvana, repose and night, forgetfulness."

The *Passage to India*, whose title has a symbolic and quite unexpected sense, does not furnish him with anything more precise about Indian thought than the poor verse:

"Old occult Brahma, interminably far back, the tender and junior Buddha...."

What he says of the Hindu and of India is still poorer in *Greeting to the World.*

The only piece whose inspiration seems to have come from an Asiatic source is in the last collection of his seventy-second year: *Good-bye my Fancy* (1891), the *Persian Lesson*, where he makes mention of Sufi. And there was no need for him to go to Persia to hear these very banal truths.

believer, Elias Hicks, to whom at the end of his life Whitman dedicated a pamphlet. He was a great religious individualist, free from all church and all *credo*, who made religion consist entirely of inner illumination, "the secret silent ecstasy."[1]

Such a moral disposition in Whitman was bound to bring about from his childhood a habit of mystic concentration, having no precise object, but filtering nevertheless through all the emotions of life. The young man's peculiar genius did the rest. His nature possessed a kind of voracious receptivity, which made him not only, like ordinary men, glean from the vine-arbour of the spectacle of the universe some grains of pleasure or pain, but he instantaneously incorporated himself with each object that he saw. He has described this rare disposition in the admirable poem, *Autumn Rivulets:*

"There was a child went forth....

And the first object he look'd upon, that object he became.

And that object became part of him for the day or a certain part of the day.

Or for many years or stretching cycles of years...."

Instinctively rather than reflectively he had reached the conclusion that the whole universe was for him not object but subject—it was he. When he suddenly in his thirties wrote an account of what appeared to him to be his real birth (probably about 1851-1852), it was a blinding flash, an ecstatic blow.

"Oh! the Joy," he said, "of my soul leaning pois'd on itself, receiving identity through materials....

---

[1] In a short address of May 31, 1889, the old poet, Whitman, said again. "Following the impulse of the spirit—for I am quite half of Quaker stock."

My soul vibrated back to me from them...."[1]

It seemed to him that he was "awake for the first
time and that all that had gone before was nothing
but a despicable sleep."[2]

Finally he heard some lectures or conferences of
Emerson's[3] and they may have intellectualised his intuition so that it came to fruition in ideas, however imperfectly determined and connected; for with this man,
always indifferent to the logic of reason and metaphysical construction,[4] his whole chain of thought brought
him inevitably to the present moment and to a degree
of illumination that made an infinity of space and time
arise from them. Hence he immediately perceived,
embraced, espoused, and became at one and the same
time each distinct object and their mighty totality, the
unrolling and the fusion of the whole Cosmos realised
in each morsel of the atom and of life. And how does
this differ from the point of ecstasy, the most intoxicated Samadhi of a Bhakti-Yogin, who, reaching in a
trice the summit of realisation and having mastered it,

[1] *A Song of Joys.*

[2] Camden Edition, III, 287.

[3] In 1887 Whitman denied that he had read Emerson before 1855.
But in 1856 he had generously written to Emerson that the latter
had been the Columbus of the "New Continent" of the Soul, and
Whitman its inspired explorer: "It is you who have discovered these
shores...." But the one does not cancel the other. It may be
said of this discovery that it was for Emerson, like that of Columbus,
the reasoned discovery of the New World, although in point of fact
the ships of the Northmen had sailed along centuries before, like the
young Whitman, without bothering to mark its position on the naval
log.

[4] "A morning-glory at my window satisfies me more than the
metaphysics of books." (*Song of Myself*).

And the beautiful part of *Calamus:* "Of the terrible doubt of
appearances." In this "terrible doubt" where everything reels, where
no idea, no reasoning is of any avail or proves anything, nothing
but the touch of a friend's hand can communicate absolute certainty:
"a hold of my hand has completely satisfied me."

comes down again to use it in all the acts and thoughts of his everyday life?[1]

Here then is a typical example of the predisposition to Vedantism, which existed in America long before the advent of Vivekananda. Indeed it is a universal disposition of the human soul in all countries and in all ages, and not contained, as Indian Vedantists are inclined to believe, in a body of doctrines belonging to one country alone. On the contrary, it is either helped or hindered by the chances of evolution among the different peoples and the creeds and customs whereon their own civilisations are built. It may be said that this attitude of mind is latent in all who carry within themselves a spark of the creative fire, and particularly is it true of great artists, in whom the universe is not only reflected (as in the cold glass of the medium), but incarnate. I have already mentioned in the case of Beethoven crises of Dionysiac union with the Mother, to use one name for the hidden Being whom the heart perceives in each earth-beat. Moreover, great European poetry in the nineteenth century, especially that of the English poets of the age of Wordsworth and Shelley, is full of such sudden gleams. But no Western poet possessed them so strongly or so consciously as Whitman, who collected all the scattered flames into a brazier, transmitting his intuition into a faith—faith in his people, faith in the world, faith in humanity as a whole.

How strange it is that faith was not brought face to face with Vivekananda's! Would he not have been struck by so many unexpected similarities—the senti-

[1] The Memoirs of Miss Helen Price (quoted by Bucke: *Whitman*, pp. 26-31) describe as an eye-witness the condition of ecstasy in which he composed some of his poems.

ment, so strong in Whitman, so insistent, so persistent,
of the journey of his ego "through trillions" of years
and incessant "incarnations"[1]—keeping the record in
double column of profit and loss of each of his previous
existences—the Atman-Brahman, the dual self wherein
no one god must debase himself before the others[2]—the
net of Maya, which he tears asunder[3] so that through

---

[1] "How can the real body ever die and be buried? Of your real
body... it will pass to future spheres, carrying what has accrued
to it from the moment of birth to that of death." (*Starting from
Paumanok*).

"The journey of the soul, not life alone, but death, many deaths,
I wish to sing...." (*Debris on the Shore*).

*Song of Myself* unfolds a magnificent panorama "from the summit
of the summits of the staircase:"—"far away at the bottom, enormous original Negation," then the march of the self, "the cycles of
ages" which ferry it "from one shore to another, rowing, rowing,
like cheerful boatmen" with the certainty that whatever happens they
will reach their destination!

"Whether I arrive at the end of today or in a hundred thousand
years or in ten millions of years."

From the poem: *To Think of Time:*
"Something long preparing and formless is arrived and form'd
in you.

You are henceforth secure, whatever comes or goes.

The law of promotion and transformation cannot be eluded."

*Song of Prudence* (in *Autumn Rivulets*) establishes according to
the Hindu law of Karma that "every move affects the births to
come," but unfortunately it introduces the word "business":
"investments for the future" (the only good ones are charity and
personal force).

Perhaps, the most striking of these songs, *Faces*, in the collection,
*From Noon to the Starry Night*, conjures up the most abject faces
like "muzzles" of a moment, which later shall be removed layer
by layer until the glorious face is revealed:

"Do you suppose I could be content with all, if I thought them
their own finale?...

I shall look again a score or two of ages."

Finally, when he was close upon death, he said, "I receive now
again of my many translations, from my avatars ascending, while others
doubtless await me." (*Farewell* from the *Songs of Parting*).

[2] "The Me myself....I believe in you, my soul, the other I am
must not abase itself to you....and you must not be abased to the
other...." (*Song of Myself*).

[3] His devoted friend, O'Connor, described him as: "The man

the widened meshes the illuminating face of God may
shine: "Thou orb of many orbs, Thou seething principle, Thou well-kept latent germ, Thou centre"[1]—the
glorious "Song of the Universal,"[2] wherein fusion is
realised by the harmony of antinomies, embracing all
religions, all beliefs, and unbeliefs, and even the doubts
of all the souls of the universe, which in India was the
very mission delegated by Ramakrishna to his disciples[3]
—his own message that "All is Truth!"[4]

And is it not true that they were alike even in some
individual characteristics, such as the high pride, com-
paring itself to God[5]—the warrior spirit of the great

who had torn aside disguises and illusions, and restored to the com-
monest things their divine significance." (Cf. Bucke: *Whitman*,
pp. 124-5.)

[1] *Inscriptions* (*To Thee Old Cause*). Might this not be culled from a
Vedic hymn?

[2] *Birds of Passage*.

[3] "I do not despise you priests, all time, the world over.
My faith is the greatest of faiths and the least of faiths.
Enclosing worship, ancient and modern cults, and all
Between ancient and modern....
Peace be to you sceptics, despairing shades....
Among you I can take my place just as well as among others...."
(*Song of Myself*).
"I believe materialism is true and spiritualism is true....."
(*With Antecedents in Birds of Passage*).
In the same collection he raises the same protest as Ramakrishna
against all attempt to found a theory or a new school upon him:
"I charge that there be no theory or school founded out of me.
I charge you to leave all free, as I have left all free."
(*Myself and Mine*).
Finally, like Ramakrishna and Vivekananda, he refused categorically
to take part in politics, and showed aversion for all social action
proceeding by exterior means. (*Cf.* the discourses delivered to H.
Traubel: *With Walt Whitman in Camden*. pp. 103 and 216.) The only
reform he sought was an inner one: "Let each man, of whatever class
or situation, cultivate and enrich humanity!"

[4] In the collection: *From Noon to Starry Night:*
"All is Truth....
I see that there are really ... no lies after all....
And that each thing exactly represents itself and what has preceded it."

[5] "Nothing, not God, is greater to one than one's self is....

Kshatriya, "the enemy of repose", and that of the brother of war, fearing neither danger nor death, but calling them rather[1]—the worship rendered to the Terrible, an interpretation recalling the dark yet magnificent confidences of Vivekananda to Sister Nivedita during their dream-like pilgrimage in the Himalayas?[2]

At the same time I can see clearly what Vivekananda would have disliked in Whitman—the ridiculous mixture of *The New York Hearld* and the Gita, which awoke the fine smile of Emerson: his metaphysical journalism, his small shopkeeper's wisdom, picked up from dictionaries—his eccentric affection of a bearded Narcissus, his colossal complacency with regard to himself and his people—his democratic Americanism, with its childish vanity and expansive vulgarity, ever seeking the limelight; all these must have roused the aristocratic disdain of the great Indian. Especially would Vivekananda have had no patience with the compromising coquettings of his idealism with the forbidden joys of "metaphysics", spiritualism, and intercourse with

I, who am curious about each, am not curious about God....
Nor do I understand who there can be more wonderful than
    myself....
Why should I wish to see God better than this day?
In the faces of men and women I see God, and in my own face
    in the glass." (*Song of Myself*).
"It is not the earth, it is not America who is so great.
It is I who am great or to be great....
The whole theory of the universe is directed unerringly to one
    single individual—namely to You."
                                      (*By Blue Ontario's Shore*).
[1] "I am the enemy of repose and give the others like for like,
My words are made of dangerous weapons, full of death.
I am born of the same elements from which war is born."
                                      (*Drum-Taps*).
[2] "I take you specially to be mine, your terrible rude forms.
    (Mother, bend down, bend close to me your face.)
I know not what these plots, and wars, and determents are for.

5

spirits, etc.... [1] But such differences would not have prevented this mighty lover from being drawn by Vivekananda's magnetic soul. And in point of fact, the contact took place later; for we have proof that Vivekananda read *Leaves of Grass* in India, and that he called Whitman "the Sannyasin of America"[2], thus acknowledging their common parentage. Is it to be believed that he did not make this discovery until the end of his stay in America, because, during the course of it, no

I know not the fruition of success, but I know that through war and crime your work goes on."

(*By Blue Ontario's Shore*).

*Cf*. Vivekananda, p. 141 of this volume.

[1] One of his last poems: *Continuities* (from the collection, *Sands at Seventy*) is inspired (he says so himself) by a conversation with a spirit. He had a firm belief repeated many times in the real return of the dead among the quick:

"The living look upon the corpse with their eyesight.

But without eyesight lingers a different living and looks curiously on the corpse." (*To Think of Time*).

"Living beings, identities, now doubtless near us in the air that we know not of." (*Starting from Paumanok*).

He was convinced of the distinction between "a real body" and an "excremental body":

"The corpse you will leave will be but excrementitious.

(But) yourself spiritual bodily, that is eternal.....will surely escape."

(*Cf. To One Shortly to Die* from the collection *Whispers of Heavenly Death*.)

"Myself discharging my excrementitious body, to be burn'd, or render'd to powder or buried.

My real body doubtless left to me for other spheres."

(*A Song of Joys*).

[2] *Cf*. the great *Life of the Swami Vivekananda* by his disciples, Vol. III, 199. It was at Lahore towards the end of 1897, a short time after his return from America, that Vivekananda found a copy of *Leaves of Grass* in the library of one of his Indian hosts, Tirtha Ram Goswami (who later went to America under the name of Swami Ramtirtha, but who was then a Professor of Mathematics at a College in Lahore). He asked leave to take it away to read or to re-read it (it is not possible to decide which, from the words of the account), and it adds: "He used to call Whitman 'the Sannyasin of America.'" But whether this judgment was prior or subsequent to that date is impossible to determine.

mention of the relationship was published by his disciples in detail?

Whatever the truth may be, the spirit of Whitman was there, attesting that America was ready to listen to Indian thought. That spirit acted as her forerunner. The old prophet of Camden had solemnly announced the arrival of India:

"To us, my city,...

The Originatress comes,

The nest of languages, the bequeather of poems, the
     race of old....

The race of Brahma comes."[1]

He opened his arms to the Pilgrim of India and confided him to America, "the nave of democracy":

"The past is also stored in thee....

Thou carriest great companions.

Venerable priestly Asia sails this day with thee."[2]

It is clear then that the Indian biographers of Vivekananda have been regrettably remiss in not putting Whitman in the front rank of those, whose thought did the honours of the New World to the stranger guest.[*]

But having put him in his proper place near Vivekananda, shoulder to shoulder and with equally broad shoulders, we must be careful not to exaggerate his influence in America. This Homer of "En-masse"[3]

---

[1] *A Broadway Pageant.*
[2] *Thou Mother with Thy Equal Brood.*
[*]Apart from the differences of view that might exist between M. Rolland and the authors of *The Life of the Swami Vivekananda* about Whitman, the plan of the *Life* itself precluded any consideration of the "forerunners" whom M. Rolland considers in this chapter. Besides M. Rolland himself admits that Whitman's influence was very little in America.—*Publisher.*
[3] "One's-Self I sing, a simple separate person.
     Yet utter the word Democratic, the word En-masse."
These are the first words of *Inscriptions* at the beginning of the book.

did not succeed in conquering the masses. The
annunciator of the great destinies of Democracy in
America died misunderstood and almost unnoticed by
the Democrats of the New World. The singer of the
"Divine Average"[1] was only loved and revered by a
small group of chosen artists and exceptional men—
and perhaps more in England than in the United States.

But this is true of almost all real precursors. And it
does not make them any the less the true representatives
of their people that their people ignore them. In them
is liberated out of due time the profound energies hidden
and compressed within the human masses: they
announce them; sooner or later they come to light.
The genius of Whitman was the index of the hidden
soul sleeping—(she is not yet wide awake)—in the
ocean depths of his people of the United States.

"And mine (my word), a word of the modern, the word
En-masse.
A word of faith that never balks...." (*Song of Myself*).
[1] "O, such themes,—equalities, O Divine average!"
(*Starting from Paumanok*).
He announces for the future "Liberty and the divine average."
(*And Walk These Broad Majestic Days of Peace* from the collection:
*From Noon to Starry Night*).
And his last word, his poem, *Good-bye my Fancy*, proclaims again,
"I chant the common bulk, the general average horde."

# V

## THE PREACHING IN AMERICA

THE whole of the spiritual manifestations that I have just explained in brief (I delegate their deep study to the future historian of the new Soul of the West), will have made it clear that the thought of the United States, thus fermenting and working for half a century, was more ready than any in the West to receive Vivekananda.

Hardly had he begun to preach than men and women athirst for his message came flocking to him. They came from all parts: from salons and universities, sincere and pure Christians and sincere free-thinkers and agnostics. What struck Vivekananda—what strikes us still today—was the existence side by side in that young and old globe, for ever the enigma, the hope and the fear of the future, of the highest and the most sinister forces, an immense thirst for truth, and an immense thirst for the false, absolute disinterestedness and an unclean worship of gold, childlike sincerity and the charlatanism of the fair. Despite sudden outbreaks of passion, to which his hot-headed character was prone, Vivekananda was great enough to keep the balance between sympathy and antipathy; he always recognised the virtues and the real energy of Anglo-Saxon America.

In point of fact, although on this soil he founded works more enduring than elsewhere in Europe, he never felt the earth so solid under his feet as he did later in England. But there was nothing great in the new America which he did not handle with respect, which he did not try to understand and to hold up to his compatriots as an example to be admired, such as economic policy, industrial organisation, public instruction, museums and art galleries, the progress of science, hygienic institutions, and social welfare work. The blood rose to his face when he compared the magnificent efforts made with regard to the last of these by the United States and the liberality of public expenditure for the public good to the social apathy of his own country. For, although he was always ready to scourge the hard pride of the West, he was still readier to humiliate that of India under the crushing example of Western social work.

"Ah! butchers!" he cried, when he came out of a model prison for women, where the delinquents were humanely treated, as he compared the cruel indifference of the Indians towards the poor and weak, unable to help themselves. "No religion on earth preaches the dignity of humanity in such a lofty strain as Hindusim, and no religion on earth treads upon the necks of the poor and the low in such a fashion as Hinduism. Religion is not in fault, but it is the Pharisees and Sadducees."

And so he never ceased to beseech, to stimulate, to harry the youth of India:

"Gird up your loins, my boys! I am called by the Lord for this.... The hope lies in you—in the meek, the lowly, but the faithful.... Feel for the miserable and look up for help—it *shall come*. I have travelled twelve years with this load in my heart and this idea in my head. I have gone from door to door of the so-called rich and great. With a bleeding heart I have

crossed half the world to this strange land seeking
for help.... The Lord... will help me. I may perish
of cold and hunger in this land, but I bequeath to
you, young men, this sympathy, this struggle for the
poor, the ignorant, the oppressed.... Go... down on
your faces before Him and make a great sacrifice, the
sacrifice of a whole life for them... these three hundred millions, going down and down every day....
Glory unto the Lord, we will succeed. Hundreds will
fall in the struggle—hundreds will be ready to take
it up.... Faith—sympathy. Life is nothing, death is
nothing.... Glory unto the Lord—march on, the Lord
is our General. Do not look back to see who falls—
forward—onward!..."

And this magnificent letter, inspired by the spectacle
of the noble social philanthropy of America, ends on a
note of hope, which shows that he who could scourge
the Tartuffes of the Christian faith, felt more than any
other the breath of *Amor-Caritas*,[1] animating this same
faith in its sincerity: "I am here amongst the children
of the Son of Mary, and the Lord Jesus will help me."[2]

No, he was never the man to trouble about religious
barriers. He was to utter this great truth:[3] "It is well
to be born into a church, but it is terrible to die there."

To the scandalised outcries of bigots—Christian or
Hindu—who felt themselves called upon to guard the
closed doors of their exclusive faiths so that no infidel
might enter, he replied, "I do not care whether they

[1] *Amor-caritas=Blessed Love.—Translator.*
[2] *The Life of the Swami Vivekananda*, Chapter LXXVII. Letter
written at the beginning of his stay in America before the opening
of the Parliament of Religions.

He translated a few chapters of *The Imitation of Christ* into Bengali
and wrote a preface to it.
[3] In London, 1895.

are Hindus, or Mohammedans, or Christians, but those that love the Lord will always command my service. Plunge into the fire, my children.... Everything will come to you, if you only have faith.... Let each one of us pray day and night for the downtrodden millions in India, who are held fast by poverty, priestcraft, and tyranny—pray day and night for them.... I am no metaphysician, no philosopher, nay, no saint. I am poor, I love the poor.... Who feels in India for the two hundred millions of men and women sunken for ever in poverty and ignorance? Where is the way out?... Who will bring the light to them? Let these people be your God.... Him I call a Mahatman (great soul) whose heart bleeds for the poor.... So long as the millions live in hunger and ignorance, I hold every man a traitor, who having been educated at their expense, pays not the least heed to them!..."[1]

And so he never forgot for a single day the primary idea of his mission, the same whose talons had gripped him as he travelled across India from the North to the South, from the South to the North between the Himalayas and Cape Comorin—to save his people, body and soul (the body first: bread first!), to mobilise the whole world to help him in his task by widening his appeal until it become the cause of the people, the cause of the poor and the oppressed of the whole world. Give and take! Let there be no more talk of the hand stretched out for charity falling in pity from above. Equality! He who receives, gives, and gives as much as he receives, if not more. He receives life, he gives life, he gives God. For all the ragged, the dying, the

---

[1] *The Life of the Swami Vivekananda,* Chapter LXXXIII. Letter to his Indian disciples about 1894-1895.

poor of India are God. Under the pressure of the suffering and outrage grinding down the peoples throughout
the ages, the wine of the Eternal Spirit flows, ferments,
and is concentrated. Take and drink! They also can
use the words of the Sacrament: "For this is my
Blood." They are the Christ of the nations.

And so in Vivekananda's eyes the task was a double
one: to take to India the money and goods acquired by
Western civilisation; to take to the West the spiritual
treasures of India. A loyal exchange. A fraternal and
mutual help.

It was not only the material goods of the West that
he counted, but social and moral goods as well. We
have just read the cry torn from him by the spirit of
humanity which a great self-respecting nation felt
bound to show even to those she had been obliged to
condemn. He was filled with admiration and emotion
by the apparent democratic equality inherent in the
spectacle of a millionaire and a working woman elbow-
ing each other in the same tramway, and he gave it
a greater significance than it deserved; for he did not
realise the remorselessness of the machine, grinding
down all who fell.[1] He therefore felt more poignantly
the murderous inequality of the castes and the outcasts

[1] Later his eyes were opened. On his second journey to America
he tore aside the mask: and the social vices and the pride of race,
of faith, and of colour appeared in all their nakedness to choke him.
He, who had said in his beautiful discourse of September 19, 1893,
at the Parliament of Religions: "Hail, Columbia, motherland of
liberty! It has been given to thee, who never dipped her hand in
her neighbour's blood..." discovered the devouring imperialism
of the Dollar, and was angry that he had been deceived. He said
to Miss MacLeod, who repeated it to me, "So America is just
the same! So she will not be the instrument to accomplish the work,
but China or Russia" (meaning: the realisation of the double allied
mission of the West and the East).

of India: "India's doom was sealed," he wrote, "the very day they invented the word MLECHCHHA (the non-Hindu, the man outside) and stopped from communion with others."

He preached the primordial necessity of "an organisation that will teach Hindus mutual help and appreciation" after the pattern of Western democracies.[1]

He further admired the high intellectual attainments of so many American women and the noble use they made of their freedom. He compared their emancipation with the seclusion of Indian women, and the memory of the hidden sufferings of one of his dead sisters made it a labour of love for him to work for their emancipation.[2]

No racial pride was allowed to prevent him from stating the social superiority of the West in so many ways;[3] for he wished his people to profit from it.

But his pride would accept nothing except on a basis of equal return. He was keenly aware that he carried to the Western world, caught in the snare of its own demon of action and practical reason (he would have said: of physical reason), freedom through the spirit, the key to God contained in man and possessed by even the most destitute of Indians. The belief in man, which he found so highly developed in young America, was for him only the first step, the point of attack. Far from wishing to lessen it, as is the case with some forms

[1] Letter quoted (1894-1895).

[2] During his first journey, part of the money earned by his lectures was sent to a foundation for Hindu widows at Baranagore. And soon the idea took shape in his mind of sending to India Western teachers devoted to the formation of a new intellectual generation of Hindu women.

[3] "In spirituality the Americans are very inferior to us. But their society is very superior to ours." (Letter to his disciples at Madras.)

of European Christianity, his energy recognised in it a younger sister of good birth, but so blinded by the new sun that she walked blindly with rash and precipitate steps along the edge of the abyss. He believed that he was called upon to endow her with sight, to guide her to the beyond, the terrace of life from whence she could see God.

*

In America, therefore, he undertook a series of apostolic campaigns with the object of spreading over this immense spiritual stretch of fallow land the Vedantic seed, and watering it with Ramakrishna's rain of love. From the former he himself was to select such parts as were appropriate to the American public on account of their logical reasoning. He had avoided all mention of the latter, his Master, although he had preached his word. This omission was due to the modesty of passionate love, and even when he decided to speak directly of him to several very intimate disciples,[1] he forbade them to make this touching act of grace public.

He quickly shook himself free from Yankee lecturing organisations with their fixed itineraries drawn up by managers, who exploited and embarrassed him by beat-

---

[1] It was in June, 1895, at Thousand Island Park, on the river St. Lawrence, that he seems to have revealed for the first time in America to a group of chosen hearers the existence of Ramakrishna. And it was on February 24, 1896, at New York, that he finished a series of lectures by his beautiful discourse: *My Master*. Even then he refused to publish it; and when on his return to India surprise was expressed at his refusal, he replied with burning humility, "I did not allow it to be published as I have done injustice to my Master. My Master never condemned anything or anybody. But while I was speaking of him, I criticised the American people for their dollar-worshipping spirit. That day I learnt the lesson that I am not yet fit to talk of him."

(Reminiscences of a disciple, published in *The Vedanta Kesari* of January-February, 1923).

ing the big drum as if he were a circus turn.[1] It was at Detroit, where he stayed for six weeks, in 1894, that he threw off the insufferable yoke of such binding engagements. He besought his friends to have the contract cancelled, though at considerable pecuniary loss.[2] It was at Detroit, too, that he met her, who, of all his Western disciples, was to be with Sister Nivedita (Miss Margaret Noble) the closest to his thought: she took the name of Sister Christine (Miss Greenstidel).

From Detroit he returned to New York at the beginning of the winter of 1894. He was at first monopolised by a group of rich friends, who were far more interested in him as the man of the day than in his message. But he could not bear much restraint. He wanted to be alone and his own master. He was tired of this kind of steeplechase, which allowed nothing lasting to be founded; he decided to form a band of disciples and to start a free course. Rich friends with their offers to "finance" him made intolerable conditions: they would have forced him to meet only the exclusive society of "the right people". He was transported with rage and cried, "Shiva! Shiva! Has it ever come to pass that a

---

[1] I have in my hands an advertising prospectus, in which the headlines announce him in large letters as "One of the Giants of the Platform." His portrait is included with four inscriptions, proclaiming at the four cardinal points, that he is: "An Orator by Divine Right; A Model Representative of his Race; A Perfect Master of the English Language; The Sensation of the World's Fair Parliament." The announcement does not fail to enumerate his moral and physical advantages, especially his physical, his bearing, his height, the colour of his skin and clothing—with attestations from those who had seen him, heard him, and tried him. So might an elephant or a patent medicine have been described.

[2] From that time he went alone from town to town, at the invitation of such or such a society, giving sometimes as many as twelve or fourteen lectures in a week. At the end of a year he had visited all the important towns from the Atlantic coast to the Mississippi.

great work has been grown by the rich! It is the brain
and heart that creates and not the purse...."[1]

Several devoted and comparatively poor students
undertook the financial responsibility of the work. In
an "undesirable" quarter some sordid rooms were
rented. They were unfurnished. One sat where one
could—he on the floor, ten or twelve standing up. Then
it became necessary to open the door leading to the
staircase; people were piled up on the steps and landing. Soon he had to consider moving into larger quarters. His first course lasted from February to June,
1895,[2] and in it he explained the Upanishads. Every
day he instructed several chosen disciples in the exercise
of the double method of Raja-Yoga and Jnana-Yoga
—the first more especially psycho-physiological, aim-
ing at concentration through control of the vital energies by the subordination of the organism to the mind,
by silence imposed on the agitation of inner currents so
that nothing but the clear voice of the Being[3] might
make itself heard—the second, purely intellectual, and
akin to scientific reason, seeking the unification of the
spirit with the Universal Law, the Absolute Reality:
the Science-Religion.

About June, 1895, he had finished writing his famous
treatise on Raja-Yoga, dictated to Miss S. E. Waldo
(afterwards Sister Haridasi), which was to attract the

[1] Sister Christine: *Unpublished Memoirs.*

[2] At the same time he gave another series of public lectures on
Hindu religion to the Brooklyn Ethical Association. The proceeds
enabled him to pay the expenses of his private classes.

[3] India has never had the monopoly of such inner discipline. The
great Christian mystics of the West both knew and practised it.
Vivekananda was aware of this fact, and often invoked their example.
But India alone has made of the practice a precise science determined
by centuries of experiment and open to all without distinction of
creed.

attention of American physiologists, like William James, and later to rouse the enthusiasm of Tolstoy.[1] In the second part of this volume I shall speak again of this mystic method, as well as of the other chief Yogas. It is to be feared that this, with its more physiological character, only exercised the great attraction it had in America because she took it in its most practical sense, as promising material power. A giant with the brain of a child, this people is only interested as a rule in ideas which they can turn to their advantage. Metaphysics and religion are transmuted into false applied sciences, their object being the attainment of power, riches, and health—the kingdom of this world. Nothing could wound Vivekananda more deeply. For all truly spiritual Hindu masters, spirituality is an end in itself, their sole object is to realise it; they cannot forgive those who subordinate its pursuit to the acquisition of all kinds of power over material means! Vivekananda was particularly bitter in his condemnation of what to him was the unpardonable sin. But perhaps it would have been better "not to tempt the devil", so to speak, but to have led American intelligence into other paths at first. He probably realised it himself; for during the following winter his lessons were concerned with the other Yoga. At this time he was still at the experimental stage. The young Master was testing his power over men of another race; and he had not yet decided how he ought to exercise that power.

It was immediately after (June-July, 1895), during

[1] *Cf.* in the most recent editions of my *Life of Tolstoy*, the additional chapter: "The Response of Asia to Tolstoy". Tolstoy came to know Vivekananda's *Raja-Yoga* in the New York edition of 1896, as well as a work dedicated by Vivekananda to Ramakrishna in a posthumous edition of 1905, Madras.

the period of summer weeks spent among a chosen band of devoted souls at the Thousand Island Park, that Vivekananda definitely decided, according to the evidence of Sister Christine, on his plan of action.[1] On a hill near a forest above the river St. Lawrence on an estate generously placed at the Master's disposal for his exposition of the Vedanta, a dozen chosen disciples were gathered together. He opened his meditations by a reading from the Gospel according to St. John. And for seven weeks, not only did he explain the sacred books of India, but (a more important education from his point of view) he sought to awaken the heroic energy of the souls placed in his hands: "liberty", "courage", "chastity", "the sin of self-depreciation", etc. Such were some of the themes of his Interviews.

"Individuality is my motto," he wrote to Abhayananda, "I have no ambition beyond training individuals."[2]

He said again:

"If I succeed in my life to help one single man to attain freedom, my labours will not have been in vain."

Following the intuitive method of Ramakrishna, he never spoke above the heads of his listeners to the vague entity called the Public by most orators and preachers; he seemed to address each one separately. For, as he said, "one single man contains within himself the whole universe."[3] The nucleus of the Cosmos is in each individ-

[1] For this vital period at the Thousand Island Park the *Unpublished Memoirs* of Sister Christine provide information of the greatest importance.

[2] Autumn, 1895.

[3] In 1890, at the beginning of his wanderings in India, he had gone into ecstasy under a banyan at the edge of a stream, where the identity of the macrocosm and the microcosm and the whole universe contained in an atom had appeared to him.

ual. Mighty founder of an Order though he was, he
remained essentially a Sannyasin to the end,[1] and he
wished to give birth to Sannyasins, free men of God.
And so his conscious and definite object in America was
to free certain chosen souls and to make them in their
turn the disseminators of liberty.

During the summer of 1895, several Western disciples
responded to his call, and he initiated some of them.[2]
But they proved themselves later to be of very different
calibre. Vivekananda does not appear to have possessed
the eagle glance of Ramakrishna, who at sight infallibly
plunged into the depths of passing souls, unveiling their

[1] He was ceaselessly consumed with a burning desire for the free
life. "I long, Oh, I long for my rags, my shaven head, my sleep
under the trees, and my food from begging...." (January, 1895.)
His beautiful *Song of the Sannyasin* dates from the middle of this
same year, 1895.

[2] Sister Christine has left us portraits, not without humour, of
the personalities of these first American disciples, disappointing, as
was only to be expected, as some of them turned out to be. Particularly noteworthy are—the tumultuous Marie Louise (who took the
name of Abhayananda), a naturalised Frenchwoman, well known in
Socialist circles of New York: the complex and tormented Leon
Landsberg (Kripananda), a Russian Jew by birth, a very intelligent
New York journalist: Stella, an old actress, who sought in Raja-
Yoga the fountain of youth: the excellent little old man, Dr. Wight,
with his sweet and modest Antigone, Miss Ruth Ellis, both athirst for
spirituality. Then there were his disciples and friends of the first
rank—Miss S. E. Waldo of Brooklyn (later Sister Haridasi), who
has preserved for us in writing Vivekananda's first lecture cycle and
to whom he accorded (Spring 1896) the privilege of instruction in
the theory and practice of Raja-Yoga: Mrs. Ole Bull, the wife of a
celebrated Norwegian artist, a friend of Andersen, who was one of
the most generous donors to Vivekananda's work: Miss Josephine
MacLeod, to whose reminiscences I owe so much: Mr. and Mrs.
Francis Leggett of New York: Prof. Wright of Harvard, the provi-
dential friend of Vivekananda's arrival in America.

Finally comes the one nearest to his heart, the quiet Mary at the
feet of her Messiah—Miss Greenstidel (Sister Christine), who gathered
and treasured within herself the spirit of the Master, as it was poured
fourth in audible monologues.

At Greenacre on the coast of Maine for several days he soliloquised
in front of Christine without seeming to notice her presence, searching

past as well as their future, seeing them naked.* The Swami gathered chaff and wheat in his wake—content to let the morrow winnow the grain and scatter the chaff to the winds. But among their number he selected some devoted disciples, the greatest prize with the exception of Sister Christine being the young Englishman, J. J. Goodwin, who gave him his whole life: from the end of 1895 he was Vivekananda's self-appointed Secretary—his right hand the Master called him—and it is especially to him that we owe the preservation of the seed sown in America.

His stay in the United States was broken from August to December, 1895, by a visit to England, of which I shall speak later. It was resumed in the winter and lasted until the middle of April, 1896. He carried on his Vedantic instruction by two series of lectures and by private classes in New York; the first in December, 1895, on the Karma-Yoga (the way of God through work), whose exposition is supposed to be his masterpiece, and the second in February, 1896, on Bhakti-Yoga (the way of Love).

He spoke in all kinds of places in New York, Boston, and Detroit, before popular audiences, before the Metaphysical Society of Hartford, before the Ethical Society

for the path and examining all the problems of his life point by point from different angles. And at the end, when she softly expressed her wonder at the contradictory judgments he had expressed, he said, "Don't you understand? I was thinking aloud."

For, Vivekananda for his own satisfaction needed to put his own inner debates into words.

*Whenever the Swami liked, he also could see clearly into the past, present, and future of those that came to him. But he deliberately refrained from doing so. (See *The Life of the Swami Vivekananda*, Vol. II. pp. 335-36.) He helped them provided there was some fitness to receive. He knew the help would not be in vain. He was too full of loving kindness to easily refuse anyone.—*Publisher*.

of Brooklyn, and before students and professors of philosophy at Harvard.[1] At Harvard he was offered the Chair of Oriental Philosophy, at Columbia the Chair of Sanskrit. At New York under the presidency of Mr. Francis Leggett he organised the Vedanta Society, which was to become the centre of the Vedantist movement in America.

His motto was: tolerance and religious universalism. The three years of travel in the New World, the perpetual contact with the thought and faith of the West, had ripened his ideal of a universal religion. But in return his Hindu intelligence had received a shock. He felt the necessity for a complete and thorough reorganisation of the great religious and philosophical thought of India, if it was to recover its conquering force and power to advance, and penetrate and fertilise the West —a view he had already stated in Madras in 1893.[2] Its jungle of ideas and interlaced forms required to be put in order and its great systems classified round several stable pivots of the universal spirit. The apparently contradictory conceptions in Indian metaphysics (the Absolute Unity of Advaitism, "qualified" Unity, and Duality), which clashed even in the Upanishads, needed to be reconciled and the bridge built joining them to the conceptions of Western metaphysics by the establishment of a table of comparison destined to set forth all the points of relationship between the profound views of the oldest Himalayan philosophy and the principles

[1] Of particular importance was the lecture he gave at Harvard on *The Philosophy of the Vedanta*, and the discussion that followed (March 25, 1896).
[2] "The time has come for the propaganda of the faith.... The Hinduism of the Rishis must become dynamic...." After having concentrated on itself for centuries it must come out of itself.

admitted by modern science. He himself wished to write this *Maximum Testamentum*, this Universal Gospel, and he urged his Indian disciples to help him in the choice of the necessary materials for this reconstruction. He maintained that it was a case of translating Hindu thought into European language, to "make out of dry Philosophy and the intricate Mythology and queer starting Psychology a religion which shall be easy, simple, popular, and at the same time meet the requirements of the highest minds."[1]

That such an enterprise was not without the risk of changing the authentic design of the age-old tapestry, might easily be said—and was said—by orthodox Hindus and European Indianists. But Vivekananda did not believe them. He claimed on the contrary that so the great lines, covered by embroideries falsifying their truth—the original and profound essence—would be cleared, and he expressed this view on many occasions.[2]

Moreover for a mind such as his, religion can never be fixed for ever in certain texts, under whatever form they may appear. It progressed. If it stopped for a single instant it died. His universal ideal was always in motion. It was to be fertilised by the constant union of the East and the West, neither of them fixed in one doctrine or one point of time, but both living and

---

[1] "The abstract Advaita must become living—poetic—in everyday life; out of the hopelessly intricate Mythology must come concrete moral forms; and out of bewildering Yogism must come the most scientific and practical Psychology.

[2] But I must add that when he returned to India, he felt anew too forcibly the beauty and the living verity of the mythological forms of his people to sacrifice them to any preconceived idea of a radical simplification for which he had been perhaps disposed in America under the direct pressure of the Western spirit. The problem thenceforward was how to harmonise everything without renouncing anything.

advancing. And one of the objects of the Vedanta
Society was to watch that a continual interchange of
men and ideas took place, so that the circulation of the
blood of thought should be regular and bathe the entire
body of humanity.

# VI

## THE MEETING OF INDIA AND EUROPE

UNDER the dry and brilliant sky of New York with its electric atmosphere, Vivekananda's genius for action burned like a torch and consumed him in the midst of a world of frenzied activity. His expenditure of power in thought, writing, and impassioned speech dangerously compromised his health. When he came out of the crowds into whom he had infused his enlightened spirit,[1] he longed for nothing but "a corner apart" and "to lie there and die". His brief life, already wasted by the illness to which he succumbed, was further shortened by the agony of such overstrain. He never recovered from it,[2] and it was about this time that he felt the approach of death. He actually said, "My day is done."

[1] All witnesses agree in attesting to his overwhelming expenditure of energy, which at these meetings was communicated to the public like an electric charge. Some hearers came out exhausted and had to rest for several days as from a nervous shock. Sister Christine said, "His power was sometimes overwhelming." He was called "the Lightning Orator." In his last session in America he gave as many as seventeen lectures a week and private classes twice a day. And his was no case of abstract and prepared dissertation. Every thought was passion, every word was faith. Every lecture was a torrential improvisation.

[2] The first symptoms of diabetes (of which he died before his fortieth year) appeared during his adolescence, when he was seventeen or eighteen. (Then he really had an attack of malaria.—*Publisher*.)

He had also suffered in India from numerous and violent attacks of malaria. He had almost died of diphtheria contracted on one of his pilgrimages. During the great journey of two years through India he had abused his powers, making excessive journeys, half naked and underfed; it had happened several times that he had fallen fainting for want of food. Then was superimposed the overwork in America.

But the great game and his heroic mission always recalled him.

It was thought that a journey to Europe would distract him, but wherever he went he always spent himself. He stayed three times in England,[1] from September to the end of November, 1895, from April to the end of July, 1896, from October to December 16, 1896.

The impression it made on him was even deeper than that made by America and much more unexpected. Certainly he had nothing to complain of in the latter; for despite antipathies that he came up against and the Vanity Fair he was obliged to avoid, he had found there the most delicate sympathy,[2] the most devoted helpers and a virgin soil crying aloud to be sown.

But from the moment that he set foot in the Old World, he breathed a quite different atmosphere of intellectuality. Here was no longer the empty and barbarous aspiration of a young people to over-estimate the will, which made it fling itself on the Yoga of energy—the Raja-Yoga—in order to demand of it, even while they deformed it, infantile and unhealthy secrets for the conquest of the world. Here the labour of a thousand years of thought was to go direct to the teachings of India, to that which for Vivekananda the Advaitist was also the essential: to the methods of knowledge, to the Jnana-Yoga. Hence in explaining it to

[1] He came through Paris in August, 1895, before going to London. But he only gave it a brief glance this first time (visiting museums, cathedrals, the tomb of Napoleon), and his dominant impression was of an artistic people, highly gifted. He was to see France more at leisure five years later from July to October, 1900. We shall return to this again.

[2] One of its expressions which touched him most was towards the end of 1894 at the close of a lecture on the Ideals of Indian Women, wherein he had rendered pious homage to his mother—a letter to his mother at Christmas from the ladies of Boston.

Europe, he could start above the primary class: for Europe was capable of judging it with science and precision.

Although in the United States Vivekananda had met several intellectuals of mark, such as Professor Wright, the philosopher William James,[1] and the great electri-

---

[1] It was Mrs. Ole Bull who brought Vivekananda and William James together. The latter invited the young Swami to visit him and followed his teaching on Raja-Yoga with close attention. It is said that he practised it.

Vivekananda's disciples tend to believe that their Master exercised an influence over William James. They quote certain passages of American philosophy (Pragmatism), recognising in Vedantism the most logical and extreme of the monist systems, and in Vivekananda the most representative of the Vedantist missionaries. But that does not mean that William James had adopted these doctrines himself. He was and always remained an observer. Although mediocrely endowed for "religious experience" (he acknowledges it frankly), he nevertheless devoted a famous book to it. [The original work, *The Varieties of Religious Experience*, appeared in New York, June, 1902. James therein reproduced two series of lectures given in 1901 and 1902 in Edinburgh.] There is no doubt that Vivekananda contributed indirectly to the birth of the book. But James only quotes him by virtue of example among many others in the Chapter X on *Mysticism*, then twice among the Indian mystics (quotation from *Raja-Yoga*), and lastly at the conclusion of all the witnesses of mysticism drawn from all countries and all times, thus rendering him just homage (*Practical Vedanta* and *The Real and the Apparent Man*). [But for further information on the subject, see pp. 444-45, Vol. II, *The Life of the Swami Vivekananda.—Publisher.*]

It does not seem, however, that James drew as much as he might have done from the Swami's experiences, nor that the latter discovered to him the source of his thought: Ramakrishna. (James quotes him in passing carelessly from Max Müller's little book.) The importance of James' book is that it seems to be at the cross-roads, where gaps are being made by mighty assaults from all sides in the scientific positivism of the last years of the nineteenth century, so naïvely sure of itself: the Subconscious of Myers, the Relativity that was being rough hewn, Christian Science, the Vedantism of Vivekananda. The turning point of Western thought had come, the eve of the discovery of new continents. Vivekananda played his definite part in the great assault. But others even in the West had preceded him. And I think that the previous researches of Professor Starbuck in California (*The Psychology of Religion*) and his considerable collection of religious witnesses had inspired William James with the idea of his book rather than his knowledge of the Indian Swami.

cian Nicolas Tesla,[1] who had shown a sympathetic interest in him,[2] they were in general novices in the field of Hindu metaphysical speculation with everything to learn, like the graduates of philosophy at Harvard.

In Europe Vivekananda was to measure himself against the masters of Indology, such as Max Müller and Paul Deussen. The greatness of philosophical and philological science in the West was revealed to him in all its patient genius and scrupulous honesty. He was touched to the depths by it and rendered a more beautiful witness of love and veneration to it than any other has done to his people in India, quite ignorant of it, as he himself had been up to that time.

But the discovery of England had reserved for him an emotion of quite a different order. He came as an enemy, and he was conquered. On his return to India he was to proclaim it with superb loyalty, "No one ever landed on English soil with more hatred in his heart for a race than I did for the English.... There is none among you...who loves the English people more than I do now...."

And in a letter from England to an American disciple (October 8, 1896): "My ideas about the English have been revolutionised."[3]

---

[1] Nicolas Tesla was especially struck in Vivekananda's teaching by the cosmogonic Sânkhya theory and its relation to the modern theories of matter and force. We shall return to this point.

[2] Vivekananda also met in New York the highest representatives of Western science: Sir William Thomson (afterwards Lord Kelvin) and Professor Helmholtz. But they were Europeans whom the chance of an Electricity Congress had brought to America.

[3] He also said with a touch of irony, "I think I am beginning to see the Divine even inside the high and mighty Anglo-Indians. I think I am slowly approaching to that state when I would be able to love the very 'Devil' himself, if there were any." (July 6, 1896).

He discovered "a nation of heroes: the true Ksha-
triyas!... brave and steady.... Their education is
to hide their feelings and never to show them. But
with all this heroic superstructure there is a deep spring
of feeling in the English heart. If you once know how
to reach it, he is your friend for ever. If he has once an
idea put into his brain, it never comes out; and the
immense practicality and energy of the race makes it
sprout up and immediately bear fruit.... They have
solved the secret of obedience without slavish cringing
—great freedom with great law-abidingness."[1]

A race worthy of envy! She forces even those whom
she oppresses to respect her. Even those who are the
burning consciences of their subjected people and who
wish to raise them—Ram Mohun Roys, the Vivekanandas, the Tagores, the Gandhis—are obliged to
recognise the greatness of the victor, and perhaps even
the utility of loyal collaboration with her. In any case
if they had to change their conquerors, they would not
choose any other. With all the monstrous abuses of her
domination she seems the one nation of all the West
(and I include the whole of Europe and America in
that term) to offer the greatest scope for the free
development of Indian ideas.

But while he admired her, Vivekananda never lost
sight of his Indian mission. He meant to make use of
England's greatness in order to realise the spiritual
dominion of India. He was to write,[2] "The British
Empire with all its drawbacks is the greatest machine
that ever existed for the dissemination of ideas. I

[1] I have composed this paragraph from extracts of the letter of
1896 and a famous lecture given in Calcutta.
[2] To Mr. Francis Leggett, July 6, 1896.

mean to put my ideas in the centre of this machine and they will spread all over the world.... Spiritual ideas have always come from the downtrodden (Jews and Greece)."

During his first journey to London he was able to write to a disciple in Madras, "In England my work is really splendid."

His success had been immediate. The Press expressed great admiration for him. The moral figure of Vivekananda was compared to those of the highest religious apparitions—not only to those of his Indian forerunners, Ram Mohun Roy and Keshab, but to Buddha and to Christ.[1] He was well received in aristocratic circles; and even the heads of the churches showed their sympathy for him.

During his second visit he opened regular classes of Vedantic instruction; and, certain of an intelligent public, he started with the Yoga of the mind: the Jnana-Yoga.[2] In addition he gave several courses of lectures in a Piccadilly Picture Gallery, at Princes' Hall, in clubs, to educational societies, at Annie Besant's lodge, and to private circles. He felt the seriousness of his English hearers, in contrast to the superficial infatuation of the American public. Less brilliant, more conservative than the Americans, the English at first reserved their adherence; but when they gave it, they did not give it by halves. Vivekananda felt more at his ease and trusted them more. He spoke of him whom he had always been careful to veil from profane eyes— of his beloved Master Ramakrishna. He said with

[1] *The Standard, The London Daily Chronicle. Cf.* also the interview that appeared in *The Westminster Gazette.*

[2] Five classes a week, and on Friday evenings in addition a class for open discussion.

passionate humility that "all he was himself came from that single source.... that he had not one infinitesimal thought of his own to unfold...." And he proclaimed him as "the spring of this phase of the earth's religious life."

It was Ramakrishna who brought him into contact with Max Müller. The old Indianist, whose young regard followed with ever fresh curiosity all the palpitations of the Hindu religious soul, had already perceived, like the Magi of old, in the East the rising star of Ramakrishna.[1] He was eager to question a direct witness of the new Incarnation; and it was at his request that Vivekananda indited his memories of the Master, afterwards used by Max Müller in his little book on Ramakrishna.[2] Vivekananda was no less attracted by the Mage of Oxford, who, from his distant observatory had announced the passage of the great swan[3] through the Bengal sky. He was invited to his house on May 28, 1896; and the young Swami of India bowed before the old sage of Europe and hailed him as a spirit of his race, the reincarnation of an ancient Rishi, recalling his first births in the ancient days of Vedic India— "a soul that is every day realising its oneness with Brahman...."[4]

*

---

[1] In an article in *The Nineteenth Century*: "A Real Mahatman".

[2] Vivekananda asked Saradananda to collect data concerning Ramakrishna.

[3] "Paramahamsa."

[4] In his enthusiasm he wrote at once on June 6, 1896, for *The Brahmavadin*, his Indian Journal: "I wish I had a hundredth part of that love for my own motherland!...He has lived and moved in the world of Indian thought for fifty years or more....(It has) coloured his whole being.... He has caught the real soul of the melody of the Vedanta....The jeweller alone can understand the worth of jewels...."

And England was to give him still more in the shape
of perhaps the most beautiful friendships of his life:
J. J. Goodwin, Margaret Noble, Mr. and Mrs. Sevier.

I have already mentioned the first of them. He met
him at the end of 1895, in New York. A good steno-
grapher was wanted to take down exactly the lessons of
the Swami; and it was not easy to find one of sufficient
education. Young Goodwin was engaged immediately
after his arrival from England. He was on trial for a
fortnight and before it was over, enlightened by the
thought he was transcribing, he left all to devote himself to the Master. He refused payment, worked night
and day, accompanied Vivekananda wherever he went
and watched over him tenderly. He took the vow of
Brahmacharya. He gave his life to the Master, in the
complete sense of the word: for he was to die pre-
maturely[1] in India, whither he followed the man who
was to become his family, his country, and to whose
faith he had given his passionate adherence.

Margaret Noble made a no less complete gift of herself. The future will always unite her name of initiation, Sister Nivedita, to that of her beloved Master
...as St. Clara to that of St. Francis... (although of
a truth the imperious Swami was far from possessing
the meekness of the *Poverello*,[2] and submitted those
who gave themselves to him to heart-searching tests
before he accepted them).[3] She was the young head-

[1] June 2, 1898.

[2] Title given to St. Francis of Assisi, meaning the Little Poor
Man.—*Translator.*

[3] But her love was so deep that Nivedita does not seem to have
kept any memory of the harshness from which she suffered to the
point of the greatest dejection. She only kept the memory of his
sweetness. Miss MacLeod tells us, "I said to Nivedita, 'He was all
energy.' She replied, 'He was all tenderness.' But I replied, 'I never

mistress of a school in London. Vivekananda spoke at her school, and she was immediately captivated by his charm.[1] But for a long time she struggled against it. She was one of those who came to Vivekananda after each lecture with the words: "Yes, Swami... *But*...."

She always argued and resisted, being one of those English souls who are hard to overcome, but once conquered, faithful for ever. Vivekananda said himself, "There are no more trustworthy souls!"

She was twenty-eight when she made up her mind to place her fate in the Swami's hands. He made her come to India[2] to devote herself to the education of Hindu women; and he forced her to make herself a Hindu, "to Hinduise her thoughts, her conceptions, her habits, and to forget even the memory of her own past." She took the vow of Brahmacharya, and was the first Western woman to be received into an Indian monastic order. We shall find her again at Vivekananda's side, and she has preserved his Interviews,[3] and done more than anyone else to popularise his figure in the West.

The friendship of the Seviers was also marked by the same love and absolute confidence that gives itself once

felt it.' 'That was because it was not shown to you.' For he was to each person according to the nature of that person and his way to the Divine."

[1] She delicately invoked the memory of their first meeting: "The time was a cold Sunday afternoon in November and the place a West End drawing-room.... He was seated facing a half circle of listeners with the fire on the hearth behind him. Twilight passed into darkness. ...He sat amongst us...as one bringing us news from a far land, with a curious habit of saying now and again, 'Shiva! Shiva!', and wearing a look of mingled gentleness and loftiness.... (Nivedita compared his look to that of the Child in the Sistine Madonna).... He chanted for us Sanskrit verses." And Nivedita listened to him, thinking of beautiful Gregorian chants.

[2] The end of January, 1898.

[3] *Notes of Some Wanderings with the Swami Vivekananda*, by Sister Nivedita of Ramakrishna-Vivekananda, Udbodhan Office, Calcutta.

and for ever. Mr. Sevier was a retired captain of forty-
nine. Both he and his wife were preoccupied with religious questions, and were struck by the thought, words,
and personality of Vivekananda. Miss MacLeod told
me, "Coming out of one of his lectures Mr. Sevier asked
me, 'You know this young man? Is he what he seems?'
'Yes.' 'In that case one must follow him and with
him find God.' He went and said to his wife. 'Will you
let me become the Swami's disciple?' She replied,
'Yes.' She asked him, 'Will you let me become the
Swami's disciple?' He replied with affectionate humour,
'I don't know. . . .' "

They became his companions, having realised the
whole of their little fortune. But Vivekananda was
more anxious for the future of his old friends than they
were for themselves, and would not allow them to give
all to his work, forcing them to keep a part for themselves. They looked upon the Swami as their own child,
and devoted themselves, as we shall see, to the building
of the Advaita Ashrama, of which he had dreamed, in
the Himalayas, for meditation on the impersonal God:
for it was Advaitism that had especially attracted them
in the thought of Vivekananda, and for him also it was
the essential. Mr. Sevier was to die in 1900 in this
monastery he had built. Mrs. Sevier survived him as
well as Vivekananda. For fifteen years she remained the

The chief work dedicated by Nivedita to her Master is: *The Master
as I saw Him, being pages from the Life of the Swami Vivekananda by his
disciple, Nivedita*, Longmans Green & Co., London and New York, 1910.

Nivedita has written many works to popularise the religious thought,
the myths, the legends and the social life of India in the West.
Several have won a well-merited fame: *The Web of Indian Life; Kali
the Mother; Cradle Tales of Hinduism* (charming tales of Hindu mythology
presented in a poetic and popular form), *Myths of the Indo-Aryan Race;*
etc.

only European woman in this remote spot in the midst
of mountains, inaccessible for long months of the year,
busying herself with the education of children.

"And do you not get bored?" Miss MacLeod asked
her.

"I think of him (Vivekananda)," she replied simply.

Such admirable friends have not been offered by
England to Vivekananda alone of Indians. Great
Hindus have always found among the English their
most valiant and faithful disciples and helpers. What a
Pearson is to Tagore, and an Andrews or 'Mirabai' to
Gandhi is well known.... Later, when free India
reckons up all she has suffered from the British Empire
and what she owes to it, such holy friendships will
more than anything else make the balance hesitate,
heavy as it is with iniquities.

But in this land where his word roused such deep
reverberations, he did not attempt to found anything
as he did in the United States, where the Ramakrishna
Mission was to grow and multiply. Is it to be believed,
as one of his American disciples said to me, that he had
to take into account the high intellectuality of England
and Europe, which required Hindu missionaries of
a spiritual quality rare among the brethren of Baranagore?[1] But I think the terrible fatigue which began
to weigh upon him at times must be taken into account.

[1] Nevertheless one of them, Saradananda, whom he sent for to
come to London (April 1896) and later sent to America, had a solid
philosophic brain, able to meet European metaphysicians on terms
of equality. Abhedananda, too, who succeeded him in London
(October 1896) was very well received. [As a matter of fact, it was
due to quite other reasons that the London work from which the
Swami had expected so much, collapsed. The Swami at least never
thought that the requisite spiritual quality was lacking among his
brother-disciples, for then he would not have placed Swami

He was tired of the world and the bondage of works. He longed for rest. The evil that consumed the walls of his body in secret, like the taredo worm, made him for long periods quite detached from existence. At such times he refused to construct anything new, declaring that he was no organiser. He wrote on August 23, 1896,[1] "I have begun the work; let others work it out! So you see, to set the work going I had to touch money and property for a time.[2] Now I am sure my part of the work is done, and I have no more interest in Vedanta, or in any philosophy in the world, or in the work itself.... Even its religious utility is beginning to pall on me.... I am getting ready to depart to return no more to this hell, this world."

A pathetic cry, whose poignancy will be felt by all who know the terrible exhaustion of the disease that was wasting him! At other times, on the contrary, it showed itself in too great exaltation: the whole universe seemed to him the exhilarating toy of a child God, devoid of reason.[3] But detachment was there just the

Abhedananda in charge of the London work when he left for India.—*Publisher*.]

[1] From Lucerne.

[2] For, where money was concerned, he shared the physical repulsion of Ramakrishna.

[3] *Cf.* the letter of July 6, 1896 to Mr. Francis Leggett, which ends in an outburst of delirious joy:

"I bless the day I was born. He (the Beloved) is my Playful Darling, I am His playfellow. There is neither rhyme nor reason in the Universe. What reason binds Him? He, the Playful One, is playing these tears and laughter over all parts of the Play! Great fun, great fun....A school of romping children let out to play in this playground of the world! Whom to praise, whom to blame?...He is brainless, nor has He any reason. He is fooling us with little brains and reason, but this time He won't find me napping. ...I have learnt a thing or two; beyond, beyond reason and learning and talking is the feeling, the 'Love', the 'Beloved'. Ay, *Saké*, fill up the cup and we will be mad."

same in joy or sorrow. The world was leaving him. The thread of the kite was breaking.[1]

*

The affectionate friends, who were watching over him, took him again for a rest to Switzerland. He spent most of the summer of 1896 there,[2] and he seems to have benefited greatly in enjoyment of the air from the snows, the torrents, and mountains, which reminded him of the Himalayas.[3] It was there in a village at the foot of the Alps, between Mont Blanc and the Little St. Bernard, that he first conceived the plan of founding in the Himalayas a monastery where his Western and Eastern disciples might be united. And the Seviers, who were with him, never let the idea lapse: it became their life-work.

To his mountain retreat there came a letter from Professor Paul Deussen, inviting him to visit him at Kiel. To see him he shortened his stay in Switzerland, and took the student path through Heidelberg, Coblenz, Cologne, Berlin: for he wished to have a glimpse at least of Germany, and he was impressed by her material power and great culture. I have already described in the *Jahrbuch* of the *Schopenhauer Gessellschaft*,[4] his visit to Kiel, to the founder of the Schopenhauer Society. His reception was as cordial, and their relations as animated as might have been expected from such an ardent Vedantist as Paul Deussen, who saw in the Vedanta not only "one of the most majestic structures

[1] *Cf.* the parable of Ramakrishna, quoted in the first volume.
[2] At Geneva, Montreux, Chillon, Chamounix, the St. Bernard, Lucerne, the Rigi, Zermatt, Schaffhausen.
[3] He claimed to discover in Swiss peasant life and its manners and customs, resemblances to the mountaineers of Northern India.
[4] 1927. According to the Memoirs of Mrs. Sevier and the notes collected in the great *Life of the Swami Vivekananda*.

and valuable products of the genius of man in his search for truth," but "the strongest support of pure morality, and the greatest consolation in the sufferings of life and death."[1]

But if Deussen was sensible to the personal charm, the spiritual gifts and the deep knowledge of the Swami, the notes in his Journal do not show that he foresaw the great destiny of his young visitor. In particular he was far from imagining the tragic seriousness at the bottom of this man, who was outwardly of robust and joyous appearance, but whose heart was obsessed by his miserable people, and whose flesh was already marred by death. He saw him in an hour of relaxation and grateful abandon, happy in the presence of the great German savant and sage, who had done so much for the cause of India. This gratitude never faded from Vivekananda's mind, and he kept a shining remembrance of his days at Kiel, as well as of others at Hamburg, Amsterdam, and London, when Deussen was his companion.[2] Their reflection is preserved in a magnificent article in *The Brahmavadin*, wherein Vivekananda later reminded his disciples of India's debt to great Europeans, who had known how to love and understand her better than she knew herself... especially to the two greatest—Max Müller and Paul Deussen.

He spent another two months in England, seeing Max Müller again, meeting Edward Carpenter, Frederick

[1] Lecture given by Deussen at Bombay on February 25, 1893, before the Indian branch of the Royal Asiatic Society. He reminded Vivekananda of these words.

[2] Mrs. Sevier says that Deussen rejoined Vivekananda at Hamburg, that they travelled together in Holland, spent three days at Amsterdam, then went to London, where for two weeks they met every day. During the same time Vivekananda saw Max Müller again at Oxford. "Thus three great minds were conversing with each other."

Myers, and Canon Wilberforce, and delivering a fresh course of lectures on the Vedanta, on the Hindu theory of Maya and on the Advaita.[1] But his stay in Europe was drawing to a close. The voice of India was calling him back. Home-sickness attacked him, and the exhausted man, who three weeks before had refused with the fury of despair to forge fresh chains[2] for himself and declared that he only desired to escape from the infernal treadmill of life and action, flung himself passionately into it, and harnessed himself with his own hands again to the mill. For, as he said to his English friends, when he was taking leave of them, "I may even find it good to get out of this body, to throw it off like a disused garment. But I shall never cease... helping mankind...."

To work, to serve in this life, in the lives to come, to be reborn, for ever reborn, to serve.... Yes, a Vivekananda is obliged to "return to this hell!" For his whole destiny and reason for living is simply to return, to return without rest, so as to fight the flames of "this hell" and to rescue its victims; for his fate it is to burn in it in order to save others.

He left England on December 16, 1896, and travelling by Dover, Calais, and the Mont Cenis, he crowned his stay in Europe by a short journey through Italy. He went to salute da Vinci's *Last Supper* at Milan, and

[1] It is noteworthy that the last lecture, the final word, was devoted to the Advaita Vedanta (December 10, 1896): the essential thought.

[2] "I have given up the bondage of iron—the family tie.... I am not to take up the golden chain of religious brotherhood. I am free, I must always be free—free as the air. As for me I am as good as retired. I have played my part in the world...."

This was written on August 23, 1896, at Lucerne at the moment when he had been rescued from the whirlpool of action, in which he had almost gone down breathless. The Swiss air had not yet had time to reinvigorate him.

was especially moved by Rome, which in his imagination held a place comparable to Delhi. At every instant
he was struck by the similarity between the Catholic
Liturgy[1] and Hindu ceremonies, being sensible of its
magnificence, and defending its symbolic beauty and
emotional appeal to the English who were with him.
He was profoundly touched by the memories of the first
Christians and martyrs in the Catacombs, and shared the
tender veneration of the Italian people for the figures
of the infant Christ and the Virgin Mother.[2] They
never ceased to dwell in his thought, as can be seen by
many words that I have already quoted in India and
America. When he was in Switzerland he came to a
little chapel in the mountains. Having plucked flowers
he placed them at the feet of the Virgin through the
hands of Mrs. Sevier, saying, "She also is the Mother."

One of his disciples had later the strange idea to
give him an image of the Sistine Madonna to bless,
but he refused in all humility, and piously touching
the feet of the Child, he said, "I would have washed
his feet, not with my tears, but with my heart's blood."

It may indeed with truth be said that there was no
other being so close as he to the Christ.[3] And nobody

[1] Everything reminded him of India: the tonsure of the priests,
the sign of the Cross, the incense, the music. He saw in the Holy
Sacrament a transformation of the Vedic Prasada—the offering of
food to the gods, after which it is immediately eaten.

[2] He was at Rome for the feast of Krishna. On the Eve he had
seen at Santa-Maria d'Ara Cœli the simple worship of the Bambino
by the children.

[3] It was not that Vivekananda was more certain of his historic
existence than of that of Krishna. A very strange dream that he had
on the boat the last night of the year, will no doubt interest the
modern iconoclasts of the historic Christ: An old man appeared to
him: "Observe carefully this place," he said. "It is the land where
Christianity began. I am one of the therapeutic Essenes, who lived
there. The truths and the ideas preached by us were presented

felt more clearly that the great Mediator between God and man was called to be the Mediator also between the East and the West: for the East recognises him as its own. It was from thence he came to us.

On the boat taking him from Europe back to India, Vivekananda brooded long over this divine bond of union between the two worlds. It was not the only one. There was the link traced by the great disinterested men of letters, who had found unaided and unguided in the darkness the path leading to the most ancient knowledge, to the purest Indian spirit. There was the unexpected flame of spirituality which rose at the first impact of the Swami's burning words from the crowds of men of goodwill in both the Old and the New Worlds! There was the upspringing of generous confidence, of richness of heart—(would he have thought the same of the new West, the conqueror of the world—or of its panoply of the sword of reason and the mailed fist of force!)—manifested through the pure and candid souls, who had given themselves to him. There were the noble friends, the slaves of love, whom he carried in his wake—(two of them, the old Sevier couple, were at his side on the same boat; they were deserting Europe and all their past to follow him...).

Indeed, when he summed up his long pilgrimage of four years and the treasures he was carrying to his

as the teaching of Jesus. But Jesus the person was never born. Various proofs attesting this fact will be brought to light when this place is dug up." At this moment (it was midnight) Vivekananda awoke, and asked a sailor where he was: he was told that the ship was fifty miles off the isle of Crete. Until that day he had never doubted the historical fact of Jesus. But for a spirit of his religious intensity, as of Ramakrishna as well, the historic reality of God was the least of His realities. God, the fruit of the soul of a people, is more real than he, who is the fruit of the womb of a Virgin. More surely is he the seed of fire flung by the Divine.

Indian people, spiritual riches, treasures of the soul, were not the least from which India was to benefit. But was it not more vital and urgent to remedy the misery of India? The urgent help he had gone to get, the handful of corn gleaned from the fields of the monstrous wealth of the West, to save the millions of India from annihilation, the monetary help he needed to rebuild the physical and moral health of his people— was he bringing it to them? No. In that respect his journey had failed.[1] His work had to be taken up again on a new basis. India was to be regenerated by India. Health was to come from within.

But for the accomplishment of this Herculean task, which he was about to undertake unhesitatingly, the journey to the West had given this young hero, marked by death, as he himself was aware, what he had previously lacked—authority.

[1] Two years later in 1899, he still had bouts of despair because all his success, all his glory, had not brought him the three hundred million rupees necessary for his dream of the material regeneration of India. But he had learnt by this time that we are not born to see success: "No rest! I shall die in harness. Life is a battle. Let me live and die fighting!"

# VII

## THE RETURN TO INDIA

THE news of Vivekananda's success at the Parliament of Religions was slow in reaching India, but once it became known, it created an outburst of joy and national pride. The news spread throughout the country. The monks of Baranagore did not hear of it for six months, and had no idea that it was their brother who was the triumphant hero of Chicago. A letter from Vivekananda told them of it; and in their joy they recalled the old prophecy of Ramakrishna: "Naren will shake the world to its foundations." Rajas, pandits, and peoples rejoiced. India celebrated its conquering champion. Enthusiasm reached its height in Madras and Bengal, their tropic imaginations afire. On September 5, 1894, a year after the Congress at Chicago, a meeting was held in the Town Hall of Calcutta: all classes of the population, all sections of Hinduism, were represented; and they had come together to celebrate Vivekananda and to thank the American people. A long letter with the signatures of famous names was sent to the United States. Certain political parties tried to make profit out of Vivekananda's work, but when Vivekananda was warned of this he protested emphatically. He refused to take part in any movement that was not disinterested.[1]

[1] "Let no political significance be ever attached falsely to any of my writings or sayings. What nonsense!" (September, 1894.)
"I will have nothing to do with nonsense. I do not believe in

"I do not care for success or non-success.... I must keep my movement pure or I will have none of it."

But he had never lost touch with his young disciples in Madras, and constantly wrote them inspiring and stimulating letters; he intended them to become God's militia, poor and faithful unto death....

"We are poor, my brothers, we are nobodies; but such have always been the instruments of the Most High."

His letters from the West laid down their plan of campaign in advance—"the sole duty of raising the masses of India"—and to that end "to centralise the individual forces, to cultivate the virtue of obedience, to learn to work unitedly for others." He watched their progress from afar, he sent them money to found a Vedantic tribune, *The Brahmavadin* of Madras, to fly his flag in his absence. And in spite of his weight of weariness, the nearer he came to the day of his return, the more do his Epistles to India sound like clarion calls:

"There are great things to do.... Do not fear, my children! Have courage!... I am coming back to India and I shall try to set on foot what there is to be done. Work on, brave hearts, the Lord is behind you."

He announced his intention of founding two general headquarters at Madras and Calcutta, and later two more in Bombay and Allahabad. Round one central organisation he would group his brethren in Rama-

politics. God and Truth are the only policy in the world. Everything else is trash." (September 9, 1895.)

His predecessor, Keshab Chandra Sen, had established the same line of demarcation between politics and his work. "He was ready to join in any public movement *which had no political character*, but whose object was the betterment of the fate of the Indian people." (Article published by *The Hindu Patriot* on the occasion of his death in 1884.)

krishna and his disciples and his lieutenants of the West
in a Mission of help and universal love, which should
conquer India and the world by serving them.

Hence he hoped to find his militia ready for his
word of command on his arrival. But he never expected
that the whole nation—the peoples of India—would
rise and lie in wait for the approach of the vessel bringing back their hero, the conqueror of the West. In the
great towns committees of all sections of society were
formed to receive him. Triumphal arches were erected,
streets and houses were decorated. The exaltation was
such that many could not await his coming, but poured
towards the South of India, towards his disembarka-
tion in Ceylon, in order to be the first to welcome him.

When he arrived on January 15, 1897, a mighty
shout arose from the human throng covering the·quays
of Colombo. A multitude flung itself upon him to touch
his feet. A procession was formed with flags at its head.
Religious hymns were chanted. Flowers were thrown
before his path. Rose water or sacred water from the
Ganga was sprinkled. Incense burned before the
houses. Hundreds of visitors, rich and poor, brought
him offerings.

And Vivekananda once again recrossed the land of
India from the South to the North,[1] as he had done
formerly as a beggar along its roads. But today his
was a triumphal progress with an escort of delirious
people. Rajas prostrated themselves before him or
drew his carriage.[2] The cannon boomed, and in the

[1] By Colombo, Kandy, Anuradhapura, Jaffna, Pamban, Rameswaram,
Ramnad, Madura, Trichinopoly, Kumbakonam, a small railway station
—where hundreds of people in the open country laid themselves on the
rails so as to stop his train—Madras, and from thence by sea to Calcutta.
[2] The Raja of Ramnad.

exotic processions wherein elephants and camels rode, choirs chanted the victory of *Judas Maccabeus*.[1]

He was not the man to flee from triumph any more than from battle. He held that not himself but his cause was honoured, and he laid public emphasis on the extraordinary character of such a national reception to a Sannyasin without worldly goods, without name, without home, who carried nothing with him but God. He collected his forces in order to raise the sacred burden on high. A sick man, who needed to nurse his vitality, he made a superhuman expenditure of energy. All along the way he scattered his seed to the winds in a series of brilliant speeches, the most beautiful and heroic India had ever heard, sending a thrill through her land. I must stop at this point, for they mark the summit of his work. Having returned from his Crusade on the other side of the world, he brought with him the sum total of his experience. His prolonged contact with the West made him feel more deeply the personality of India. And in contrast this made him value the strong and multiple personality of the West. Both seemed to him equally necessary, for they were complementary, awaiting the word to unite them, the common Gospel, and it was he, who was to open the path to union.

*

Moving as were his lectures at Colombo (*India the Holy Land, The Vedanta Philosophy*), the one given in the shade of the fig tree of Anuradhapura, where, in spite of a mob of Buddhist fanatics, he celebrated "the Universal Religion", and the preaching to the people of Rameswaram this great word, so closely akin to the

[1] Choruses from Handel (also fêtes at Ramnad).

teaching of Christ: "Worship Shiva in the poor, the diseased and the weak!"—with the result that the pious Raja was transported to a delirium of charity[1]— it was for Madras that he reserved his greatest efforts. Madras had been expecting him for weeks in a kind of passionate delirium. She erected for him seventeen triumphal arches, presented him with twenty-four Addresses in various languages of Hindustan,[2] and suspended her whole public life at his coming—nine days of roaring fêtes.....

He replied to the frenzied expectancy of the people by his Message to India, a conch sounding the resurrection of the land of Rama, of Shiva, of Krishna, and calling the heroic Spirit, the immortal Atman, to march to war. He was a general, explaining his *Plan of Campaign*,[3] and calling his people to rise *en masse*:

"My India, arise! Where is your vital force? In your Immortal Soul....

"Each nation, like each individual, has one theme in this life, which is its centre, the principal note round which every other note comes to form the harmony. ... If any one nation attempts to throw off its national vitality, the direction which has become its own through the transmission of centuries, that nation dies.... In one nation political power is its vitality, as in England. Artistic life in another and so on. In India religious life forms the centre, the keynote of the whole music

[1] The next day he fed thousands of the poor and began to raise a monument of victory.

[2] Besides these Indian Addresses—among which was one from Vivekananda's sponsor, the Maharaja of Khetri—there were Addresses from England and America, signed by William James and professors of Harvard University. That of the Brooklyn Ethical Association was addressed "To our Indian brothers of the great Aryan Family."

[3] *My Plan of Campaign*—the title of his first lecture in Madras.

of national life.... And, therefore, if you succeed in the attempt to throw off your religion and take up either politics or society,... the result will be that you will become extinct.... Social reform... and politics has to be preached...through that vitality of your religion.... Every man has to make his own choice; so has every nation. We made our choice ages ago. ... And it is the faith in an Immortal Soul.... I challenge anyone to give it up.... How can you change your nature?"[1]

Do not complain! Yours is the better part. Make use of the power that is in your hands! It is so great that if you only realise it and are worthy of it, you are called to revolutionise the world. India is a Ganga of spirituality. The material conquests of the Anglo-Saxon races, far from being able to dam its current, have helped it. England's power has united the nations of the world, she has opened the paths across the seas so that the waves of the spirit of India may spread until they have bathed the ends of the earth. (So, Vivekananda might have added—for he knew its truth—the Roman Empire was constructed for the victory of Christ....)

What then is the spirit of India? What is this new faith, this word, that the world is awaiting?...

"The other great idea that the world wants from us today—more perhaps the lower classes than the higher, more the uneducated than the educated, more the weak than the strong—is that eternal grand idea of the spiritual oneness of the whole universe...the

---

[1] Extracts from the Madras lecture: *My Plan of Campaign*. The passages in inverted commas are quoted exactly. The others are summarised and condense the arguments of the discourse.

only Infinite Reality, that exists in you and in all, in
the self, in the soul. The infinite oneness of the Soul
is the eternal sanction of all morality, that you and I
are not only brothers...but that you and I are really
one... Europe wants it today just as much as our
downtrodden races do, and this great principle is even
now unconsciously forming the basis of all the latest
social and political aspirations that are coming up in
England, in Germany, in France, and in America."[1]

Moreover this is the foundation of the old Vedantic
faith, of the great Advaitism, the deepest and purest
expression of the ancient spirit of India....

"I heard once the complaint made that I was preaching too much of Advaita (absolute Monism) and too
little of Dualism. Ay, I know what grandeur, what
oceans of love, what infinite ecstatic blessings and joy
there are in the dualistic...religion. I know it all.
But this is not the time with us to weep, even in joy;
we have had weeping enough; no more is this the time
for us to become soft. This softness has been with us
till we have become like masses of cotton.... What
our country now wants are muscles of iron and nerves
of steel, gigantic wills, which nothing can resist, which
...will accomplish their purpose in any fashion, even
if it meant going down to the bottom of the ocean and
meeting death face to face. That is what we want, and
that can only be created, established, and strengthened,
by understanding and realising the ideal of the Advaita,
that ideal of the oneness of all. Faith, faith, faith in
ourselves.... If you have faith in the three hundred
and thirty millions of your mythological gods, and in
all the gods which foreigners...have introduced into

[1] *The Mission of the Vedanta.* Extracts from the lecture.

your midst, and still have no faith in yourselves, there is no salvation for you. Have faith in yourselves and stand up on that faith.... Why is it that we, three hundred and thirty millions of people, have been ruled for the last thousand years by any and every handful of foreigners?... Because they had faith in themselves and we had not.... I read in the newspapers how when one of our poor fellows is murdered or ill-treated by an Englishman, howls go all over the country; I read and I weep, and the next moment comes to my mind who is responsible for it all.... Not the English...it is we who are responsible for all our... degradation. Our aristocratic ancestors went on treading the common masses of our country underfoot, till they became helpless, till under this torment the poor, poor people nearly forgot that they were human beings. They have been compelled to be merely hewers of wood and drawers of water for centuries, so...that they are made to believe that they are born as slaves, born as hewers of wood and drawers of water."[1]

"Feel, therefore, my would-be reformers, my would-be patriots! Do you feel? Do you feel that millions and millions of the descendants of gods and of sages have become next-door neighbours to brutes? Do you feel that millions are starving today, and millions have been starving for ages? Do you feel that ignorance has come over the land as a dark cloud? Does it make you restless? Does it make you sleepless?... Has it made you almost mad? Are you seized with that one idea of the misery of ruin, and have you forgotten all about your name, your fame, your wives, your children, your property, even your own bodies?... That is the

[1] Extracts from *The Mission of the Vedanta.*

first step to become a patriot!...For centuries people have been taught theories of degradation. They have been told that they are nothing. The masses have been told all over the world that they are not human beings. They have been so frightened for centuries till they have nearly become animals. Never were they allowed to hear of the Atman. Let them hear of the Atman—that even the lowest of the low have the Atman within, who never dies and never is born—Him whom the sword cannot pierce, nor the fire burn, nor the air dry, immortal, without beginning or end, the all-pure, omnipotent, and omnipresent Atman...."[1]

"Ay, let every man and woman and child, without respect of caste or birth, weakness or strength, hear and learn that behind the strong and the weak, behind the high and the low, behind every one, there is that Infinite Soul, assuring the infinite possibility and the infinite capacity of all to become great and good. Let us proclaim to every soul: Arise, awake, and stop not till the goal is reached. Arise, awake! Awake from this hypnotism of weakness. *None* is really weak; the soul is infinite, omnipotent, and omniscient. Stand up, assert yourself, proclaim the God within you, do not deny Him!..."[2]

"It is a man-making religion that we want.... It is man-making education all round that we want. It is man-making theories that we want. And here is the test of truth—anything that makes you weak physically, intellectually, and spiritually, reject as poison, there is no life in it, it cannot be true. Truth is strengthening. Truth is purity, truth is all-knowledge...truth must

[1] *My Plan of Campaign.*
[2] *The Mission of the Vedanta.*

be strengthening, must be enlightening, must be invigo-rating.... Give up these weakening mysticisms, and be strong.... the greatest truths are the simplest things in the world, simple as your own existence...."[1]

"Therefore... my plan is to start institutions in India to train our young men as preachers of the truths of our scriptures in India and outside India. Men, men, these are wanted: everything else will be ready, but strong, vigorous, believing young men, sincere to the backbone, are wanted. A hundred such and the world becomes revolutionised. The will is stronger than anything else. Everything must go down before the will, for that comes from God...a pure and strong will is omnipotent...."[2]

"If the Brahmin has more aptitude for learning on the ground of heredity than the Pariah, spend no more money on the Brahmin's education, but spend all on the Pariah. Give to the weak, for there all the gift is needed. If the Brahmin is born clever, he can educate himself without help.... This is justice and reason as I understand it."[3]

"For the next fifty years...let all other vain Gods disappear for that time from our minds. This is the only God that is awake, our own race—everywhere His hands, everywhere His feet, everywhere His ears, He covers everything. All other Gods are sleeping. What vain Gods shall we go after and yet cannot wor-ship the God that we see all round us, the Virat?... The first of all worship is the worship of the Virat— of those all around us.... These are all our Gods—

---

[1] *My Plan of Campaign.*
[2] Ibid.
[3] *The Mission of the Vedanta.*

men and animals, and the first Gods we have to worship are our own countrymen...."[1]

Imagine the thunderous reverberations of these
words! The reader almost says with the Indian masses
and with Vivekananda himself, "Shiva!...Shiva!"

The storm passed; it scattered its cataracts of water
and fire over the plain, and its formidable appeal to
the Force of the Soul, to the God sleeping in man and
His illimitable possibilities! I can see the Mage erect,
his arm raised, like Jesus above the tomb of Lazarus in
Rembrandt's engraving:[2] with energy flowing from his
gesture of command to raise the dead and bring him
to life....

Did the dead arise? Did India, thrilling to the sound
of his words, reply to the hope of her herald? Was
her noisy enthusiasm translated into deeds? At the
time nearly all this flame seemed to have been lost in
smoke. Two years afterwards Vivekananda declared
bitterly that the harvests of young men necessary for
his army had not come from India. It is impossible to
change in a moment the habits of a people buried in a
Dream, enslaved by prejudice, and allowing themselves
to fail under the weight of the slightest effort. But the
Master's rough scourge made her turn for the first time
in her sleep, and for the first time the heroic trumpet
sounded in the midst of her dream the Forward March
of India, conscious of her God. She never forgot it.
From that day the awakening of the torpid Colossus
began. If the generation that followed, saw, three
years after Vivekananda's death, the revolt of Bengal,

[1] *The Future of India.*
[2] An allusion to a famous engraving of Rembrandt: the Resurrection
of Lazarus.

8

the prelude to the great movement of Tilak and Gandhi, if India today has definitely taken part in the collective action of organised masses, it is due to the initial shock, to the mighty "Lazarus, come forth!" of the Message from Madras.

This message of energy had a double meaning: a national and a universal. Although, for the great monk of the Advaita, it was the universal meaning that predominated, it was the other that revived the sinews of India. For she replied to the urge of the fever which has taken possession of the world at this moment of history—the fatal urge of Nationalism, whose monstrous effects we see today. It was, therefore, at its very inception fraught with danger. There was ground for fearing that its high spirituality would be twisted to the profit of a purely animal pride in race or nation, with all its stupid ferocities. We know the danger, we who have seen too many of such ideals—however pure they may have been—employed in the service of the most dirty national passions! But how else was it possible to bring about within the disorganised Indian masses a sense of human Unity, without first making them feel such unity within the bounds of their own nation? The one is the way to the other. All the same I should have preferred another way, a more arduous way, but a more direct, for I know too well that the great majority of those who pass through the nation stage remain there. They have spent all their powers of faith and love on the way.... But such was not the intention of Vivekananda, who, like Gandhi in this, only thought of the awakening of India in relation to its service for humanity. Yet a Vivekananda, more cautious than a Gandhi, would have disavowed the desperate efforts of the latter to make the religious spirit dominate political action: for on every occasion—as we have already seen in his letters from America—he placed a naked sword between himself and politics.... "*Noli me tangere!*" "I will have nothing to do with the nonsense of politics." But a Vivekananda would have always had to take into account his temperament as well as his spirit; and the proud Indian, who so often fell foul of the exactions or the stupid insults of the conquering Anglo-Saxons, reacted with a violence, which would have made him in spite of himself take part in the dangerous passions of nationalism, although condemned by his faith. This inner combat was to last until the crisis of the early days of October, 1898, when, having withdrawn alone in Kashmir to a sanctuary of Kali (he was then the prey of a flood of emotion caused by the sufferings and the devastation of India),[1] he came out transfigured and said to Nivedita, "All my patriotism is gone.... I have been wrong.... Mother (Kali) said to me, 'What even if unbelievers should enter My temples and defile My images? What is that to you? Do *you* protect Me? Or do *I* protect you?' So there is no more patriotism. I am only a little child!"

But through the tumult of the flood, the noise of the cataract of his Madras discourses, the people were incapable of hearing the disdainful words and serene voice of Kali, curbing human pride. The people were carried away by the exhilaration and fury of the current.

---

[1] The sight of the ruins and desecration of Mother's temple, the result of Mohammedan vandalism. He thought to himself: "How could such things be allowed? If I had been there, I would have given my life to protect my Mother." Several days before, his national pride had been roused by brutal abuse of English power.

# VIII

## THE FOUNDING OF
## THE RAMAKRISHNA MISSION

A real leader of men does not omit the smallest detail.
Vivekananda knew that if he was to lead the peoples
to the conquest of an ideal, it was not enough to inflame
their ardour; he had to enrol them in a spiritual militia.
The chosen few must be presented to the people as
types of the new man; for their very existence was the
pledge of the order that was to be.

That is why Vivekananda, as soon as he was free
from his triumphs in Madras and Calcutta,[1] immediately turned his attention to his monastery of
Alambazar.[2]

It was with difficulty that he raised his Gurubhais[3]
to the level of his own thoughts! The great bird of
passage had flown over the world, and his glance had
measured vast horizons, while they had remained

---

[1] At Calcutta his reception was no less magnificent than at Madras,
with triumphal arches and unharnessed carriage dragged by enthusiastic
students in the midst of processions of Sankirtanas, songs, and dances,
while a princely residence was placed at his disposal. On February
28, 1897, there was a presentation to the victor of an Address of Welcome from the city before an audience of 5000, followed by patriotic
discourses from Vivekananda: a fresh panegyric of energy in the name
of the Upanishads and the repudiation of all debilitating doctrines
and practices.

[2] Ramakrishna's monks had betaken themselves in 1892 from Baranagore to Alambazar near Dakshineswar, Ramakrishna's sanctuary.
Several had come to meet Vivekananda at Colombo: Sadananda, his
first disciple (see note p. 16), had traversed the whole of India to
be the first to welcome him.

[3] His brother-monks.

piously at home and kept their timorous ways. They loved their great brother, but they hardly recognised him. They could not understand the new ideal of social and national service, which fired him. It was painful to them to sacrifice their orthodox prejudices, and their religious individualism, their free and quiet life of peaceful meditation; and in all sincerity it was easy for them to find holy reasons in support of their devout egoism. They even invoked the example of their Master Ramakrishna and his detachment from the world. But Vivekananda claimed to be the true depositary of Ramakrishna's most profound thought. In his ringing discourses at Madras and Calcutta[1] he had spoken constantly in the name of Ramakrishna: "My Master, my ideal, my hero, my God in this life." He claimed to be the voice of the Paramahamsa, and went so far as to refuse the merit of all initiative, of all new thought, and to claim that he was merely a faithful steward, exactly carrrying out his Master's orders:

"If there has been anything achieved by me, by my thoughts or words, or deeds, if from my lips has ever fallen one word that has helped anyone in the world, I lay no claim to it; it was his.... All that has been weak has been mine, and all that has been life-giving, strengthening, pure, and holy, has been his inspiration, his word—and he himself."

The two Ramakrishnas—the one whose out-spread wings had brooded over the disciples left behind in the dovecote—and the other who, carried on those same wings, had covered the world in the shape of his great disciple—were bound to come into conflict. But the

[1] Lectures on *The Sages of India* (Madras) and *The Vedanta in All Its Phases* (Calcutta).

victory was never in doubt: it was a foregone conclusion, not only on account of the immense ascendancy of
the young conqueror, the superiority of his genius and
the prestige of India's acclamation, but on account of
the love his brethren bore him and that Ramakrishna
had shown for him. He was the Master's anointed.

So they obeyed the orders Vivekananda imposed
upon them without always agreeing with them from
the bottom of their hearts. He forced his brethren to
receive the European disciples into their community,
and to take up the mission of service and social help.
He sternly forbade them to think any longer of themselves and their own salvation. He came, so he declared, to create a new order of Sannyasins, who would
go down into hell, if need be, to save others.[1] There
had been enough of the sterile God of solitary prayers!
Let them worship the Living God, the Coming God,
the Virat, dwelling in all living souls! And let "the
lion of Brahman" sleeping in the heart of each man
awake at their call![2]

So urgent was the tone of the young Master's injunc-
tions that the excellent brothers, of whom several were
his elders, obeyed perhaps before they really believed
him.[3] The first to set the example of leaving the
monastic home was just the one who felt his departure
the most, for he had never left it for a single day in

[1] He added this theological argument: "To think of his liberation
is unworthy of the disciple of an Avatara" (of a Divine Incarnation,
as Ramakrishna was in their eyes): for his liberation is secured by
that fact alone. (Such an argument, though perhaps effective for the
weak, diminishes the cost of the devotional act in our eyes.)

[2] Words spoken by Vivekananda at the ceremony of initiation of
four young disciples.

[3] We shall see later in a pathetic scene the objection that they never
ceased to raise.

twelve years: Ramakrishnananda. He went to Madras and founded a centre for the propagation of Vedantic principles in Southern India.* Next followed he, who was most deeply penetrated with the spirit of Service, Akhandananda (Gangadhar). He went to Murshidabad, where famine was raging, and devoted himself to the relief of the victims.[1]

Different paths of Service on behalf of the great Indian community were tried haphazard at first.

But Vivekananda was feverishly anxious that order and plan should be established once and for all. There was not a day to lose. The superhuman expenditure of strength that he had had to make during the first months of his return to India in stirring the masses, had brought on a severe attack of his disease. During the spring of the same year he had been forced to retire twice into the mountains for rest—to Darjeeling the first time for several weeks—and to Almora the second time (from May 6 to the end of July) for two and a half months.

In the interval he had had sufficient energy to found the new Order, the Ramakrishna Mission, which lives and carries on his work to this day.

*

On May 1, 1897, all Ramakrishna's monastic and lay disciples were summoned to Calcutta to the home of one of their number, Balaram. Vivekananda spoke as the master. He said that without strict organisation nothing lasting could be established. In a country like India it was not wise to begin such an organisation on the

---

* Before him Swamis Saradananda and Abhedananda had gone to the West at the call of Swami Vivekananda.—*Publisher*.

[1] It was he, who in 1894, had been so moved by Vivekananda's words that he had begun his work of service by going to Khetri to undertake the education of the masses. (See p. 30, note 1.)

republican system, wherein each had an equal voice and where decisions were according to the vote of a majority. It would be high time for that when the members had learnt to subordinate their interests and their particular prejudices to the public weal. What they wanted for the time being was a dictator. Moreover, he himself was only acting in the capacity of a servant of the common Master—*In nomine et in signo Ramakrishna*[1]— as were they all.

The following resolutions were passed at his instigation:[2]

1. An association is to be founded under the name of the *Ramakrishna Mission*.

2. Its *aim* is to preach the truths which Ramakrishna, for the good of humanity, preached and taught by the practice of his own life, and to help others to put them into practice in their lives for their temporal, mental, and spiritual progress.

3. Its *duty* is to direct in a fitting spirit the activities of this movement, inaugurated by Ramakrishna "*for the establishment of fellowship among the followers of different religions, knowing them all to be only so many forms of one undying Eternal Religion.*"

4. Its *methods of action are*: I. "*to train men so as to make them competent to teach such knowledge or sciences as are conducive to the material and spiritual welfare of the masses;* II. *to promote and encourage arts and industries;*" III. to introduce and spread among the people in general Vedantic and other religious ideas as elucidated in the life of Ramakrishna.

---

[1] In the name of and under the sign of Ramakrishna.—*Translator.*
[2] I have thought it sufficient to give a summary. I have italicised the passages which are of most interest to Western minds.

5. It was to have two branches of action: The first to be Indian: *Maths* (monasteries) and *Ashramas* (convents for retreat) were to be established in different parts of India for the education of Sannyasins and lay brethren (householders) *"as may be willing to devote their lives to the teaching of others."* The second foreign: it was to send members of the Order into countries outside India for the foundation of spiritual centres, and *"for creating a close relationship and spirit of mutual help and sympathy between the foreign and the Indian centres."*

6. *"The Aims and Ideals of the Mission being purely spiritual and humanitarian, it would have no connection with politics."*

The definitely social, humanitarian, and "panhuman" apostolic nature of the Order founded by Vivekananda is obvious. Instead of opposing, as do most religions, faith to reason and the stress and necessity of modern life, it was to take its place with science in the front rank; it was to co-operate with progress, material as well as spiritual, and to encourage arts and industries. But its real object was the good of the masses. It laid down that the essence of its faith was the establishment of brotherhood among the different religions, since their harmony constituted the Eternal Religion. The whole was under the aegis of Ramakrishna, whose great heart had embraced all mankind within its love.

"The sacred swan" had taken its flight. The first stroke of his wings overspread the whole earth. If the reader wishes to observe in the spirit of the founder the dream of this full flight, he will find it in the visionary interview between Vivekananda and Sharatchandra Chakravarti.[1]

---

[1] In March, 1898, at Belur.

For the moment the next business was the election of the heads. Vivekananda, the General President, made Brahmananda and Yogananda President and Vice-President of the Calcutta centre, and they were to meet every Sunday at Balaram's house.[1] Vivekananda then without further delay inaugurated the twofold task of public Service and Vedantic teaching.[2]

The monks, though they obeyed him, found it difficult to follow him, and occasionally very lively debates took place between them, although these were always of a fraternal character. Vivekananda's passion and humour were not always under control, for both were overexcited by his latent malady; and sometimes those who contradicted him felt the scratch of his claws. But they took it all in good part; for such was only "king's play".[3] Both sides were assured of their mutual devotion.

---

[1] This condition lasted two years. In April, 1898, the building of the central Math of the Order was begun at Belur near Calcutta. The dedication took place on December 9 of the same year, and the final occupation on January 2, 1899. The Association divided into two twin institutions, with a considerable difference between them: for the first, the *Ramakrishna Math*, is a purely monastic body with its Maths and Ashramas; its legal status was established during 1899; it is vowed to the maintenance and the diffusion of the Universal Religion; the second institution is the *Ramakrishna Mission*, which exercises jurisdiction over all works of public utility, both philanthropic and charitable: it is open to laymen as well as to religious, and is under the government of the trustees and President of the Math. It was legally registered in April, 1909, after Vivekananda's death. The two organisations are at once akin, allied, and yet separate. In the *Appendices* of this volume we shall devote a chapter to the Ramakrishna Math and Mission and its development up to the present time.

[2] He himself gave lessons to the brethren, and instituted discussions upon the Vedanta. Here again, in spite of his learned attachment to the ancient doctrines, he showed the breadth of his mind; he called the division between Aryans and "Gentiles" ignorance. He loved to see in a Max Müller a reincarnation of some ancient commentator on the Vedas.

[3] Allusion to one of La Fontaine's fables.

At times they were still seized with longing for their contemplative life and for *their* Ramakrishna, the King of Ecstasy. They would have felt it sweet to turn the Ramakrishna Mission again into a cult of the Temple with its contemplative inaction. But Vivekananda roughly shattered their dream:

"Do you want to shut Shri Ramakrishna up within your own limits?... Shri Ramakrishna is far greater than what his disciples understand him to be.[1] He is the embodiment of infinite spirtual ideas capable of development in infinite ways. One glance of his gracious eyes can create a hundred thousand Vivekanandas at this instant. I shall scatter his ideas broadcast over the world...."

For dear as Ramakrishna the man was to him, his word was still more precious. He had no intention of raising an altar to a new God,[2] but of shedding on mankind the manna of his thought—thought that first and foremost was to be expressed in action. "Religion, if it is a true religion, must be practical."[3] Moreover, in his eyes the best form of "religion" was "to see Shiva represented in living men, and especially in the poor." He would have liked everyone each day to take a hungry Narayana, or a lame Narayana, or a blind

---

[1] Vivekananda was right not to allow this pious egotism and contemplative idleness to claim Ramakrishna as an example. It must be remembered that Ramakrishna himself often strove against his ecstatic leanings, which prevented him from giving adequate help to others. (See in Vol. I, *5th edition*, of this work, p. 295.) One of his prayers was: "Let me be born again and again, even in the form of a dog, if so I can be of use to one single soul!..."

[2] "I was not born to create a new sect in this world, too full of sects already." These were the very words of Ramakrishna. (*Cf. Life of Ramakrishna*, pp. 207-8.)

[3] This was the theme of his lectures in the Punjab, October-November, 1897.

Narayana, or six or twelve, as their means permitted, into their own houses, there to feed them and to offer them the same worship which they would to Shiva or to Vishnu in the temple.[1]

Moreover he took great care lest sentimentalism in some form or another should creep in, for he detested all forms of it. A sentimental trend of mind was only too prone to expand in Bengal, where its result had been to stifle virility. Vivekananda was adamant on the subject, all the more bitterly because (the following scene gives pathetic evidence of this fact) he had had to drag it out of himself as well as others before he could begin his work.

One day one of his brother-monks reproached him jestingly for having introduced into Ramakrishna's ecstatic teaching Western ideas of organisation, action, and service, of which Ramakrishna had not approved. Vivekananda retorted ironically at first and with rather rough humour to his antagonist and through him to the other hearers (for he felt that they were in sympathy with the speaker):

"What do you know? You are an ignorant man. ... Your study ended like that of Prahlada at seeing the first Bengali alphabet, *Ka*, for it reminded Prahlada of Krishna and he could not proceed further because of the tears that came into his eyes.... You are sentimental fools! What do you understand of religion? You are only good at praying with folded hands, 'O

---

[1] Public lecture at Lahore. There was no question of charity in the European sense: "Here, take this and go away"—an entire misconception which had a bad effect alike on the giver and the receiver. Vivekananda repudiated it. "In the religion of Service," such as he conceived it, "the receiver is greater than the giver," because for the time being the receiver was God Himself.

Lord! how beautiful is Your nose! How sweet are Your eyes!' and all such nonsense...and you think your salvation is secured and Shri Ramakrishna will come at the final hour and take you by the hand to the highest heaven.... Study, public preaching, and doing humanitarian works are, according to you, Maya, because he said to someone, 'Seek and find God first; doing good in the world is a presumption!'... As if God is such an easy thing to be achieved! As if He is such a fool as to make Himself a plaything in the hands of an imbecile!"

Then suddenly he declared, "You think you have understood Shri Ramakrishna better than myself! You think Jnana is dry knowledge to be attained by a desert path, killing out the tenderest faculties of the heart! Your Bhakti is sentimental nonsense, which makes one impotent. You want to preach Ramakrishna as you have understood him, which is mighty little! Hands off! Who cares for *your* Ramakrishna? Who cares for your Bhakti and Mukti? Who cares what your Scriptures say? I will go into a thousand hells cheerfully, if I can rouse my countrymen, immersed in Tamas, to stand on their own feet and be *men* inspired with the spirit of Karma-Yoga.... I am not a servant of Ramakrishna, or anyone, but of him only who serves and helps others, without caring for his own Bhakti or Mukti!"

His face was on fire, says a witness, his eyes flashed, his voice was choked, his body shaken and trembling. Suddenly he fled to his own room. The others, completely overwhelmed, remained silent. After a few minutes one or two of them went and looked into his room. Vivekananda was deep in meditation. They

waited in silence.... An hour afterwards Vivekananda
returned. His features still bore the traces of the violent
storm, but he had recovered his calm. He said softly,
"When one attains Bhakti, one's heart and nerves
become so soft and delicate that they cannot bear even
the touch of a flower! Do you know that I cannot even
read a novel nowadays? I cannot think or talk of Shri
Ramakrishna long, without being overwhelmed. So I
am trying and trying always to keep down the welling
rush of Bhakti within me. I am trying to bind and bind
myself with iron chains of Jnana, for still my work
for my motherland is unfinished, and my message to
the world not yet fully delivered. So, as soon as I find
that Bhakti feelings are trying to come up and sweep
me off my feet, I give a hard knock to them and make
myself as firm as adamant by bringing up austere Jnana.
Oh, I have work to do! I am a slave of Ramakrishna,
who left his work to be done by me and will not give
me rest till I have finished it!... Oh, his love for
me!..."

He was again unable to proceed from emotion. Yogananda thereupon tried to distract his thoughts, for they
feared a fresh outburst.[1]

From that day onwards there was never a word of
protest against Vivekananda's methods. What could
they object to him that he had not already thought
himself? They had read to the depths of his great
tortured soul.

*

Every mission is dramatic, for it is accomplished at
the expense of him who receives it, at the expense of
one part of his nature, of his rest, of his health, often

[1] *The Life of the Swami Vivekananda*, III, pp. 159-61.

of his deepest aspirations. Vivekananda shared his countrymen's nature with their vision of God, their need to flee from life and the world as wandering monks, either for meditation, for study, or driven by the ecstasy of love, to the everlasting flight of the unattached soul which has no resting place, in order never to lose contact with the Universal One. Those who watched him closely often heard a sigh of weariness and regret coming from the depths of his heart.[1]

But he had not chosen his way of life. His mission had chosen him.

"There is no rest for me. What Ramakrishna called Kali took possession of my soul and body three or four days before he left this earth. And that forces me to work, work, and never allows me to busy myself with my own personal needs."[2]

[1] "I was born for the life of the scholar, retired, quiet, poring over my books. But the Mother dispenses otherwise. Yet the tendency is there...." (June 3, 1897, Almora).

He had hours of intense religious vision, "when work seemed to him more than illusion." (October, 1898).

One day he had been arguing with considerable irritation with one of his monks, Virajananda, in order to tear him away from his meditations and force him to useful action:

"How could you think of meditating for hours? Enough if you can concentrate your mind for five minutes or even one minute. For the rest of the time one has to occupy himself with studies and some work for the general good."

Virajananda did not agree and went away in silence. Vivekananda said to another monk that he understood only too well. "The memories of the Parivrajaka (wandering) days were among the sweetest and the happiest of his whole life, and he would give anything if he could again have that unknownness freed from all cares of public life." (January 13, 1901).

[2] It was shortly before his death that, speaking to a disciple, Sharat-chandra Chakravarti, Vivekananda told him about this mysterious transmission which took place in him three or four days before Ramakrishna's death:

"Ramakrishna made me come alone and sit in front of him, while he gazed into my eyes, and passed into Samadhi. Then I perceived a powerful current of subtle force, like an electric shock. My body

It made him forget himself and his desires, his well-being, even his health for the good of others.[1]

And he had to inculcate the same faith in his apostolic militia. This was only possible by stirring in them the energy of action. He had to deal with a nation of "dyspeptics", drunk with their own sentimentality.[2] That is why he could be harsh sometimes in order to harden them. He wished "in all fields of activity to awaken that austere elevation of spirit which arouses heroism." This was to be accomplished by both manual and spiritual work, scientific research, and the service of man. If he attached so much importance to the teaching of the Vedanta, it was because he saw in it a sovereign tonic: "To revivify the country through the thundering notes of the Vedic rhythm."

He violated the heart not only of others, but also his own, although he was only too aware that the heart is a source of the divine. As a leader of men he did not want to stifle it, but to put it in its proper place. Where

was transpierced. I also lost consciousness. For how long I do not know.... When I returned to myself, I saw the Master weeping. He said to me with an infinite tenderness, 'O my Naren, I am nothing now but a poor fakir. I have given thee all. By virtue of this gift thou wilt do great things in this world; and not till afterwards will it be permitted to thee to return....' It seems to me that it was this force which carried me into the turmoil and makes me work, work...."

[1] "I should consider it a great honour, if I had to go through hell in doing good to my country." (October, 1897).

"The Sannyasin takes two vows: I. to realise truth, II. to help the world. Above all he renounces all thoughts of heaven!" (To Nivedita, July, 1899).

In Indian thought heaven is lower than communion with Brahman. From heaven there is a return.

[2] "A nation of dyspeptics, indulging in antics to the accompaniment of Khol and Karatal and singing Kirtanas and other songs of sentimental type.... I wish to stimulate energy, even by means of martial music, and proscribe everything that titillates languorous sentiments...." (Dialogue with Sharatchandra, 1901).

the heart had the ascendancy, he debased it, where it was in an inferior position, he exalted it.[1] He desired an exact equilibrium of inner powers,[2] in view of the work to be done in the direction of human service, for that was the most pressing: the ignorance, suffering, and misery of the masses could not wait.

It is true that equilibrium is never stable. It is particularly difficult to acquire, and even more difficult to maintain, in those extreme races, who pass immediately from the red heat of exaltation to the dead ashes of desire; and it was a harder task still in the case of a man such as Vivekananda, torn between twenty contradictory demons—faith, science, art, all the passions of victory and action. It was wonderful that he kept in his feverish hands to the end the equal balance between the two poles: a burning love of the Absolute (the Advaita) and the irresistible appeal of suffering Humanity. And what makes him so appealing to us is that at those times when equilibrium was no longer possible, and he had to make a choice, it was the latter that won the day: he sacrificed everything else to Pity,[3] to "poor

[1] In the Punjab, the country of fighting races, he encouraged Bhakti, though he condemned it in Bengal. He went so far as to long in Lahore for the processions of dances and religious songs, the Sankirtanas, which he had held up to derision in Calcutta. For "this land of the Five Rivers (Punjab) is spiritually dry," and it needed watering. (November, 1897).

[2] Before his second journey to the West, when he was tracing for his monks his ideal of religious life, he said to them, "You must try to combine in your life immense idealism with immense practicality. You must be prepared to go into deep meditation now, and the next moment you must be ready to go and cultivate those fields. You must be prepared to explain the intricacies of the Shastras now, and the next moment to go and sell the produce of the fields in the market." The object of the monastery was man-making. "The true man is he who is strong as strength itself and yet possesses a woman's heart." (June, 1899).

[3] Speaking to his monks at Belur, he said once (1899), "If your brain and your heart come into conflict, follow your heart."

suffering Humanity", as Beethoven, his great European brother, said.

The beautiful episode of Girish is a moving example:

It will be remembered that this disciple of Rama-krishna—the celebrated Bengali dramatist, writer, and comedian, who had led the life of a "libertine" in the double sense of the classic age until the moment when the tolerant and mischievous fisher of the Ganga took him upon his hook—had since, without leaving the world, become the most ardent and sincere of the converts; he spent his days in a constant transport of faith through love, of Bhakti-Yoga. But he had kept his freedom of speech; and all Ramakrishna's disciples showed him great respect for the sake of their Master's memory.

One day he came in while Vivekananda was discussing the most abstract philosophy with a disciple. Vivekananda broke off and said to him in a mockingly affectionate tone, "Well, Girish, you did not care to make a study of these things, but passed your days with your 'Krishnas and your Vishnus'."

Girish replied, "Well, Naren, let me ask you one thing. Of Vedas and Vedanta you have read enough. But are there remedies prescribed in them for these wailings, these cries of hungry mouths, these abominable sins. . . and the many other evils and miseries that one meets with every day? The mother of the house there, who at one time fed daily fifty mouths, has not the wherewithal to cook even for herself and her children for the last three days! The lady of such-and-such a family has been violated by ruffians and tortured to death. The young widow of so-and-so has succumbed from causing abortion to hide her shame!... I ask

you, Naren, have you found in the Vedas any preven-
tive for these evils?..."

And as Girish continued in this vein of sharp irony,
depicting the dark and dismal side of society, Vivekananda sat speechless and deeply moved. Thinking of
the pain and misery of the world, tears came into his
eyes and to hide his feelings he walked out of the
room.

Girish said to the disciple, "Now, did you see with
your own eyes what a large heart your Guru possesses?
I do not esteem him so much for being a scholar and
intellectual giant, as for that large-heartedness which
made him walk out shedding tears for the misery of
mankind. As soon as he heard it, mark you, all his
Vedas and Vedanta vanished out of sight as it were,
all the learning and the scholarship that he was dis-
playing a moment ago was cast aside and his whole
being was filled to overflow with the milk of loving
kindness. Your Swamiji is as much a Jnani and a
pandit as a lover of God and humanity."

Vivekananda returned, and said to Sadananda that
his heart was gnawing with pain at the poverty and
distress of his countrymen, and exhorted him to do
something by opening a small relief centre at least.
And turning to Girish, he said, "Ah, Girish, the thought
comes to me that even if I have to undergo a thousand
births to relieve the misery of the world, ay, even to
remove the least pain from anyone, I shall cheerfully
do it!..."[1]

*

The generous passion of his pitiful heart mastered
his brethren and disciples, and one and all, they

[1] *The Life of the Swami Vivekananda*, III, pp. 165-7.

dedicated themselves to the multiple forms of human Service, which he pointed out to them.

During the summer of 1897 Akhandananda, with the help of two disciples sent him by Vivekananda, for four or five months fed and nursed hundreds of poor people suffering from famine in the district of Murshidabad in Bengal; he collected abandoned children and founded an orphanage at Mohula, removed afterwards to Sargachhi. With Franciscan patience and love Akhandananda devoted himself to the education of these poor children without distinction of caste or belief. In 1899 he taught them the trades of weaving, tailoring, joinery, and silk-culture, and reading, writing, arithmetic, and English.

The same year, 1897, Trigunatita opened a famine centre at Dinajpur. In two months he came to the rescue of eighty-four villages. Other centres were established at Deoghar, Dakshineswar, and Calcutta.

The following year, April-May, 1898, a mobilisation of the whole Ramakrishna Mission against the plague that had broken out in Calcutta took place. Vivekananda, ill though he was, hastily returned from the Himalayas to put himself at the head of the relief work. Money was lacking. All that they had at their disposal had been spent on the purchase of a site for the construction of a new monastery. Vivekananda did not hesitate for an instant:

"Sell it, if necessary," he ordered. "We are Sannyasins, we ought always to be ready to sleep under the trees and live on what we beg every day."

A big stretch of ground was rented and sanitary camps laid out upon it. Vivekananda came to live in a poor locality to inspire courage in the people and cheer up the workers. The management of the work was entrusted to Sister Nivedita (Margaret Noble), recently arrived from Europe, and to the Swamis Sadananda and Shivananda with several other helpers.* They supervised the disinfection and the cleansing of four of the main poor quarters of Calcutta. Vivekananda called the students to a meeting (April, 1899), and reminded them of their duty in times of calamity. They organised themselves into bands to inspect poor houses, to distribute pamphlets of hygiene and to set the example of scavenging. Every Sunday they came to the meetings of the Ramakrishna Mission to report to Sister Nivedita.

The Mission also adopted the holy custom of making the anniversary of Ramakrishna a festival for the poor, and of feeding thousands on that day at all the centres of the Order.

And so a new spirit of solidarity and brotherly communion between all classes of the nation was formed in India.

Parallel to this work of social mutual aid, education and Vedantic preaching were undertaken; for, to use his own words, Vivekananda wanted India to have "an Islamic body and a Vedantic heart." During 1897 Ramakrishnananda, who was giving lectures in Madras and the neighbourhood, opened eleven classes in different parts of the city; side by side he carried on teaching work and cared for the starving. In the middle of the same year Vivekananda sent Shivananda to Ceylon to preach the Vedanta. Educationalists were seized with a holy passion. Vivekananda rejoiced to hear the

* This was done on the occasion of the second plague outbreak in 1899.—*Publisher*.

headmistress of a school for young girls say to him, "I adore these young girls as the Divine Mother (Bhagavati). I do not know any other worship."

Soon after the founding of the Ramakrishna Mission Vivekananda was obliged to stop his own activities and undergo a course of treatment for several weeks at Almora. Nevertheless he was able to write, "The movement is begun. It will never stop." (July 9, 1897.)

"Only one idea was burning in my brain—to start the machine for elevating the Indian masses and that I have succeeded in doing to a certain extent. It would have made your heart glad to see how my boys are working in the midst of famine and disease and misery —nursing by the mat-bed of the cholera-stricken Pariah and feeding the starving Chandala, and the Lord sends help to me and to them all.... He is with me, the Beloved, as he was when I was in America, in England, when I was roaming about unknown from place to place in India.... I feel my task is done—at most three or four years more of life is left.[1] I have lost all wish for my salvation. I never wanted earthly enjoyments. I must see my machine in strong working order, and then, knowing for certain that I have put in a lever for the good of humanity, in India at least, which no power can drive back, I will sleep without caring what will be next. And may I be born again and again, and suffer thousands of miseries, so that I 'may worship the only God that exists, the only God I believe in, the sum total of all souls."[2]

[1] There remained exactly five. He died in July, 1902.
[2] *Cf. The Life of the Swami Vivekananda*, III, p. 178. Here comes the admirable confession of faith that I have already quoted in p. 26 and to which I shall return again in my final examination of Vivekananda's thought.

He made use of the least respite from his illness to increase his work tenfold. From August to December, 1897, he went like a whirlwind through Northern India from the Punjab to Kashmir, sowing his seed wherever he went. He discussed with the Maharaja the possibility of founding a great Advaitist monastery in Kashmir, he preached to the students of the Lahore colleges, urging strength and belief in man as a preparation for belief in God, and he formed among them an association, purely unsectarian, for the relief, hygiene, and education of the people. Wherever he went he never wearied of trying to rebuild individual character in India, by helping each man to be delivered of the God within him. He constantly subjected faith to the test of action. He tried to remedy social injustices by preaching intermarriage between the castes and subdivisions of castes, so that they might draw near to each other, by ameliorating the condition of outcasts, by occupying himself with the fate of unmarried women and of Hindu widows, by fighting sectarianism wherever it was to be found, and vain formalism, the "don't-touchisms", as he called them. At the same time—(the two tasks were complementary)—he worked for the reconstruction of the Hindu intellect by spreading a real knowledge of Sanskrit, by seeking to integrate Western science in it, and by reviving the Indian universities so that they might produce men rather than diplomas and officials.

There was no thought of *Hind Swaraj*,* of the political independence of India, having risen against England. He depended on British co-operation as on

* But the Swami wanted the political independence of India—*Publisher*.

the co-operation of the universe. And as a matter of fact England helped his work: in default of the State, Anglo-Saxon disciples from London and New York brought the Swami their personal devotion and sufficient funds to buy land and build the great monastery of Belur.[1]

The year 1898 was chiefly devoted to arrangements for the new working of the Ramakrishna Math, and to the founding of journals or reviews which were to be the intellectual organs of the Order and a means for the education of India.[2]

*

But the chief importance of this year, 1898, was Vivekananda's training of his Western disciples.

[1] On fifteen acres of land situated upon the other bank of the Ganga opposite the old building of Baranagore, near Calcutta. The purchase took place during the first months of 1898: the building was begun in April under the architect who became Swami Vijnanananda.

[2] *Prabuddha Bharata*, already in existence, had been suspended as a result of the death of its young editor. It was taken over by Sevier, and transferred from Madras to Almora, under the editorship of a remarkable man who had withdrawn from the world, and whose kindred passion for the public weal had attracted him to Vivekananda, who had initiated him into his Order after only a few days of preparation under the name of Swami Swarupananda. He was the master of Miss Noble (Nivedita) in Hindu religious literature. He was to become the President of the Advaita Ashrama.

At the beginning of 1899, another monthly review was founded, *Udbodhan*, under the direction of Swami Trigunatita. Its guiding principles were never to attack anybody's faith, to present the doctrine of the Vedas in the simplest form so that it might be accessible to all, to find room for definite questions of hygiene and education, and the physical and spiritual betterment of the race, and to spread ideas of moral purity, mutual aid, and universal harmony.

For the first of these magazines Vivekananda published in August, 1898, his beautiful poem, *To the Awakened India*, which is a real manifesto of active energy and realised faith:

"Awake, arise, and dream no more!
This is the land of dreams, where Karma
Weaves unthreaded garlands with our thoughts,
Of flowers sweet or noxious—and none

They had come at his call—Miss Margaret Noble at
the end of January—to found in conjunction with Miss
Müller model institutions for the education of Indian
women—Mrs. Ole Bull and Miss Josephine MacLeod
in February.[1] In March Margaret Noble took the vow
of Brahmacharya and the name of Nivedita (the Consecrated One). Vivekananda introduced her in warm
terms to the Calcutta public as a gift of England to
India, and that he might the better root out all trace
of the memories, prejudices, and customs of her

> Has root or stem, being born in naught, which
> The softest breath of Truth drives back to
> Primal nothingness. Be bold, and face
> The Truth! Be one with it! Let visions cease.
> Or, if you cannot, dream but truer dreams,
> Which are Eternal Love and Service Free."

(*The Complete Works of Swami Vivekananda*, IV, pp. 388-89. Only the
last verse of the poem has been given here.)

[1] Miss MacLeod, who has done me the honour of communicating
her memories, had known Vivekananda for more than four years,
and he had been her guest for months at a time. But though she was
devoted to him, she never renounced her independence, nor did he
demand it. He always gave full liberty to those who had not voluntarily
contracted vows. So she remained a friend and a free helper, not an
initiated disciple like Nivedita. She told me that she had asked his
permission before she came to rejoin the Swami in India. He had
replied with this imperious message (which I quote from memory),
"Come, if you wish to see poverty, degradation, dirt, and men in
rags, who speak of God! But if you want anything else, do not come!
For we cannot bear one more word of criticism."

She conformed strictly to this reservation, imposed by the compassionate love of Vivekananda for his debased people, whose humi-
liations he resented with wounded pride. But on one occasion she
happened to make a laughing remark with regard to a Brahmin of
grotesque appearance whom they met in the Himalayas. Vivekananda "turned on her like a lion," withered her with a glance and
cried, "Hands off! Who are you? What have you ever done?"

She remained silent, disconcerted. Later she learnt that this very
same poor Brahmin had been one of those who by begging had collected the sum to make it possible for Vivekananda to undertake his
journey to the West. And she realised that a man's real self is not
what he appears, but what he does.

"How can I best help you?" she asked when she had arrived.
"Love India."

country,[1] he took her with a group of disciples on a journey of several months through historic India.[2]

But—and this is curious—while plunging the souls of his companions into the religious abyss of his race, he lost himself in it until he seemed to be submerged. Men saw the great Advaitist, the fervent worshipper of the Absolute without form or face, go through a phase of devouring passion for the legendary Gods, for the sovereign pair: Shiva and the Mother. Undoubtedly in this he was only following the example of his Master Ramakrishna, in whose heart there was room for the formless God and for the forms of all Gods, and who for years on end had experienced the bliss of passionate abandon to the beautiful Goddess. But the striking point in Vivekananda's case is that he came to it *after*, not *before*, he had mastered the Absolute;* and he

[1] This was no manifestation of the evil spirit of chauvinism or hostility to the West. In 1900, when he established the Swami Turiyananda in California, he said to him, "From this day, destroy even the memory of India within you." In order to work profoundly upon a people for its real betterment, it is necessary to become one with that people and forget oneself in it: that was the principle Vivekananda imposed on his disciples.

[2] She has left an account of this journey and the talks with Vivekananda in her *Notes of Some Wanderings with the Swami Vivekananda*. I also owe to Miss MacLeod's reminiscences (also of the party) many precious notes, especially on the moral discipline to which Vivekananda subjected Nivedita. He had not the slightest respect for her instinctive national loyalty, for her habits or her dislikes as a Westerner; he constantly humiliated her proud and logical English character. Perhaps in this way he wished to defend himself and her against the passionate adoration she had for him; although Nivedita's feelings for him were always absolutely pure, he perhaps saw their danger. He snubbed her mercilessly and found fault with all she did. He hurt her. She came back to her companions overwhelmed and in tears. Eventually they remonstrated with Vivekananda for his excessive severity, and from that time it was softened, and light entered Nivedita's heart. She only felt more deeply the price of the Master's confidence, and the happiness of submitting to his rules of thought.

* The Swami had been devoted to Kali even before he had realised the Absolute.—*Publisher.*

brought to his passion for them all the tragic vehe-
mence of his nature, so that he clothed the Gods,
especially Kali, in a quite different atmosphere from the
one in which the ecstatic tenderness of Ramakrishna
had enveloped them.

After a stay at Almora, where the Seviers were already established and where the Advaita Ashrama was
about to be built—then after a journey to Kashmir in
three house-boats up the river through the Vale of
Srinagar—Vivekananda with Nivedita at the end of
July, 1898, undertook the great pilgrimage to the cave
of Amarnath in a glacial valley of the Western Himalayas. They were part of a crowd of two or three thousand
pilgrims, forming at each halting place a whole town
of tents. Nivedita noticed a sudden change come over
her Master. He became one of the thousands, scrupulously observing the most humble practices demanded
by custom. In order to reach their goal it was necessary to climb for days up rocky slopes, along dangerous
paths, to cross several miles of glacier, and to bathe in
the sacred torrents in spite of the cold. On August 2,
the day of the annual festival, they arrived at the enormous cavern large enough to contain a vast cathedral:
at the back rose the ice-lingam—great Shiva Himself.
Everyone had to enter naked, his body smeared with
ashes. Behind the others, trembling with emotion,
Vivekananda entered in an almost fainting condition;
and there, prostrate, in the darkness of the cave, before
that whiteness, surrounded by the music of hundreds
of voices singing, he had a vision.... Shiva appeared
to him. He would never say what he had seen and
heard.... But the blow of the apparition on his tense
nerves was such that he almost died. When he emerged

from the grotto, there was a clot of blood in his left eye, and his heart was dilated and never regained its normal condition. For days afterwards he spoke of nothing but Shiva, he saw Shiva everywhere; he was saturated by Him; the snowy Himalaya was Shiva seated on His throne....

A month later he was possessed in turn by the Mother, Kali. The Divine Maternity was omnipresent. He worshipped Her even in the person of a little girl of four years old. But it was not only in such peaceful guise that She appeared to him. His intense meditation led him to the dark face of the symbol. He had a terrible vision of Kali—the mighty Destructress, lurking behind the veil of life—the terrible One hidden by the dust of the living who pass by, and all the appearances raised by their feet. During the evening in a fever he groped in the dark for pencil and paper, and wrote his famous poem, *Kali the Mother;* then he fell exhausted:

> "The stars are blotted out,
>   The clouds are covering clouds,
> It is darkness vibrant, sonant.
>   In the roaring, whirling wind
> Are the souls of a million lunatics—
>   Just loose from the prison house—
> Wrenching trees by the roots,
>   Sweeping all from the path.
> The sea has joined the fray,
>   And swirls up mountain-waves,
> To reach the pitchy sky.
>   The flash of lurid light
> Reveals on every side
>   A thousand, thousand shades

Of Death begrimed and black—
    Scattering plagues and sorrows,
Dancing mad with joy.
Come, Mother, come!
For Terror is Thy name,
    Death is in Thy breath,
And every shaking step
    Destroys a world for e'er.
Thou 'Time', the All-Destroyer!
    Come, O Mother, come!
Who dares misery love
    And hug the form of Death,
Dance in Destruction's dance,
    To him the Mother comes."[1]

He said to Nivedita, "Learn to recognise the Mother as instinctively in evil, terror, sorrow, and annihilation, as in that which makes for sweetness and joy. Fools put a garland of flowers around Thy neck, O Mother, and then start back in terror and call Thee 'The Merciful'.... Meditate on death. Worship the Terrible. Only by the worship of the Terrible can the Terrible itself be overcome and Immortality gained.... There could be bliss in torture too.... The Mother Herself is Brahman. Even Her curse is blessing. The heart must become a cremation ground—pride, selfishness, desire, all burnt to ashes. Then and then alone, will the Mother come!"

And the Englishwoman, shaken and bewildered by the storm, saw the good order and comfort of her Western faith disappearing in the typhoon of the Cosmos invoked by the Indian visionary. She wrote:

"As he spoke, the underlying egoism of worship that

[1] *The Complete Works of Swami Vivekananda*, IV, p. 384.

is devoted to the kind God, to Providence, the consoling Divinity, without a heart for God in the earthquake, or God in the volcano, overwhelmed the listener. One saw that such worship was at bottom, as the Hindu calls it, merely 'shopkeeping', and one realised the infinitely greater boldness and truth of the teaching that God manifests through evil *as well as* through good. One saw that the true attitude of mind and will, that are not to be baffled by the personal self, was in fact that determination, in stern words of the Swami Vivekananda, 'to seek death, not life, to hurl oneself upon the sword's point, to become one with the Terrible for evermore!' "[1]

Once more we see in this paroxysm the will to heroism, which to Vivekananda was the soul of action. Ultimate Truth, desiring to be seen in all its terrible nakedness and refusing to be softened. Faith, which expects nothing in return for its free bestowing and scorns the bargain of "giving to get in return" and all its promise of Paradise—for its indestructible energy is like steel forged upon the anvil by the blows of the hammer.[2]

[1] *The Master as I Saw Him*, by Nivedita of Ramakrishna-Vivekananda, p. 162.

[2] Even the tender Ramakrishna knew the terrible face of the Mother. But he loved Her smile better.

"One day," so Shivanath Shastri, one of the founders and heads of the Sadharan Brahmo Samaj, relates, "I was present when several men began to argue about the attributes of God, and if they were more or less according to reason. Ramakrishna stopped them, saying, 'Enough, enough. What is the use of disputing whether the Divine attributes are reasonable or not?... 'You say that God is good: can you convince me of His goodness by this reasoning? Look at the flood that has just caused the death of thousands. How can you prove that a benevolent God ordered it? You will perhaps reply that this same flood swept away uncleannesses and watered the earth...etc. But could not a good God do that without drowning thousands of innocent men, women, and children?' Thereupon one of the disputants

Our great Christian ascetics knew and still experience this virile pleasure. Even Pascal tasted of it. But instead of its leading to detachment from action, Vivekananda was inspired by it with a red-hot zeal, that steeled his will and flung him into the thick of the fight with tenfold renewed zest.

He espoused all the sufferings of the world. "One had the impression," wrote Nivedita, "as if no blow to any in the world could pass and leave our Master's heart untouched: as if no pain even to that of death could elicit anything but love and blessing."[1]

"I have hugged," he said, "the Form of Death."

He was possessed by it for several months. He heard no other voice but that of the Mother, and it had a terrible reaction upon his health. When he returned, his monks were terrified by the change. He remained plunged in concentration so intense that a question ten times repeated would invoke no answer. He recognised that its cause was "an intense Tapasya" (the fire of asceticism).

"Shiva Himself has entered into my brain. He *will not* go!"

For the rationalist minds of Europe who find such obsession by personal Gods repugnant, it may be useful

said, 'Then, ought we to believe that God is cruel?' 'O idiot,' cried Ramakrishna, 'who said that? Fold your hands and say humbly, "O God, we are too feeble and too weak to understand Thy nature and Thy deeds. Deign to enlighten us !"...Do not argue. Love!' " (*Reminiscences of Ramakrishna* by Shivanath Shastri). The knowledge of the terrible God was the same both with Ramakrishna and Vivekananda. But their attitude was different. Ramakrishna bowed his head and kissed the Divine foot which trampled on his heart. Vivekananda, head erect, looked death in the eyes; and his sombre joy of action rejoiced in it. He ran to hurl himself "upon the point of the sword."

[1] Probably the moral upheaval caused shortly before by the death of his faithful friend, Goodwin, and of Pavhari Baba (June, 1898), prepared the way for this inner irruption of the terrible Goddess.

to recall the explanation Vivekananda had given a year after to his companions: "The Totality of all souls— not the human alone—is the Personal God. The will of the Totality nothing can resist. It is what we know as Law. And that is what we mean by Shiva, Kali and so on."[1]

But the powerful emotivity of the great Indian projected in images of fire that which in European brains remains at the reasoning stage. Never for an instant was his profound faith in the Advaita shaken. But by the inverse road to Ramakrishna, he reached the same pitch of universal comprehension—the same belvedere of thought—where man is at the same time the circumference and the centre: the totality of souls and each individual soul—the AUM[2] containing them and becoming reabsorbed in the eternal Nada—the starting point and the end of the double unending movement. His brother-monks from this time had some obscure inkling of his identity with Ramakrishna. Premananda said to him once, "Is there any difference between you and Ramakrishna?"

He returned to the monastery, to the new Math of Belur, and consecrated it on December 9, 1898. At Calcutta a few days before, on November 12, the day of the festival of the Mother, Nivedita's school for girls was opened. In spite of illness and suffocating attacks

[1] During his second voyage to Europe on the boat in sight of the coast of Sicily. (*Cf.* Talks with Nivedita, in the book: *The Master as I Saw Him.*)

[2] Or OM, the sacred word. It is, according to the old Hindu belief and the definition of Vivekananda himself, "the kernel of all sounds and the symbol of Brahman.... The Universe is created of this sound." "Nada-Brahman," he said, "is the Brahman Sound,...the most subtle in the Universe." (*Cf.* "The Mantra: Om: Word and Wisdom" in *Bhakti-Yoga: The Complete Works of Swami Vivekananda*, III, pp. 56-59.)

of asthma from which he emerged with his face blue
like that of a drowning man, he pushed on the organisation of his Mission with Saradananda's help. The
swarm was at work. Sanskrit. Oriental and Western
philosophy, manual work and meditation alike were
taught there. He himself set the example. After his
lessons on metaphysics he tilled the garden, dug a well,
and kneaded bread.[1] He was a living hymn of Work.

"Only a great monk (in the widest sense: a man
vowed to the service of the Absolute) can be a great
worker; for he is without attachment.... There were
no greater workers than Buddha and Christ.... No work
is secular. All work is adoration and worship...."

Moreover there was no hierarchy in the forms of
work. All useful work was noble....

"If my Gurubhais told me that I was to pass the rest
of my life cleaning the drains of the Math, assuredly I
should do it. He alone is a great leader who knows
how to obey for the public good...."

The first duty was "renunciation".

"Without renunciation no religion (he might have
said, 'no deep foundation of the spirit') can endure."

And the man who has "renounced", the "Sannyasin", so say the Vedas, "stands on the head of the
Vedas," for he is freed from sects, churches, and
prophets." He dwells in God. God dwells in him. Let
him only believe!

"The history of the world is the history of a few men
who had faith in themselves. That faith calls out the
Divinity within. You can do anything. You fail only

[1] He attached importance to physical exercise: "I want sappers and
miners in the army of religion. So, boys, set yourselves to the task of
training your muscles. For ascetics mortification is all right. For workers
well-developed bodies, muscles of iron and nerves of steel!"

when you do not strive sufficiently to manifest infinite power. As soon as a man or a nation loses faith in himself, death comes. Believe first in yourself, and then in God. A handful of strong men will move the world...."

Then be brave. Bravery is the highest virtue. Dare to speak the whole truth always, "to all without distinction, without equivocation, without fear, without compromise." Do not trouble about the rich and great. The Sannyasin should have nothing to do with the rich. To pay respects to the rich and hang on to them for support is conduct which becomes a public woman. The Sannyasin's duty is with the poor. He should treat the poor with loving care and serve them joyfully with all his might.

"If you seek your own salvation, you will go to hell. It is the salvation of others that you must seek...and even if you have to go to hell in working for others, that is worth more than to gain heaven by seeking your own salvation.... Shri Ramakrishna came and gave his life for the world. I will also sacrifice my life; you also, every one of you, should do the same. All these works and so forth are only a beginning. Believe me, from the shedding of our life-blood will arise gigantic, heroic workers and warriors of God who will revolutionise the whole world."

His words are great music, phrases in the style of Beethoven, stirring rhythms like the march of Handel choruses. I cannot touch these sayings of his, scattered as they are through the pages of books at thirty years' distance, without receiving a thrill through my body like an electric shock. And what shocks, what transports must have been produced when in burning words they issued from the lips of the hero!

He felt himself dying. But "... Life is a battle. Let me die fighting. Two years of physical suffering have taken from me twenty years of life. But the soul is unchanged. It is always there, the same fool, the fool with a single idea: Atman...."

# IX

## THE SECOND JOURNEY
## TO THE WEST

HE set out upon a second journey to the West in order
to inspect the works he had founded and to fan the
flame. This time he took with him[1] one of the most
learned of his brethren, Turiyananda, a man of high
caste and noble life, and learned in Sanskrit studies.

"The last time," he said, "they saw a warrior. Now
I want to show them a Brahmin."

"He left[2] under very different conditions from those
of his return: in his emaciated body he carried a brazier
of energy, breathing out action and combat, and so
disgusted with the supineness of his devitalised people
that on the boat in sight of Corsica he celebrated "the
Lord of War" (Napoleon).[3]

In his contempt for moral cowardice he went so far
as to prefer the vigour of crime,[4] and the older he grew,

[1] Nivedita went with them.

[2] On June 20, 1899 he travelled from Calcutta by Madras, Colombo,
Aden, Naples, Marseilles. On July 31, he was in London. On August
16, he left Glasgow for New York. He stayed in the United States
until July 20, 1900, chiefly in California. From August 1 to October 24,
he visited France, and went to Paris and Brittany. Then by Vienna,
the Balkans, Constantinople, Greece, and Egypt he returned to India
and arrived at the beginning of December, 1900.

[3] He recalled also the energy of Robespierre  He was full of the epic
history of Europe. Before Gibraltar his imagination saw on the shore the
galloping horses of the Moors and the great Arab invasion disembarking.

[4] When people spoke of the rarity of crime in India, he cried, "Would
God it were otherwise in my land! For this is verily the virtuousness of
death." "The older I grow," he added, "the more everything seems
to me to lie in manliness: this is my new Gospel." He went so far as to
say, "Do even evil like a man. Be wicked if you must on a great scale."

the deeper was his conviction that the East and the West must espouse each other. He saw in India and Europe "two organisms in full youth...two great experiments neither of which is yet complete." They ought to be mutually helpful, but at the same time each should respect the free development of the other. He did not allow himself to criticise their weaknesses: both of them were at the ungrateful age. They ought to grow up hand in hand.[1] When he returned to India a year and a half later, he was almost entirely detached from life, and all violence had gone out of him, exorcised by the brutal face he had this time unveiled in Western Imperialism; he had looked into its eyes, full of rapacious hatred. He had realised that during his first journey he had been caught by the power, the organisation and the apparent democracy of America and Europe. Now he had discovered the spirit of lucre, of greed, of Mammon, with its enormous combinations and ferocious struggle for supremacy. He was capable of rendering homage to the grandeur of a mighty association....

These words must be taken, it goes without saying, (spoken as they were on the boat to sure and tried friends, who were not likely to misunderstand them), as one of the linguistic thunderbolts, whereby the Kshatriya, the spiritual warrior, fulminated against the shifting sands of the East. The true sense is probably that which I read in an old Italian motto: *Ignavia est jacere*—The vilest of crimes is not to act.

[1] *Cf.* the Interviews recorded by Nivedita. That which emerges most clearly is his "universal" sense. He had hopes of democratic America, he was enthusiastic over the Italy of art, culture, and liberty—the great mother of Mazzini. He spoke of China as the treasury of the world. He fraternised with the martyred Babists of Persia. He embraced in equal love the India of the Hindus, the Mohammedans, and the Buddhists. He was fired by the Mogul Empire: when he spoke of Akbar the tears came into his eyes. He could comprehend and defend the grandeur of Genghis Khan and his dream of Asiatic unity. He made Buddha the subject of magnificent eulogy: "I am the servant of the servants of Buddha...."

"But what beauty was there amongst a pack of wolves?"

"Western life," said a witness, "seemed hell to him...."

Material brilliance no longer deceived him. He saw the hidden tragedy, the weariness under the forced expenditure of energy, the deep sorrow under the frivolous mask. He said to Nivedita, "Social life in the West is like a peal of laughter: but underneath it is a wail. It ends in a sob. The fun and frivolity are all on the surface; really it is full of tragic intensity.... Here (in India) it is sad and gloomy on the surface, but underneath are carelessness and merriment."[1]

How had this all too prophetic vision come to him? When and where had his glance, stripping the bark from the tree and revealing the canker gnawing at the heart of the West despite all its outward glory, foreseen the monster of the days of hate and agony that were approaching, and the years of wars and revolutions?[2] Nobody knows. The record of his journey was only

His intuition of the unity of the human race did not stop at the arbitrary divisions of races and nations. It made him say that he had seen in the West some of the best Hindu types, and in India the best Christians.

[1] *The Master as I Saw Him*, p. 145, 3rd edition.

[2] Sister Christine has just revealed to us in her unpublished Memoirs that even during his first journey in 1895, Vivekananda had seen the tragedy of the West:

"Europe is on the edge of a volcano. If the fire is not extinguished by a flood of spirituality, it will erupt."

Sister Christine has also given us another striking instance of prophetic intuition:

"Thirty-two years ago (that is, in 1896) he said to me: 'The next upheaval that is to usher in another era, will come from Russia or from China. I cannot see clearly which, but it will be either the one or the other.'"

And again: " 'The world is in the third epoch under the domination of Vaishya (the merchant, the third estate). The fourth epoch will be under that of Shudra (the proletariat.)'"

kept spasmodically. This time there was no Goodwin
with him. Apart from one or two private letters, the
most beautiful being one from Alameda to Miss
MacLeod, we have to regret that nothing is known
save his movements and the success of his mission.

After having broken his journey only in London, he
went to the United States and stayed for almost a year.
There he found Abhedananda with his Vedantic work
in full swing. He settled Turiyananda down at Mont
Clair near New York. He himself decided to go to
California on account of its climate, from which he
regained several months of health. There he gave
numerous lectures.[1] He founded new Vedantic centres
at San Francisco, Oakland, and Alameda. He received
the gift of a property of one hundred and sixty acres
of forest land in the district of Santa Clara and there
he created an Ashrama, where Turiyananda trained a
select band of students in the monastic life. Nivedita,
who rejoined him, also spoke in New York on the
ideals of Hindu women, and on the ancient arts of
India. Ramakrishna's small but well-chosen band was
very active. The work prospered and its ideas spread.

But their leader, three parts of him, no longer belonged to this world. The shadows were rising round
the oak.... Were they shadows, or reflections of
another light? They were no longer those of our sun....

[1] Notably at Pasadena on *Christ the Messenger*, at Los Angeles on
*Powers of the Mind*, at San Francisco on *The Ideal of a Universal Religion*,
on the *Gita*, on *The Message of Buddha, Christ and Krishna to the World*,
on the *Arts and Sciences of India*, on *Mind and its Powers and Possibilities*,
etc. He also spoke in other places of California.

Unfortunately many of the lectures have been lost. He did not find
a second Goodwin to write them down. Some lectures, re-written by
Ida Ansell from the shorthand notes she took at that time, have since
been included in *The Complete Works of Swami Vivekananda.—
Publisher*.

"Pray for me that my work stops for ever, and my whole soul be absorbed in the Mother.... I am well, very well mentally. I feel the rest of the soul more than that of the body. The battles are lost and won! I have bundled my things, and am waiting for the Great Deliverer. Shiva, O Shiva, carry my boat to the other shore!... I am only the young boy who used to listen with rapt wonderment to the wonderful words of Ramakrishna under the Banyan of Dakshineswar. That is my true nature; works and activities, doing good and so forth are all superimpositions.... Now I again hear his voice, the same old voice thrilling my soul. Bonds are breaking, love dying, work becoming tasteless; the glamour is off life. Now only the voice of the Master calling:... 'Let the dead bury the dead. Follow thou Me.'...'I come, my Beloved Lord, I come!' Nirvana is before me...the same Ocean of peace, without a ripple, or a breath.... I am glad I was born, glad I suffered so, glad I did make big blunders—glad to enter Peace. I leave none bound; I take no bonds.... The old man is gone for ever. The guide, the Guru, the leader, has passed away...."

In that marvellous climate, under the glorious sun of California, among its tropical vegetation, his athletic will relaxed its hold, his weary being sank into a dream, body and soul let themselves drift....

"I dare not make a splash with my hands or feet, for fear of breaking the wonderful stillness—stillness that makes you feel sure it is an illusion! Behind my work was ambition, behind my love was personality, behind my purity fear, behind my guidance the thirst for power! Now they are vanishing and I drift.... I come, Mother, I come in Thy warm bosom—floating wheresoever Thou takest me—in the voiceless, the strange, in the wonderland. I come, a spectator, no more an actor. Oh, it is so calm! My thoughts seem to come from a great, great distance in the interior of my heart. They seem like faint distant whispers, and Peace is upon everything—sweet, sweet peace, like that one feels for a few moments just before falling asleep, when things are seen and felt like shadows, without fear, without love, without emotion.... I come, Lord! The world *is*, but not beautiful nor ugly, but as sensations without exciting any emotion. Oh the blessedness of it! Everything is good and beautiful, for they are all losing their relative proportions to me—my body among the first. Om—That Existence!"[1]

The arrow was still flying, carried by the original impetus of movement, but it was reaching the dead end where it knew that it would fall to the ground.... How sweet was the moment, "a few moments just before falling into sleep"—the downfall—when the tyrannous urge of destiny that had driven him was spent; and the arrow floated in the air, free from both the bow and the mark....

The arrow of Vivekananda was finishing its trajectory. He crossed the ocean on July 20, 1900. He went to Paris, where he had been invited to a Congress on the History of Religions, held on the occasion of the Universal Exposition. This was no Parliament of Religions as at Chicago. The Catholic power would not have allowed it. It was a purely historical and scientific Congress. At the point of liberation at which Vivekananda's life had arrived, his intellectual interest, but not his real passion nor his entire being, could find

[1] Letter to Miss MacLeod, April 18, 1900, Alameda.

nourishment in it. He was charged by the Committee of the Congress to argue the question whether the Vedic religion came from Nature-worship. He debated with Oppert. He spoke on the Vedas, the common basis of Hinduism and Buddhism. He upheld the priority of the Gita and of Krishna over Buddhism, and rejected the thesis of Hellenic influence on the drama, the arts, and the sciences of India.

But most of his time was given up to French culture. He was struck by the intellectual and social importance of Paris. In an article for India,[1] he said that "Paris is the centre and the source of European culture," that there the ethics and society of the West were formed, that its University was the model of all other Universities. "Paris is the home of liberty, and she has infused new life into Europe."

He also spent some time at Lannion, with his friend Mrs. Ole Bull, and Sister Nivedita.[2] On St. Michael's Day he visited Mont St. Michael. He became more and more convinced of the resemblances between Hinduism and Roman Catholicism.[3] Moreover he discovered Asiatic blood mingled in different degrees even in the races of Europe. Far from feeling that there was a fundamental natural difference between Europe and Asia, he was convinced that deep contact between Europe and Asia would inevitably lead to a renaissance of Europe; for she would renew her vital stock of spiritual ideas from the East.

[1] "*The East and the West.*"

[2] Nivedita went away a short time afterwards to speak in England for the cause of Hindu women. Vivekananda, when he blessed her at her departure, said these mighty words to her, "If I made you, be destroyed! If the Mother made you, live."

[3] He loved to say that "Christianity was not alien to the Hindu spirit."

It is to be regretted that only Father Hyacinthe and Jules Bois should have been the guides of so penetrating a spectator of the moral life of the West in Paris in his researches into the mind of France.[1]

He left again on October 24 for the East by Vienna and Constantinople.[2] But no other town interested him after Paris. He made a striking remark about Austria as he passed through it: he said that "if the Turk was the sick man, she was the sick woman of Europe." Europe both repelled and wearied him. He smelt war. The stench of it rose on all sides. "Europe," he said, "is a vast military camp...."

Although he halted a short time on the shores of the Bosphorus to have interviews with Sufi monks—then in Greece with its memories of Athens and Eleusis—and finally in the museum of Cairo, he was more and more detached from the spectacle of external things and buried in meditation. Nivedita said that during his last months in the West he sometimes gave the impression of being completely indifferent to all that was going on. His soul was soaring towards wider horizons. In Egypt he seemed to be turning the last pages of experience.

Suddenly he heard the imperious call to return. With-

---

[1] But he met Patrick Geddes in Paris, and his great compatriot, the biologist Jagadish Chandra Bose, whose genius he admired, and defended against all attack. He also met the strange Hiram Maxim, whose name is commemorated in an engine of destruction, but who deserves a better fate than such murderous fame, against which he himself protested: he was a great connoisseur and lover of China and India.

[2] Miss MacLeod, Father Hyacinthe who wished to work for a rapprochment between Christians and Mohammedans in the East, Madame Loyson, Jules Bois, and Madame Calvé accompanied him— a strange escort for a Sannyasin, who was leaving the world and life with giant strides. Perhaps his detachment itself made him more indulgent, or perhaps more indifferent.

out waiting a single day he took the first steamer and came back alone to India.[1] He had brought his body back to the funeral pyre.

[1] At the beginning of December, 1900.

# X

## THE DEPARTURE

His old and faithful friend had just gone before him. Mr. Sevier had died on October 28 in the Himalayas at the Ashrama he had built. Vivekananda heard the news on his arrival, but he had a presentiment of it during his return voyage. Without stopping to rest at Belur, he telegraphed to Mayavati that he was coming to the Ashrama. At that time of the year access to the Himalayas was difficult and dangerous, especially for a man in Vivekananda's state of health. It necessitated a four days' march through the snow, and the winter was particularly severe that year. Without waiting for coolies and necessary porters to be collected, he departed with two of his monks; and was joined on the way by an escort sent from the Ashrama; but amid the falling snow and the mist and the clouds he could scarcely walk; he was suffocated; his anxious companions carried him to the monastery of Mayavati with great difficulty. He arrived on January 3, 1901, and despite the mingled joy and emotion he felt at meeting Mrs. Sevier again, in seeing the work finished, and in contemplating the beautiful Ashrama perched on the mountains, he could only stay for a fortnight; asthma suffocated him; the least physical effort exhausted him. "My body is done for," he said. And on January 13, he celebrated his thirty-eighth birthday. His spirit, however, was always vigorous.[1] In this Advaita

---

[1] He wrote from Mayavati between attacks of suffocation three

Ashrama, consecrated by his wish to the contemplation of the Absolute, he discovered a hall dedicated to the worship of Ramakrishna. And he, the passionate disciple of Ramakrishna, who had never shown more complete adoration for the Master than in these last years, was indignant at this cult, a sacrilege in such a place. He vehemently reminded his followers that no dualistic religious weakness ought to find a foothold in a sanctuary devoted to the highest spiritual Monism.[1]

The same fever that had driven him to come, drove him to go. Nothing could hold him back. He left Mayavati on January 18, travelled for four days over slippery slopes, partly through the snow, and re-entered his monastery of Belur on January 24.[2]

Apart from a last pilgrimage that he made with his mother to the holy places of Eastern Bengal and Assam, to Dacca and Shillong,[3] and whence he returned exhausted, he only left Belur for a short stay at Varanasi at the beginning of 1902. The great journey of his life was ended. . . .

Essays for *Prabuddha Bharata* (of which one was on Theosophy, never a friend of his).

[1] On his return to Belur, he again almost despairingly reiterated his dissatisfaction at having found "the old man established at the Ashrama." Surely it was possible for one single centre to exist free from dualism! He reminded them that such worship was against Ramakrishna's own thought. It was through the teaching and at the wish of Ramakrishna that Vivekananda had become an Advaitist. "Ramakrishna was all Advaita, he preached Advaita. Why do you not follow the Advaita?" (Words of the "Holy Mother.")

[2] Certainly the Kshatriya had lost none of his fighting spirit. In the train coming back an English colonel rudely showed his disgust at having a Hindu in his compartment and tried to make him get out. Vivekananda's rage burst forth and it was the colonel who had to give up his place and go elsewhere.

[3] In March, 1901. He gave several lectures at Dacca. At Shillong, the seat of the Assam Government, he found broad-minded Englishmen, among them the Chief Commissioner, Sir Henry Cotton, a defender of the Indian cause. This last tour through countries of fanatical religious

"What does it matter?" he said proudly. "I have done enough for fifteen hundred years."

*

At the monastery he occupied a big airy room on the first floor with three doors and four windows.[1]

"In front the broad river (the Ganga) is dancing in the bright sunshine, only now and then an occasional cargo-boat breaking the silence with the splashing of the oars.... Everything is green and gold, and the grass is like velvet...."[2]

He led a country life, a kind of sacred bucolic like a Franciscan monk. He worked in the garden and the stables. Like the ascetics of *Shakuntala* he was surrounded by his favourite animals: the dog Bagha, the she-goat Hansi, the kid Matru, with a collar of little bells, with whom he ran and played like a child, an antelope, a stork, ducks and geese, cows and sheep.[3] He walked about as in an ecstasy, singing in his beautiful, rich, deep voice, or repeating certain words that charmed him, without heeding the passage of time.

conservatism threw into high relief the manly liberty of his own conceptions. He reminded these Hindu bigots that the true God was to see Him in man, that it was useless to veget— —however glorious it might be—that it was necessary to become even greater Rishis. He treated beings who from Avataras most irreverently. He advised them to ed their brains and muscles.

[1] It has been kept as at the day of his de yesterday.... he rarely reclined, preferring the ground for meditation, a great mirror.... His Ramakrishna have been added.

[2] Letter of December 19, 1900

[3] "The rains have come down pouring, pouring, night and returned from lending a ha water.... My huge stork the Math.... One of One of the geese is

But he knew also how to be the great abbot guiding the monastery with a firm hand in spite of his sufferings. Almost daily until his death he held Vedantic classes to teach the novices the methods of meditation, he inspired the workers with a spirit of virile confidence in themselves, paid strict attention to discipline and cleanliness, drew up a weekly time-table and kept a watchful eye over the regularity of all the acts of the day; no negligence escaped the eye of the Master.[1] Round him he maintained a heroic atmosphere, a "burning bush"[2] of the soul, in the midst whereof God was always present. Once when he saw them going to worship as he was in the middle of the court under a tree, he said to them: "Where shall you go to seek Brahman?... He is immanent in all beings. *Here*, *here* is the visible Brahman! Shame to those who, neglecting the visible Brahman, set their minds on other things. Here is the Brahman before you, as tangible as a fruit

The animals adored him. Matru, the little kid, who had been (so he pretended) a relation of his in a previous existence, slept in his room. Before milking Hansi, he always asked her permission. Bagha, who took part in Hindu ceremonies, went to bathe in the Ganga when the gongs and conchs announced the end of an eclipse.

[1] The bell sounded at fixed hours. For awakening at four in the morning. Half an hour afterwards the monks had to be in chapel for meditation. But he was always before them. He got up at three, and went to the hall of worship, where he sat, facing the north, meditating motionless for more than two hours. Nobody got up from his place ... til he set the example, saying, "Shiva, Shiva...." He walked about ...ate of serene exaltation, communicating it to all around him. ...y when he came in unexpectedly and found only two monks ... he imposed on the whole convent, even on the greatest ...tial fast for the rest of the day, and forced them to ...pervised in like manner the publications of the ...e of what he called "these stupidities" to ...d sentimentalism or strict sectarianism, ...found it most difficult to forgive. ...of Moses from the Old Testament. ...e burning bush. (*Exodus*, III).

in one's hand. Can't you see? Here, here, here is the Brahman!..."

And so forceful was his utterance that each received a kind of shock and remained for nearly a quarter of an hour glued to the spot as if petrified. Vivekananda at last had to say to them, "Now go to worship!"[1]

But his illness steadily increased. Diabetes took the form of hydropsy: his feet swelled and certain parts of his body became keenly hypersensitive. He hardly slept at all. The doctor wished to stop all exertion, and made him follow a most painful regime; although forbidden to drink any water, he submitted with stoical patience. For twenty-one days he did not swallow a single drop, even when he rinsed out his mouth. He declared, "The body is only a mask of the mind. What the mind dictates, the body *will have* to obey. Now I do not even *think* of water, I do not miss it at all....I see I can do anything."

The illness of its head did not stop the work or the festivals of the monastery. He wished the latter to be ritualistic and sumptuous; for his free mind, which paid no attention to scandal if it was a case of social reform, kept a tender regard for the legendary poetry of beautiful ceremonies, which maintained the stream of living faith[2] in the heart of simple believers, however much

---

[1] The end of 1901.
[2] Miss MacLeod told me, "Vivekananda was personally indifferent to ritualistic customs, and refused to be bound by them in social life. But he authorised ritualism, even in Hindu meals, where part is offered to the Gods, and on festival days of the holy dead, when a place is reserved for them at table and food served to them. He said that he realised such ritualism was necessary for the weakness of man; for, without prescribed and repeated acts he is incapable of keeping the memory and living impression of religious experience. He said, 'Without it there would be nothing but intellect here, (and he touched his forehead), and dry thought.' "

11

he fell foul of the inhuman orthodoxy of the bigots.[1]

So in October, 1901, the great festival of Durgâ-Pujâ —the adoration of the Mother[2]—the national festival of Bengal, corresponding to our Christmas, celebrated with great magnificence the joys of the scented autumn, when men are reconciled to each other and exchange gifts, and the monastery feeds hundreds of poor for three days. In February 1902, the festival of Rama-krishna brought together more than thirty thousand pilgrims to Belur. But the Swami was feverish and confined to his room by the swelling of his legs. From his window he watched the dances, the Sankirtanas, and sought to comfort the tears of the disciple who was nursing him; alone with his memories he lived again the days he had spent in the past at the feet of the Master at Dakshineswar.

One great joy still remained to him. Okakura,[3] an illustrious visitor, came to see him. He arrived with the Japanese abbot of a Buddhist convent, Oda, who invited him to the next Congress of Religions. The meeting was a moving one. The two men acknowledged their kinship.

"We are," said Vivekananda, "two brothers who meet again, having come from the ends of the earth."[4]

Okakura begged Vivekananda to accompany him to the ruins of Bodh-Gaya of famous memory, and

---

[1] During the early days of the monastery the orthodox of the neighbouring villages were scandalised, and slandered the monks of Belur. Vivekananda, when he heard of it, said, "That is good. It is a law of nature. That is the case with all founders of religion. Without persecution superior ideas cannot penetrate into the heart of society."

[2] But the sacrifice of animals was abolished.

[3] At the end of 1901.

[4] Told by Miss MacLeod, to whom Vivekananda confided the emotion he felt at this meeting.

Vivekananda, taking advantage of several weeks' respite from his malady, accepted his invitation and went to see Varanasi for the last time.[1]

\*

The talks, plans, and desires expressed during his last year were faithfully collected by the disciples. He was always preoccupied with the regeneration of India, while two of the projects nearest his heart were the foundation at Calcutta of a Vedic college, where eminent professors should teach the ancient Aryan culture and Sanskrit learning—and a monastery for women, analogous to that of Belur on the banks of the Ganga, under the direction of the "Holy Mother" (Ramakrishna's widow).

But his true spiritual testament is to be found in the beautiful confidences he made out of the abundance of his heart one day when he was talking to some Santal workmen. They were poor folk, employed about the monastery in digging the ground. Vivekananda loved them dearly; he mingled with a group of them, talking

[1] In January and February, 1902. They visited Bodh-Gaya together on Vivekananda's last birthday. At Varanasi Okakura left him. The two men, although they loved each other and acknowledged the grandeur of their mutual tasks, recognised their differences. Okakura had his own kingdom, that of art. At Varanasi Vivekananda found an association of young people, which had been formed under his inspiration to help, feed, and care for sick pilgrims. He was proud of these children, and wrote an *Appeal for the Ramakrishna Home of Service* for them.

Count Keyserling, who visited the Ramakrishna Mission at Varanasi, carried away with him a deep impression: "I have never been in a hospital with a more cheerful atmosphere. The certainty of salvation sweetens all sufferings. And the quality of the love for one's neighbour which animated the male nurses, was exquisite. These men are truly real followers of Ramakrishna, the 'God-elated'!" (*The Travel Diary of a Philosopher*, Vol. I, p. 248). Keyserling forgot that they had received their inspiration from Vivekananda whom he leaves completely in the dark, although he speaks all too briefly—but with understanding sympathy—of Ramakrishna.

to them, making them talk, weeping in sympathy as they related their simple sorrows. One day he served a beautiful feast for them at which he said, "You are Narayanas; today I have entertained Narayana Himself...."

Then turning towards his disciples, he said to them, "See how simple-hearted these poor illiterate people are! Will you be able to relieve their miseries to some extent at least? Otherwise of what use is our wearing the gerua (the ochre robe of the Sannyasin)?... Sometimes I think within myself, 'What is the good of building monasteries and so forth? Why not sell them and distribute the money among the poor, indigent Narayanas? What homes should we care for, we who have made the tree our shelter? Alas! How can we have the heart to put a morsel into our mouths, when our countrymen have not enough wherewith to feed or clothe themselves?'...Mother, shall there be no redress for them? One of the purposes of my going out to preach religion to the West, as you know, was to see if I could find any means of providing for the people of my country. Seeing their poverty and distress I think sometimes, 'Let us throw away all this paraphernalia of worship—blowing the conch and ringing the bell, and waving the lights before the Image.... Let us throw away all pride of learning and study of the Shastras and all Sadhanas for the attainment of personal Mukti—and going from village to village devote our lives to the service of the poor, and by convincing the rich men about their duties to the masses, through the force of our character and spirituality and our austere living, get money and the means wherewith to serve the poor and distressed....' Alas! Nobody in our country thinks for the low, the poor, and the miserable! Those that are the backbone of the nation, whose labour produces food, those whose one day's strike from work raises a cry of general distress in the city—where is the man in our country who sympathises with them, who shares in their joys and sorrows? Look, how for want of sympathy on the part of the Hindus, thousands of Pariahs are becoming Christians in the Madras Presidency! Don't think that it is merely the pinch of hunger that drives them to embrace Christianity. It is simply because they do not get your sympathy. You are continually telling them, 'Don't touch me!' 'Don't touch this or that!' Is there any fellow-feeling or sense of Dharma left in the country? There is only 'Don't-touchism' now! Kick out all such degrading usages! How I wish to demolish the barriers of 'Don't-touchism' and go out and bring them together one and all, crying, 'Come, all ye that are poor and destitute, fallen and downtrodden! We are one in the name of Ramakrishna!' Unless they are elevated, the Great Mother (India) will never awake! What are we good for, if we cannot provide facilities for their food and clothing? Alas, they are ignorant of the ways of the world and hence fail to eke out a living though labouring hard day and night for it. Gather all your forces together to remove the veil from their eyes. What I see clear as daylight is, that the same Brahman, the same Shakti *is* in them as in me! Only there is a difference in the degree of manifestation—that is all. Have you ever seen a country in the whole history of the world rise unless there was a uniform circulation of the national blood all over its body? Know this for certain, that no great work can be done by that body one limb of which is paralysed...."

One of the lay disciples pointed out the difficulty of establishing unity and harmony in India. Vivekananda replied with irritation, "Don't come here any more if you think any task too difficult. Through the grace of the Lord, everything becomes easy of achievement. Your duty is to serve the poor and the distressed, without distinction of caste and creed. What business have you to consider the fruits of your action? Your duty is to go on working, and everything will set itself right in time and work by itself....You are all intelligent boys and profess to be my disciples— tell me *what* you have done. Couldn't you give away one life for the sake of others? Let the reading of the Vedanta and the practising of meditation and the like be left to be done in the next life! Let this body go in the service of others—and then I shall know you have not come to me in vain!"

A little later he said, "After so much Tapasya (asceticism) I have known that the highest truth is this: '*He* is present in every being! These are all the manifold forms of Him. There is no other God to seek for! He alone is worshipping God, who serves all beings!'"

The great thought is there in all its nakedness. Like the setting sun it breaks forth from the clouds before disappearing in resplendent glory: the Equality of all men, all sons of the same God, all bearing the same God. And there is no other God. He who wishes to serve God, must serve man—and in the first instance man in the humblest, poorest, most degraded form. Break down the barriers. Reply to the inhumanity of "Untouchability", which though most cruelly apparent in India is not peculiar to that country (the hypocrisy

of Europe has also its Pariahs, whose contact she flees),
by outstretched hand and the cry of the *Ode to Joy*—
"Brothers!"...

Vivekananda's disciples have obeyed the call. The
Ramakrishna Mission has been unremitting in coming
to the help of the poor and the outcast[1] and in particular
it watches over the Santals, whom its dying Swami confided to its care.

Another has received the torch from the hands of him
who cried, "Come, all ye, the poor and the disinherited!
Come, ye who are trampled under foot! We are One!"
and has taken up the holy struggle to give back to
the untouchables their rights and their dignity—M. K.
Gandhi.

*

As he lay dying, his great pride realised the vanity
of pride, and discovered that true greatness lay in little
things: "The humble, heroic life."[2]

"As I grow older," he had said to Nivedita, "I find
that I look more and more for greatness in *little* things.
...Anyone will be great in a great position. Even the
coward will grow brave in the glare of the footlights.
The world looks on! More and more the true greatness
seems to me that of the worm doing its duty silently,
steadily from moment to moment and hour to hour."

He looked death in the face unafraid, as it drew near,
and remembered all his disciples, even those across the
seas. His tranquillity was a delusion to them: they
thought that he had still three or four years of life,
when he himself knew that he was on the eve of depar-

[1] A chapter devoted to the works of the Ramakrishna Mission will
be found in the *Appendices* of this volume.
[2] I have given this title to a collection of thoughts.

ture. But he showed no regret for having to leave his work in other hands:

"How often," he said, "does a man ruin his disciples by remaining always with them!"

He felt it necessary that he should go away from them, so that they might develop by themselves. He refused to express any opinion on the questions of the day:

"I can no more enter into outside affairs," he said, "I am already on the way."

On the supreme day, Friday, July 4, 1902, he was more vigorous and joyous than he had been for years. He rose very early. Going to the chapel, contrary to his wont of opening everything, he shut the windows and bolted the doors. There he meditated alone from eight to eleven o'clock in the morning, and sang a beautiful hymn to Kali. When he went out into the court he was transfigured. He ate his meal with an appetite in the midst of his disciples. Immediately afterwards he gave the novices a Sanskrit lesson for three hours and was full of life and humour. Then he walked with Premananda along the Belur road for nearly two miles; he spoke of his plan of Vedic College and talked of Vedic study: "It will kill superstition," he said.

Evening came—he had a last affectionate interview with his monks, and spoke of the rise and fall of nations.

"India is immortal," he said, "if she persists in her search for God. But if she goes in for politics and social conflict, she will die."[1]

Seven o'clock.... The convent bell sounded for Ârati (worship)....He went into his room and looked out over the Ganga. Then he sent away the

[1] Miss MacLeod repeated these words to me.

novice who was with him, desiring that his meditation should be undisturbed. Forty-five minutes later he called in the monk, had all the windows opened, lay down quietly on the floor on his left side and remained motionless. He seemed to be meditating. At the end of an hour he turned round, gave a deep sigh—there was silence for several seconds—his eyes were fixed in the middle of his eyelids—a second deep sigh...and eternal silence fell.

"There was," said a brother-disciple of the Swami, "a little blood in his nostrils, about his mouth, and in his eyes."

It seemed as if he had gone away in a voluntary fit of Kundalini Shakti[1]—in the final great ecstasy, which Ramakrishna had promised him only when his task was completed.[2]

He was thirty-nine.[3]

The next day, like Ramakrishna, he was carried to the pyre on the shoulders of the Sannyasins, his brothers and disciples, amid shouts of victory.

And in thought I can hear, as in his triumphal progress at Ramnad, the chorus of *Judas Maccabeus*, greeting the mighty athlete after his last contest.

---

[1] One of the talks of the day had been concerned with the current Sushumna, which rises through the six "Lotuses" of the body.

[2] I have tried to combine in my account the different accounts of eye-witnesses, which only differ in details. The doctors consulted, of whom one arrived two hours after life had completely expired, said that death was due to heart-failure and apoplexy. But the monks keep the firm belief that the death was an act of will. And the two explanations do not clash. Sister Nivedita only arrived the next day.

[3] He had said, "I shall not live to be forty years old."

# PART II

## THE UNIVERSAL GOSPEL

" 'I AM THE THREAD THAT RUNS THROUGH ALL THESE VARIOUS IDEAS, EACH OF WHICH IS LIKE A PEARL,' SAYS THE LORD KRISHNA."

VIVEKANANDA: *Maya and the Evolution of the Conception of God.*

# I

## MAYA AND THE MARCH TOWARDS FREEDOM

It is no part of my present intention to enter into an argument about the thought of the two great Indians, whose lives I have just related. The material of Vivekananda's ideas was no more his own personal conquest than in the case of Ramakrishna. It belongs to the thought inherent in the depths of Hinduism. The simple and modest Ramakrishna made no claim to the honour of founding a school of metaphysics. And Vivekananda, though more intellectual and therefore more conscious of his doctrine, knew and maintained that there was nothing new in it. On the contrary he would have been inclined to defend it on the strength of its exalted spiritual ancestry.

"I am Shankara," he said.

They would both have smiled at the illusion, so general in this age, that makes a man believe himself the inventor or proprietor of some form of thought. We know that the thoughts of mankind move within a narrow circle, and that, although they alternately appear and disappear, they are always there. Moreover, those which seem to us the newest are often in reality the most ancient; it is only that they have been longer forgotten by the world.

So I am not prepared to embark upon the vast and profitless task of discussing the Hinduism of the Paramahamsa and his great disciple; for if I wished to probe to the depths of the question, I should be unable to confine myself to Hinduism. The essential part of their experience and mystic conception, as well as the metaphysical construction of which these are at the same time the foundation and the keystone, far from being peculiar to India as she tends to believe, are held by her in common with the two great religious metaphysical systems of the West, the Hellenic and the Christian. The Divine Infinity, the absolute God, immanent and transcendent, who is poured out in the constant flood of the *Natura Rerum*, and yet is concentrated in the most minute of its particles—the Divine Revelation, diffused throughout the universe and yet inscribed in the centre of each soul—the great Paths of reunion with the Infinite Force, in particular that of total Negation— the "deification" of the enlightened soul, after its identification with Unity—these are all explained by Plotinus of Alexandria and by the early masters of Christian mysticism with an ordered power and beauty, which need fear no comparison with the monumental structure of India. On the other hand Indian mystics would do well to study it.*

But obviously within the limits of this work, I cannot give so much as a bird's-eye view of the historic variations that have taken place in the conception of the Divine Infinity and in the great science of union with the Absolute. It would require a history of the whole world; for such ideas belong to the very flesh of humanity—past, present, and future. Their character is universal and eternal. I cannot begin to discuss even the

* See the pamphlet: *The influence of Indian Thought on the Thought of the West* by Swami Ashokananda, as also *Eastern Religions and Western Thoughts* by S. Radhakrishnan—*Publisher.*

question of their worth (problematical as are all the ideas of the human spirit without exception), or the question bound up with it, that of the great scientific problem of "Introversion". They would need a whole work to themselves. I shall content myself with referring the reader to a twofold and fairly lengthy Note at the end of the Volume.[1] The first part deals with Mystic "Introversion" and the singular mistakes made in its appreciation by modern psycho-pathologists: for they ignore its strictly scientific elements, and the considerable weight of evidence already registered for its true perception and understanding. The second part is devoted to the Hellenic-Christian Mysticism of the first centuries (Plotinus, Denis and Areopagite) and its relation to Indian Mysticism. I shall confine myself here to a summary of Vedantic thought, as it has been explained in these modern days through the mouth of Vivekananda.

All great doctrine, as it recurs periodically in the course of the centuries, is coloured by reflections of the age wherein it reappears; and it further receives the imprint of the individual soul through which it runs. Thus it emerges anew to work upon men of the age. Every idea as a pure idea remains in an elementary stage, like electricity dispersed in the atmosphere, unless it finds the mighty condenser of personality. It must become incarnate like the Gods. *"Et caro facta est."*[2]

It is this mortal flesh of the immortal idea that gives it its temporary aspect of belonging to a day or a century, whereby it is communicated to us.

I shall try to show how closely allied is this aspect of

[1] *Notes II* and *III* in *Appendices*.
[2] "And was made flesh."

Vivekananda's thought to our own, with our special needs, torments, aspirations, and doubts, urging us ever forward, like a blind mole, by instinct upon the road leading to the light. Naturally I hope to be able to make other Westerners, who resemble me, feel the attraction that I feel for this elder brother, the son of the Ganga, who of all modern men achieved the highest equilibrium between the diverse forces of thought, and was one of the first to sign a treaty of peace between the two forces eternally warring within us, the forces of reason and faith.

*

If there is one sentiment that is absolutely essential to me (and I speak as the representative of thousands of Europeans), it is that of Freedom. Without it nothing has any value..."*Das Wesen des Geistes ist die Freiheit.*"[1]

But those who are best qualified to estimate its unique value are those who have known most fully the suffering of chains, either those of especially crushing circumstances or the torments of their own nature. Before I was seven years old the universe of a sudden seemed to me to be a vast rat-trap wherein I was caught. From that moment all my efforts were directed to escape through the bars—until one day in my youth under slow and constant pressure one bar suddenly gave way and I sprang to freedom.[2]

These spiritual experiences which marked me for life, brought me singularly near to the spirit of India when later I came to know it. For thousands of years she has

---

[1] "The essence of the spirit is liberty." (Hegel)
[2] I have related these experiences in a chapter of intimate memories as yet unpublished: *The Inner Voyage*, which so far has only been shown to my Indian friends.

felt herself entangled in a gigantic net, and for thousands of years she has sought for some way to escape through the meshes. This ceaseless effort to escape from a closed trap has communicated a passion for freedom, ever fresh, ardent, and untiring (for it is always in danger) to all Indian geniuses whether Divine Incarnations, wise philosophers, or poets; but I know few examples so striking as the personality of Vivekananda.

The sweeping strokes of his wild bird's wings took him, like Pascal, across the whole heaven of thought from one pole to the other, from the abyss of servitude to the gulf of freedom. Listen to his tragic cry as he conjures up the chain of rebirth:

"Why! the memory of one life is like millions of years of confinement, and they want to wake up the memory of many lives! Sufficient unto the day is the evil thereof...."[1]

But later he extols the splendour of existence:

"Never forget the glory of human nature! We are the greatest God that ever was or ever will be. Christs and Buddhas are but waves on the boundless ocean which *I am*."[2]

Therein lies no contradiction. For Vivekananda the two conditions are coexistent in man. "What is this universe?...In freedom it rises, in freedom it rests."[3] And yet with each movement every living being makes the chains of slavery eat more deeply into his flesh. But the dissonance of the two sentiments blends into harmony—a harmonious dissonance as in Heraclitus, which is the opposite of the serene and sovereign homophony of

---

[1] 1899, during his second journey to the West.
[2] 1895, in an interview at the Thousand Island Park, U. S. A.
[3] 1896, lectures on Maya, delivered in London.

the Buddha. Buddhism says to men, "Realise that all this is illusion," while the Advaita Vedanta says, "Realise that in illusion is the real!"[1]

Nothing in the world is to be denied, for Maya, illusion, has its own reality. We are caught in the network of phenomena. Perhaps it would be a higher and radical wisdom to cut the net, like Buddha, by total negation, and to say, "They do not exist."

But in the light of the poignant joys and tragic sorrows, without which life would be poor indeed, it is more human, more precious to say, "They exist. They are a snare," and to raise the eyes from this mirror, like that used to snare larks, and to discover that it is all a play of the sun. The play of the sun, Brahman, is Maya the huntress, with Nature her net.[2]

Before going further let us rid ourselves of the equivocation, inherent in the very name of Maya for even the most learned men of the West, and see how she is conceived by the intellectual Vedantism of the present day; for as it stands it raises a fictitious barrier between us. We are wrong to think of it as total illusion, pure hallucination, vain smoke without a fire: for it is this idea that makes us hold the derogatory opinion that the East is incapable of facing the reality of life, and sees in it nothing but the stuff that dreams are made of—a conception that leads it to float through life, half asleep, motionless and supine, eyes fixed on the blue

[1] Talks of Vivekananda with Nivedita in London.

[2] In his first lecture upon "*Maya and Illusion*" Vivekananda went back to the original meaning of the word in India, where it implied a kind of magic illusion, a fog covering reality; and he quoted from one of the last Upanishads (the Shvetashvatara Upanishad): "Know Nature to be Maya and the Ruler of this Maya is the Lord Himself." (*Complete Works*, Vol. II, pp. 88-89).

depths, like webs of wandering spiders floating in the autumn breeze.

But I believe I am faithful to the real thought of modern Vedantism, as it was incarnate in Vivekananda, when I prove that his conception of Nature was not vastly different from that of modern science.[1]

The true Vedantic spirit does not start out with a system of preconceived ideas. It possesses absolute liberty and unrivalled courage among religions with regard to the facts to be observed and the diverse hypotheses it has laid down for their co-ordination. Never having been hampered by a priestly order, each man has been entirely free to search wherever he pleased for the spiritual explanation of the spectacle of the universe. As Vivekananda reminded his listeners, there was a time when believers, atheists, and downright materialists could be found preaching their doctrines side by side, in the same temple; and further on I shall show what esteem Vivekananda publicly professed for the great materialists of Western science. "Liberty," he said, "is the sole condition of spiritual progress." Europe has known how to achieve it (or to demand it) more effectively than India in the realm of politics,[2] but she has attained it and even imagined it infinitely less in the spiritual realm. The mutual misunderstanding and intolerance of our so-called "free-thinkers" and of

---

[1] Vivekananda has devoted to the special study of Maya a set of four lectures delivered in London in 1896: (1) *Maya and Illusion;* (2) *Maya and the Evolution of the Conception of God;* (3) *Maya and Freedom;* (4) *The Absolute and Manifestation* (that is to say, the phenomenal world). He returned frequently to the subject in the course of his interviews and his other philosophic and religious treatises.

[2] At the moment she is using the same energy to crush it. And *bourgeois* democracies, while still maintaining "parliamentary" etiquette, are not in this respect behind communist or fascist dictators.

our diverse religious professions has no longer the power to astonish us: the normal attitude of the average European may be summed up as "I am Truth!", while the great Vedantist would prefer as his motto Whitman's "All is Truth."[1] He does not reject any one of the proposed attempts at explanation, but from each he seeks to extract the grain of permanent reality; hence when brought face to face with modern science he regards it as the purest manifestation of real religious sense—for it is seeking to seize the essence of Truth by profound and sincere effort.

The conception of Maya is viewed from this standpoint. "It is not," said Vivekananda, "a theory for the explanation of the world.[2] It is purely and simply a statement of fact" to be observed of all observers. "It is what we are, and what we see," so let us experiment. We are placed in a world which can be reached only through the doubtful medium of the mind and senses. This world only exists in relation to them. If they change it will also change. The existence we give it has no unchangeable, immovable, absolute reality. It is an undefinable mixture of reality and appearance, of certainty and illusion. It cannot be the one without the other. And there is nothing Platonic about this contradiction! It seizes us by the throat at every minute throughout our life of passion and action—it has been perceived throughout the ages by all the clear-thinking

[1] In the collection, *From Noon to Starry Night* from *Leaves of Grass*.

[2] It would be more exact to say, if criticism is allowed, that it is a fact of observation, insufficiently explained, if not actually unexplained, as most Vedantic philosophers agree. (*Cf.* for example the most recent exposition of Vedantism by Dr. Mahendranath Sircar, M.A., Ph.D., Professor of Philosophy at the Sanskrit College, Calcutta: *Comparative Studies in Vedantism*, Oxford University Press, Calcutta, Bombay, and Madras, 1928).

minds of the universe. It is the very condition of our knowledge. Though we are unceasingly called to the solution of insoluble problems the key to which seems as necessary to our existence as love or food, we cannot pass the circle of atmosphere imposed by nature itself upon our lungs. And the eternal contradiction between our aspirations and the wall enclosing them—between two orders having no common measure, between contradictory realities, the implacable and real fact of death and the no less real, immediate, and undeniable consciousness of life—between the irrevocable working of certain intellectual and moral laws and the perpetual flux of all the conceptions of the spirit and heart, the incessant variations of good and evil, of truth and falsehood on both sides of a line in space and time[1]— the whole coil of serpents wherein from the beginning of time the Laocoon of human thought has found itself intertwined so that as it unties itself on one side it only ties its knots more tightly on the other— all this is the real world. And the real world is Maya.

How then can it be defined? Only by a word that science has made fashionable in these latter days— Relativity. In Vivekananda's day it had hardly appeared above the horizon; its light was not yet bright enough to fill the dark sky of scientific thought;

---

[1] "Good and bad are not two cut-and-dried, separate existences. The very phenomenon which is appearing to be good now, may appear to be bad tomorrow. The fire that burns the child, may cook a good meal for a starving man....The only way to stop evil, therefore, is to stop good also....To stop death, we shall have to stop life also...each (of the two opposing terms) is but a different manifestation of the same thing....The Vedanta says, there must come a time when we shall look back and laugh at the ideals which make us afraid of giving up our individuality."

(Lecture on "*Maya and Illusion*", *Complete Works*, II, pp. 97-8)

and Vivekananda only uses it incidentally.[1] But it is clear that it gives the precise meaning of his conception; and the passage I have just quoted in the form of a note, leaves no room for doubt on the subject. Nothing but the mode of expression differs. Vedantic Advaitism (that is to say, impersonal and absolute Monism), of which he is the greatest modern representative, declares that Maya cannot be defined as non-existence any more than it can be defined as existence. It is an intermediate form between the equally absolute Being and non-Being. Hence it is the Relative. It is not existence, for, says the Hindu Vedantist, it is the sport of the Absolute. It is not non-Existence, because this sport exists, and we cannot deny it. For the type of man, so common in the West, who is content with the game from which he derives profit, it is the sum total of existence: the great revolving Wheel bounds their horizon. But for great hearts the only existence worthy of the name is that of the Absolute. They are impelled to lay hold of it to escape from the Wheel. The cry of humanity comes across the centuries, as it sees the sand of its days running through its fingers together with all that it has constructed: love, ambition, work, and life itself.

"This world's wheel within wheel is a terrible mechanism; if we put our hands to it, as soon as we are caught, we are gone.... We are all being dragged along by this mighty, complex world-machine."[2]

*

How then can we find the path to liberty?
For in the case of a Vivekananda or of any other man

[1] From the fourth lecture on Maya.
[2] *Karma-Yoga*, Chapter VIII.

cast in the heroic mould, there can be no question of throwing up the arms in advance, raising the hands and resigning himself to despair—still less is it possible to cover the eyes as do some agnostics, while they chant "What do I know?", and to gulp down the fleeting and passing pleasures which brush past our bodies like ghosts floating along the edge of the river!...What is it that will assuage the cry of the soul, the Great Hunger? Certainly such rags of flesh will not fill up the gulf: all the Epicure's roses will not keep him from starting back, like the horses of Orcagna in the Campo Santo,[1] from the stench of putrefying corpses. He must get out of the graveyard, out of the circle of tombs, away from the crematorium. He must win freedom or die: and better to die, if need arises, for freedom![2] "Better to die on the battlefield than to live a life of defeat!"

This trumpet call from ancient India,[3] sounded again by Vivekananda, is, according to him, the motto, the word of command written on the starting post of all religions, whence they set out on their age-long march. But it is also the motto of the great scientific spirit:

[1] Allusion to the famous fresco of Orcagna in the Campo Santo of Pisa.

[2] This brings out the error made by the psycho-pathologist in attributing to genuine Introversion a character of *flight*, misunderstanding its true character of *combat*. Great mystics, of the type of Ruysbroeck, Eckhart, Jean de la Croix, and Vivekananda, do not flee. The look reality straight in the face, and then close in battle.

[3] Vivekananda attributed this saying to Buddha. The idea of a struggle for freedom is emphasised in pure Christian thought. Denis the Areopagite goes so far as to make Jesus Christ the chief fighter, and the "first athlete": "It was Christ who as God instituted this struggle....And this is yet more Divine....He devotedly entered the lists with them, contending on behalf of their freedom....The initiated will enter the contests, as those of God, rejoicing...following in the divine steps of the first of athletes."

(*Concerning the Ecclesiastical Hierarchy,* Chapter II, Part III: "Contemplation", 6).

"I shall hew out a way for myself. I will know the truth, or give up my life in the attempt."[1] With both science and religion the original impulse is the same—and so too is the end to be achieved—Freedom. Is it not true that the learned man who believes in nature's laws seeks to discover them solely for the purpose of mastering them, so that he may use them in the service of the spirit that their knowledge has set free? And what have all the religions in the world been seeking? They project this same sovereign freedom, which is refused to every individual being, into a God, into a higher, greater, more powerful Being who is not bound —(in whatever form they may imagine Him)—and freedom is to be won by the meditation of the Conqueror: God, the Gods, the Absolute, or the idol; all are the agents of power set up by humanity, in order to realise in its stead those gigantic aspirations, for which it can find no assuagement in a life that it knows is ever slipping away: for they are its bread of life, the reason for its very existence.

"And so all are marching towards freedom. We are all journeying towards freedom."[2]

And Vivekananda recalled the mysterious answer of the Upanishads to the question they propounded:

"The question is: 'What is this universe? From what does it arise? Into what does it go?' And the answer is: 'In freedom it rises, in freedom it rests, and into freedom it melts away.'"

"You cannot give up this idea of freedom," so Vivekananda continued. Without it your being is lost. It is no question of science or religion, of unreason or

[1] Lecture on *Maya and Freedom*.
[2] Ibid.

reason, of good or evil, of hatred or love—all beings without any exception hear the voice that calls them to freedom. And all follow it like the children who followed the Piper of Hamelin.[1] The ferocious struggle of the world comes from the fact that all are striving among themselves, as to who can follow the enchanter most closely and attain the promised end. But all these millions fight blindly without understanding the real meaning of the voice. But those to whom understanding is given, realise in the same instant not only its meaning, but the harmony of the battlefield, whereon the planets, the brethren of the peoples, revolve, where all living beings, saints and sinners, good and bad (so called according to whether they stumble or walk erect —but all towards the same end), struggling or united, press on, towards the one goal: Freedom.[2]

There can be then no question of opening up an unknown way for them. Rather distracted mankind must learn that there are a thousand paths more or less certain, more or less straight, but all going there—and must be helped to free themselves from the quagmire wherein they are walking, or from the thickets whereon they are being torn, and shown among all these multitudinous ways the most direct, the *Viae Romanae*, the royal roads: the great Yogas: Work (Karma-Yoga), Love (Bhakti-Yoga), Knowledge (Jnana-Yoga).

[1] Allusion to the old Rhenish legend, told by Goethe, of the "Rat-catcher" whose flute captivated all who heard it and forced them to follow him. (The story is used by Browning in the *Pied Piper of Hamelin.—Translator*.)

[2] And this *object*, as the Advaita Vedanta shows, is the *subject* itself, the real nature and essence of each one. It is MYSELF.

## II

## THE GREAT PATHS

### The Four Yogas

The term Yoga[1] has been compromised in the West by the many charlatans and gull-catchers who have degraded its use. These spiritual methods, based on psycho-physiological genius experimenting for centuries past, assure to those who have assimilated them a spiritual mastery, which is inevitably and openly manifested in a mighty power of action—(a sane and complete soul is the lever of Archimedes: find its fulcrum and it will raise the world). Hence the interested pragmatism of thousands of dupes has rushed[2] to seize upon these real or faked methods with a gross spiritualism differing but little from a commercial transaction; with them faith is the medium of exchange whereby they may acquire the goods of this world: money, power, health, beauty, virility.... (One has only to open the papers to see the claims of debased doctors, and spurious fakirs.) There is no Hindu of sincere faith who does not feel

---

[1] Vivekananda derives the word from the same Sanskrit root as the English *yoke*, in the sense of *joining*. It implies *union* with God and the means to attain that union. (*Cf.* Vol. V of *The Complete Works of Swami Vivekananda*, p. 292; *Notes from Lectures and Discourses*.)

[2] Here at first I had written (and I ask my American friends to forgive me for it, for among them I have met the freest minds and the purest character):—"Among such dupes, the Anglo-Saxons of America hold the first place." But I am not so sure in these days. In this as in many other things America merely went ahead of the Old World. But the latter is now in a fair way to catch her up, and when it comes to extravagances the oldest are not always the last.

an equal disgust for such base exploitation; and not one of them has expressed it more forcibly than Vivekananda. In the eyes of all disinterested believers, it is the sign of a fallen soul to put to base uses the way which has been proved to be the way of liberation, and to turn the Appeal of the Eternal Soul and the way of its attainment into a means for the pursuit of the worst desires of the flesh, pride, and lust for power.

The real Vedantic Yogas, such as Vivekananda has described them in his treatises,[1] are a spiritual discipline, such as our Western philosophers have sought for in their "Discourse of Method",[2] for the purpose of travelling along the straight way leading to truth. And this straight way, as in the West, is the way of experiment and reason.[3]

But the chief differences are that in the first place, for the Eastern philosopher, the spirit is not limited to the intelligence; and that in the second place, thought is action, and only action can make thought of any

[1] I am aware that the definition of it given by the great living master of Yoga, Aurobindo Ghose, differs slightly from that of Vivekananda, although he quoted the latter as his authority in the first article he published on the *Synthesis of Yoga* (*Arya*, Pondicherry, August 15, 1914). Aurobindo does not confine himself only to the properly Vedic or Vedantic Yogas, which are always founded on Knowledge (of the spirit or the heart or the will). He adds Tantric Yogas after having cleansed and purified their polluted source. This introduces the Dionysiac elements as distinct from the Apollinian— Prakriti, Energy, and Soul of Nature in opposition to Purusha, the conscious Soul, which observes, understands, and controls. The very originality of Aurobindo Ghose is that he achieves the synthesis of the diverse forces of life.

[2] Allusion to the title of a famous treatise of Descartes, the foundation-stone of modern Western philosophy.

[3] "No one of these Yogas gives up reason, no one of them asks you to be hoodwinked or to deliver your reason into the hands of priests of any type whatsoever....Each one of them tells you to *cling* to your reason, to hold fast to it." (*Jnana-Yoga*: "*The Ideal of a Universal Religion*").

value. The Indian, whom the average European always considers a blind believer in comparison to himself, carries in his faith demands as sceptical as those of St. Thomas the Apostle: he must touch; abstract proof is not enough; and he is right to tax the Westerner who contents himself with such abstract proof as a visionary.... "If God exists it must be possible to reach Him.... Religion is neither word nor doctrine. It is realisation. It is not hearing and accepting. It is being and becoming. It begins with the exercise of the faculty of religious realisation."[1]

You will have noticed in the preceding pages that the search for "truth" is combined with the search for "freedom". The two terms are really identical—for the Westerner[2] there are two distinct worlds; speculation and action, pure reason and practical reason—(and we are well aware of the trench with its barbed wire fortifications that Germany, the most philosophic of Euro-

---

[1] *Cf.* Vivekananda: *A Study of Religion; My Master.* Many texts exist. This idea, a common one in India, is explained by Vivekananda in all its forms—especially in his great lecture on Hinduism at the Congress of Chicago, in September 1893, and in a series of lectures in the Punjab in October 1897. There, one of his leit-motifs was "Religion, to be worthy the name, must be action." This explains the vast spiritual tolerance which makes the followers of Ramakrishna embrace all the diverse and even opposite forms of religion: for "religion being concentrated in realisation, and not in any doctrinal affirmation", it is natural that the same Verity changes when it is adapted to the different needs of the most diverse human natures.

[2] I always except the Catholic Christian Mysticism of the West, whose ancient and profound affinity to that of India I shall often have occasion to show throughout these pages For a great Christian perfect "adherence" to the supreme Truth procures true freedom. For true freedom "presupposes a certain condition of indifference, illimitation, and independence with regard to outside things founded on perfect union with and adherence to God." (*Cf.* the treatise of Séguenot, the disciple of Bérulle, Cardinal and great French mystic theologian of the seventeenth century: "*Conduite d'oraison...*", anno 1634, analysed by Henri Brémond in *Métaphysique des Saints*, Vol. I, p. 138).

pean peoples, has dug between them); but for the Indian they are one and the same world: knowledge implies power and will to action. "Who knows, is." Hence "true knowledge is salvation."

But before true knowledge can be efficacious—otherwise there is always the danger that it might degenerate into a mere exercise of dialectics—it must be prepared to influence mankind in general, divided as it is into three great types: the Active, the Emotional, and the Reflective. True science has accordingly taken the three forms of Work, Love, and Knowledge—Karma, Bhakti, and Jnana,[1] and the Propylaeum, the motive Force of all three is the science of inner forces, consciously controlled and mastered: the science of Raja-Yoga.[2]

Hindu belief as explained by Count Keyserling, who is in aristocratic agreement with it, is that Work

[1] Before Vivekananda and Ramakrishna, Keshab Chandra Sen, who in many directions opened out new paths, had already adopted the system of adapting the ways of the soul to the different temperaments of his disciples. About 1875 when he inaugurated his new spiritual culture, he recommended Yoga (that is to say, Raja) to some, Bhakti to others, Jnana to a third set. And he attached different forms of devotion to diverse names or attributes of God—composing in the same way litanies to celebrate the different perfections of the unique Good. (Cf. P. C. Mazoomdar).

(Neither Keshab Chandra Sen, nor his predecessors or successors in the Brahmo Samaj believed or believe—and much less practised or practise—the Raja and Jnana Yogas. Keshab used the name Yoga in a sense quite different from its proper meaning.—Publisher.)

[2] Of all forms of Yoga the one most abused, exploited, and monstrously deformed by degraded Anglo-Saxon pragmatism, which looks upon it as an end in itself, whereas it ought to be a wise applied method of concentration to prepare for the mastery of the mind and to make the whole psycho-physiological organism a supple and docile instrument, so that it may be able to advance further along one of the paths of Knowledge in the sense of truth realised by the mind—or of real and complete Liberty. Need I remind my readers that great Christian mysticism has also its Raja-Yoga, experimented and controlled by a series of masters in the past?

Aurobindo Ghose defined it thus: "All Raja-Yoga depends on this perception and experience—that our inner elements, combinations,

(Karma-Yoga) is "the lowest"[1] of the three ways. But I do not believe that there was a "high road" and a "low road" for the boundless heart of Ramakrishna. Everything that led to God was of God. And I am certain that to Vivekananda, the passionate brother of the humble and the poor, the way trodden by their naked feet was holy: " 'Fools alone say that work and philosophy are different, not the learned.' ... Each one of our Yogas—the Yogas of work, of wisdom, and of devotion are all capable of serving as direct and independent means for the attainment of Moksha (freedom, salvation)."[2]

And how admirably independent are these great religious minds of India, how far removed from the caste-pride of our learned men and believers in the West! Vivekananda, aristocrat, savant, and prophet, does not hesitate to write, "Although a man has not attained a single system of philosophy, although he does not believe in any God and never has believed, although he has not prayed even once in his whole life, if the simple power of good actions has brought him to the state where he is ready to give up his life and all else for others, he has arrived at the same point to which the religious man will come through his prayers and the philosopher through his knowledge"—to know *Nivritti*, entire self-abnegation.[3]

functions, forces, can be separated or dissolved, can be newly combined and set to novel and formerly impossible uses or can be transformed and resolved into a new general synthesis by fixed internal processes." (*op. cit.*).

[1] Naturally "the highest" is the philosophical. (*Cf.* pp. 234-5 of Vol. I of the English Translation of *The Travel Diary of a Philosopher*, Jonathan Cape, 1925). But Aurobindo Ghose makes Bhakti-Yoga the highest. (*Essays on the Gita*).

[2] *Karma-Yoga*, Chapter VI.

[3] Ibid.

Here Indian wisdom and the pure Gospel of Galilee[1] without the slightest effort find common ground in the kinship existing between all great souls.

## I. Karma-Yoga

Of the four Gospels of Vivekananda—his four Yogas —I find the most deep and moving tone in the Gospel of Work—Karma-Yoga.

Here follow several extracts coupled to the dark saying I have already quoted about the blind Wheel of the Universe, whereon mankind is bound and broken:

---

[1] Let us put down here the connection between the two systems of religious thought. William James, who has studied *"Religious Experiences"* with praiseworthy zeal, but—he confesses it himself— without any personal fitness for the task ("My temperament," he writes, "prohibits me from almost all mystic experience, and I can only give the evidence of others"), is apt to attribute to Western mysticism a character of "sporadic" exception which he opposes to the "methodically cultivated mysticism" of the East; and as a result he considers that the form is alien to the daily life of the average man and woman in the West. In fact, like most Protestants he knows little of the daily "methodical mysticism" of Western Catholicism. The union with God that Indians seek through the Yogas, is a natural state with the true Christian, imbued with the essence of his faith. It is perhaps even more innate and spontaneous; for, according to the Christian faith "the centre of the soul" is God, "the Son of God" is woven into the very texture of Christian thought and he has therefore only to offer this thought to God in prayer to "adhere" to Christ and find communion with God.

The difference (I prefer to believe) is that God in the West plays a more active part than in India, where the human soul has to make all the effort. By "common and ordinary grace" the "mystic career" is open to all, as Brémond rightly shows, and the chief business of Christian mysticism throughout the ages has been to open this door of mystic union with God to the rest of the world. Seen from this standpoint the seventeenth century in France was astonishingly democratic. (I refer the reader again to the *Métaphysique des Saints* by H. Brémond, and in particular to two curious portraits: one of the Franciscan "panmystic", Paul de Lagny, and the other of the "Vigneron de Montmorency" [the wine-grower of Montmorency], Jean Aumont, whose robust Gallic common sense revolted against the

"...This world's wheel within wheel is a terrible mechanism; if we put our hands in it, as soon as we are caught we are gone....We are all being dragged along by this mighty complex world-machine. There are only two ways out of it. One is to give up all concern with the machine, to let it go and stand aside.... That is very easy to say, but it is almost impossible to do. I do not know whether in twenty millions of men one can do that. ..."

idea that "mysticism" was not for everybody—"Our Lord refused it to none except the man who was too lazy to have the courage to stoop down and drink." The great Salesien [disciple of the great seventeenth century mystic, St. Francois de Sales, Bishop of Annecy in Savoy], Jean-Pierre Camus, achieved the difficult task of watering down the potent mystic liquor of Denis the Areopagite, into an innocuous table wine of slightly diluted truth for all good people.) This democratisation of mysticism is a striking phenomenon of our Classic Age, as the French call the intellectual seventeenth century. Not for the first time does it appear that great transformations in the soul of humanity always come forth from the depths. Religion and metaphysics precede literary and political thought by one or several centuries. But the latter, being ignorant of spiritual things, flatter themselves that they are the inventors or discoverers of truths that have formed part of the substructure of the mind for a long time before their advent.

[The comparison that M. Rolland has made between Indian and Christian mysticism in this note, is rather unfortunate. Union with God means approximation to and identification with the Divine nature and being. That doctrine which helps most the assertion of the Divine being of man, is the best. Does Christianity help this assertion better than Hinduism? In India the vast majority of people, if not all, believe that God is the soul of their soul, that all men and beings are God Himself, and that they themselves are God. Hindus simply deny at the very outset that they are other than Divine. Can there be any union with God more intimate, innate, and spontaneous? Hindus also have their "Sons of God"—their Divine incarnations. But does not the mediation of a Christ make the union with God less direct? On the other hand, the Christian idea of man—a born sinner—is itself a great bar to the conception of an innate and intimate relationship with God: it is the denial of the Divinity of man. The idea of the soul—Atman—as existing in India, is infinitely superior to it and far more helpful in the realisation of God. The Hindu ideas of the relationship between God and soul are undoubtedly more perfect and helpful than the Christian—Publisher.]

"If we give up our attachment to this little universe of the senses, we shall be free immediately. The only way to come out of bondage is to go beyond the limitations of law, to go beyond causation. But it is a most difficult thing to give up the clinging to the universe: few ever attain to that....

"The other way is not negative but positive.... It is to plunge into the world and learn the secret of work. ... Do not fly away from the wheel of the world-machine but stand inside it and learn the secret of work, and that is the way of Karma-Yoga.... Through proper work done inside, it is also possible to come out.

"Every one must work in the universe.... A current rushing down of its own nature falls into a hollow and makes a whirlpool, and after running a little in that whirlpool, it emerges again in the form of the free current to go on unchecked. Each human life is like that current. It gets into the whirl, gets involved in the world of space, time, and causation, whirls round a little, crying out, 'my father, my brother, my name, my fame' and so on, and at last emerges out of it and regains its original freedom. The whole universe is doing that. Whether we know it or not...we are all working to get out of the dream of the world. Man's experience in the world is to enable him to get out of its whirlpool....

"We see that the whole universe is working. For what?... For liberty; from the atom to the highest being working for the one end, liberty for the mind, for the body, for the spirit. All things are always trying to get freedom, flying away from bondage. The sun, the moon, the earth, the planets, all are trying to fly away from bondage. The centrifugal and centripetal forces of nature are indeed typical of our universe.... We learn from Karma-Yoga the secret of work, the organising power of work.... Work is inevitable... but we should work to the highest purpose...."

And what is this highest purpose? Does it lie in moral or social Duty? Is it the passion for work which consumed the insatiable Faust so that with failing eyesight he strove up to the very threshold of the tomb to remodel the universe according to his own way of thinking (as if that would have been for the general good!)?[1]

No! Vivekananda would have replied almost in the words of Mephistopheles as he saw Faust fall, "He persists in chasing with his love nothing but phantoms. Up to the last miserable, empty instant, the unfortunate man has kept it up!"[2]

"Karma-Yoga says, 'Work incessantly, but give up all attachment to work'.... Hold your mind free.[3]

---

[1] And even he, Faust, in those last seconds of life, evoked the phantom of Liberty pursued unceasingly:
"He alone is worthy of liberty, who knows how to conquer it each day...."

[2] In re-reading this scene from Goethe, it is striking to find in it thought and expression often closely akin to the Hindu Maya:
*Mephistopheles* (looking at the corpse of Faust):
"Gone! What a stupid word!...He is worth exactly as much as if he had never existed; and nevertheless man strives and moves as if he did exist....In his place I should prefer eternal annihilation."

[3] This is the classic doctrine of the Gita: "The ignorant work by attachment to the act; the wise man also works but beyond all attachment and solely for the good of the world....Referring all action to Me, let the spirit, withdrawn into itself and free from all hope and interested motives, strive without troubling itself with scruples...."
*Cf.* Christian mysticism: "Do not strive...either for some useful end, or temporal profit, or for hell, or for paradise, or for Grace, or to become the beloved of God...but purely and simply

Do not project into it the tentacle of selfishness...
'I and mine.' "

There must even be freedom from all belief in Duty.
... He keeps his greatest irony for Duty, the last
shabby and tiresome fetish of the small shopkeeper:

"Karma-Yoga teaches us that the ordinary idea of
duty is on the lower plane; nevertheless, all of us have
to do our duty.[1] Yet we may see that this peculiar
sense of duty is very often a cause of great misery.
Duty becomes a disease with us.... It is the bane of
human life.... Look at those poor slaves to duty!
Duty leaves them no time to say prayers, no time to
bathe. Duty is ever on them. They go out and work.
Duty is on them! They come home and think of work
for the next day. Duty is on them! It is living a
slave's life, at last dropping down in the street and
dying in harness like a horse. This is duty as it is
understood.... The only true duty is to be unattached and to work as free beings, to give up all work unto
God. All our duties are His. Blessed are we that we

to the glory of God." (*Conduite d'oraison*, by the Bérullian, Claude
Séguenot, 1634).

But with more courage still Vivekananda expressly stipulates that
such renunciation is not conditional upon faith in any God whatsoever. Faith merely makes it easier. But he appeals first to "those
who do not believe in God or in any outside help. They are left to
their own devices; they have simply to work with their own will,
with the powers of the mind and with discrimination, saying, 'I must
be non-attached.' "

[1] Vivekananda devotes a whole chapter to the definition of real
duty. But he refuses to give it an objective reality: "It is not the
thing done that defines a duty.... Yet duty exists from the sub-
jective side. Any action that makes us go Godward is a good action
...; any action that makes us go downward is evil.... There is,
however, only one idea of duty which has been universally accepted
by all mankind, of all ages and sects and countries, and that has been
summed up in a Sanskrit aphorism thus: 'Do not injure any being;
not injuring any being is virtue; injuring any being is sin.' " (*Karma-
Yoga*, Chap. IV).

are ordered out here. We serve our time; whether we
do it ill or well who knows? If we do it well we do
not get the fruits.[1] If we do it ill, neither do we get
the care. Be at rest, be free and work....

"This kind of freedom is a very hard thing to attain.
How easy it is to interpret slavery as duty, the morbid
attachment of flesh for flesh as duty! Men go out into
the world and struggle and fight for money (or ambition). Ask them why they do it. They say, 'It is a
duty.' It is the absurd greed for gold and gain, and
they try to cover it with a few flowers.... When an
attachment has become established (marriage, for
example) we call it duty.... It is, so to say, a sort of
chronic disease. When it is acute we call it disease,
when it is chronic we call it nature.... We baptise
it with the high-sounding name of duty. We strew
flowers upon it, trumpets sound for it, sacred texts are
said over it, and then the whole world fights, and men
earnestly rob each other for this duty's sake.... To
the lowest kinds of men, who cannot have any other
ideal, it is of some good, but those who want to be
Karma-Yogis must throw this idea of duty overboard.
There is no duty for you and me. Whatever you have
to give to the world, do give by all means, but not as
a duty. Do not take any thought of that. Be not compelled. Why should you be compelled? *Everything
that you do under compulsion goes to build up attachment.*
Why should you have any duty? Resign everything
unto God.[2] In this tremendous fiery furnace where the
fire of duty scorches everything, drink this cup of

[1] "We have the right to the work, not to the fruits thereof," says
the Gita.
[2] "Men who aspire to nothing, neither honours nor usefulness, nor
inner sacrifice, nor reward, nor to the kingdom of heaven, but who

nectar and be happy. We are all simply working out His will, and have nothing to do with rewards and punishments.[1] If you want the reward you must also have the punishment; the only way to get out of the punishment is to give up the reward. The only way of getting out of misery is by giving up the idea of happiness, because these two are linked to each other. The only way to get beyond death is to give up the love of life. Life and death are the same thing, looked at from different points. So the idea of happiness without misery or of life without death is very good for school boys or children; but the thinker sees that it is all a contradiction in terms and gives up both."

To what a pitch of human detachment does this intoxication with boundless Liberty lead! Moreover, it is obvious that such an ideal is not only beyond most men, but that, if badly interpreted, by its very excess it may lead to indifference to one's neighbour as well as to oneself and hence to the end of all social action. Death may lose its sting, but so also does life, and then what remains as a stimulus to that doctrine of service which is so essential a part of Vivekananda's teaching and personality?*

But it is always important to notice *to whom*

have renounced all these things and all that is their own—God is honoured by such men." (Meister Eckhart).

[1] "...He only is fit to contemplate the Divine light who is the slave to nothing, not even to his virtues." (Ruysbroeck: *De Ornatu Spiritualium Nuptiarum*).

"Every man who counts anything as merit, virtue, or wisdom except only humility, is an idiot." (Ruysbroeck: *De Praecipuis Quibusdam Virtutibus*).

* Only when one has attained a state beyond life and death, can one truly love and feel for mankind. Compare the life of Buddha who preached compassion after attaining Nirvana. An understanding of this paradox is the key to the understanding of India and her wisdom.—*Publisher*.

Vivekananda was addressing each of his lectures or writings. Because his religion was essentially realistic and practical with action as its object, its expression varied with his public. So vast and complex a system of thought could not be swallowed whole at one gulp. It was necessary to choose between different points of view. In this case Vivekananda was addressing Americans, and there was no danger that they would sin by excess of self-forgetfulness and action; the Swami therefore emphasised the opposite extreme, the virtues of other lands beyond the sea.

On the other hand when he spoke to his Indians, he was the first to denounce the inhuman extravagance to which a religion of detachment might lead. Directly after his return from America in 1897, when an old Bengali professor, one of Ramakrishna's pupils, raised the objection: "All that you say about charity, service, and the good that is to be accomplished in the world, belongs after all to the realm of Maya. Does not the Vedanta teach us that our object is to break all our chains? Why then should we make unto ourselves others?"—Vivekananda replied with this sarcasm, "At that rate does not even the idea of liberation (Mukti) belong to the realm of Maya? Does not the Vedanta teach us that the Atman is always free? Why then struggle for liberation?"

And later alone with his disciples he said bitterly that such interpretation of the Vedanta had done incalculable harm to the country.[1]

[1] There were many similar episodes. One was his turbulent interview with a devotee who refused to think about a terrible famine to which Central India was a prey (9,00,000 dead). The devotee maintained it was a matter concerning only the victims' Karma and was none of his business. Vivekananda went scarlet with anger. The

He knew only too well that there is no form of
detachment where selfishness cannot find means to
enter in and that there is no more repulsive form of
it than the conscious or unconscious hypocrisy involved
in a "liberation" sought only for self and not for
others.* He never ceased to repeat to his Sannyasins
that they had taken two vows, and that although the
first was "to liberate oneself", the second was "to help
the world". His own mission and that of his followers
was to rescue the great teachings of the Vedanta from
their selfish retreat among a few privileged persons
and to spread them among all sorts and conditions of
men as they were fitted to assimilate them.[1] During
his last days, when his body was ravaged by disease
and his soul had won the right of being three parts
detached from all human preoccupations—for he had
finished his work at the sacrifice of his whole life—at
the very hour when he was being asked about questions
of the day, and replied that "his mind could not
enter into them for it was too far gone in death"—he

---

blood rose to his face, his eyes flashed, and he thundered against the
hard heart of the Pharisee. Turning to his disciples, he exclaimed,
"This, this is how our country is being ruined! To what extremes
has this doctrine of Karma fallen! Are they men, those who have no
pity for men?"

His whole body was shaken with anger and disgust.

Another memorable scene related above will be remembered, when
Vivekananda loftily castigated his own disciples and fellow monks,
spurning under foot their preoccupation with and their doctrine of
individual holiness, and mocked even their authority, Ramakrishna.
For he reminded them that there was no law or religion higher than
the command to "Serve Mankind."

\* That was not the Swami's idea.—*Publisher.*

[1] "Knowledge of the Advaita has been hidden too long in caves
and forests. It has been given to me to rescue it from its seclusion and
to carry it into the midst of family and social life....The drum of
the Advaita shall be sounded in all places, in the bazaars, from the
hill-tops, and on the plains."

still made one exception, "his work, his life-work."[1]

Every human epoch has been set its own particular work. Our task is, or ought to be, to raise the masses, so long shamefully betrayed, exploited, and degraded by the very men who should have been their guides and sustainers. Even the hero or the saint, who has reached the threshold of final liberation, must retrace his steps to help his brethren who have fallen by the way or who are lagging behind. The greatest man is he who is willing to renounce his own realisations— Karma-Yoga—in order to help others to realise it instead.[2]

So then there was no danger that the Master of Karma-Yoga would ever sacrifice his flock to his own ideal, however sublime, but inhuman for the majority of mankind, being beyond their nature. And no other religious doctrine has ever showed so much sympathetic understanding of the spiritual needs of all men from the humblest to the highest. It regarded all fanaticism and intolerance as a source of slavery and spiritual death.[3] The only possible line of conduct for the achievement of liberation was for each man to know

---

[1] The Sunday before his death: "You know the work is always my weak point. When I think *that* might come to an end, I am all undone!"

[2] "Help men to stand upright, by themselves, and to accomplish their Karma-Yoga for themselves." (Vivekananda to his monks, 1897).

[3] "One must first know how to work without attachment, then he will not be a fanatic....If there were no fanaticism in the world, it would make much more progress than it does now.... It is a retarding element....When you have avoided fanaticism, then alone will you work well....You hear fanatics glibly saying, 'I do not hate the sinner, I hate the sin'; but I am prepared to go any distance to see the face of that man who can really make a distinction between the sin and the sinner...." (*Karma-Yoga,* Chapter V).

his own ideal and to seek to accomplish it; or, if he were incapable of discovering it alone, it was for a master to help him, but never to substitute his own. Always and everywhere the constantly repeated principle of true Karma-Yoga is "to work freely", "to work for freedom", "to work as a master and not as a slave."[1] That is why it can never be a question of working at the command of a master. His word can only be effectual if the master forgets himself in him whom he is counselling, if he espouses his nature and helps it to discern and accomplish its own destiny by the powers innate in every man.

Such is the real duty of all great organisers of human work like Vivekananda. He comprehended the entire hierarchy of Karma-Yoga, where as in a vast workshop different types and forms of associated labour work, each in its own place, at the one great task.

But those words, "workshop", "types", and "ranks" do not imply any idea of superiority or inferiority among the different kinds of workmen. These are vain prejudices, that the great aristocrat repudiated. He would allow no castes among the workers, but only differences between the tasks allotted to them.[2] The most showy and apparently important do not consti-tute a real title to greatness. And if Vivekananda can be said to have any preference, it was for the humblest

[1] "The whole gist of this teaching is that you should work like a *master* and not as a *slave*....Work through freedom!... When we ourselves work for the things of this world as slaves... our work is not true work....Selfish work is slave's work.... Work without attachment." (Ibid., Chapter III).

[2] The important thing is to recognise that there are gradations of Karma-Yoga. The duty of one condition of life in an accumulation of given circumstances is not and cannot be the same as in another. ...Each man must learn his own ideal and try to accomplish it:

and simplest: "If you really want to judge of the character of a man look not at his great performances. Every fool may become a hero at one time or another. Watch a man do his most common action; those are indeed the things which will tell you the real character of a great man. Great occasions rouse even the lowest of human beings to some kind of greatness, but he alone is really the great man whose character is great always, the same wherever he be."[1]

In speaking of classes among workers, it is small matter for wonder that Vivekananda places first, not the illustrious, those crowned with the halo of glory and veneration—no, not even the Christs and the Buddhas. But rather the nameless, the silent ones—the "unknown soldiers".

The page is a striking one, not easily forgotten when read: "The greatest men in the world have passed away unknown. The Buddhas and the Christs that we know, are but second-rate heroes in comparison with the greatest men of whom the world knows nothing. Hundreds of these unknown heroes have lived in every country working silently. Silently they live and silently they pass away; and in time their thoughts find expression in Buddhas or Christs; and it is these latter that become known to us. The highest men do not seek to get any name or fame from their knowledge. They leave their ideas to the world; they put forth no claims for themselves and establish no schools or systems in their name. Their whole nature shrinks from such a thing. They are the pure Sâttvikas, who can

that is a surer way of progress than to take the ideas of another, for they can never be realised.

[1] *Karma-Yoga*, Chapter I.

never make any stir, but only melt down in love.... [1]
In the life of Gautama Buddha we notice him constantly saying that he is the twenty-fifth Buddha.
The twenty-four before him are unknown to history
although the Buddha known to history must have built
upon foundations laid by them. The highest men are
calm, silent, and unknown. They are the men who
really know the power of thought; they are sure that
even if they go into a cave and close the door and
simply think five true thoughts and then pass away,
these five thoughts of theirs will live throughout
eternity. Indeed such thoughts will penetrate through
the mountains, cross the oceans, and travel through
the world. They will enter deep into human hearts
and brains and raise up men and women who will
give them practical expression in the workings of
human life.... The Buddhas and the Christs will go
from place to place preaching these truths.... These
Sâttvika men are too near the Lord to be active
and to fight, to be working, struggling, preaching,
and doing good, as they say, here on earth to
humanity...."[2]

Vivekananda did not claim a place among them but
relegated himself to the second, or the third rank,

[1] Vivekananda added an example from his own personal observation:
"I have seen one such Yogi, who lives in a cave in India....He
has so completely lost the sense of his own individuality that we may
say that the man in him is completely gone, leaving behind only the
all-comprehending sense of the Divine...."
He was speaking of Pavhari Baba of Ghazipur, who had fascinated
him at the beginning of his pilgrimage in India in 1889-90, and whose
influence only just failed to drag him back from the mission Ramakrishna
had traced for him (see pp. 14-15). Pavhari Baba maintained that
all work in the ordinary sense was bondage; and he was certain
that nothing but the spirit without the action of the body could help
other men.
[2] *Karma-Yoga,* Chapter VII.

among those who work without any interested motive.[1]
For those Sâttvikas who have passed the stage of
Karma-Yoga, have already reached the other side,
and Vivekananda remains on ours.

His ideal of the active omnipotence that radiates
from intense and withdrawn mystic thought is certainly
not one to astonish the religious soul of the West;
all our great contemplative orders have known it. And
our highest form of modern lay thought can recognise
itself in it as well; for wherein lies the difference from
the homage we render in a democratic form from
the bottom of our hearts to the thousands of silent
workers, whose humble life of toil and meditation is
the reserve of heroism and the genius of the nations?[2]
He who wrote these lines and who can, in default of
any other merit, attest to sixty years' unceasing work,
is a living witness to these generations of silent workers,
of whom he is at once the product and the voice. Toil-
ing along and bending over himself, striving to hear the
inner voice, he has heard the voices of those nameless
ones rising, like the sound of the sea whence clouds
and rivers are born—the dumb thousands whose
unexpressed knowledge is the substance of my thoughts
and the mainspring of my will. When outside noises
cease, I can hear the beating of their pulse in the night.

[1] "He works best who works without any motive, neither for
money, nor for fame, nor for anything else; and when a man can
do that, he will be a Buddha, and out of him will come the power
to work in such a manner as will transform the world. This man
represents the very highest ideal of Karma-Yoga." (Ibid., end of
Chapter VIII).
[2] The Hindu genius has the same intuition, but explains it by the
doctrine of Reincarnation, of a long series of works collected during
a succession of lives: "The men of mighty will have all been
tremendous workers . . . with wide wills, . . . they got by persistent work, through ages and ages." The Buddhas and the Christs

## II. Bhakti-Yoga

The second path leading to Truth—to Freedom—is the way of the heart: Bhakti-Yoga. Here again I seem to hear the parrot cry of our learned ones: "There is no truth except through reason; and the heart does not and cannot lead to anything but slavery and confusion." Let me beg of them to remain in their own path, where I will return to them anon; it is the only one that suits them and so they do well to stick to it; but it is not well to claim that all minds can be contained in it. They underestimate not only the rich diversity of the human spirit but the essentially *living* character of truth. They are not wrong to denounce the dangers of servitude and error lurking in the way of the heart; but they make a mistake when they think that the same dangers are absent from the path of intellectual knowledge. To the great "Discriminator" (Viveka) by whatever path a man travels, the spirit ascends by a series of partial errors and partial truths, ridding itself one after the other of the vestments of slavery until it reaches the whole and pure light of liberty and truth, called by the Vedantist *Sat-Chit-Ananda* (Existence, Knowledge, Bliss absolute): it enfolds within its empire the two distinct realms of heart and reason.

But for the benefit of Western intellectuals it should be clearly stated that not one of them is more on his guard against ambushes on the road of the heart than Vivekananda; for he knew them better than any.

have been possible, thanks only to their accumulation of power, which comes from the work of centuries. (*Karma-Yoga*).

However chimerical this theory of Reincarnation may appear to a Westerner, it establishes the closest relationship between the men of all ages, and is akin to our modern faith in universal brotherhood.

Although Bhakti-Yoga under different names has seen the feet of the great mystic pilgrims of the West passing by, and thousands of humble believers following in their footsteps, the spirit of law and order, bequeathed by ancient Rome to our Churches as well as to our States, has effectively kept the crusaders of Love in the right path, without permitting dangerous excursions outside its limits. In passing, it is worthy of note that this fact explains Count von Keyserling's specious judgment upon Bhakti as compared to Europe.[1] The mobile and brilliant genius of the "Wandering Philosopher", with its lack of tenderness that leads him to depreciate what he is pleased to call "super-annuated feminine ideals", because they are beyond the limits of his nature, has made him exaggerate the lack of heart in the West, of which he claims to be the most perfect representative.[2] In reality he has a very superficial knowledge of the Catholic Bhakti of Europe. His judgment seems to be based on the wild mystics of the sixteenth century in Flanders and Germany, such as the violent Meister Eckhart and Ruysbroeck, but can he equally distrust the delicate treasures of sensitive love and religious emotion in France and the Latin countries? To tax the Western mystic with "poverty", with "paltriness", with a lack of nicety and refinement[3] is to cast asper-

[1] *The Travel Diary of a Philosopher*, English Translation, Vol. I, p. 225, *et seq*.

[2] "Yesterday as today the word of Rabindranath Tagore is true: 'Of all the Westerners that I know, Keyserling is the most violently Western.'" (Quoted complaisantly by himself in the Preface to his "*Travel Diary*").

Further having generalised the whole West from his own temperament, he raises what is lacking in himself into a virtue, nay more, into the "mission" of the West.

[3] "The heart, no matter, what they say, is only poorly developed

sions at the same time upon the perfection attained in France by a whole galaxy of religious thinkers during the seventeenth century—the equals if not the superiors of the psychological masters of the French Classical Age and of their successors, the modern novelists, in analysing the most secret feelings of mankind.[1]

With regard to the ardour of this faith of love, I refuse to believe that in the case of a great European believer it can be inferior in quality to that of a great Asiatic believer. The excessive desire shown always by the latter for "Realisation" in my opinion is not the mark of the highest and purest religious soul. It is hardly possible that India could have invented "*Noli me tangere!*" ... In order to believe she must see, touch, and taste. And she would be perilously near to unbelief if she had not at least the hope that one day she would attain her goal in this life. Vivekananda himself gave utterance to some words almost disconcerting and brutal in their frankness.[2] Their hunger for God is all-powerful; but there is a lofty and aristocratic bashfulness of love exemplified

in the Westerner. We imagine, because we have professed for one and a half thousand years a religion of love, that for this reason love animates us. That is not true....How meagre is the effect of Thomas à Kempis by the side of Ramakrishna! How poor is the highest European Bhakti beside that, for instance, of the Persian mystics. Western feeling is stronger than that of the East in so far as it possesses more kinetic energy. But it is not nearly so rich, so delicate or so differentiated." (Ibid., p. 227 *et seq.*).

[1] *Cf.* the books devoted to "*The Mystic Invasion in France*", and to "*Mystic Conquest*", in the admirable *Histoire littéraire du sentiment religieux en France, depuis la fin des guerres de religion jusqu'à nos jours*, by Henri Brémond.

[2] "Only the man who has actually perceived God and soul has religion....We are all atheists; let us confess it. Mere intellectual assent does not make us religious....All knowledge must stand on perception of certain facts....Religion is a question of fact." (*Jnana-Yoga: "Realisation"*).

by one of our saints, who, when shown a miracle,
turned away his eyes and said, "Let me have the
sweetness of believing without having seen."

We like to give credit to our ideals and we do not
ask them to pay in advance. There are some most noble
souls, whom I know, who give until they are bankrupt
without thought of return.[1]

But let us not establish degrees; for there is more
than one way of loving. If a man gives all that he has,
it does not matter if his gift differs from that of his
neighbour. They are equal.

Nevertheless we must recognise that by exercising a
strict control over mysticism, our Western churches
have curbed its emotional expression so that it is less
obvious than in India, where it flows with no limitation. A great Hindu with the wisdom of Vivekananda, the responsible leader of his people's conscience, knew that he had little necessity to stimulate
among his own people such dispositions of heart. On
the other hand care was needed to keep them within
bounds. They had too great a tendency to degenerate
into morbid sentimentality. On many occasions I
have already shown that Vivekananda reacted violently
against anything of the kind. The scene with his monks

[1] One of the most touching characteristics of our Western mysticism is the intelligent pity of souls, truly religious themselves, that
has driven them to understand, to accept, and even to love absence
of God, so-called "hardness" of heart in others. It has been often
described, perhaps most strikingly, in the celebrated pages of St. Jean
de la Croix in *La Nuit Obscure* and of Francois de Sales, in the ninth
book of his *Traité de l'Amour de Dieu* ("On the Purity of 'Indifference' "). It is difficult to know which to admire most, whether
their acuteness of analysis, or the tender brotherly understanding
hovering over the sufferings of the loving and devoted soul, and
teaching it—(as in the beautiful story of the deaf musician who
played the lute for his prince's pleasure and did not stop singing
even when the prince, in order to try him, left the room)—to find

is a memorable one when he insulted their "sentimental imbecility" and was implacable in his
condemnation of Bhakti—and then suddenly confessed
that he himself was a prey to it. It was for that very
reason that he took up arms against it, and was ever
watchful to guard his spiritual flock against the abuses
of the heart. His particular duty as a guide along the
path of Bhakti-Yoga was to throw light on the wind-
ings of the road and the snares of sentiment.

The Religion of Love[1] covers an immense territory.
Its complete exploration would entail a kind of *Itinéraire
à Jérusalem*,[2] being the march of the soul through the
different stages of love towards the Supreme Love. It
is a long and dangerous journey, and few arrive at the
goal.

". . . There is a power behind impelling us forward,
we do not know where to seek for the real object, but
this love is sending us forward in search of it. Again and
again we find out our mistake. We grasp something
and find it slips through our fingers and then we grip

joy in its pain and to offer to God its very forlornness as a proof of
its supreme love:

"While, O God, I see Your sweet face, and know that the song
of my love pleases You, alas, what comfort I find!...But when You
turn away Your eyes, and I no longer see in Your sweet favour
that You were taking pleasure in my song, O true God, how my soul
suffers! But I do not stop loving You...or singing the hymn
of my love, not for the pleasure I find in it, for I have none, but for
the pure love of Your pleasure." (Francois de Sales).

We shall see further on that India also has its lovers of God, who
give all without expecting any reward; for "they have passed the
stage of recompense and sorrow." The human heart is the same
everywhere.

[1] *Religion of Love* was the usual title given to a series of lectures
given in England and the United States. Vivekananda there condensed in a universal form his teachings on Bhakti-Yoga. (A pamphlet
of 124 pages, Udbodhan Office, Calcutta, 1922).

[2] Allusion to the title of Chateaubriand's famous work.

something else. Thus on and on we go, till at last comes light; we come to God, the only One who loves. His love knows no change....[1] All the others are mere stages.... But the path to God is long and difficult...."

And the majority lose themselves on the way. Turning towards his Indians, Vivekananda said to them (let the humanitarians and Christians of the West mark his words!), "Millions of people make a trade of that religion of love. A few men in a century attain to that love of God and the whole country becomes blessed and hallowed.... When at last the Sun comes, all the lesser lights vanish...." "But," he hastened to add, "you have all to pass through these smaller loves...."

But do not stop at these intermediary stages, and before all things be sincere! Never walk in a vain and hypocritical pride that makes you believe you love God, when in reality you are attached to this world. And on the other hand—(and this is still more essential)—do not scorn other honest travellers who find it difficult to advance! Your first duty is to understand and to love those whose views are not the same as your own.

"Not only that we would not tell others that they are wrong, but that we would tell them that they are right, all of these who follow their own ways; that way which your nature makes it absolutely necessary for

[1] "Wherever there is any love it is He, the Lord, is present there. Where the husband kisses the wife, He is there in the kiss; where the mother kisses the child, He is there in the kiss; and where friends clasp hands, He, the Lord, is present...in the sacrifice of a great man (who) loves and wishes to help mankind."

"The ideal of man is to see God in everything. But if you cannot see Him in everything, see Him in one thing, in that thing which you like best, and then see Him in another. So on you go. There is infinite life before the soul. Take your time and you will achieve your end." (God in Everything).

you to take, is the right way.[1]... It is useless to quarrel with people who think differently from you.... There may be millions of radii converging towards the same centre in the sun. The further they are from the centre the greater is the distance between any two. But as they all meet at the centre all difference vanishes. The only solution is to march ahead and go towards the centre...."

It follows that Vivekananda vigorously took up the cudgels against all dogmatic education, and nobody has more strenuously defended the freedom of the child. His soul, like his limbs, should be free from all bounds. To stifle the soul of a child is the worst crime of all, and yet we commit it daily.

"... I can never teach you anything: you will have to teach yourself, but I can help you perhaps in giving expression to that thought.... I must teach myself religion. What right had my father to put all sorts of nonsense into my head?... or my master? ...Perhaps they are good, but they may not be *my* way. Think of the appalling evil that is in the world today, of the millions and millions of innocent children perverted by the wrong ways of teaching. How many beautiful spiritual truths have been nipped in the bud by this horrible idea of a family religion, a social religion, a national religion, and so forth. Think of what a mass of superstition is in your head just now about your childhood's religion, or your country's religion, and what an amount of evil it does or can do!..."

Then must one simply fold one's arms? Why did Vivekananda busy himself with education with so

[1] What the Hindu calls the "Ishta" of each man.

much ardour and what happens to the teacher? He then becomes a liberator, who allows each one to work according to his capacities in his own way, at the same time instilling into each a proper respect for the way of his neighbours.

"There are so many ideals; I have no right to say what shall be your ideal, to force my ideal on you. My duty should be to lay before you all the ideals I know of and enable you to see by your own constitution what you like best, and which is most fitted to you. Take up that one which suits you best and persevere in it. This is your Ishta."

That is why Vivekananda was the enemy of all so-called "established" religion, (of what he calls "congregational" religion)—the religion of a Church. "Let the Churches preach doctrines, theories, philosophies to their heart's content." All these are unimportant. But no Church has the right to interfere with *real* religion, with "higher religion", with the religion of action called prayer, with "adoration", the real contact of the soul with God. These things are matters between the soul and God. "When it comes to worship, the real practical part of religion, it should be as Jesus says, 'When thou prayest, enter into thy closet, and when thou hast shut the door, pray to thy Father which is in secret.'" Deep religion "cannot be made public.... I cannot get ready my religious feelings at a moment's notice. What is the result of this mummery and mockery? It is making a joke of religion, the worst of blasphemy.... How can human beings stand this religious drilling? It is like soldiers in a barrack. Shoulder arms, kneel down, take a book, all regulated exactly. Five minutes of feeling, five minutes of reason, five minutes of prayer all arranged beforehand. These parades have driven out religion, and if they continue for centuries, religion will cease to exist."

Religion consists solely of an inner life, and this inner life is a forest peopled by very diverse fauna, so that it is impossible to choose between the kings of the jungle. "There is such a thing as instinct in us, which we have in common with the animals.... There is again a higher form of guidance, which we call reason, when the intellect obtains facts and then generalises them. There is the still higher form...which we call inspiration, which does not reason, but knows things by flashes. But how shall we know it from instinct? That is the great difficulty. Everyone comes to you, nowadays, and says he is inspired, and puts forth superhuman claims. How are we to distinguish between inspiration and deception?"

The answer is a striking one for the Western reader; for it is the same that a Western rationalist would give: "In the first place, inspiration must not contradict reason. The old man does not contradict the child, he is the development of the child. What we call inspiration is the development of reason. The way to intuition is through reason.... No genuine inspiration ever contradicts reason. Where it does it is no inspiration."

The second condition is no less prudent and sane: "Secondly, inspiration must be for the good of one and all; and not for name or fame or personal gain. It should always be for the good of the world, and perfectly unselfish."

It is only after subjecting inspiration to these two tests that it may be accepted. "But you must remember that there is not one in a million that is inspired in the present state of the world."

Vivekananda cannot be accused of allowing too wide loopholes to credulity; for he knew his people and the abuse they made of it.* He knew, moreover, that sentimental devotion is too often a mask for weakness of character, and he had no pity for such weakness. "Be strong and stand up and seek the God of Love. This is the highest strength. What power is higher than the power of purity?... This love of God cannot be reached by the weak; therefore be not weak, either physically, mentally, morally, or spiritually."[1]

Strength, virile reason, constant preoccupation with universal good and complete disinterestedness are the conditions for reaching the goal. And there is still another: it is the will to arrive. Most men who call themselves religious are not really so at bottom; they are too lazy, too fearful, too insincere; they prefer to linger on the way and not to look too closely at what is awaiting them; hence they stagnate in the lotus-land of formal devotion. "Temples or churches, books or forms are just for the child's play, so as to make the spiritual man strong enough to take yet higher steps, and these first steps are necessary to be taken if he wants religion."

It is useless to urge that such stagnation is a sign of wise prudence, and that those who stand still would

---

* These addresses were given in England and America.—*Publisher*.

[1] *Cf.* the "heroic" character imprinted on Divine Love by the great Christian mystics:—"the Combat" by Ruysbroeck, where the spirit and God grapple and strive savagely (*De Ornatu Spiritualium Nuptiarum*, II, 56, 57),—the "*irascibilis*" soul of Meister Eckhart, seizing God by force. According to Eckhart, of the three highest forces of the soul, the first is knowledge (*Erkenntnis*); the second, "*irascibilis*", the "violent aspiration towards the Most High" (*die*

be in danger of losing their faith and their God, if they come out of their sheltering "Kindergarten". The truth is that they have nothing to lose, being in reality only false devotees; true unbelievers are preferable, for they are nearer to God. Here is the tribute paid by the greatest believer to sincere and exalted atheism:

"The vast majority of men (*and he was speaking of devotees*) are atheists. I am glad that in modern times another set of atheists has come up in the Western world, the materialists, because they are *sincere* atheists.[1] They are better than these religious atheists, who are insincere, who *talk* about religion, and fight about it, yet never *want* it, never try to realise it, never try to understand it. Remember the words of Christ: 'Ask and ye shall receive, seek and ye shall find, knock and it shall be opened to you....' These words

---

*aufstrebende Kraft*); the third, will-power (*der Wille*). One of the symbols of this mystic encounter with God is Jacob wrestling with the angel. (*Cf.* the beautiful paraphrase made by the French Dominican of the seventeenth century, Chardon: pp. 75-77 of Vol. I of Brémond's *Métaphysique des Saints.*) Even the gentle Francois de Sales says, "Love is the standard of the army of the virtues, they must all rally to her." (*Traité de l'Amour de Dieu*).

Here there is nothing effeminate. The virile soul flings itself into the thick of the fight courting wounds and death.

[1] More recent homage has been paid to modern materialism by the great Hindu mystic Aurobindo Ghose. In his articles in the *Arya* Review (No. 2, September 15, 1914) on *The Life Divine* and *The Synthesis of Yoga*, he sees in the scientific and economic materialism of the day a necessary stage of Nature and her work for the progress of the human spirit and of society:

"The whole trend of modern thought and modern endeavour reveals itself to the observant eye as a large conscious effort of Nature in man to effect a general level of intellectual equipment, capacity, and further possibility of universalising the opportunities which modern civilisation affords for the mental life. Even the preoccupation of the European intellect, the protagonist of this tendency, with material Nature and the externals of existence, is a necessary part of the effort. It seeks to prepare a sufficient basis in man's physical being

are literally true, not figures or pictures.... But who wants God? ... We want everything but God...."

Western devotees, as well as Eastern, may profit by this rough lesson. The unmasker of religious dishonesty fearlessly reveals such camouflaged atheists to themselves.

"Every one says: 'Love God!' ... Men do not know what it is to love.... Where is love? Wherever there is neither traffic, nor fear, nor any interest,

and vital energies and in his material environment for his full mental possibilities."

"The right or at least the ultimate means may not always be employed, but their aim is the right preliminary aim—a sound individual and social body and the satisfaction of the legitimate needs and demands of the material mind, sufficient ease, leisure, equal opportunity, so that the whole of mankind and no longer only the favoured race, class, or individual, may be free to develop the emotional and intellectual being to its full capacity. At present the material and economic aim may predominate, but always behind there works or there waits in reserve the higher and major impulse."

Further he recognises "the enormous, the indispensable utility of the very brief period of rationalistic Materialism through which humanity has been passing. For that vast field of evidence and experience which now begins to reopen its gates to us, can only be safely entered when the intellect has been severely trained to a strict austerity. It became necessary for a time to make a clean sweep at once of the truth and its disguises in order that the road might be clear for a new departure and a surer advance. It is necessary that advancing knowledge should base herself on a clear, pure, and disciplined intellect. It is necessary, too, that she should correct her errors sometimes by a return to the restraint of sensible fact, the concrete realities of the physical world. It may even be said that the supra-physical can only be really mastered in its fullness, when we keep our feet firmly on the physical. 'Earth is His footing,' says the Upanishad whenever it images the Self that is manifested in the universe. And it is certainly the fact that the wider we extend and the surer we make our knowledge of the physical world, the wider and surer becomes our foundation for the higher knowledge, even for the highest, even for the *Brahmavidya*."

Here the rationalistic materialism of Europe is accepted and used by Indian thought as a stepping-stone to complete knowledge and to the mastery of the Atman.

where there is nothing but love for the love of love."[1]

When the last stage has been reached, you will no longer need to know what is going to happen to you, or if God, the creator of the universe, an almighty and pitiful God, a God who rewards the merits of humanity, exists; it will not matter to you even if God is a tyrant or a good God.... "The lover has passed beyond all these things, beyond rewards and punishments, beyond fears, or doubts, or scientific or any other demonstration...." He loves, he has attained the fact of Love "of which the whole universe is only a manifestation...."

For at this pitch love has lost all human limitations and has taken on a Cosmic meaning: "What is it that makes atoms come and join atoms, molecule molecules, sets big planets flying towards each other, attracts man to woman, woman to man, human beings to human beings, animals to animals, drawing the whole universe, as it were, towards one centre? That is what is called love. Its manifestation is from the lowest atom to the highest ideal: omnipresent, all-pervading, everywhere is the love.... It is the one motive power that is in the universe. Under the impetus of that love, Christ stands to give up his life for humanity, Buddha for an animal, the mother for the child, the husband for the wife. It is under the

[1] In another place, in *Notes of Class Talks and Lectures* (Vol. VI of the *Complete Works*, p. 90 *et seq.*), Vivekananda enumerates five stages in the path of Divine Love:

(1) Man is fearful and needs help.

(2) He sees God as father.

(3) He sees God as mother. (And it is only from this stage that real love begins, for only then does it become intimate and fearless.)

(4) He loves for the sake of love—beyond all other qualities and beyond good and evil.

(5) He realises love in Divine union, Unity.

impetus of the same love that men are ready to give up
their lives for their country, and strange to say, under
the impetus of that same love, the thief goes to steal,
the murderer to murder; for in these cases, the spirit
is the same.... The thief has love for gold; the love
was there but it was misdirected. So, in all crimes, as
well as in all virtuous actions, behind stands that eternal
love.... The motive power of the universe is love,
without which the universe will fall to pieces in a
moment, and this love is God."

Here also, as at the end of Karma-Yoga, we come to
an outburst of liberation or ecstasy—supreme Bhakti,
where ties uniting men to ordinary existence seem to
be so broken that it must either be destroyed or thrown
out of equilibrium. The Bhakta has shed forms and
symbols and no sect or church holds him any longer;
none of them are big enough, for he has attained the
zone of limitless Love, and has become ONE with it.
The Light floods his entire being, annihilating desire,
selfishness, and egoism. The man has passed along the
whole path, through all its stages: he has been son,
friend, lover, husband, father, and mother, and is now
ONE with his Beloved. "I am you and you are me.
..." And everything is but ONE....[1]

But is there nothing to follow?

He comes down voluntarily from the mountain-tops
bathed in Light, and turns again to those who have

---

[1] Aurobindo Ghose has dedicated some beautiful pages to a new
theory of supreme Bhakti which he claims to have deduced from the
teachings of the Gita. According to him this super-eminent Bhakti,
which is the highest degree of the ascent of the soul, is accompanied
by knowledge and does not renounce a single one of the powers of
being, but accomplishes them all in their integrity. (*Essays on the Gita*).
It seems to me that in many pages of these *Essays* the thought of
Aurobindo Ghose is very close to that of Christian mysticism.

remained at the bottom so that he may help them to ascend.[1]

## III. Raja-Yoga

Although Vivekananda preached as his ideal the harmonious practice of the four kinds of Yoga,[2] there was one peculiarly his own, which might almost be called

[1] "After attaining super-consciousness the Bhakta descends again to love and worship....Pure love has no motive. It has nothing to gain" (*Notes from Lectures*, Vol. VI, *loc. cit.*).

"Come down! Come down!" Ramakrishna said in order to bring himself back from ecstasy, and he reproached himself and refused to have the happiness attained in union with God so that he might render service to others: "O Mother, let me not attain these delights, let me remain in my normal state, so that I can be of more use to the world!..." Is it necessary to recall that the Christian Bhakta always knows how to tear himself from the delights of ecstasy, in order to serve his neighbour? Even the wildest transports of the impassioned Ruysbroeck, who embraced his God like the spoils of love won in battle, sank at the name of "Charity": "...If you are ravished in ecstasy as highly as St. Peter or St. Paul or as anybody you like, and if you hear that a sick man is in need of hot soup, I counsel you to wake from your ecstasy and warm the soup for him. Leave God to serve God: find Him and serve Him in His members; you will lose nothing by the change...." (*De praecipuis quibusdam virtutibus*).

In this form of divine Love, directed towards the human community, the Christianity of Europe has no rival: for its faith teaches it to consider all humanity as the mystic body of Christ. Vivekananda's wish that his Indian disciples should sacrifice, not only their lives, but their salvation itself in order to save others, has often been realised in the West by pure and ardent souls, like Catherine of Sienna and Marie des Vallées, the simple peasant of Coutances in the fourteenth century. Her marvellous story has been recently recorded for us by Emile Dermenghen. She demanded of God the pains of hell in order to deliver the unfortunate. "Our Lord refused her, and the more He refused, the more she offered herself. 'I fear,' she said to Him, 'that you have not enough torments to give me.' "

[2] It was this characteristic that struck both Ramakrishna and later Girish. "Your Swami," said the latter to the monks of Alambazar, "is as much Jnani and pandit as the lover of God and humanity."

Vivekananda held the reins of the four paths of Truth, love, action, knowledge and energy, as in a quadriga and travelled simultaneously along them all towards Unity.

after him, or it is the way of "Discrimination" (Viveka).
Further, it is the one that should be able to unite
the West and the East—Jnana-Yoga—the way of
"realisation" by "Knowledge", or in other words, the
exploration and conquest of the ultimate Essence or
Brahman through the mind.

But the conquest of the Poles is child's play compared
to this heroic expedition, wherein science and religion
compete the one with the other, and it demands hard
and careful training. It cannot be undertaken haphazard, as can the two preceding paths of Work and Love
(Karma and Bhakti). A man must be fully armed,
equipped and drilled. And that is the office of Raja-
Yoga. Although it is self-sufficient in its own sphere,
it also plays the part of a preparatory school to the
supreme Yoga of Knowledge. That is why I have put
it at this point in my exposition, and also because it
was where Vivekananda put it.[1]

Raja-Yoga is the raja, the king, of Yogas, and as
a sign of royalty it is often spoken of as Yoga without
any further qualification or designation. It is the Yoga

---

[1] In *Jnana-Yoga*, the chapter on the "*The Ideal of a Universal
Religion*," I have instinctively followed Vivekananda in the order
he laid down for the four types of temperament and their corresponding Yogas. It is, however, a curious fact that Vivekananda did
not apply to the second, Bhakti-Yoga, the emotional one, the name
of "Mysticism", given to it in the West. He reserves this name for
the third, the Raja-Yoga, the one that analyses and conquers the
inner human self. He is thus more faithful/than we to the classic
meaning of the word "Mystic", which in the feminine is "the study
of spirituality" (*Cf.* Bossuet) and which we have wrongly used, or
rather restricted to the effusions of the heart. In the masculine
it seems to me to be the correct term for the Raja-Yogi,
"myste", the initiated. Aurobindo Ghose puts them in a different order in his *Essays on the Gita*. He superimposes these three
degrees:

(1) Karma-Yoga, which realises disinterested self-sacrifice by
works;

*par excellence*. If by Yoga we mean union with the supreme object (and subject) of Knowledge, Raja-Yoga is the experimental psycho-physiological method for its direct attainment.[1] Vivekananda called it "the psychological Yoga", since its field of action is the control and absolute mastery of the mind—the first condition of all knowledge. It achieves its end by concentration.[2]

Normally we waste our energies. Not only are they squandered in all directions by the tornado of exterior impressions; but even when we manage to shut doors and windows, we find chaos within ourselves, a multitude like the one that greeted Julius Caesar in the Roman Forum; thousands of unexpected and mostly "undesirable" guests invade and trouble us. No inner activity can be seriously effective and continuous until we have first reduced our house to order, and then have recalled and reassembled our herd of scattered energies. "The powers of the mind are like rays of dissipated light; when they are concentrated they illumine. This is our only means of Knowledge." In all

(2) Jnana-Yoga, which is the knowledge of the true nature of self and the world;

(3) Bhakti-Yoga, which is the search for and the realisation of the supreme Self, the fullness of the possession of the Divine Being. (*Essays on the Gita*, first series, Chapter 4, 1921).

[1] "The science of Raja-Yoga proposes to lay before humanity a practical and scientifically worked-out method of reaching the truth" (in the Hindu sense of the living and individual "realisation" of the truth). (*Raja-Yoga*, Chapter I).

I have said above that Aurobindo Ghose widens the field of Raja-Yoga from knowledge to power, from speculation to action. But I am speaking here only of speculative Raja-Yoga as understood by the great authorities on the Vedanta.

[2] Inspired by Patanjali, the great classical theorist of Raja-Yoga (whose Sutras are placed by Western Indological science between 400 and 450 A.D. *Cf.* P. Masson-Oursel, *op. cit.*, p. 184 *et seq.*). Vivekananda defined this operation as "the science of restraining the Chitta (the mind) from breaking into Vrittis (modifications)".— Vol. VII of *The Complete Works of Swami Vivekananda*, p. 61.

countries and at all times learned men, or artists, great
men of action or of intense meditation, have known
and practised it instinctively each in his own way,
either consciously or subconsciously, as experience dictated. I have shown in the case of Beethoven, to what
degree this can be achieved by a Western genius living
in complete ignorance of Raja-Yoga in the strict sense
of the word. But this same example is a signal warn-
ing of the dangers of such individual practice when
insufficiently understood and controlled.[1]

The originality of Indian Raja-Yoga lies in the fact
that it has been the subject for centuries past of a
minutely elaborated and experimental science for the
conquest of concentration and mastery of the mind.
By mind, the Hindu Yogi understands the instrument
as well as the object of knowledge, and in what concerns the object he goes very far, farther than I can
follow him. It is not that I deny on principle the
boundless powers he claims for his science, not only
over the soul but over all nature (in Hindu belief they
are indistinguishable). The really scientific attitude is
one of reserve with regard to the future possibilities
of the mind, since neither its bounds nor extent, by
which term I mean its limits, have yet been scientifically fixed. But I rightly condemn* the Indian Yogi
for taking as proved what nobody as yet has been able

---

[1] *Cf.* my study on the *Deafness of Beethoven*, in Vol. I of *Beethoven:
The Great Creative Epochs*, p. 335 *et seq.* The Yogis were well aware of
it:—"All inspired persons," wrote Vivekananda, "who stumbled upon
this superconscious state...generally had some quaint superstitions
along with their knowledge. They laid themselves open to halluci-
nations" and ran the risk of madness. (*Raja-Yoga*, Chapter VII).

* The supernatural powers claimed by the Yogis are not hypothetical. The argument advanced by Sir J. C. Bose seems to us beside
the point. Only a Yogi knows, and not an ordinary man like us,
what our human world—a mere speck, albeit *our* world, in the vast

to prove experimentally. For if such extraordinary
powers exist, there seems to be no reason why the
ancient Rishis made no use of them to refashion the
world[1] (as even the great Indian who is both a learned
genius and a convinced believer, Sir Jagadish C. Bose,
said to me). And the worst feature of such foolish
promises, such as might have been made by the fabulous genii of the Arabian Nights, is that they are seized
upon by greedy and empty brains. Even Vivekananda
could not always resist this kind of preaching, with
its attraction for the dangerous and gluttonous appetite
of the most sensuous souls.[2]

But Vivekananda was always careful to surround the

universe of reality opened before the Yogi's vision—counts to him and
if this world requires to be refashioned in the way Sir J. C. Bose suggests.
Innumerable witnesses are available of the truth of the extraordinary
Yogic powers. Swami Vivekananda himself witnessed many. See
Volume II of his *Complete Works*: *"The Powers of the Mind"*. It is wrong
to wish that the truth about Raja-Yoga should not be taught, simply
because some foolish persons may abuse it. If some of those who listened
to the Swami, were guided by worldly motives, there were others who
were quite earnest and noble. No truth can be spared abuse or misuse
by unworthy minds. Do we not see how material science also has been
subjected to the same misuse?

M. Rolland seems to have overlooked the fact that supernatural
powers come to all who have made appreciable progress towards
spirituality, whether they travel along the path of Bhakti, Karma,
Jnana, or Raja-Yoga.—*Publisher.*

[1] I am well aware that Aurobindo Ghose, who has devoted years
of his life to these researches in absolute seclusion from the world,
has, it is said, achieved "realisations" that are destined to transform
the realm of the mind as it is known up to the present. But while
credit must be given to his philosophic genius, we are waiting for
the discoveries announced by his entourage to be presented to the
full light of scientific investigation. Strict analysis has never accepted
experiences of which the experimentalist, however authoritative, was
the sole judge and participator. (Disciples do not count, for they are
merely the reflection of the master.)

[2] In his *Raja-Yoga*, one of his first works published in America,
he spoke rashly (Chapter I) of the powers that could be obtained
over nature in a relatively short time (several months) by those who
perseveringly followed the practice of Raja-Yoga. And the intimate

coveted object, like Brünhilde's rock,[1] with a fivefold ring of fire.[2] None but the hero can bear away the prize. Even the first stage is unattainable—the Yama or mastery—without the fulfilment of five indispensable conditions, each one sufficient to make a saint:

1. *Ahimsa*, the great aim of Gandhi, which the old Yogis considered to be the highest virtue and happiness of mankind: "no hurt" to all nature, the "doing no evil" in act, word, thought to any living being;

2. *Absolute truth*: "truth in action, word, thought"; for truth is the foundation of all things whereby all things are attained;

3. *Perfect chastity* or Brahmacharya;

4. *Absolute non-covetousness;*

5. *Purity of soul and absolute disinterestedness*: not

memories that have been communicated to me by his most deeply religious American disciple, Sister Christine, make it discreetly evident, reading between the lines, that mundane preoccupations formed the kernel of the meditations of those, especially the women, who practised Raja-Yoga in America (*Cf*. Chapter V of Vivekananda's treatise—the effects derived from the Yogic practice on beauty of voice and face). It is true that the young Swami, filled as he was with faith, could hardly have foreseen the frivolous interpretation put upon his words. As soon as he saw it, he protested emphatically. But one must never "tempt the devil", as one of our proverbs has it. If we do, the devil takes advantage of us, and we are fortunate if we escape with nothing worse than ridicule, which often enough is only a step away from the obscene. There are other and less scrupulous Yogis who have traded upon its attractions and made Raja-Yogism a receiving office for men and women greedy for this totally different kind of conquest.

[1] Allusion to the Nibelungen Legend in Wagner's opera—the Valkyrie.

[2] Far from recognising supernatural powers as the reward of Yogic efforts, Vivekananda, like all great Yogis, regarded them as a temptation similar to that borne by Jesus on the top of the mountain when the devil offered him the kingdoms of this world. (It is clear to me that in the legend of Christ that moment corresponded to the last stage but one of his personal Yoga.) If he had not rejected this temptation all the fruits of Yoga would have been lost.... (*Raja-Yoga*, Chapter VII):

"Different powers will come to the Yogi, and if he yields to the

to accept or to expect any gift: every accepted gift is prejudicial to independence and is death to the soul.[1]

Hence it is clear that the common herd who sought in Yoga a fraudulent means to "success", those who wished to cheat fate, dabblers in the occult and clients of Beauty Parlours, found "No road" barring the way at the outer ring of fortifications. But most of them were careful not to read the notice; and they tried to coax the more or less authentic Guru, who guarded the door, to allow them to enter.

That is why Vivekananda, as he became aware of the danger of certain words for weak and unscrupulous moral natures,* avoided their use.[2] And he tended more and more to restrict his instruction in Raja-Yoga to the conquest of Knowledge by the most perfect

temptations of any one of these, the road to his further progress will be barred.... But if he is strong enough to reject even these miraculous powers he will attain... the complete suppression of the waves in the ocean of the mind." He will attain Divine Union. But it is only too evident that the ordinary man troubles himself little about this union and prefers the good things of the world.

(I would add that to an idealistic free-thinker, as I am, who naturally unites scientific scepticism to spiritual faith, such so-called "supernatural power", as come to the Yogi and are repulsed by him, are in fact illusory, since he has never tried them. But this is unimportant. What matters is that the mind is convinced of their reality and voluntarily makes the sacrifice; for the sacrifice is the only reality that counts.)

[1] Cf. Raja-Yoga, Chapter VIII, the summing up of Kurma Purana; and Vol. VI of The Complete Works of Swami Vivekananda, P. 89 et seq.

* The Swami always thought that very few are fit to practise Raja-Yoga.—Publisher.

[2] He recognised this more and more as he gained experience. To an Indian disciple who asked him about the different ways of salvation, he said, "The path of Bhakti or devotion to God is a slow process, but is easy of practice. In the path of Yoga (Raja) there are many obstacles; perhaps the mind runs after psychic powers and thus draws you away from attaining your real nature. Only the path of Jnana is of quick fruition and the rationale of all other creeds; hence it is equally esteemed in all countries and all ages." (Vol. VII, Complete Works, p. 198 et seq.)

instrument of scientific method: absolute Concentration.[1]

And in this we are all interested. Whatever may be the effect upon the mind produced by this instrument on the part of the Hindu seeker after truth, all seekers after truth, whether of the West or the East, are obliged to use that instrument; and it is to their advantage that it should be as exact and perfect as possible. There is nothing of the occult in it. Vivekananda's sane intelligence had the same aversion to all that was secret and hidden in the searchings of the mind as the most devoted and erudite Westerner: "... There is no mystery in what I teach.... Anything that is secret and mysterious in these systems of Yoga should be at once rejected.... Discard everything that weakens you. Mystery-mongering weakens the human brain. It has wellnigh destroyed Yoga—one of the grandest of sciences.... You must practise and see whether these things happen or not.... There is neither mystery nor danger in it.[2] ... It is wrong to believe blindly...."[3]

Nobody condemns more categorically the slightest abdication of self-mastery, however partial or transient, into the hands of strangers. And it is this that makes him protest so violently against all kinds of suggestion however honest and well-intentioned: "The so-called hypnotic suggestion can only act upon a weak mind

[1] "Give up... this nibbling at things. Take up one idea. Make that one idea your life; think of it; dream of it; live on that idea" until it becomes the substance of your whole body. (*Raja-Yoga*, Chapter VI.)

[2] All the same Vivekananda elsewhere lays down wise and prudent rules for the physical and moral hygiene of those who wish to practise Yoga.

[3] *Raja-Yoga*, Chapter I.

... and excite in the patient a sort of morbid
Pratyâhâra.... It is not really controlling the brain
centres by the power of one's own will, but is, as
it were, stunning the patient's mind for the time
being by sudden blows which another's will delivers
to it.... Every attempt at control which is not
voluntary is ... disastrous, it ... only rivets one
link more to the already existing heavy chain of
bondage.... Therefore beware how you let yourselves
be acted upon by others ... even if they succeed
in doing good ... for a time.... Use your own
minds ... control body and mind yourselves, remember that until you are a diseased person, no
extraneous will can work upon you; avoid everyone,
however great and good he may be, who asks you to
believe blindly. It is healthier for the individual or the
race to remain wicked than to be made apparently
good by such morbid extraneous control.... Beware
of everything that takes away your freedom."[1]

In his unwavering passion for mental freedom he, like
Tolstoy, although an artist by race and a born musician,
went so far as to reject the dangerous power of artistic
emotion, especially that produced by music, over the
exact working of the mind.[2] Anything that runs the

---

[1] Ibid., Chapter VI.
[2] It is not that a real Yoga of art does not exist in India. And
here Vivekananda's own brother, Mohendra Nath Dutt, a profound
thinker, has filled in the lines indicated by the Master. I cannot urge
European aesthetes too strongly to read his *Dissertation on Painting*
(dedicated to the memory of Brahmananda, the first Abbot of the
Ramakrishna Mission, with a preface by Abanindranath Tagore, 1922,
Calcutta, Seva Series Publishing Home). The great Indian religious
artist places himself face to face with the object he wishes to represent
in the attitude of a Yogi in search of Truth: to him the object
becomes the subject; and the process of contemplation is that of the
strictest Yogic "discrimination".

risk of making the mind less independent to carry out its own observations and experiments, even if it seems to bring about temporary relief and well-being, has in it the "seed of future decadence, of crime, of folly, and of death."

I do not believe that the most exacting scientific mind ever gave utterance to more pronounced views; and Western reason must agree with the principles laid down by Vivekananda.

It makes it all the more astonishing that Western reason has taken so little into account the experimental research of Indian Raja-Yogis, and that it has not tried to use the methods of control and mastery, which they offer in broad daylight without any mystery, over the one infinitely fragile and constantly warped instrument that is our only means of discovering what exists.

While admitting, with no possibility of contradiction, that Yogist psycho-physiology uses explanations—and still more terms—that are both controvertible and obsolete, it should be easy to rectify them by readjusting (as Vivekananda tried to do) the experiments of past centuries to modern science. To make up for their lack of laboratories Hindu observers have possessed age-long patience and a genius for intuition. There can be no doubt on this point in the light of such pregnant lines

"In representing an ideal the painter really represents his own spirit, his dual self, through the medium of exterior objects. In a profound state of identification the inner and outer layers of the spirit are separated; the external layer or the variable part of the spirit is identified with the object observed, and the constant or un-changing part remains the serene observer. The one is 'Lila' (the play), the other 'Nitya' (Eternity). We cannot say what is beyond, for it is 'Avyakta', the inexpressible state...."

It is not astonishing that many great Indian artists, who have passed through this discipline, finally become saints. (*Cf.* also *Dance of Shiva*, by A. Coomaraswamy).

as the following on the nature of living bodies from the most ancient sacred texts:

"The body is the name given to a series of changes. ... As in a river the mass of water changes every moment and other masses come to take its place, so is it with the body."[1]

Religious faith in the case of Indians has never been allowed to run counter to scientific laws; moreover the former is never made a preliminary condition for the knowledge they teach; but they are always scrupulously careful to take into consideration the possibility that lay reason, both agnostic and atheist, may attain truth in its own way. Thus Raja-Yoga admits two distinct divisions: Mahâ-Yoga, which imagines the unity of the Ego with God, and Abhâva-Yoga (Abhava=non-existence), which studies the Ego "as zero and bereft of duality,"[2]—and both may be the object of pure and strict scientific observation.[3] Such tolerance may be surprising to religious believers in the West, but it is an integral part of Vedantic belief to regard the human spirit as God, who is as yet unaware of himself, but who is capable of being brought to know himself.[4]

[1] It is unnecessary to underline the similarity of this conception to that of the Eleates. Deussen, in his *System of the Vedanta*, has compared Heraclitus' doctrine of the perpetual instability of soul "complex" to Hindu doctrines.

The fundamental idea is that the universe is made out of one substance, whose form is perpetually changing. "The sum total of energies remains always the same." (*Raja-Yoga*, Chapter III).

[2] *Raja-Yoga*, Chapter VIII (summary from *Kurma Purana*).

[3] "In the study of this Raja-Yoga no faith or belief is necessary. Believe nothing until you find it out for yourself. ... Every human being has the right and the power to seek for religion." (*Raja-Yoga*, Chapter I).

[4] For Hindus, as for Buddhists, human birth is the highest stage that the Being has reached on the road to realisation; and that is why a man must make haste to profit by it. Even the gods, or *Devas* in the polytheistic sense, only achieve freedom by passing through human birth. (Ibid., Chapter III).

Such a *Credo* is not far from the secret or avowed aim
of Science, and so is not strange to us.

Further, Hindu religious psycho-physiology is entirely
materialistic up to a certain stage of being which is
placed very high, since it goes beyond the "mind". In
tracing the genesis of perception—from the impressions
received of exterior objects to the nerve and brain
centres where they are stored and thence to the mind
—all the stages are material, but the mind is made of
more subtle matter, although it does not differ in
essence from the body. It is only in the higher state
that the non-material *soul* occurs, the Purusha, which
receives its perceptions from its instrument, the mind,
and then transmits its orders to the motive centres.
As a result, positive science can walk hand in hand with
Hindu faith for three-quarters of the way. It is only
at the last stage but one that she will cry "Halt!"
And so all I ask here is that the two shall go the first
three-quarters of the way together. For I believe it is
possible that Hindu explorers in the course of their
journeying have seen many objects which have escaped
our eyes. Let us profit by their discoveries without
renouncing in any way our right to the free exercise of
our critical faculties with regard to them.

\*

I cannot find room within the limits of this book for
a detailed examination of Raja-Yogic methods. But I
recommend it to Western masters of the new psychology, and of pedagogy in so far as it is scientifically
founded on the physiology of the mind. I myself have
derived much benefit from their remarkable analysis;
and although it is too late to apply their teachings in
my own life, I admire the way they have explained the

past experiences of my life with all its mistakes and obscure instincts towards salvation.

But the three first psychological stages in the concentration of the mind must be mentioned:[1]—*Pratyâhâra*,[2] which turns the organs of sense away from exterior things and directs them towards entirely mental impressions;—*Dhâranâ*, which forces the mind to fix its attention on a special and given point, either outwardly or inwardly;—*Dhyâna* (properly speaking, meditation), when the mind, trained by the preceding exercises has acquired the power of "flowing in an unbroken current towards a chosen point."

It is only when the first stage has been mastered that character begins to form, according to Vivekananda. But "how hard it is to control the mind! Well has it been compared to the maddened monkey.... Incessantly active by its own nature; then it becomes drunk with the wine of desire... the sting... of jealousy... and pride enters the mind." Then what does the Master advise? The exercise of the will? No, he came earlier than our psychological doctors who have but tardily realised that the clumsy application of the will against some mental habit often provokes that habit to a violent reaction. He teaches mastery of the "monkey" by letting it grow quiet under the calm inner regard that judges it impartially. The ancient Yogis did not wait for Dr. Freud to

[1] They are preceded by exercises of a physiological nature—of great interest to medical science: *Asana* (or posture), and *Prânâyâma* (control of the breath). These are followed by the higher state of the mind, *Samâdhi*, where "the *Dhyâna* is intensified to the point of rejecting the exterior part of meditation and all sensible forms" and is absorbed in Unity. We shall return to this condition when we study the Yoga of knowledge (Jnana).

[2] The meaning of the word is: "gathering towards".

teach them that the best cure for the mind is to make
it look its deeply hidden monsters straight in the face:

"The first lesson then is to sit for some time and let
the mind run on. The mind is bubbling up all the
time. It is like that monkey jumping about. Let the
monkey jump as much as he can—you simply wait and
watch.... Many hideous thoughts may come into it;
knowledge is power...you will find that each day
the mind's vagaries are becoming less and less violent.
... It is tremendous work.... Only after a patient,
continuous struggle for years can we succeed."[1]

Hence before proceeding to the next stage, the Yogi
must have learnt to use the play of imagination in order
to discipline the mind to fix itself on one point.

But the Master was always preoccupied with matters
physiological. Avoid fatigue. "Such exercises are not
designed to follow the rough work of the day." Pay
attention to diet. "A strict diet from the first; milk
and cereals;" all stimulant is forbidden.[2] Inner phenomena are observed and described with praiseworthy

[1] Even prescriptions analogous to those of Dr. Coué are to be found
with the Yogis—the method of auto-suggestion, which makes the
patient repeat a beneficent statement. The Yogis counsel the novice
to repeat mentally at the beginning of his exercises: "May all beings
be happy!" so as to surround himself with an atmosphere of peace.

[2] Absolute chastity. Without it Raja-Yoga is attended with the
greatest dangers. Hindu observers maintain that each man possesses
a constant quantity of total energy: but that this energy can be transferred from one centre to another; sexual energy when used by the
brain is transformed into mental energy. But if, to use one of our popular expressions, a man "burns the candle at both ends," physical
and mental ruin is the result. Yoga followed under such conditions
leads to worse aberrations.

Add what contemplative souls in Europe have too often neglected,
hygiene and perfect cleanliness. The "purity" demanded by the rules
of Yoga embraces the double "obligation of the two purities, moral
and physical. No one can be a Yogi until he has both." (Raja-Yoga,
Chapter, VIII, summary of the Kurma Purana).

acumen.[1] At first during the conquest of concentration
the least sensation is like a stupendous wave. "A pin
dropping makes a noise like thunder.". . . Hence it is
very important to watch the organism closely, and to
keep it absolutely calm, since that is the desired aim.
It is obvious that constant care must be taken to avoid
all unhealthy overstrain. Otherwise the result will be
the deranged system and unbalanced mind, which
Western clumsiness hastily concludes to be the inevitable and exaggerated characteristics of an ecstatic or of
an inspired artist like Beethoven.[2]

The master Yogi on the other hand maintains that
physical health benefits from his discipline as much as
moral health. He says that its effects ought to become
quickly apparent in repose of body, relaxation of
features, and even in the tone of the voice. It is only
natural that these have been the advantages emphasised
by the worldly disciples of all Yogis whether true or
false. Let them do so! From so rich a storehouse of
experience, embracing as it does so many different
aspects of the body and mind, each may glean for his
own granary. Our concern here is only with psychologists and learned men![3]

---

[1] Sometimes sounds like those of a distant *carillon* are heard fading
into one continuous accord. Points of light appear. . . etc.

[2] "He who fasts, he who keeps awake, he who sleeps much, he who
works too much, he who does no work, none of these can be a *Yogi*."
(*Raja-Yoga*, Chapter I).
  "Do not practise when the body feels very lazy or ill, or when the
mind is very miserable or sorrowful." (Ibid., Chapter VIII).

[3] Without going outside the plane of the observable and probable,
it has actually been proved that sovereign control of the inner life
is able to put into our hands (partially if not entirely) our unconscious or subconscious life. "Almost every action of which we are
now unconscious can be brought to the plane of consciousness."
(*Raja-Yoga*, Chapter VII). It is a well-known fact that the Yogis
have the power to stop or provoke physiological acts that are quite

## IV. JNANA-YOGA

The upward surge of the spirit towards the truth
wherein it may find freedom, can occur—as we have
seen—under different forms: as *Amor Caritas*,[1] or disinterested Work, or mind-control having as object the
conquest of the laws governing the inner mechanism.
To each of these forms Raja-Yoga teaches the fingering
whereby the psycho-physiological piano may be played;
for nothing firm and lasting is possible without the
preliminary apprenticeship of concentration. But it is
peculiarly essential for one of them, if mastery is to be
attained, although it possesses its own independent
path. This brings us to the last we have to examine,
the one closely bound up with Raja-Yoga: Jnana-
Yoga, the rationalist and philosophical Yoga. In so far
as Raja-Yoga is the science of the control of inner
conditions, the philosopher has to go to it in order to
control his instrument of thought. Even Vivekananda,
the great "Discriminator", recognised that in this path,
so essentially his own—that of "discrimination" in the

beyond the scope of will-power, such as the beating of the heart.
Strict scientific observation has established the reality of these facts
and we ourselves have proved them. The Yogi is convinced that
"every being, however small he may be, has in reserve an immense
storehouse of energies." And this eminently virile and strengthening
belief contains nothing that can be denied on principle; the constant
progress of science rather tends to confirm it. But the Yogi's peculiar
quality (and this should be viewed with caution) is to think that he
can, by his methods of intensified concentration, quicken the rhythm
of individual progress and shorten the time necessary for the complete
evolution of humanity. That belief is the basis of the new researches
of Aurobindo Ghose (based upon a saying of Vivekananda) in his *The
Synthesis of Yoga*: "Yoga may be regarded as a means of compressing
one's evolution into a single life of a few years or even a few months of
bodily existence." I very much doubt it. But my doubt is scientific.
It does not deny. It waits for the proof of facts.
[1] Divine love. See note 1, p. 71.—*Publisher*.

sense of philosophic analysis and experiment—Jnana—
"the spirit can be caught in the endless net-work of
vain disputation," and that nothing but the practice of
Raja-Yogic concentration can enable it to escape
through the net.

It is, therefore, only logical that our exposition should
come last to this high method of the mind, which was
at the same time the one pre-eminently dear to
Vivekananda. He devoted so much more study to it
and so many lectures that he was unable to condense
them into treatises, as was the case with Raja-Yoga and
Karma-Yoga, both written at his dictation.[1]

The first striking thing about it is that, although,
like the other Yogas, its aim is the absolute Being, its
starting point and methods are much more like those
of the scientific than the religious spirit of the West.
It invokes both science and reason in no uncertain
tones.

"Experience is the only source of knowledge."[2]

"No one of these Yogas gives up reason... or asks
you to deliever your reason into the hands of priests of
any type whatsoever.... Each one of them tells you
to *cling* to your reason, to hold fast to it."[3]

And Jnana-Yoga magnifies reason, its devoted help-
mate, to the highest degree. It follows therefore that
religion must be tested by the same laws as the other
sciences.

[1] The voluminous compilation of *Jnana-Yoga* is a somewhat artificial collection of separate lectures, most of them given in London
in 1896. They are to be found in Volume II of the *Complete Works*, pp.
57-396. Other fragments scattered throughout the *Complete Works* must
be added: that of *Introduction to Jnana-Yoga*, Vol. VI, p. 41 *et seq.*,
*Discourses on the Yogas*, Vol. VI, p. 89 *et seq.*

[2] *Religion and Science*, VI, 81.

[3] *The Ideal of a Universal Religion*, II, 375.

"The same methods of investigation which we apply to the sciences and to exterior knowledge, should they be applied to the science of religion? I say, 'Yes,' and I would add, 'The sooner the better.' If a religion is destroyed by such investigation it was nothing but a useless and unworthy superstition; the sooner it disappeared the better. I am absolutely convinced that its destruction would be the best thing that could happen.[1] All that was dross would be taken away; but the essential parts would emerge triumphant for such investigation."[2]

What right has religion to claim to be above the control of reason?

"Why religions should claim that they are not bound to abide by the standpoint of reason no one knows.... For it is better that mankind should become atheist by following reason than blindly believe in two hundred millions of gods on the authority of anybody. It degrades human nature and brings it to the level of the beast. We must reason.... Perhaps there are prophets, who have passed the limits of sense and obtained a glimpse of the beyond. We shall believe it only when we can do the same ourselves; not before."[3]

---

[1] I am not certain that his good master, Ramakrishna, who was always the "brother" of the weak, would have approved of the uncompromising attitude adopted by his great intellectual and imperious disciple. He would have reminded him again that there is more than one door to a house, and that it is impossible to make everyone come in by the front entrance. In this I believe that Gandhi is nearer than Vivekananda to the universal "welcome" of Ramakrishna. But the fiery disciple would have been the first to blame himself afterwards in great humility.

[2] *Jnana-Yoga.*

[3] Fifteen years before, Keshab Ch. Sen said the same thing in his *Epistle to his Indian Brethren* (1880), "You must accept nothing on trust as do the superstitious. Science will be your religion, as said the Lord, Our God. You will respect science above all other things; the science

"It has been said that reason is not strong enough; it does not always help us to get the Truth; many times it makes mistakes, and therefore the conclusion is that we must believe in the authority of a church. That was said to me by a Roman Catholic, but I could not see the logic of it. On the other hand I should say, if reason be so weak, a body of priests would be weaker, and I am not going to accept their verdict, but I will abide by my reason, because with all its weakness there is some chance of my getting at truth through it.... We should, therefore, follow reason, and also sympathise with those who do not come to any sort of belief, following reason. For it is better that mankind should become atheist by following reason than blindly believe in millions of gods on the authority of anybody. What we want is progress.... No theories ever made man higher.... The only power is in realisation and that lies in ourselves and comes from thinking. Let men think.... The glory of man is that he is a thinking being.... I believe in reason and follow reason, having seen enough of the evils of authority, for I was born in a country where they have gone to the extreme of authority."[1]

The basis of both science and religion (as Vivekananda understood it) being the same—knowledge or

of matter above the Vedas, and the science of the spirit above the Bible. Astronomy and geology, anatomy and physiology, botany and chemistry are the Living Scriptures of the God of nature. Philosophy, logic, ethics, yoga, inspiration, and prayers are the Scriptures of the God of the soul. In the 'New Faith' (*that is to say, the one that he was preaching*) everything is scientific. Do not mystify your mind with occult mysteries. Do not give yourselves up to dreams and fantasies. But with clear vision and sound judgment, untroubled, prove all things and hold fast what has been proved. In all your beliefs and prayers, faith and reason ought to harmonise into a true Science."

[1] *Practical Vedanta* III, Vol. II, pp. 335-36.

reason—there is no essential difference between them, except in their application; Vivekananda even regarded them as having the same acceptation. He said once that "All human knowledge is but a part of religion."[1] Here he made religion the sum of all knowledge. But at other times with proud independence he extolled "those expressions of religion whose heads, as it were, are penetrating more into the secrets of heaven, though their feet are clinging to earth, I mean the so-called materialistic sciences."[2] "Science and religion are both attempts to help us out of the slavery; only religion is the more ancient, and we have the superstition (*notice this word in the mouth of a passionate believer!*) that it is the more holy...."[3] In what then do they differ? In the field of their application.

"Religion deals with the truths of the metaphysical world, just as chemistry and the other natural sciences deal with the truths of the physical world."[4]

---

[1] *Complete Works*, Vol. VII, p. 103.

[2] Ibid., II, pp. 68-69.

[3] Ibid., VII, p. 103. Vivekananda, it is true, adds that "in a sense it is, because it makes morality a vital point: and science neglects this side." But this expression: "in a sense" safeguards the independence of other points of view.

[4] Ibid., VI, 81. Let us not forget the vital word "combat", already mentioned. It is characteristic of Vivekananda's warrior spirit. To him the work both of science and religion is no cold search for truth, but a hand to hand struggle.

"*Man is man, so long as he is struggling to rise above nature,* and this nature is both internal and external. Not only does it comprise the laws that govern the particles of matter outside us and in our bodies, but also the more subtle nature within, which is, in fact, the motive power governing the external. It is good and very grand to conquer external nature, but grander still to conquer our internal nature. It is grand and good to know the laws that govern the stars and planets; it is infinitely grander and better to know the laws that govern the passions, the feelings, the will, of mankind....This conquering of the inner man belongs entirely to religion." (*Jnana-Yoga: "The Necessity of Religion"*).

And because the field is different, so the method of investigation ought to be different too. That laid down by Vivekananda for religious science, the one belonging to Jnana-Yoga, is opposed to what he thinks defective in that modern science, the comparative history of religions, as studied in the West. Without underrating the interest of such historic researches and their ingenious theories about the origin of ancestral religions, Vivekananda maintains that their methods are too "exterior" to account for so essentially "interior" an order of facts. It is true that the outward appearance of the body and face can, to the practised eye, reveal the constitution and state of health. But without a knowledge of anatomy and physiology it is impossible to know the nature of a living being. In the same way a religious fact can only be known through the acquired practice of introspective observation; this method is essentially psychological, even infra-psychological; a chemistry of the spirit—the purpose is to discover the first element, the cell, the atom!

"If I know a particle of a lump of clay, I should know the whole of its nature, its birth, its growth, its decline, and its end. Between the part and the whole there is no difference but time. The cycle is completed more or less rapidly."

In this case the first essential is to practise inner analysis in order to discover the spiritual atom. When it has been discovered and sifted into its primary elements, they can then be rearranged, and the next step is to attempt to deduce the principles. "The intellect has to build the house; but it cannot do so without brick, and alone it cannot make bricks."[1]

---

[1] Introduction to Jnana-Yoga, Vol. VI, p. 41 et seq.

Jnana-Yoga is the surest method of penetrating to the bottom of the elemental facts, and it is at this stage that it uses the practical methods of Raja-Yoga.

First the physiology of the mind, the sensorial and motor organs, the brain centres, must be studied minutely. Then the mind-substance, which according to the Sankhya philosophy is part of matter distinct from the soul, must be analysed, followed by the mechanism of the perceptions and their intellectual processes. The real exterior universe is an unknown $x$. The universe that we know is $x+$ (or$-$) the mind (in its function of perceptive faculty) which gives it the imprint of its own conditions. The mind can only know itself through the medium of the mind. It is an unknown $y+$ (or$-$) the conditions of the mind. Kant's analysis was familiar to Vivekananda. But centuries before Kant, Vedantic philosophy had already predicated and even surpassed it,[1] according to Vivekananda's testimony.

Spiritual work groups itself into two different and complementary stages; Pravritti, Nivritti; to advance and then retire in a circular movement. Wise metaphysical and religious method begins with the second of them: Negation or Limitation.[2] Like Descartes, the Jnani makes a clean sweep and seeks a point of stability before he starts rebuilding. The first essential is to test the foundations and to eliminate all causes of illusion and error. The Jnana-Yoga, is, therefore, primarily a searching critic of the conditions of knowledge—time, space, causality, etc.; and it reconnoitres

[1] Lecture given at Harvard on the *Vedanta Philosophy* (March 25, 1896) and *Introduction to Jnana-Yoga*.

[2] Lectures given in London on *Maya*, II, October 1896; *Maya and the Evolution of the Conception of God*.

the frontiers of the mind in detail before it crosses them.

\*

But who gives him permission to cross them? What is it that convinces him that beyond the conditions of the mind the real $x$ or $y$ exists, the only reality? Here is obviously the point of bifurcation between the religious and the scientific spirit that have travelled so far as companions. But even here at the parting of the ways they are still very close to each other. For what is implied in the two pursuits of religion and science? The search for Unity—whatever may be its nature—and a tacit faith in itself—that by means of the mind it will be able to lay down provisionally such a pregnant hypothesis that it will be capable of being immediately perceived and definitely accepted, and such an intense and profound intuition that it will enlighten all future investigation.

"Do you not see whither science is tending? The Hindu nation proceeded through the study of the mind, through metaphysics and logic. The European nations start from external nature, and now they too are coming to the same results. We find that searching through the mind we at last come to that Oneness, that Universal One, the Internal Soul of everything, the Essence, the Reality of everything.... Through material science we come to the same Oneness...."[1]

"Science is nothing but the finding of Unity. As soon as science would reach perfect unity, it would stop from further progress because it would reach the goal. Thus chemistry could not progress further, when it would discover one element out of which all others could be made. Physics would stop when it would be

[1] *Complete Works*, Vol. II, p. 140.

able to fulfil its services in discovering one energy of
which all the others are but manifestations...and the
science of religion become perfect when it would discover Him who is the one life in the universe of death.
...Religion can go no farther. This is the goal of all
science.''[1]

Unity then is the necessary hypothesis upon which
the constructions of science rest. In the science of religion this supposed, essential Unity has the value of the
Absolute.[2] And the work of Jnana-Yoga, when it has
explored and delimited the finite, is to connect itself
to this keystone of the infinite, by parting the fragile
and closely interwoven spider's webs of the intersecting
arcs.

But it is in this web of the mind that the religious
savant of India definitely parts company with the only
methods acceptable to the European rationalist. In
order to bridge the gulf between the bounds of his
senses and the Absolute, he appeals within his own
organism to a new order of experiences that have never
been countenanced by Western science. And this to
him is Religious Experience, in the true meaning of
the term.

I have just spoken of the "bricks" with which "the
intellect has to build the house." Those of the Indian
Yogi have lain unused in our workshops.

Western science proceeds by experiment and reason.
In neither case does it attempt to come out of the circle
of relativity, either with regard to external nature
or its own mind. Its hypothesis of Unity as the pivot
of phenomena remains suspended in the void; it is

[1] *Complete Works*, Vol. I, pp. 14-15.
[2] Lectures on Maya: IV, *The Absolute and Manifestation.*

less an essence than a provisional premiss, although it is the vital link in the chain of reason and fact. But as long as the nail holds, nobody either knows or cares to know to what it is fixed.

The Vedantic sage admires the divinatory courage (however it may seek to excuse itself) of Western science and the integrity of its work; but he does not believe that its methods can ever lead him to the attainment of that Unity which is absolutely essential to him.[1] It appears to him that Western religions can no more free themselves from the anthropomorphic conception of their Gods,[2] than the sciences can rise beyond a reality having the same stature as the human mind.[3] But the universe that contains all the universes must be found. The solution of the problem is the discovery of the *nescio quid* which is to be the common property

[1] He is perhaps wrong. Science has not said its last word. Einstein has appeared since Vivekananda. He never foresaw the "Transcendental Pluralism" whose latent germs in the new thought of the West are rising from the furrow ploughed by wars and revolutions. *Cf.* Boris Yakowenko: *Vom Wesen des Pluralismus*, (1928, Bonn), which has taken as its motto the words of H. Rickert: "*Das All ist nur als Vielheit zu begreifen.*" ("The whole is only intelligible in multiplicity.")

[2] Here he is quite wrong. Unfortunately the Indian Vedanta is ignorant of the deep meaning of great Christian mysticism, which transcends, just as does the highest Vedantism, the limits of the images and forms employed by and for popular anthropomorphism. But it is to be feared that Christian teachers of the second rank with whom he has had to deal are almost as ignorant.

[3] It would not appear that Vivekananda was familiar with the high speculations of modern science, or with mathematics of several dimensions, non-Euclidian geometry, the "logic of the infinite", and epistemology, "the science of sciences" of the Cantorians, "which ought to teach us what the sciences would be if there were no learned men." (*Cf.* Henri Poincaré: *Dernières Pensées* and *La Science et l' Hypothèse*). But it is probable that he would have sought to turn them in some way to the science of religion. And as a matter of fact I can see in them flashes of a religion as yet unaware of itself, the most vital flame of modern Western faith.

of the whole universe, of the lower as well as of the higher worlds. The ancient thinkers of India declared that the further they went from the centre, the more marked was differentiation, and the nearer they approached to the centre, the more they perceived the nearness of Unity. "The external world is far away from the centre; and so there is no common ground in it where all the phenomena of existence can meet." There are other phenomena besides that of the external world: mental, moral, and intellectual phenomena; there are various planes of existence: if only one is explored the whole cannot be explained. The necessary condition is then to attain the centre from which all the diverse planes of existence begin. This centre is within us. The ancient Vedantists, in the course of their explorations, finally discovered that at the innermost core of the soul was the centre of the whole universe.[1] Therefore it must be reached. The mine must be drilled, dug, seen, and touched. And that is the real function of religion, in the Hindu sense, since,

[But it must be remembered that scientific *speculation* is not really science which must demonstrate every truth by experiment and observation before it can accept it. All these that M. Rolland mentions, are rather speculations than actual scientific facts. The superconscious and transcendental truths cannot be scientifically tested. Hence the inherent deficiency of science.—*Publisher*.]

[1] *Jnana-Yoga: "Realisation"* (October 29, 1896). Vivekananda gives a general analysis of the Katha Upanishad, and in particular paraphrases the profound legend of young Nachiketas, a seeker after truth, talking to the beautiful God of death, Yama.

Christian mysticism has made the same discovery. It is the rock-bottom of soul, "*der allerverborgenste, innerste, tiefe Grund der Seele*." Sometimes it is called the ground, sometimes the peak of the soul," said the great Tauler. "The soul in this profundity has a likeness and ineffable nearness to God.... In this deepest, most inner, and most secret depth of the soul, God essentially, really, and substantially exists."

And by God the whole universe is necessarily implied.

"The particular quality of this centre (of the soul)," so writes the Salesian, J. P. Camus, "is to assemble in a lofty fashion the whole action

as we have seen, it is primarily if not entirely a question of *fact*. Vivekananda goes so far as to dare to write: "It is better not to believe than not to have felt," (that is to say, perceived and experimented). Here the strange scientific need that was always mixed with his religion emerges clearly.

Further, this special science claims to make use of special transcendental experiments.

"Religion," says Vivekananda, "proceeds from the struggle to transcend the limitations of the senses." It must there discover its "true germ."[1] "In all organised religions their founders...are declared to have gone into states of mind...in which they came face to face with a new series of facts, relating to what is called the spiritual kingdom.[2] Thus a tremendous statement is made by all religions: that the human mind at certain moments transcends not only the limitations of the senses, but also the power of reasoning," and

of the powers and to give them the same impetus that the first motive power gave to the spheres inferior to it."

(*Traité de la Réformation intérieure selon l'esprit du B. Francois de Sales*, Paris, 1631. *Cf.* Brémond: *Métaphysique des Saints*, Vol. I, p. 56.)

The whole treatise is devoted to the exploration of this "centre of the soul." And this voyage of exploration has naturally a cosmic character as with the Vedantists.

[1] *Jnana-Yoga: "The Necessity of Religion"* (a lecture given in London).

Vivekananda imagined that the first impulsion to this research came to man through dreams that communicated to him the first confused notion of immortality. "Mankind found out...that during the dream state it is not that man has a fresh existence....But by this time the search had begun...and they continued inquiring more deeply into the different stages of the mind, and discovered higher stages than either the waking or the dreaming."

[2] Ibid. "Some exception," adds Vivekananda, "may be taken in the case of the Buddhists....But even the Buddhists find an eternal moral law, and that moral law was not reasoned out in our sense of the word, but Buddha found it, discovered it, in a supersensuous state."

that it then comes into the presence of facts outside
the realm of the senses and reason.[1]

Naturally we are not obliged to believe these facts
without having seen and proved them. Our Hindu

[1] It is worth noticing that, after Vivekananda, Aurobindo Ghose has
gone one step further, and has replaced intuition among the normal
processes of the scientific mind:

"The fault of practical reason is its excessive submission to the
apparent fact, the reality of which it can test at once, and its lack of
sufficient courage to carry the deepest facts of potentialities to their
logical conclusion. That which is, is only the realisation of an anterior
potentiality in the same way that the present potentiality is only an
index of a posterior realisation." (*The Life Divine*).

"Intuition exists, as veiled, behind our mental operations. Intuition
brings to man those brilliant messages from the Unknown, which are
only the beginning of his higher consciousness. Logical reason only steps
in afterwards to see what profit it can make from this rich harvest.
Intuition gives us the idea of something behind and beyond all that
we know and seem to be: this something always seems to us to be in
contradiction to our less advanced reason and to our normal experience;
and it drives us to include the formless perception in our positive ideas
of God, of Immortality, etc., and we use it to explain Him within the
mind."

So intuition plays the part of quartermaster and intelligence of the
Mind, while reason is the rank and file of the army bringing up the
rear. The two are not separated, as in Vivekananda's case, by a kind
of ceiling between two floors. There is continuity as of a wave, or of all
currents belonging to the regular river of Knowledge. The limits of
science have disappeared. Even the ideas of God and Immortality etc.,
and all that constituted religion properly speaking, in Aurobindo's
exposition, are no more than means whereby the soul expresses that
distant life of Reality, which today precedes logical reason, but which
reason will attain on the morrow.

This is the stage of progress arrived at in these days by the mind of
India in its conception of the "living", the "living whole", wherein
religious intuition is incorporated in the strict limits of science.

[Swami Vivekananda refers to the superconscious states in which one
experiences truths and realities which neither one's senses nor reason
can ever perceive and conceive. Even Aurobindo cannot deny this. As
regards the subsequent systematisation of those experiences, the Swami
also repeatedly said that the superconscious realisations are not *against*
reason. In fact the entire Vedanta philosophy is the rationalisation of
superconscious experiences. But one cannot stick to the normal life
and yet expect superconscious revelations. This barrier there will
always be, unless men are normally born with superconscious
perception.—*Publisher*.]

friends will not be surprised if we maintain a sane reserve with regard to them. We merely follow their own rule of scientific doubt: "If thou hast not touched, believe not!" And Vivekananda lays down the scientific rule that if one single experience has ever taken place in some branch of knowledge, it might have taken place before and should be possible to reproduce afterwards. The inspired person has no right to claim the special privilege that it should not be repeated. If then certain truths (those of the highest order) are the fruits of the religious experience of certain "chosen" people, such religious experience must inevitably happen again. And the object of the science of Raja-Yoga is to lead the mind to this same experimental region.[1]

---

[1] "Fixing the mind on the lotus of the heart or on the centre of the head, is what is called *Dhâranâ*. Limited to one spot, making that spot the base, a particular kind of mental wave rises; these are not swallowed up by other kinds of waves, but by degrees become prominent while all the others recede and finally disappear; next the multiplicity of these waves gives place to unity and one wave only is left in the mind, this is *Dhyâna*, meditation. When no basis is necessary, when the whole of the mind has become one wave, one-formedness, it is called *Samâdhi*. Bereft of all help from places and centres, only the meaning of thought is present (that is to say, the inner part of perception, of which the object was the effect). If the mind can be fixed on the centre for twelve seconds it will be a *Dhâranâ*, twelve such *Dhâranâs* will be *Dhyâna*, and twelve such *Dhyânas* will be a *Samâdhi*." And that is pure bliss of spirit. (*Raja-Yoga*, Chapter VIII, summary from the *Kurma Purana*).

For curiosity's sake I have given this ancient summary of the mechanics of intellectual operation, but would not urge anybody to abandon themselves to it without due consideration; for such exercises of lofty inward tension are never without danger. Indian masters have never ceased to put rash experimenters on their guard. For my part I hold that reason is so weak in modern post-war Europe that what remains should not be endangered by abnormalities—at least unless the scientific will has been developed rigorously to control their effects. It is for observers of this order that I have given the above train of objective research. I am appealing to free and firm reason. I have no ulterior motive to let loose a new sect of "Enlightened Ones" upon Europe! But he who believes in science cannot bear that it should leave one path of research unexplored through ignorance, indifference, contempt, or prejudice.

It is open to every single person to attempt this auto-education! But here I merely wish to show the final result of these observations, namely that in all organised religions of a higher order, when abstract spiritual facts have been discovered and perceived, they are then condensed into one Unity, "either in the form of an Abstract Presence, of an Omnipresent Being, of an Abstract Personality called God, of a Moral Law, or of an Abstract Essence underlying every existence."[1]

And in this last form which is that of Vedantic Advaitism, we find ourselves so close to the aim of pure Science that they can hardly be distinguished. The main difference is in the gesture with which the runners arrive at the tape: Science accepts and envisages Unity as the hypothetical term for its stages of thought, giving them their right bearings and co-ordinating them. Yoga embraces Unity and becomes covered with it as with ivy. But the spiritual results are practically the same. Modern science and the philosophical Advaita conclude that "the explanations of things are to be found within their own nature, and that no external beings or existences are required to explain what is going on in the Universe." And the corollary of this same principle, that "everything comes from within," is "the modern law of Evolution. The whole meaning of evolution is simply that the nature of the things is reproduced (in its growth), that the effect is nothing but the cause in another form, that all the potentialities of the effect were present in the cause, that the whole of creation is but an evolution and not a creation."[2]

[1] *Jnana-Yoga:* "*The Necessity of Religion.*"
[2] *Complete Works,* Vol I, p. 372.

Vivekananda frequently insists on the close relationship between the modern theory of evolution and the
theories of ancient metaphysics and Vedantic cosmog-
ony.[1] But there is this fundamental distinction between the evolutionary hypothesis and the Hindu
hypothesis: that the first is as compared to the second
only one wing of the whole building, and that Evolution
has as counterpart (or buttress) in Vedantism the same
periodic Involution that Vedantism itself possesses. All
Hindu theory is in its very nature founded on the theory
of Cycles. Progression presents itself in the form of
successive sets of waves. Each wave rises and falls; and
each wave is followed by another wave which in its
turn rises and falls:

"Even on the grounds of modern research, men
cannot be simply an evolution. Every evolution presupposes an involution. The modern scientific man
will tell you that you can only get the amount of
energy out of a machine that you have put into it.
Something cannot be produced out of nothing. If a
man is an evolution of the mollusc, then the perfect man,
the Buddha-man, the Christ-man was involved in the
mollusc.... Thus we are in the position of reconciling
the scriptures with modern light. That energy, which
manifests itself slowly through various stages until it
becomes the perfect man, cannot come out of nothing.
It existed somewhere; and if... the protoplasm is

[1] In his lecture on the Vedanta: "Replies to Questions," he tried
to establish a rapprochement between Evolutionism and the ancient
theory of the Creation, or, more precisely, the "projection" of the
universe by the action of Prâna (primordial Force) on Âkâsha
(primordial Matter) beyond which is Mahat, or the Cosmic Mind, in
which they can both be reabsorbed. He cites the celebrated commentaries of the old Patanjali, speaking of the change of one kind of being
into another kind of being "by the filling in of nature."

the first point to which you can trace it, that protoplasm must have contained the energy."[1] Discussions
are futile between "those who claim that the aggregate
of materials we call the body is the cause of the manifestation of the force we call the soul," and those who
make the soul the cause of the body. They explain
nothing. "Where did the force come from, which is
the source of these combinations we call the soul or
the body?...It is more logical to say that the force
which takes up the matter and forms the body is the
same which manifests through that body....It is
possible to demonstrate that what we call matter does
not exist at all. It is only a certain state of force. What
is the force which manifests itself through the body?
...In old times in all the ancient scriptures this
power, this manifestation of power, was thought to be
of bright substance, having the form of this body, and
which remained even after this body fell. Later on,
however, we find a higher idea coming—that this
bright body did not represent the force. Whatever has
form...requires something else....So, that something was called the soul, the Atman, in Sanskrit...
One, omnipresent, the Infinite."[2]

[1] In one of his lectures on *Jnana-Yoga* (*"Realisation"*, October 29,
1896) Vivekananda gave to this conception of Evolution-Involution a
striking, terrifying form akin to that of Wells, that of *Contrary
Evolution:* "If we are developed from animals, the animals also
may be degraded men. How do you know that it is not so?...You
find a series of bodies, rising in gradually ascending scale. But
from that how can you insist that it is always from the lower up-
wards, and never from the higher downwards?...I believe that
the series is repeating itself in going up and down." Certain words
of Goethe give colour to the new thought that these lines would have
found echoes within him, of which he was aware but which he
repulsed with anger and horror.

[2] *Jnana-Yoga:* II. *"The Real Nature of Man"* (Lecture delivered
in London).

But how did the Infinite become finite? The great
metaphysical problem[1] wherein the genius of the centuries has been spent in tirelessly building up again its
crumbling scaffoldings! For to suppose the Infinite, to
prove it and touch it, is only a beginning. It must be
united to that which by its own definition is fated never
to attain it. Christian metaphysicians[2] in this direction
have brought to the task an architectural genius of intelligence, order, and harmony, akin to that of their
companions, the master builders of our cathedrals;
and their magnificent constructions seem to me as
superior in beauty (there can be no certitude on this
point) to Hindu metaphysical creations as Chartres or
Amiens to a European, compared to Madura with its
mountains of sculptured stone piled into pinnacles like
white-ant-heaps. (But there can be no question of
higher or lower between two fruits of Nature equally
gigantic, and corresponding to the laws of expression
arising from two different mental climates.)

The reply of India is that of the Hindu Sphinx—
Maya. It was by transmitting the laws of the spirit
through the screen of Maya that "the Infinite" became "finite". Maya, her screen, her laws, and the
spirit are the product of a sort of "Degeneracy of the
Absolute", diluted into "phenomena". Will is situated one stage higher, although Vivekananda does not
accord it the place of honour claimed for it by Schopenhauer.[3] He places it at the threshold of the Absolute:

[1] And the mathematical as well (*Cf.* H. Poincaré: *Dernières
Pensées.*)
[2] Here again this great art with its Gothic vaulting, spanning the
Infinite and the finite, would seem to have been inherited from
Alexandria and the East, through Plotinus and Denis the Areopagite.
[3] He quotes him and contradicts him in his lecture on *Maya*: IV.
"*The Absolute and Manifestation.*"

it guards the door. It is both its first manifestation and
its first limitation. It is a composite of the real Self,
beyond causality, and the minds that dwell on this side.
Now, no composite is permanent. The will to live
implies the necessity of death. The words "Immortal
Life" are then a contradiction in terms. The real
eternal being is beyond life and death.

But how has this absolute Being become mingled
with the will, the mind, the relative? Vivekananda
replies from the Vedanta: "It has never been mingled.
You are this absolute Being, you have never changed.
All that changes is Maya, the Screen held between the
real Me and you." And the very object of Life, of individual life, of the life of generations, of all human
evolution, of the unceasing ascension of Nature from
the lowest order where dawns existence—is the gradual
elimination of the Screen. The very first illumination
of the mind makes a tiny hole, through which the
glance of the Absolute filters. As the mind grows, the
hole grows larger, so that, although it is not true to
say that what is seen through it tomorrow is truer or
more real than what is seen today (it is all equally
real), each day a wider surface is covered until the
whole Screen is lost, and nothing remains but the
Absolute.[1]

"Calmed are the clamours of the urgent flesh;
The tumult of the boastful mind is hushed;
Cords of the heart are loosened and set free;
Unfastened are the bondages that bind;
Attachment and delusion are no more!
Ay! There sounds sonorous the Sound

[1] *Introduction to Jnana-Yoga*, Vol. VI of *Complete Works*, p. 41
*et seq.*

Void of Vibration. Verily! Thy Voice!"[1]

At that evocation the spirit rises up....

"People are frightened when they are told this."
This immense ONE will submerge them. "They will
again and again ask you if they are not going to keep
their individuality. What is individuality? I should
like to see it." Everything is in a state of flux, everything changes...."There is no more individuality"
except at the end of the way. "We are not yet individuals. We are struggling towards individuality: and
that is the Infinite, our real nature.[2] He alone lives
whose life is the whole universe, and the more we concentrate on limited things the faster we go towards
death. Those moments alone we live, when our lives
are in the universe, in others; living in this little life is
death, simply death, and that is why the fear of death
comes. The fear of death can only be conquered, when
man realises that so long as there is one life in this universe, he is living....The apparent man is merely a
struggle to express, to manifest this individuality, which
is beyond...."

[1] Lines from the Bengali poem of Vivekananda: *A Song I Sing to
Thee. Complete Works*, Vol. IV, p. 511.

[2] The same affirmation that Christian Mysticism makes, when it
reassures those who tremble at the idea of their "inexistent"
individuality being swamped. In his beautiful classical style, the
Dominican Chardon writes:

"Divine Love transforms the creature into God in such a way
that it is engulfed in Deified being, in the depths of Divine perfection; nevertheless the creature being does not there cast off its being,
but rather loses its non-being, and, like a drop of water mingling
with the sea wherein it is engulfed, it loses the fear of becoming
less....It takes on divine being in the being of God in whose
abyss it is submerged...like a sponge soaked and filled with
water to its full capacity, floating on the bosom of a sea, whose very
dimension, height, depth, length, and breadth are infinite...."
(*La Croix de Jésus*, 1647. *Cf.* Brémond: *Métaphysique des Saints*,
II, pp. 46-47.)

And this struggle is accomplished by the evolution of nature leading step by step to the manifestation of the Absolute.[1]

But an important corrective must be added to the doctrine of Evolution. Vivekananda takes it from Patanjali's theory on "the Filling in of Nature."[2] The struggle for life, the struggle for existence, and natural selection have only their full and rigorous application in the inferior orders of nature, where they play the determining part in the evolution of species. But at the next stage, which is the human order, struggle and competition are a retrogression rather than a contribution to progress. For, according to pure Vedantic doctrine, the aim of all progress, its absolute fulfilment, being the real nature inherent in man, nothing but certain obstacles can prevent him from reaching it. If he can successfully avoid them, his highest nature will manifest itself immediately. And this triumph of man can be attained by education, by self-culture, by meditation and concentration, above all, by renunciation and sacrifice. The greatest sages, the sons of God, are those who have attained. Hence Hindu doctrine, although it respects the general law of scientific Evolution, offers to the human spirit the possibility of escape from the slow ascent of thousands of years, by means of rushing great wings sweeping it up to the summit of the staircase.[3] And so it matters little whether or not we discuss the philosophic probability of the whole system, and the

---

[1] *Jnana-Yoga:* II. *"The Real Nature of Man."*

[2] It was in the course of discussions on Darwinism that Vivekananda expressed these ideas at Calcutta towards the end of 1898. (*The Life of the Swami Vivekananda*, Chapter xxxiv).

[3] The evening of the day on which Vivekananda had made this statement to the superintendent of the Zoological Gardens at Calcutta, who was much struck by it, he took up the discussion again at the

strange hypothesis of Maya on which it depends—this explanation is undoubtedly fascinating and corresponds to certain hallucinated instincts of universal sensibility, but it demands an explanation in its turn; and no one has made it, no one has been able to make it; each person comes back in the last resort to this argument: "I feel that it is so. Do you not feel the same?"[1] Yes,

house of Balaram, before a group of friends. He was asked whether it was true that Darwinism applied to the vegetable and animal orders and not to the human, and if so why during his campaigns of oratory he insisted so much on the primordial necessity of bettering the material conditions of life for the Indians. He then had one of his outbreaks of passionate anger and cried, "Are you men? You are no better than animals, satisfied with eating, sleeping, and propagating and haunted by fear! If you had not had in you a little rationality you would have been turned into quadrupeds by this time. Throw aside your vain bragging, your theories and so forth, and reflect calmly on the doings and dealings of your every-day life. Because you are governed by animal nature, therefore I teach you to seek for success first in the struggle for existence, and to attend to the building up of your physique, so that you shall be able to wrestle all the better with your mind. The physically weak, I say again and again, are unfit for the realisation of the Self! When once the mind is controlled and man is master of his self, it does not matter whether the body remains strong or not, for then he is not dominated by it...."

Here once again it is clear that whatever criticisms may be levelled at Vivekananda's mysticism, lack of virility can never be one of them.

[1] Here is the kernel, the "experience" of the Infinite and Illusion. The rest is only the outer shell. The science of religion has taken a wrong turning if it confines itself to the comparative study of ideas and rites. Why does the influence of ideas and religious systems spread from one human group to the other? Because they depend on certain personal experiences. For instance the likenesses between the doctrines of Philo, Plotinus, and the first Christians may be examined. But this fact is not emphasised that Philo, Plotinus, and the first Christians realised similar "Illuminations". Now the chief point of interest is that these religious "experiences" often took place under the same forms in the case of men of different race and time. How is it possible to estimate the value of such experiences? Perhaps by a new science of the mind, armed with a more supple, and finer instrument of analysis than the incomplete rough methods of the psycho-analyst and his fashionable descendants. Certainly not by the dialectic of ideas. The systems constructed by Plotinus or Denis have a value as intellectual architecture, which is open to dispute; but

I do. I have often perceived with flaming clarity the unreality of this apparent world, the spider's web bathed in sunlight, where, Ariel-fashion, Liluli balances herself,[1] "Lila" the player, Maya, the laughing one —I have seen the screen! And for a long time I have seen through it—ever since as a child, with beating heart I surreptitiously made the hole of light bigger with my fingers. But I have no intention of adducing that as a proof. It is a vision. And I should have to lend my eyes to other people before I could communicate it to them. Maya or Nature (what matters the name?) has given each man his own eyes. And they all belong to Maya, whether we say mine, thine, or yours, and all are clothed with the rays of our Lady of Illusion. I am no longer sufficiently interested in myself to attribute to myself any special privileges. Love your eyes and what they see just as much as I love my own. Let them remain as free as mine!

It therefore follows, my European friends, that I am not trying to prove to you the truth of a system, which, like all others, being human, is only hypothesis. But what I hope I have shown you is the loftiness of the hypothesis, and that, whatever it may be worth as a metaphysical explanation of the universe, in the realm of fact it is not contrary to the most recent findings of modern Western science.

---

this architecture always goes back ultimately to the perception of the Infinite and to the efforts of reason to build a fitting temple for it. Rational criticism only reaches the superstructure of the church. It leaves the foundations and the crypt intact.

[1] Allusion to an Aristophanesque Comedy of Romain Rolland: *Liluli*, which symbolises "Illusion".

## III

## THE UNIVERSAL SCIENCE-RELIGION

OF a truth, religion, as Vivekananda understood it, had such vast wings that when it was at rest it could brood over all the eggs of the liberated Spirit. He repudiated no part of sincere and sane forms of Knowledge. To him religion was the fellow citizen of every thinking man, and its only enemy was intolerance.

"All narrow, limited, fighting ideas of religion must be given up.... The religious ideals of the future must embrace all that exists in the world and is good and great, and at the same time, have infinite scope for future development. All that was good in the past must be preserved; and the doors must be kept open for future additions to the already existing store. Religions (*and sciences are included under this name*) must also be inclusive, and not look down with contempt upon one another, because their particular ideals of God are different. In my life, I have seen a great many spiritual men, a great many sensible persons, who did not believe in God at all, that is to say, not in our sense of the word. Perhaps they understood God better than we can ever do. The Personal idea of God or the Impersonal, the Infinite, Moral Law or the Ideal Man— these all have come under the definition of religion...."[1]

"Religion", for Vivekananda, is synonymous with "Universalism" of the spirit. And it is not until "religious" conceptions have attained to this universalism,

[1] *The Necessity of Religion.*

17

that religion is fully realised. For, contrary to the belief of all who know it not, religion is a matter for the future far more than for the past. It has only just begun.

"...It is said sometimes that religions are dying out, that spiritual ideas are dying out of the world. To me it seems that they have just begun to grow.... So long as religion was in the hands of a chosen few, or of a body of priests, it was in temples, churches, books, dogmas, ceremonials, forms, and rituals. But when we come to the real, spiritual, universal concept, then and then alone religion will become real and living; it will come into our very nature, live in our every moment, penetrate every pore of our society, and be infinitely more a power for good than it has ever been before."[1]

The task awaiting us today is to join the hands of the two brothers who are now at law with each other over a field, the perfect exploitation of which needs their united efforts—religion and science. It is a matter of urgent necessity to re-establish "a fellow-feeling between the different types of religion...and between types of religious expression coming from the study of mental phenomena—unfortunately even now laying exclusive claim to the name of religion—and those expressions of religion whose heads...are penetrating more into the secrets of heaven...the so-called materialistic sciences."[2]

It is hopeless to attempt to turn one brother out for the benefit of the other. You can dispense with neither science nor religion.

"Materialism prevails in Europe today. You may

[1] *The Necessity of Religion.*
[2] Ibid.

pray for the salvation of the modern sceptics, but they do not yield, they want reason."[1]

What then is the solution? To find a *modus vivendi* between the two. Human history made that discovery long ago, but forgetful man forgets and then has to re-find his most precious discoveries at great cost.

"The salvation of Europe depends on a rationalistic religion."

And such a religion exists; it is the Advaita of India, Non-Dualism, Unity, the idea of the Absolute, of the Impersonal God,[2] "the only religion that can have any hold on intellectual people."

"The Advaita has twice saved India from materialism. By the coming of Buddha, who appeared in a time of most hideous and widespread materialism.... By the coming of Shankara, who when materialism had reconquered India in the form of the demoralisation of the governing classes and of superstition in the lower orders, put fresh life into Vedânta, by making a rational philosophy emerge from it." "We want today that bright sun of intellectuality, joined with the heart of Buddha, the wonderful, infinite heart

---

[1] *The Absolute and Manifestation*, Vol. II of *The Complete Works of Swami Vivekananda*, p. 139.

[2] Vivekananda merely made the mistake common to most Indians of thinking that the Advaita was the sole possession of India. The Absolute is the keystone of the great arch of Christian metaphysics as well as of certain of the highest philosophies of the ancient world. It is to be hoped that India will study these other expressions of the Divine Absolute at first hand and so enrich her own conception.

[Swami Vivekananda was aware of the few Christian saints who reached the state analogous to the Advaita. But a mere recognition of the Absolute in any metaphysics is not Advaita. The crucial point is the conception of the individual as that Absolute and the outlook of life that follows from that conception. Does Christianity consider that the individual is the Absolute? Does it permit man to say, "I am God Himself"? We think not.—*Publisher*.]

of love and mercy. This union will give us the highest philosophy. Science and religion will meet and shake hands. Poetry and philosophy will become friends. This will be the religion of the future, and if we can work it out we may be sure that it will be for all times and all peoples. This is the one way that will prove acceptable to modern science, for it has almost come to it. When the scientific teacher asserts that all things are the manifestations of one force, does it not remind you of the God of whom you hear in the Upanishads: 'As the one fire entering into the universe expresses itself in various forms, even so that One Soul is expressing itself in every soul and yet is infinitely more besides'? "[1]

The Advaita must be superadded to science without yielding anything to the latter, but without demanding that it should change its teachings. Let us recall once again their common principles:

"The first principle of reasoning is that the particular is explained by the general—until we come to the universal.... A second explanation of knowledge is that the explanation of a thing must come from inside and not from outside."[2] The Advaita satisfies these two principles, and pursues their application into its own chosen field. "It pushes it to the ultimate generalisation," and claims to attain to Unity, not only in its radiation and its effects, rationally deduced from experiments, but in itself, in its own source. It is for you to control its observations! It does not avoid control, rather it seeks for it. For it does not belong to those religious camps that entrench themselves behind the mystery of their revelations. Its doors and windows are

---

[1] *The Absolute and Manifestation*, Vol. II of the *Complete Works*, p. 140.
[2] *Reason and Religion*, Vol. I of the *Complete Works*, pp. 369-70.

wide open to all. Come and see! It is possible that
it is mistaken—so may you be, so may we all. But
whether it is mistaken or not, it works with us to build
the same house on the same foundations.

*

At bottom, although its Mission is to unite, the
stumbling block to mutual understanding, the great
obstacle to the coincidence of mankind is the word
"God", for that word embraces all possible ambiguities
of thought, and is used oppressively to bandage the
clear eyes of Freedom. Vivekananda was fully aware of
this fact: "...I have been asked many times, 'Why do
you use that old word God?' Because it is the best
word for our purpose,[1]... because all the hopes, aspirations, and happiness of humanity have been centred in
that word. It is impossible now to change the word.
Words like these were first coined by great saints, who
realised their import and understood their meaning.
But as they become current in society, ignorant people
take these words, and the result is, they lose their spirit
and glory. The word God has been used from time
immemorial, and the idea of this cosmic intelligence,
and all that is great and holy associated with it." If we
reject it, each man will offer a different word, and the
result will be a confusion of tongue, a new tower of
Babel. "Use the old word, only use it in the true spirit,
cleanse it of superstition, and realise fully what this
great ancient word means.... You will know that
these words are associated with innumerable majestic
and powerful ideas; they have been used and worshipped by millions of human souls and associated by

---

[1] At the end of this chapter will be found the final definition of
his "purpose" by Vivekananda.

them with all that is highest and best, all that is rational, all that is lovable, and all that is great and grand in human nature...."

Vivekananda specifies for us that "it is the sum total of intelligence manifested in the universe," concentrated in its own centre. It is "the universal intelligence." And "all the various forms of cosmic energy, such as matter, thought, force, intelligence, and so forth, are simply the manifestation of that cosmic intelligence."[1]

This "cosmic intelligence" is tacitly implied in scientific reasoning. The chief difference is that with science it remains a piece of mechanism, while Vivekananda breathes life into it. Pygmalion's statue comes alive. Even if the learned man can accuse the religious man of an induction not scientifically proven, the induction itself is not necessarily anti-scientific. It is as easy to say that Pygmalion modelled the statue as that Pygmalion was modelled by it. In any case they both came out of the same workshop; it would be surprising indeed if life was only to be found in the one while the other was an automaton. Human intelligence implies universal intelligence (to a higher degree than it can either deny or prove). And the reasoning of a religious and learned man like Vivekananda does not seem to me very different in scientific quality from that "Logic of the Infinite" which admits one part of science, and which Henri Poincaré maintains against the Cantorians.

*

But it is a matter of indifference to the calm pride of him who deems himself the stronger whether Science

[1] *Jnana-Yoga:* "*The Cosmos: The Macrocosm.*" (New York, Jan. 19, 1896.)

accepts free Religion, in Vivekananda's sense of the term, or not: for his Religion accepts Science. It is vast enough to find a place at its table for all loyal seekers after truth. It has its dreams of Empire, but it respects the liberties of all, provided that there is mutual respect. One of Vivekananda's most beautiful visions, the one to which he devotes the final Essays of his *Jnana-Yoga*, is his invocation to a "Universal Religion".[1]

Now that the reader has learnt so much about him, he will not apprehend any Taylorism of thought that seeks to impose its own colour upon the rainbow of the world, not even perfect white, the only one that could claim to replace the other colours since it contains them all. Vivekananda could not have too many spiritual modes for the music of Brahman. Uniformity for him spelt death. He rejoiced in the immense diversity of religions and ideas. Let them ever grow and multiply!...

"I do not want to live in a grave-like land: I want to be a man, in a world of men....Variation is the sign of life....Difference is the first sign of thought. ...I pray that they (sects) may multiply so that at last there will be as many sects as human beings.... Whirlpools and eddies occur only in a rushing, living stream....It is the clash of thought that awakes thought....Let each have his individual method of thought in religion....This thing exists already. Each one of us is thinking in his own way, but this natural course has been obstructed all the time and is still being obstructed."

---

[1] I. *The Way to the Realisation of a Universal Religion;* II. *The Ideal of a Universal Religion.* (Lectures given in Pasadena, California, Jan., 1900, and in Detroit, 1896.)

And so unsilt the souls of men! Open again the "bysses",[1] as my neighbours of Valais say, when they release the running water to irrigate their fields. But it is different from the thirsty Valais which has to economise water and pass the pitcher from hand to hand, turn and turn about.... The water of the soul is never scarce. It flows on all sides. In every religion in the world a mighty reservoir of life is contained and accumulated, however much those who deny it in the name of the lay religion of reason may seek to deceive themselves. No single great religion, said Vivekananda, throughout the course of twenty centuries has died, with the possible exception of Zoroastrianism. (And was he sure of this? On the contrary he was certainly mistaken on this point).[2] Buddhism, Hinduism, Islam, Christianity, continue to grow in numbers and quality.

[1] This is a system of irrigation used by the Swiss peasants in the mountains. The water is released at fixed times over the fields by each peasant in turn.

[2] Within the last few months a very interesting study by Dr. J. G. S. Taraporewala has appeared in the beautiful Review published by Rabindranath Tagore's University at Santiniketan: *The Visva-Bharati Quarterly*, January, 1929, which vindicates "The Place of Iran in Asiatic Culture," and traces the evolution of Zoroastrianism and the schools founded upon it not only in the East but in the West. It would appear that in the first century B.C. several currents flowed from their source in Asia Minor, where the cult of Ahura-Mazda was preserved. From one of them in the age of Pompey sprang the cult of Mithra, which almost conquered the West. The other, passing through the South-West of Arabia and Egypt, influenced the beginnings of the Gnostic school, whose capital importance for Christian metaphysics is well known; and this same current gave birth in Arabia to a school of mystics, known to Mahomet; Musulman Sufis have their origin in this mixture of Zoroastrianism and Islam. Hence the vital energy possessed by these religious germs, which seemed to have been stamped out and to have vanished, becomes apparent.

[This, however, does not show that Zoroastrianism has not dwindled away. Zoroastrianism survives only in India where "a handful of Parsis is all that remains." This is the fact and cannot be denied.—*Publisher*.]

(Further, the religion of science, of liberty, and of human solidarity is also growing.) What is growing less in mankind is the death of the spirit, absolute darkness, negation of thought, absence of light: the very feeblest ray is faith, although it is unaware of itself. Each great system of faith, whether "religious" or "lay", "represents one portion of Universal Truth and spends its force in converting that into a type." Each, therefore, should unite with the others, instead of being mutually exclusive. But petty individual vanities, due mainly to ignorance, upheld by the pride and interest of priestly castes, have always in all countries and all ages made the part claim to be the whole. "A man goes out into the world, God's menagerie, with a little cage in his hand," and thinks he can shut everything inside it. What old children they are! Let them chatter and mock at each other. Despite their foolishness, each group has a living, beating heart, its own mission, and its own note in the complete harmony of sound; each one has conceived its own splendid but incomplete ideal: Christianity its dream of moral purity; Hinduism, spirituality; Islam, social equality;...etc.[1] And each group is divided into families each with a different temperament: rationalism, puritanism, scepticism, worship of the senses or of the mind....They are all of diverse and graded powers in the divine economy of the Being, as it ceaselessly advances. Vivekananda uttered this profound saying, which we should do well to read, mark, learn, and inwardly digest:

"Man never progresses from error to truth, but

[1] It goes without saying that here he has emphasised only the characteristic aspects of much more vast and complex structures of thought. The responsibility for this simplification is Vivekananda's.

from truth to truth, from lesser truth to higher truth."

If we have understood him properly, our watchword should be: "Acceptance", and not exclusion—"not even toleration, which is an insult and blasphemy": for each man grasps what he can of Truth. You have no right to "tolerate" him, any more than he has the right to tolerate you or me. We all have equal rights, and equal shares in Truth. We are fellow-workers; let us fraternise.

"I accept all religions that were in the past, and worship with them all; I worship God with every one of them....Is God's book finished or is it still a continuous revelation going on? It is a marvellous book, —these Spiritual Revelations of the world. The Bible, the Vedas, the Koran, and all other sacred books are but so many pages, and an infinite number of pages remain yet to be unfolded....We stand in the present, but open ourselves to the infinite future. We take in all that has been in the past, enjoy the light of the present, and open every window of the heart for all that will come in the future. Salutation to all the prophets of the past, to all the great ones of the present, and to all that are to come in the future!"[1]

\*

These ideas of universalism and spiritual brotherhood are in the air today. But each man, consciously or

[1] *The Way to the Realisation of a Universal Religion.*

These ideas were the same as Ramakrishna's, and also of Keshab Ch. Sen, who played the part of a forerunner. About 1866 in his Lecture on *Great Men*, Keshab said:

"Hindu brethren, as ye honour your prophets, honour ye likewise the illustrious reformers and great men of Christendom....To you, my Christian brethren, also, I humbly say—As ye honour your prophets, honour ye likewise the prophets of the East."

"One religion shall be acknowledged by all men,...yet each

unconsciously, seeks to turn them to his own profit. Vivekananda had no need to live in the age of the memorable "War of Right and Liberty", to denounce and expose the exploitation of idealism, and the colossal hypocrisy, which has culminated in this modern age in Geneva, Paris, London, Berlin, Washington and their satellites, either allied or enemy. "Patriotism," he said, "is a phase of a profession of quasi-religious faith." But it is too often a mask for selfishness. "Love, Peace, Brotherhood, etc. have become to us mere words....Each one cries: 'Universal Brotherhood! We are all equal....'" And then immediately afterwards: "Let us form a sect!" The need for exclusivism re-appears at a gallop with a badly concealed fanatical passion, which makes secret appeal to all the wickedness in men: "it is a disease."[1]

Do not then be deceived by words! "The world is too full of blustering talk." Men who really feel the brotherhood of men do not talk much about it; they do not make speeches to the "Society of Nations", they

nation shall have its own peculiar and free mode of action...so shall the various races and tribes, and nations of the world, with their own peculiar voice and music, sing His glory; but all their different voices and modes of chanting shall commingle in one sweet and swelling chorus—one universal anthem."

This was the *leit-motif* of all his lectures in England (1870)— to embrace in one communion all nations and races, and so to found a Universal Religion—for each religion to share with the others whatever it had of good—so that in time the Future Church of the world might be built.

Finally, in the *Epistle to my Indian Brethren*, (1880), these words occur, which might have come from Vivekananda, or from the soul of Ramakrishna:

"Let your word of command be the infinite progression of the spirit!...Let your faith be all-embracing, not exclusive! Let your love be universal charity!...Do not form a new sect. But accept all sects. Harmonise all beliefs...."

[1] For all the preceding and following portions *cf.* "*The Ideal of a Universal Religion.*"

do not organise Leagues: they work and they live.
Diversity of ritual, myths, and doctrines (both clerical
and lay) does not trouble them. They feel the thread
passing through them all, linking the pearls into a
necklace.[1] Like the rest, they go to draw water from
the well, each with his own pitcher or receptacle whose
form is taken by the water. But they do not quarrel
about the form. It is all the same water.[2]

By what practical means can silence and peace be
secured among the brawling throng squabbling round
the well? Let each one drink his own water and
allow the rest to drink theirs! There is plenty for
everybody. And it is stupid to want everyone to drink
God out of the same pitcher. Vivekananda breaks in
in the midst of the hubbub and tries to make the disputants listen to at least two maxims of conduct, two
provisional rules:

The first: "Do not destroy!"—Build, if you can
help to build. But if you cannot, do not interfere!
It is better to do nothing than to do ill. Never speak
a word against any sincere conviction. If you have one,
serve it, but without harming the servants of different
convictions. If you have none, look on! Be content
with the role of a spectator.

The second: "Take man as he stands, and from
thence give him a lift" along his own road. You need
not fear that that road will take you out of your way.
God is the centre of all the radii, and each of us is

---

[1] "I am the thread that runs through all these different ideas, and
each one is a pearl," said the Lord Krishna. (Quoted by Vivekananda
in his lecture on *Maya and the Evolution of the Conception of God*.)

[2] Vivekananda took this beautiful figure from his Master Ramakrishna, who clothed it in still more picturesque colour. (*Cf.* Vol. I,
p. 79.)

converging towards Him along one of them. And so, as Tolstoy says, "We shall all meet again, when we have arrived." The differences disappear at the centre —but only at the centre; and variety is a necessity of nature: without it there would be no life. So, help her, but do not get it into your head that you can produce or even lead her! All that you can do is to put a protective hedge round the tender plant. Remove the obstacles to its growth and give it enough air and space so that it can develop, but nothing else. Its growth must come from within. Abandon the idea that you can give spirituality to others.[1] Each man's master is his own soul. Each has to learn for himself. Each has to make himself. The only duty another can have is to help him to do so.

This respect for human individuality and its freedom is admirable. No other religion has possessed it to this degree, and with Vivekananda it was part of the very essence of his religion. His God was no less than all living beings, and every living being ought therefore to be free to develop. One of the most ancient Upanishads says, "Whatever exists in this universe, is to be covered with the Lord." And Vivekananda explained this saying thus: "We have to cover everything with the Lord Himself, not by a false sort of optimism, not by blinding our eyes to the evil, but by really seeing God in everything:" in good and

---

[1] I think that it is necessary to add the following correction to the phrase—which corresponds to the intimate thought of Vivekananda:
"Spirituality is in everybody, but more or less latent, suppressed, or freely poured out. He who is a fountain of it, is by his presence alone, by the very music of his gushing waters, a call, an awakener of hidden springs, which did not know of their own existence or were afraid to avow it. In this sense there is certainly a gift—a living communication of spirituality."

evil, in sin and in the sinner, in happiness and misery, in life and in death. "If you have a wife it does not mean that you are to abandon her, but that you are to see God in your wife." He is in her, in you, in your child. He is everywhere.

Such a sentiment does not rob life of any of its riches; but it makes its riches and its miseries the same.

"Desire and evil itself have their uses. There is a glory in happiness, there is a glory in suffering.... As for me, I am glad I have done something good and many things bad; glad I have done something right, and glad I have committed many errors, because every one of them has been a great lesson....Not that you should not have property, have all you want...only know the truth and realise it....All belongs to the Lord, put God in your every movement....The whole scene changes and the world, instead of appearing as one of woe and misery, will become a heaven."

This is the meaning of the great saying of Jesus: "The Kingdom of Heaven is within you." Heaven is not beyond. It is here and now. Everything is heaven. You have only to open your eyes.[1]

"Awake, arise and dream no more!
...Be bold, and face
The Truth! Be one with it! Let visions cease,
Or, if you cannot, dream but truer dreams,
Which are Eternal Love and Service free."[2]

[1] The preceding belongs to the seventh lecture on *Jnana-Yoga: "God in Everything."* (London, October 27, 1896).

[2] This undated poem of Vivekananda embraces within these five lines all the principal forms of Yoga: the abstract Advaita, and in the last two verses the Yoga of Bhakti and of Karma.

"Each soul," he commented again,[1] "is potentially divine. The goal is to manifest this Divine within, by controlling nature external and internal. Do this, either by work, or worship, or psychic control, or philosophy[2]—by one or more or all of these—and be free. This is the whole of religion. Doctrines or dogmas, or rituals or books, or temples or forms are but secondary details."

And the great artist, that he was at bottom,[3] compared the universe to a picture, only to be enjoyed by the man who had devoured it with his eyes without any interested intention of buying or selling it:

"I never read of any more beautiful conception of God than the following: 'He is the Great Poet, the Ancient Poet: the whole Universe is His poem, coming in verses and rhythms, written in infinite bliss.' "[4]

\*

But it is to be feared that such a conception will seem too aesthetic and inaccessible except for those artistic spirits who are produced with less parsimony by the torrents of Shiva watering the races of Bengal than by our pale smoke-begrimed sun. And there is another danger—its direct opposite—that races accessible to this ideal of ecstatic enjoyment will remain

[1] *Raja-Yoga*, (*Complete Works*, Vol. I).

[2] Hence by one of the four Yogas—Karma, Bhakti, Raja, Jnana, or by all four.

[3] "Do you not see," he said to Miss MacLeod, "that I am first and foremost a poet?"—a word that may be misunderstood by Europeans; for they have lost the meaning of true poetry—the flight of faith—without which a bird becomes a mere mechanical toy.

In London in 1895, he said, "The artist is a witness of the beautiful. Art is the least selfish form of pleasure in the world."

And again, "If you cannot appreciate harmony in Nature, how can you appreciate God, who is the sum of all harmony?"

And finally, "Of a truth, Art is Brahman."

[4] *God in Everything*.

inactive spectators of it, enervated and enslaved by the *Summus Artifex*[1] in the same way that the Roman Emperor enervated and enslaved his subjects by the games.... "*Circenses*".

Those who have followed me up to this point, know enough of Vivekananda's nature, with its tragic compassion binding him to all the sufferings of the universe, and the fury of action, wherewith he flung himself to the rescue, to be certain that he would never permit nor tolerate in others any assumption of the right to lose themselves in an ecstasy of art or contemplation.

And because he knew in his own case and in that of his companions the dangerous attraction of this sovereign Game,[2] he constantly forbade it to those who

---

[1] It will be remembered that Nero so styled himself: "The Supreme Artist"—and that the people of Rome submitted to all his tyrannies provided he gave them "*panem et circenses*" (bread and circuses).

[2] Lila—the Game of God.

"You know," he said to Sister Nivedita, "we have a theory that the universe is God's manifestation of Himself just for fun, that the Incarnations came and lived here 'just for fun'! Play—it was all play. Why was Christ crucified? It was mere play....Just play with the Lord. Say: it (life) is all play, it is all play."

And this profound and terrible doctrine is at the bottom of the thought of all great Hindus—as of many mystics of all ages and all climes. Is not the same idea to be found in Plotinus, who visualised this life as a theatre, where "the actor continually changes his costume," where the crumbling of empires and civilisations "are changes of scene or personages, the cries and tears of the actors..."?

But in what concerns Vivekananda and his thought, the time and place of his teaching must never be forgotten. Often he wished to create a reaction against a tendency that he considered diseased in his auditors, and he used excess against excess, although for him harmony was the final truth.

On this occasion he was rather embarrassed by the emotionalism of the excellent Nivedita who was saying good-bye to him in too sentimental a way. He said to her, "Why not part with a smile? You worship sorrow..." And in order to rebuke his English friend who took everything too seriously, he showed her the doctrine of the Game.

were dependent upon his guidance, and he sought by preaching to turn their dreaming eyes to what he called a "practical Vedanta".[1]

With him it was true that "the knowledge of Brahman is the ultimate purpose, the highest destiny of man. But man cannot remain absorbed in Brahman all the time."[2] Such absorption is only for exceptional moments. "When he emerges from that Ocean of rest and without a name," he must go back to his buoy. And it is less the egoism of *"carpe diem!"* than that of *"Memento quia pulvis es"*[3] and considerations of safety that keep him afloat in the water.

"If a man plunges headlong into foolish luxuries of the world without knowing the truth, he has missed his footing....And if a man curses the world, goes out into a forest, mortifies his flesh, and kills himself little by little by starvation, makes his heart a barren

His antipathy to morose devotion, to the spirit of self-crucifying grief, was explained in the curious apologue of Nârada:

There are great Yogis among the gods. Nârada was one. One day he was passing through a forest and saw a man who had been meditating until the white ants had built a large mound round him. Further on he saw another man jumping about for joy under a tree. They asked Nârada, who had gone to heaven, when they would be judged worthy to attain freedom. To the man surrounded by the ant-heap Nârada said, "After four more births," and the man wept. To the dancer, he said, "After as many births as there are leaves on that tree." And knowing that deliverance was coming so soon, the dancer went on jumping for joy....Immediately he was free. (*Cf.* the conclusion of *Raja-Yoga*.)

[1] The title given to four lectures in *Jnana-Yoga* (London, November, 1896). *Cf.* also his lectures in the same collection: *The Real and the Apparent Man, Realisation, God in Everything,* and the *Conversations and Dialogues* (with Sharat Chandra Chakravarty, 1898, Belur), Vol. VII of the *Complete Works,* p. 107 *et seq.*

[2] Conversations and Dialogues, Vol. VII of the *Complete Works,* p. 197 *et seq.*

[3] The meaning of these two phrases is well known: "Enjoy the day," is the Epicurean: the second, "Remember you are but dust," is the Christian.

waste, kills out feeling, and becomes harsh, stern, and dried up, that man also has missed the way."[1]

The great motto we must take back into the world from illuminations, that have revealed to us for an instant the Ocean of Being in the full and Biblical sense—the word that sooner or later will allow us to attain our End—is also the motto of the highest code of ethics: "Not me, but thou!"

This "Me" is the product of the hidden Infinite in its process of exterior manifestation. We have to remake the path the inverse way towards our original state of infinitude. And each time that we say, "Not me, my brother, but thou!" we take one step forward.[2]

"But," says the selfish disciple to whose objections Vivekananda on that day replied with the patience of an angel—(a thing contrary to his habit)—"but if I must always think of others, when shall I contemplate the Atman? If I am always occupied with something particular and relative, how can I realise the Absolute?"

"My son," replied the Swami sweetly, "I have told

---

[1] *God in Everything.*

[2] "Religious realisation does all the good to the world. People are afraid that when they attain to it, when they realise that there is but One, the fountains of love will be dried up, that everything in life will go away, and that all they love will vanish for them.... People never stop to think that those who bestowed the least thought on their own individualities have been the greatest workers in the world. Then alone a man loves when he finds that the object of his love is not a clod of earth, but the veritable God Himself. The husband will love the wife...that mother will love the children more who thinks that the children are God Himself.... That man will love his greatest enemy....Such a man becomes a world-mover for whom his little self is dead and God stands in his place.... If one-millionth part of the men and women who live in this world simply sit down and for a few minutes say, 'You are all God, O ye men and O ye animals, and living beings, you are all manifestations of the one living Deity!' the whole world will be changed in half an hour." (*The Real and the Apparent Man*).

you that by thinking intensely of the good of others, by devoting yourself to their service, you will purify your heart by that work and through it you will arrive at the vision of Self which penetrates all living beings. Then what more will you have to attain to? Would you rather that Realisation of Self consisted in existing in an inert way like a wall or a piece of wood?"[1]

"But," insisted the disciple, "all the same, that which the Scriptures describe as the Self withdrawing into its real nature, consists in the stopping of all the functions of the mind and all the work."

"Oh!" said Vivekananda, "that is a very rare condition and difficult to attain and does not last long. How then will you spend the rest of the time? That is why, having realised this state, the saint sees the Self in all beings, and possessed of this knowledge he devotes himself to their service, so that thus he uses up all the Karma (work) that remains to be expended by the body. That is the condition that the Shastras describe as Jivan-Mukti (Freedom in Life)."[2]

An old Persian tale describes in an exquisite form this state of bliss wherein a man, already free through knowledge, gives himself to others so naturally that he forgets everything else in them. A lover came to knock at the door of his well-beloved. She asked, "Who is there?" He replied, "It is I." The door did not open. He came a second time, and called, "It is I, I am here!" The door remained closed. The third time the voice asked from within, "Who is there?" He replied, "Well-beloved, I am thou!" And the door opened.[3]

---

[1] I have condensed the conversation.
[2] Vol. VII of *Complete Works*, p. 111 *et seq.*
[3] Quoted by Vivekananda, second lecture on the *Practical Vedanta.*

But this lovely parable, whose charm Vivekananda could appreciate more highly than most, represented too passive an ideal of love to contain the virile energy of a leader of the people. We have seen how constantly he flagellated and abused the greedy bliss of the Bhaktas. To love with him meant to love actively, to serve, to help. And the loved one was not to be chosen, but was to be the nearest, whoever he happened to be, even the enemy in process of beating you, or the wicked or unfortunate—particularly such; for their need was the greatest.[1]

"My child, if you will only believe me," he said to a young man of middle class, who vainly sought peace of mind by shutting himself up in his house, "first of all you must begin by opening the door of your room, and looking about you.... There are some miserable people in the neighbourhood of your house. You will serve them with your best. One is ill: you will nurse him. Another is starving: you will feed him. A third is ignorant: you will teach him. If you wish peace of mind serve others! That is what I have to say!"[2]

[1] "Do you not remember what the Bible says, 'If you cannot love your brother whom you have seen, how can you love God whom you have not seen?'...I shall call you religious from the day you begin to see God in men and women, and then you will understand what is meant by turning the left cheek to the man who strikes you on the right." (*Practical Vedanta*—II in *Complete Works*, Vol. II.)

This was the thought constantly expressed during his last years in Tolstoy's *Journal*.

[2] On his return from the West in 1897.

"The watchword of all well-being...is not I, but thou. Who cares whether there is a heaven or a hell, who cares if there is a soul or not, who cares if there is an unchangeable God or not? Here is the world and it is full of misery. Go out into it as Buddha did, and struggle to lessen it or die in the attempt. Forget yourselves, this is the first lesson to be learnt, whether you are a theist or an

We have insisted enough upon this aspect of his teaching and need not dwell upon it further.

But there is another aspect that must never be forgotten. Usually in European thought "to serve" implies a feeling of voluntary debasement, of humility. It is the "*Dienen, dienen*" of Kundry in *Parsifal*. This sentiment is completely absent from the Vedantism of Vivekananda. To serve, to love, is to be the equal of the one served or loved. Far from abasement, Vivekananda always regarded it as the fullness of life. The words "Not me, but thou!" do not spell suicide, but the conquest of a vast empire. And if we see God in our neighbour, it is because we know that God is in us. Such is the first teaching of the Vedanta. It does not say to us, "Prostrate yourselves!" It tells us, "Lift up your head! For each one of you carries God within him. Be worthy of Him! Be proud of it!" The Vedanta is the bread of the strong. And it says to the weak, "There are no weak. You are weak because you wish to be."[1] First have faith in yourselves. You yourselves are the proof of God![2] "Thou art That!" Each of the pulsations of your blood sings it. "And the universe with its myriads of suns with one voice repeats the word: 'Thou art that!'"

---

atheist, whether you are an agnostic or a Vedantist, a Christian or a Mohammedan." (*Practical Vedanta*—IV).

[1] "As soon as you say, 'I am a little mortal being', you are saying something which is not true, you are giving the lie to yourselves, you are hypnotising yourselves into something vile and weak and wretched." (*Practical Vedanta*—I).

*Cf.* the last Interviews with Sharat Chandra: "Say to yourself, 'I am full of power, I am the happy Brahman.'...Brahman never awakes in those who have no self-esteem."

[2] "How do you know that a book teaches truth? Because you are truth and feel it....Your godhead is the proof of God Himself." (*Practical Vedanta*—I).

Vivekananda proudly proclaims, "He who does not
believe in himself is an atheist."[1]

But he goes on to add, "But it is not a selfish faith.
...It means faith in all, because you are all. Love
for yourselves means love for all, for you are all one."[2]

And this thought is the foundation of all ethics:

"Unity is the test of truth. Everything that makes
for Oneness is truth. Love is truth, and hatred is false,
because hatred makes for multiplicity. It is a disinte-
grating power."

Love then goes in front.[3] But love, here, is the
heart-beat, the circulation of blood without which the
members of the body would be paralysed. Love still
implies the Force.

At the basis of everything then is Force, Divine
Force. It is in all things and in all men. It is at the
centre of the Sphere and at all the points of the circumference. And between the two each radius diffuses
it. He who enters and plunges into the vestibule is
thrown out in flames, but he who reaches the centre

---

[1] Boshi Sen quoted to me the brave words that go far to explain
Vivekananda's religion—uttered in contradicting the Christian
hypothesis that we should bear a human hell here to gain a Paradise
hereafter:

"I do not believe in a God who will give me eternal bliss in heaven,
and who cannot give me bread here."

This fearlessness in the great Indian belief with regard to God must
never be forgotten. The West, which likes to represent the East as
passive, is infinitely more so in its dealings with the Divinity. If,
as an Indian Vedantist believes, God is in me, why should I accept
the indignities of the world? Rather it is my business to abolish
them.

[2] *Practical Vedanta*—I.

[3] Intellect here is relegated to the second place. "The intellect is
necessary, but...is only the street-cleaner, the policeman"; and the
road will remain empty if the torrent of love does not pour down it.
And then the Vedantist went on to quote Shankara and *The Imitation
of Christ*.

returns with hundredfold increased energy, and he who realises it in contemplation, will then realise it in action.[1] The gods are part of it. For God is all in all. He who has seen God will live for all.[2]

Hence by a perpetual coming and going between the infinite Self of perfect knowledge and the Ego implied in the Game of Maya, we maintain the union

[1] Here again Christian mysticism arrives at the same results. Having achieved the fact of union with God, the soul has never been freer to direct its other activities of life without violating any single one of them. One of the most perfect examples of this mastery is a Tourangelle of the seventeenth century, our St. Theresa of France, Madame Martin—Marie of the Incarnation—to whom the Abbé Brémond has devoted some of the most beautiful pages (half a volume) of his monumental *Histoire littéraire du sentiment religieux en France*, Vol. IV, particularly Chapter 5: "*La vie intense des mystiques*". This great soul, who in a strictly Christian setting went through all the stages of mystic union like Ramakrishna: sensibility, love, intelligence (up to the highest intellectual intuition), came down from them to practical action without for a single instant losing contact with the God she had realised. She said of herself,

"A divine intercourse was established between God and the soul by the most intimate union that can be imagined....If the person has important occupations she will strive ceaselessly to cultivate what God was doing in her. That itself comforted her, because when the senses were occupied and diverted, the soul was free of them.... The third state of passive prayer is the most sublime....The senses are then so free that the soul who has reached it, can work without distraction in any employment required by its condition....God shines at the depth of the soul...."

And her son, who was also a saint, Don Claude, wrote:

"As exterior occupations did not in the least interrupt interior union in her case, so inner union did not prevent her exterior functions. Martha and Mary were never in better accord in what they did, and the contemplation of the one did not put any hindrance in the way of the action of the other...."

I cannot too strongly urge my Indian friends—(and those of my European friends who are usually ignorant of these riches)—to make a careful study of these admirable texts. I do not believe that so perfect a genius of psychological analysis has been allied in any mysticism to the vigour of profound intuition as in the life of this bourgeoisie from the valley of the Loire in the time of Louis XIII.

[2] So said the present great Abbot of the Math of Belur, Shivananda, in his presidential address to the first Convention of the Ramakrishna Math and Mission (April 1, 1926):

of all the forces of life. In the bosom of contemplation we receive the necessary energy for love and work, for faith and joy in action, for the framework of our days. But each deed is transposed into the key of Eternity. At the heart of intense action reigns eternal calm,[1] and the Spirit at the same time partakes of the struggles of life, and yet floats above the strife. Sovereign equilibrium has been realised, the ideal of the Gita and of Heraclitus!

" Εξ των διαφεροντων καλλιστην αρμονιαν." [2]

"If the highest illumination aims at nothing short of effacing all the distinctions between the individual soul and the universal soul, and if its ideal be to establish a total identity of one's own self with Brahman existing everywhere, then it naturally follows that the highest spiritual experience of the aspirant cannot but lead him to a state of exalted self-dedication to the welfare of all. He makes the last divine sacrifice by embracing the universe after transcending its limitations, which are the outcome of ignorance."

[1] *Cf.* the Gita, which here is the inspiration of the *Practical Vedanta*—I.

[2] That is to say, "from discords (weave) the most beautiful harmony."

# IV

## CIVITAS DEI
## THE CITY OF MANKIND

In the two words equilibrium and synthesis Vivekananda's constructive genius may be summed up. He embraced all the paths of the spirit: the four Yogas in their entirety, renunciation and service, art and science, religion and action from the most spiritual to the most practical. Each of the ways that he taught had its own limits, but he himself had been through them all, and embraced them all. As in a quadriga, he held the reins of all four ways of truth, and he travelled towards Unity[1] along them all simultaneously. He was the personification of the harmony of all human Energy.

But the formula could not have been discovered by the brilliant intellect of the "Discriminator", if his own eyes had not seen its realisation in the harmonious personality of Ramakrishna. The angelic Master had instinctively resolved all the dissonances of life into a Mozartian harmony, as rich and sweet as the Music of the Spheres. And hence the work and the thought of the great disciple was all carried out under the Sign of Ramakrishna.

"The time was ripe for one to be born, who in one

---

[1] It was precisely this faculty in him that struck Ramakrishna, and later Girish Ghose who said of him to the disciples: "Your Swami is as much Jnani and pandit as the lover of God and humanity." He realised the four forms of Yoga—Love, Action, Knowledge, and Energy—and maintained the balance among them.

body would have the brilliant intellect of Shankara and
the wonderfully expansive infinite heart of Chaitanya;
one who would see in every sect the same spirit working,
the same God; one who would see God in every being,
one whose heart would weep for the poor, for the weak,
for the downtrodden, for every one in this world,
inside India or outside India; and at the same time
whose grand brilliant intellect would conceive of such
noble thoughts as would harmonise all conflicting sects,
not only in India but outside of India, and bring a
marvellous harmony....The time was ripe, it was
necessary that such a man should be born...and I
had the good fortune to sit at his feet....He came,
the living spirit of the Upanishads, the accomplishment of Indian sages, the sage for the present day...
the harmony...."[1]

Vivekananda wished this harmony, that had come to
fruition in one privileged being and had been enjoyed
by a few select souls, to be extended to the whole of
India and the world. Therein lies his courage and originality. He may not have produced one single fresh
idea: he was essentially the offspring of the womb of
India, one of the many eggs laid by that indefatigable
queen ant throughout the course of ages....But all
her different ants never combined into an ant-hill.
Their separate thoughts seemed to be incompatible,
until they appeared in Ramakrishna as a symphony.
The secret of their divine order was thus revealed to
Vivekananda,[2] and he set out to build the City—

---

[1] Lecture on the *Sages of India. Cf.* the lectures on the *Vedanta
in its Application to Indian Life* (on his return from America) and
on the *Vedanta in all its Phases* (Calcutta), from which I have taken
some phrases and inserted them in the main text.

[2] "It was given to me to live with a man who was as ardent a

*Civitas Dei—the City of Mankind* on the foundation of this golden concrete.

But he had not only to build the city, but the souls of its inhabitants as well.

The Indian representatives, who are the authorities for his thought, have acknowledged that he was inspired in its construction by the modern discipline and organised effort of the West* as well as by the Buddhist organisation of ancient India.[1]

He conceived the plan of an Order whose central Math, the mother house, was to "represent" for centuries to come "the physical body of Ramakrishna."[2]

This Math was to serve the double purpose of providing men with the means "to attain their own liberation, so that they might prepare themselves for the progress of the world and the betterment of its conditions." A second Math was to realise the same object for women. These two were to be disseminated throughout the world; for the Swami's journeys and his cosmopolitan education had convinced him that the

Dualist, as ardent an Advaitist, as ardent a Bhakta as a Jnani. And living with this man first put it into my head to understand the Upanishads and the texts of the Scriptures from an independent and better basis than by blindly following the commentators....I came to the conclusion that these texts are not all contradictory....The one fact I found is, that...they begin with Dualistic ideas... and end with a grand flourish of Advaitic ideas. I have seen the harmony which is at the back of all the faiths of India, and the necessity of the two interpretations—as the geocentric and the heliocentric theories of astronomy...." (*The Vedanta in its Application to Indian Life. Cf. The Vedanta in all its Phases.*)

\* As regards the *form* only and that also to a certain extent.— *Publisher.*

[1] It was also the ideal of the Vedas: "Truth is one, but it is called by different names."

[2] According to Swami Shivananda. They are the very expressions reproduced by the present Abbot of the Math, Shivananda, and their nearness to the conception of the Church of Christ is obvious.

aspirations and needs of humanity at the present time
are universally one. The day seemed to have dawned
for the "great India" of old to resume its ancient
mission: that of evangelising the earth. But unlike
"God's chosen peoples" in the past, who have interpreted their duty in the narrow sense of spiritual imperialism, implying the right to inflict their own uniform and tight-fitting casque, the Vedantist missionary
according to his own law respects the natural faith of
each individual. He desires only to reawaken the Spirit
in man, "to guide individuals and nations to the conquest of their inner kingdom, by their own ways which
are best suited to them, by the means corresponding
best to the needs from which they suffer most." There
is nothing in this to which the proudest nationalism
can take exception. No nation is asked to forsake
its own ways.[1] It is asked rather to develop the God
that is in them, to the fullest, highest degree.

But, like Tolstoy, whose thought, the offspring of
his good sense and kind heart, was unknown to him,
Vivekananda saw that his first duty was towards his
nearest neighbour, his own people. Throughout the
pages of this book the trembling of India incarnate in
him has appeared again and again. His universal soul
was rooted in its human soul; and the smallest pang
suffered by its inarticulate flesh sent a repercussion
through the whole tree.

He himself was the embodied unity of a nation
containing a hundred different nations, wherein each
nation, divided and subdivided into castes and sub-

---

[1] "We ought never to think of taking away the characteristics of
a nation, even if it can be proved that its character is composed of
faults." (Vivekananda, 1899-1900).

castes, seems like one of those diseased persons whose blood is too liquid to congeal—and his ideal was unity, both of thought and of action. His claim to greatness lies in the fact that he not only *proved* its unity by reason, but *stamped* it upon the heart of India in flashes of illumination. He had a genius for arresting words and burning phrases hammered out white-hot in the forge of his soul so that they transpierced thousands. The one that made the deepest impression was the famous phrase: "Daridra-Nârâyana" (the beggar God).... "The only God that exists, the only God in whom I believe...my God the miserable, my God the poor of all races." It may justly be said that India's destiny was changed by him, and that this teaching re-echoed throughout Humanity.

Its mark is to be found, a burning scar—like the spear-thrust that pierced the heart of the Son of Man on the Cross—in the most significant happenings in India during the last twenty years. When the Swarajist party of the Indian National Congress (a purely political body) triumphed in the Calcutta Municipal Council, they drew up a programme of communal work called the "Daridra-Narayana" Programme. And the striking words have been taken up again by Gandhi and are constantly used by him. At one and the same time the knot was tied between religious contemplation and service of the lower orders. "He surrounded service with a divine aureole and raised it to the dignity of a religion." The idea seized upon the imagination of India; and relief works for famine, flood, fire, and epidemic, such as were practically unknown thirty years before, Sevâshramas and Sevâ-samitis (retreats and societies for social service) have multiplied throughout the country. A rude blow had been struck at the selfishness of a purely contemplative faith. The rough words, which I have already quoted, uttered by the kindly Ramakrishna: "Religion is not for empty bellies...," embody the teaching that the desire to awaken spirituality in the heart of the people must be deferred until they have first been fed. Moreover, to bring them food is not enough; they must be taught how to procure it and work for it themselves. It is necessary to provide the wherewithal and the education. Thus it embraced a complete programme of social reform, although it held strictly aloof, in accordance with the wishes of Vivekananda, from all political parties. On the other hand it was the solution of the age-long conflict in India between spiritual life and active life. The service of the poor did not only help the poor, but it helped their helpers even more effectively. According to the old saying, "He who gives, receives." If Service is done in the true spirit of worship, it is the most efficacious means to spiritual progress. For, "without doubt man is the highest symbol of God and his worship is the highest form of worship on earth."[1]

"Begin by giving your life to save the life of the dying, that is the essence of religion."[2]

So India was hauled out of the shifting sands of barren speculation wherein she had been engulfed for centuries, by the hand of one of her own Sannyasins; and the result was that the whole reservoir of mysticism, sleeping beneath, broke its bounds and spread by

[1] Recalled by Shivananda, the Abbot of the Math, in his Presidential Address of 1926.
[2] Words spoken by Vivekananda during the epidemic of 1899 to a pandit, who complained of not being able to talk to him of religion

a series of great ripples into action. The West ought to be aware of the tremendous energies liberated by these means.

The world finds itself face to face with an awakening India. Its huge prostrate body, lying along the whole length of the immense peninsula, is stretching its limbs and collecting its scattered forces. Whatever the part played in this reawakening by the three generations of trumpeters during the previous century— (the greatest of whom we salute, the genial Precursor: Ram Mohun Roy), the decisive call was the trumpet blast of the lectures delivered at Colombo and Madras.

And the magic watchword was Unity. Unity of every Indian man and woman (and world-unity as well); of all the powers of the spirit—dream and action; reason, love, and work. Unity of the hundred races of India with their hundred different tongues and hundred thousand gods springing from the same religious centre, the core of present and future reconstruction.[1] Unity of the thousand sects of Hinduism.[2] Unity within the vast Ocean of all religious thought and all rivers past and present, Western and Eastern. For—and herein lies the difference between the awakening of Ramakrishna and Vivekananda and that of Ram Mohun Roy and the Brahmo Samaj—in these days India refuses allegiance to the imperious civilisation of

when he came to see him. He replied, "So long as even a single dog in my country is without food, my whole religion will be to feed it."

[1] In his last hour he repeated, "India is immortal if she persists in her search for God. If she gives it up for politics, she will die." The first Indian national movement, the Swadeshi Movement, desired to found its work on this spiritual basis, and one of its leaders, Aurobindo Ghose, vindicated Vivekananda's ideas.

[2] The discovery and declaration of the unity of Hinduism is one of the chief and most original features of Vivekananda's work.

the West, she defends her own ideas, she has stepped into her age-long heritage with the firm intention not to sacrifice any part of it, but to allow the rest of the world to profit by it, and to receive in return the intellectual conquests of the West. The time is past for the pre-eminence of one incomplete and partial civilisation. Asia and Europe, the two giants, are standing face to face as equals for the first time. If they are wise they will work together, and the fruit of their labours will be for all.

This "greater India", this new India—whose growth politicians and learned men have, ostrich fashion, hidden from us and whose striking effects are now apparent—is impregnated with the soul of Ramakrishna. The twin star of the Paramahamsa and the hero who translated his thoughts into action, dominates and guides her present destinies. Its warm radiance is the leaven working within the soil of India and fertilising it. The present leaders of India: the king of thinkers, the king of poets, and the Mahatma—Aurobindo Ghose, Tagore, and Gandhi—have grown, flowered, and borne fruit under the double constellation of the Swan and the Eagle—a fact publicly acknowledged by Aurobindo and Gandhi.[1]

---

[1] Gandhi affirmed in public that the study of the Swami's books had been a great help to him, and that they had increased his love and understanding of India. He wrote an Introduction to the English edition of the *Life of Sri Ramakrishna*, and has attended some anniversary festivals of Ramakrishna and Vivekananda celebrated by the Ramakrishna Mission.

"The spiritual and intellectual life of Aurobindo Ghose," Swami Ashokananda wrote to me, "has been strongly influenced by the life and teaching of Ramakrishna and Vivekananda. He is never tired of showing the importance of Vivekananda's ideas."

As for Tagore, whose Goethe-like genius stands at the junction of all the rivers of India, it is permissible to presume that in him are

The time seems to me to have come for the rest of
the world, ignorant as yet, except for isolated groups
of Anglo-Saxons, of this marvellous movement, to
profit by it. Those who have followed me in this work
must certainly have noticed how closely the views of
the Indian Swami and his Master are in accord with
many of our secret thoughts. I can bear witness to it,
not only on my own account, but as a result of the
intellectual avowal that has been made to me for the
last twenty years by the hundreds of souls of Europe
and America, who have made me their confidant and
confessor. It is not because they and I have unwittingly been subject to infiltrations of the Indian spirit
which predisposed us to the contagion—as certain
representatives of the Ramakrishna Mission appear to
believe. On this subject I have had courteous discussion with Swami Ashokananda, who starting from the
assumption of the fact that Vedantic ideas are disseminated throughout the world, concluded that this was,
partly at least, the work of Vivekananda and his
Mission. I am quite convinced of the contrary. The
work, thought, and even the name of Vivekananda[1]
are practically unknown to the world in general (a

united and harmonised the two currents of the Brahmo Samaj (transmitted to him by his father, the Maharshi) and of the new Vedantism
of Ramakrishna and Vivekananda. Rich in both, free in both, he
has serenely wedded the West and the East in his own spirit. From
the social and national point of view his only public announcement
of his ideas was, if I am not mistaken, about 1906 at the beginning
of the Swadeshi movement, four years after Vivekananda's death.
There is no doubt that the breath of such a Forerunner must have
played some part in his evolution.

[1] One of the most significant facts has been his complete oblivion
in the philosophic and learned circles that knew him as he travelled
in Europe: thus in the circle of the *Schopenhauer Gesellschaft* I have
had to re-teach, so to speak, Vivekananda's name to the disciples and
successors of Paul Deussen, his host and friend.

fault that I am trying to rectify), and if, among the
deluge of ideas that come to water with their substance the burning soil of Europe and America in these
days, one of the most life-giving and fertilising streams
may be called "Vedantic", that is so in the same way
that the natural speech of Monsieur Jourdain[1] was
"prose" without his knowing it, because it is a natural
medium of thought for mankind.*

What are the so-called essentially Vedantic ideas?
According to the definition of one of the most authoritative spokesmen of modern Ramakrishnite Vedantism, they can be reduced to two principles:

I. *The Divinity of man.*
II. *The essential spirituality of Life.*

And the immediate consequences deduced from them
are:

1. That every society, every state, every religion
ought to be based on the recognition of this All-
Powerful presence latent in man.

2. That, in order to be fruitful, all human interests
ought to be guided and controlled according to the
ultimate idea of the spirituality of life.[2]

These ideas and aspirations are none of them alien
to the West. Our Asiatic friends, who judge Europe
by our bankrupts—our politicians, our traders, our
narrow-minded officials, our "ravening wolves whose
gospel is their maw", the whole of our colonial

---

[1] A popular character in France from Moliere's comedy, *Le Bourgeois
Gentilhomme.*

* On this and the subsequent observations of M. Rolland, see the
book: *The Influence of Indian Thought on the Thought of the West,*
by Swami Ashokananda, Advaita Ashrama, Mayavati, Almora, U.P.—
*Publisher.*

[2] I depend here on a remarkable letter from Swami Ashokananda
(Sept. 11, 1927), which possesses all the weight and value of a mani-

personnel (both the men and their ideas)—have good reason to doubt our spirituality. Nevertheless it is deep and real, and has never ceased to water the subsoil and roots of our great Western nations. The oak of Europe would long ago have been hurled to the ground by the tempests that have raged round it, if it had not been for the mighty spiritual sap rising ceaselessly from its silent reservoir. They accord us a genius for action. But the unflagging feverishness of this age-long action would be impossible without inner fires—not the lamp of the Vestal Virgins, but a Cyclopian crater where the igneous substance is tirelessly amassed and fed. The writer of this work has denounced and disavowed the "Market Place"[1] of Europe, the smoke and cinders of the volcano, with sufficient severity to be able to vindicate the burning sources of our inexhaustible spirituality. He has never ceased to recall their existence and the persistence of "better Europe", both to outsiders, who misunderstand her, and to herself, as she sits wrapped in silence. "*Silet sed loquitur!*"[2] But her silence speaks more loudly than the babel of charlatans. Beneath the frenzy of enjoyment and power consuming themselves in surface eddies of a day or of an hour, there is a persistent and immovable treasure made up of abnegation, sacrifice, and faith in the Spirit.

As for the Divinity of man, such a conception is possibly not one of the fruits of Christianity or of

festo on the Ramakrishna Mission. It was published together with my replies in the journals and reviews of the Mission.

[1] Allusion to the name of one volume of *Jean Christophe* by Romain Rolland, which castigates the ephemeral masters of the West, with their new-fangled ideas.

[2] "She is silent, but she speaks."

Greço-Roman culture,[1] if they are considered separately. But it is the fruit of the engrafted tree of Greco-Roman heroism superimposed upon the vine, whose golden juice is the blood of the Son of God.[2] And whether or no it has forgotten the Christian vine stalk and wine press, the heroic idealism of our democracies in their great moments and their great leaders have retained its taste and scent.[3] A religion whose God has been familiar for nineteen hundred years to the peoples of Europe by the name of the "Son of Man", cannot wonder that man should have taken it at its word and claimed Divinity for himself. The new consciousness

[1] "How did the West come by these ideas?" Swami Ashokananda wrote to me. "I do not think that Christianity and Greco-Roman culture were specially favourable to them. . . ."

But it is possible to answer Swami Ashokananda with the fact that Europe has not been solely made up of Christianised Greco-Roman culture. That is a pretension of the Mediterranean school, which we do not admit. The groundwork of the autochthonous races of the West has been ignored, as well as the tides of the Great Invasions that covered France and *Mittel Europa* with their fertile alluvion. The *"Hochgefühl"* of Meister Eckhart and the great Gothics has been allowed to fall into oblivion:

*"Gott hat alle Ding durch mich gemacht, als ich stand in dem unergrundeten Grunde Gottes."* (Eckhart).

("God has created all things through me, when I stand in the bottomless deeps of God.")

And is it not a phenomenon proving the extraordinary immanence of these flashing intuitions dwelling deep within the soul of the West that they re-emerge at the beginning of the nineteenth century with Fichte, who knew nothing of Hindu thought? (*Die Anweisung zum seeligen Leben*, 1806). Whole passages of Fichte and of Shankara can be placed side by side to show their complete identity. (*Cf.* a study of Rudolf Otto on *Fichte and the Advaita*.)

[2] I have already pointed out that at the beginning of its great religious thought—from its double source of Greece, and Jewish-Christianity—the West rests on similar foundations to those of Vedantism. I propose to devote a long Note in the *Appendices* to a demonstration of this kinship in the great Hellenic systems and those of Alexandrine Christianity: Plotinus and Denis the Areopagite.

[3] The mighty sayings of our great French revolutionaries, such as St. Just, which bear strangely enough the double imprint of the Gospel and of Plutarch, are a striking example.

of his power and the intoxication of his young liberty,
were still more exalted by the fabulous conquests of
science, which in half a century have transformed the
face of the earth. Man came to believe himself God,
without the help of India.[1] He was only too ready to
bow down and worship himself. This state of over-
valuation of his power lasted up to the very eve of the
catastrophe of 1914, which shattered all his foundations. And it is from that very moment that the
attraction and domination of Indian thought over him
can be traced. How is this to be explained?

Very simply. His own paths had led the Westerner
by his reason, his science, and his giant will to the
cross-roads where he met the Vedantic thought, that
was the issue of our great common ancestors, the Aryan
demi-gods, who in the flower of their heroic youth saw
from their high Himalayan plateaus, like Bonaparte
when he had completed the conquest of Italy, the
whole world at their feet. But at that critical moment,
when the test of the strong awaited them (as it appears
under various names in the myths of all countries, and
which our Gospel relates as the Temptation of Jesus
on the mountain), the Westerner made the wrong
choice. He listened to the tempter, who offered him
the empire of the world spread out beneath him. From
the divinity that he attributed to himself he saw and
sought for nothing but that material power represented
by the wisdom of India as the secondary and dangerous

[1] There is ample testimony to the thrill of joy that idealistic
thinkers like Michelet have felt when they have recognised in India
the forgotten ancestor of the *Gospel of Humanity*, which they have
themselves brought forth. This was true in my own case as well.

(*The Gospel of Humanity* is a book by Michelet, from which I
have taken the foreword of my *Life of Ramakrishna*.)

attribute of the inner force that alone can lead man to the Goal.[1] The result is that today the European "Apprentice Sorcerer"[2] sees himself overwhelmed by the elemental powers he has blindly unloosed. For he has nothing but the letter of the formula to control them. He has not been concerned with the Spirit. Our civilisation in its dire peril has vainly invoked the spell of great words: Right, Liberty, Co-operation, the Peace of Geneva or Washington—but such words are void or filled with poisonous gas. Nobody believes in them. People mistrust explosives. Words bring evils in their train, and have made confusion worse confounded. At the present time it is only a profound misunderstanding of the mortal illness from which a whole generation in the West has been suffering that makes it possible for the dregs and the scum who have known how to profit from the situation to murmur: "After us, the Deluge!" But millions of unsatisfied beings find themselves fatally driven to the cross-roads where they must choose between the abdication of what remains of their freedom—implied by the return of the discouraged soul to the park of the dead order of things wherein, though imprisoned, it is warmed and protected by the grease of the flock—and the great void in the

[1] These attributes, these powers, I must remind my readers, were not denied by Vivekananda. He did not underestimate them, as a Christian ascetic might do; they constitute a superior stage than that of ignoble quietude, of the weakness of body and soul which he was never tired of denouncing; but they constitute a lower stage than the terrace whence there is a commanding view of the whole house and the wide circle of the horizon. It must be attained by climbing without stopping. I refer to what I have said in the preceding pages about Raja-Yoga.

[2] The title of a famous and often quoted poem of Goethe, "The Apprentice Sorcerer", who in the absence of his master managed to unloose the magic powers, but was incapable of putting them again under the yoke, and so became their prey.

night leading to the heart of the stronghold of the besieged Soul, where it may rejoin its still intact reserves
and establish itself firmly in the *Feste Burg*[1] of the Spirit.

And that is where we find the hand of our allies,
the thinkers of India, stretched out to meet us: for they
have known for centuries past how to entrench themselves in this *Feste Burg* and how to defend it, while
we, their brethren of the Great Invasions, have spent
our strength in conquering the rest of the world. Let us
stop and recover our breath! Let us lick our wounds!
Let us return to our eagle's nest in the Himalayas.
It is waiting for us, for it is ours. Eaglets of Europe, we
need not renounce any part of our real nature. Our
real nature is in the nest, whence we formerly took our
flight; it dwells within those who have known how to
keep the keys of our keep—the Sovereign Self. We
have only to rest our tired limbs in the great inner lake.
Afterwards, my companions, with fever abated and
new power flowing through your muscles, you will
again resume your Invasions, if you wish to do so. Let a
new cycle begin, if it is the Law. But this is the moment
to touch Earth again, like Anteus, before beginning a
new flight! Embrace it! Let your thoughts return to
the Mother! Drink her milk! Her breasts can still
nourish all the races of the world.

Among the spiritual ruins strewn all over Europe,
our "Mother India" will teach you to excavate the
unshakable foundations of your Capitole. She possesses
the calculations and the plans of the "Master Craftsman."[2] Let us rebuild our house with our own materials.

[1] "A stronghold sure." (The words of Luther's Chorale.)
[2] The term "Master Craftsman" was used for the architect of our
Gothic cathedrals.

# V

## CAVE CANEM!

I have no intention of concealing it: the great lesson taught by India is not without its own dangers, a fact that must be recognised. The idea of the Atman (the Sovereign Soul) is such strong wine that weak brains run the risk of being turned by it. And I am not sure that Vivekananda himself in his more juvenile moments was not intoxicated by its fumes, for example in the rodomontades of his adolescence, which Durgacharan has recorded, and to which Ramakrishna, the indulgent, listened, an ironic smile on his lips. Nag the pious, adopting the meek attitude Christianity has taught us, said on one occasion, "Everything happens according to the will of the Mother. She is the Universal Will. She moves, but men imagine that it is they who move."

But the impetuous Naren replied, "I do not agree with you, with your He or She. I am the Soul. In me is the Universe. In me it is born, it floats and disappears."

NAG: "You have not power enough to change one single black hair into a white one, and yet you speak of the Universe! Without God's will not one blade of grass dies!"

NAREN: "Without my will the Sun and the Moon could not move. At my will the Universe goes like a machine."[1]

[1] And Ramakrishna with a smile at his youthful pride, said to Nag, "Truly Naren can say that; for he is like a drawn sword."

Such pride is only a hair's breadth removed from the bragging of the Matamore,[1] and yet there is a world of difference—for he who spoke these words was Vivekananda, an intellectual hero who weighed the exact meaning of his audacious statements. Here is no foolish self-glorification or utterance of a delirious "Superman" taking his call before the curtain. This *Soul*, this *Atman*, this *Self* are not only those enclosed in the shell of my body with its transient and fleeting life. The soul is the Self within me, within you, within all, within the universe and before and beyond it. It can only be attained through detachment from

And the pious Nag bowed down before the young Elect of the Mother. (*Cf. The Saint Durgacharan Nag; the Life of an Ideal Householder*, 1920, Ramakrishna Math, Madras.)

Girish Ch. Ghose described the two wrestlers with his usual humour. "Mahâmâyâ (the Great Illusion) would have found it exceedingly difficult to hold them in Her toils. If She had tried to capture Naren, he would have made himself greater and still greater, so great that no chain was long enough....And if She had tried Her tricks on Nag, he would have made himself smaller and smaller, so small that he would have escaped between the meshes."

[1] A comic character in ancient Spanish and French comedy: the trumpeter who boasted of imaginary victories.

But there is also a strange likeness to the rodomontades of the young "Baccalaureate" who plucked the bread of Mephistopheles in *The Second Faust*. The expressions are practically the same, and the similarity would be still more surprising unless it is remembered that Goethe very probably was caricaturing the "*gigantische Gefühl*" of Fichte, so closely though unconsciously akin to the intoxication of the Indian Atman:

> "*Die Welt, sie war nicht, eh ich sie erschuf;*
> *Die Sonne führt ich aus dem Meer herauf;*
> *Mit mir begann der Mond des Wechsels Lauf;*
> *Da schmuckte sich der Tag auf meinen Wegen,*
> *Die Erde grünte, blühte mir entgegen.*
> *Auf meinen Wink, in jener ersten Nacht,*
> *Entfaltete sich aller Sterne Pracht....*"

("The world was not before I created it. It was I who made the sun rise from the sea. With me the moon began her alternate course. Then day sprang beneath my feet. The earth grew green and blossomed before my face. At my gesture the splendour of the stars was unfolded in the first night.")

the ego. The words "All is the Soul, It is the only
Reality" do not mean that you, a man, are everything,
but that it depends upon yourself whether you return
your flask of stale water to the source of the snows
whence flow all the streams of water.[1] It is within
you, you are the source, if you know how to renounce
the flask. And so it is a lesson of supreme disinterestedness and not of pride.

It is none the less true that it contains an exhilarating
lesson, and that in the impetus of ascension it lends to
the soul, the latter is apt to forget the humble starting
point, to remember nothing but the final achievement
and to boast of its Godlike plumes.[2] The air of great
heights must be treated with caution. When all the
gods have been dethroned and nothing is left but the
"Self", beware of vertigo![3] It was this that made
Vivekananda careful in his ascent not to hurry the
whole mass of souls as yet uninured to the precipices
and the wind of the chasms. He made each one climb
by small stages leaning upon the staff of his own reli-

[1] "The Power behind me is not Vivekananda, but He, the
Lord...." (Letter of Vivekananda, July 9, 1897, *The Life of Swami
Vivekananda*, p. 518).

In spite of this very definite limitation the Brahmo Samajists of
India on several occasions have treated Vivekananda's claim to
Divinity as blasphemy. (*Cf.* Chap. V. of the pamphlet of B. Mozoomdar:
*Vivekananda, the Informer of Max Müller.*)

[2] A popular French expression referring to one of La Fontaine's
Fables: "The Jay who Preened her Peacock's Feathers."

[3] The wise and simple Ramakrishna gave more earnest warnings
against the danger of spiritual pride than Vivekananda. He said,
"To claim that 'I am He'...is not a sane attitude. Whoever has
this ideal before having overcome the consciousness of the physical
self, will receive great hurt from it, and it will retard his progress, and
little by little he will be drawn down. He deceives others and himself
in absolute ignorance of his real lamentable condition...."

(*The Gospel of Sri Ramakrishna*, II, Chapter IV, p. 67, 1928
edition).

gion or of the provisional spiritual *Credos* of his age and country. But too often his followers were impatient and sought to gain the summits without due rest and preparation. Hence it was hardly surprising that some fell, and in their fall they were not only a danger to themselves, but to those who knew themselves to be inferior. The exaltations caused by the sudden realisation of inner power may provoke social upheavals, whose effect and range of disturbance are difficult to calculate beforehand. It is therefore perhaps all to the good that Vivekananda and his monastic Order have consistently and resolutely kept aloof from all political action, although Indian Revolutionaries have more than once invoked his teaching and preached the Omnipotence of the Atman according to his words.

All great doctrine becomes fatally deformed. Each man twists it to his own profit and even the Church founded to defend it from usury and change is always tempted to stifle it and shut it up within its own proprietary walls. But considered in its unaltered greatness, it is a magnificent reservoir of moral force. Since everything is within ourselves and nothing outside, we assume full responsibility for our thoughts and deeds; there is no longer a God or a Destiny onto whom we can basely shift it. No more Jahveh, no more Eumenides, no more "Ghosts."[1] Each one of us has to reckon only with himself. Each one is the creator of his own destiny. It rests upon his shoulders alone. He is strong enough to bear it. "Man has never lost his empire. The soul has never been bound. It is free by nature. It is without cause. It is beyond cause.

[1] Allusion to one of Ibsen's plays.

Nothing can work upon it from without....Believe that you are free and you will be!..."[1]

"The wind is blowing; those vessels whose sails are unfurled, catch it and so they go forward on their way, but those whose sails are furled, do not catch the wind. Is that the fault of the wind?...Blame neither man, nor God, nor anyone in the world....Blame yourselves, and try to do better....All the strength and succour you need is within yourselves. Therefore make your own future."[2]

You call yourselves helpless, resourceless, abandoned, despoiled?... Cowards! You have within yourselves the Force, the Joy, and the Freedom—the whole of Infinite Existence. You have only to drink it.[3]

From it you will not only imbibe torrents of energy, sufficient to water the world, but you will also imbibe the aspirations of a world athirst for those torrents and you will water it. For "He who is within you works through all hands, walks with the feet of all." He "is the mighty and the humble, the saint and the sinner, God and the earthworm." He is everything, and He is above all, "the miserable and the poor of all kinds and all races;"[4] "for it is the poor who have done all the gigantic work of the world."[5]

If we will realise only a small part of this vast con-

---

[1] *The Freedom of the Soul*, (Nov. 5, 1896), Vol. II of *Complete Works*.

[2] *Jnana-Yoga: "Cosmos"* (II. Microcosm).

[3] "There is only one Infinite Existence which is at the same time Sat-Chit-Ananda (Existence, Knowledge, Bliss absolute). And that is the inner nature of man. This inner nature is in its essence eternally free and divine." (Lecture in London, Oct. 1896). And Vivekananda added, "On this rationalistic religion the safety of Europe depends."

[4] Letter of July 9, 1897.

[5] March 11, 1898, Calcutta.

ception, "If one-millionth part of the men and women who live in this world, simply sit down and for a few minutes say, 'You are all God, O ye men... and living beings, you are all manifestation of the one living Deity!' the whole world will be changed in half an hour. Instead of throwing tremendous bomb-shells of hatred into every corner, instead of projecting currents of jealousy and evil thought, in every country people will think that it is all He."[1]

\*

Is it necessary to repeat that this is no new thought? (And therein lies its force!) Vivekananda was not the first (such a belief would be childish) to conceive the Universe of the human Spirit and to desire its realisation. But he was the first to conceive it in all its fullness with no exception or limit. And it would have been impossible for him to do so, if he had not had before his eyes the extraordinary example of Ramakrishna.

It is no rare thing in these days to see occasional efforts by Congresses or Societies, when a few noble representatives of the great religions speak of union in the shape of a drawing together of all its different branches. Along parallel lines lay thinkers have tried to rediscover the thread, so many times broken, so many times renewed, running through blind evolution, connecting the separate attempts—successful and unsuccessful—of reason; and they have again and again affirmed the unity of power and hope that exists in the Self of Humanity.[2]

[1] *Jnana-Yoga: "The Real and the Apparent Man."*
[2] A warmer heart never existed than Michelet's: "*Omnia submagna labentia flumina terra*.... The Choir Universal.... The eternal communion of the human race...."

But neither attempt, isolated as it has been (perhaps that explains its failure), has yet arrived at the point of bridging the gap between the most religious of secular thought and the most secular of religious thought. Even the most generous have never succeeded in ridding themselves completely of the mental prejudice that convinces them of the superiority of their own spiritual family—however vast and magnanimous it may be—and makes them view the others with suspicion, because they also claim the right of primogeniture. Michelet's large heart would not have been able to maintain that it had "neither combated nor criticised": even in his *Bible of Humanity*, he distinguished between two classes: the people of light and the people of darkness. And, naturally, he had a preference for his own races and his own small pond, the Mediterranean. The genial Ram Mohun Roy, when about 1828 he began to found his high "Universalism" with the intention of embracing Hindus, Mohammedans, and Christians, erected the impenetrable barrier of theism —"God, the one and only, without equal"—the enemy of polytheism. Such prejudice is still upheld by the Brahmo Samaj, and I find it again, veiled it is true, but none the less deep-rooted, in my most freethinking friends of the Tagore circle, and in the most chivalrous champions of the reconciliation of religions—for example in the estimable *Federation of International Fellowships*, founded four or five years ago in Madras, which includes the most disinterested Anglo-Indian representatives of Protestant Christianity, and those of purified Hinduism, Jainism, and Theosophy: the

*Cf.* his *Origines du Droit francais*, 1837, and the beautiful book devoted to him by Jean Guéhenno: *L'Evangile Eternal*, 1927.

popular religions of India are excluded from it and (characteristic omission) in the accounts of its meetings for several years the names of Vivekananda and Ramakrishna do not appear. Silence on that score! It might prove embarrassing....

I can well imagine it! Our European devotees of reason would do just the same. Reason and the one God, and the God of the Bible and of the Koran would find it easier to come to an understanding than any one of them to understand the multiple gods and to admit them into their temple. The tribe of *Monos*[1] at a pinch will admit that *Monos* may be a man of God; but it will not tolerate the proliferation of the One, on the ground that anything of the kind is a scandal and a danger! I can discover traces of the same thing in the sorrowful revolt of my dearest Indian friends, who have been brought up like their glorious Roy on absolute Vedantism and highest Western reason. They believed at last after long pain and conflict they had succeeded in integrating the latter in all the best Indian thought of the end of the nineteenth century—and then Ramakrishna and his trumpeter Vivekananda appeared on the scene calling alike the privileged and the common herd to worship and love all forms of the ideal, even to the millions of faces that they hoped they had thrust into oblivion!... In their eyes this was a mental retrogression.

But in mine it is a step in advance, a mighty Hanumân-leap over the strait separating the continents.[2]

---

[1] That is, personal Unity—both secular and religious.

[2] At the same time I do not want my Indian friends to interpret this vast comprehension of all forms of the religious spirit, from the lowest to the highest, as preference in favour of the lower and less developed. Therein lies the opposite danger of reaction, which

I have never seen anything fresher or more potent in the religious spirit of all ages than this enfolding of all the gods existing in humanity, of all the faces of Truth, of the entire body of human Dreams, in the heart and the brain, in the Paramahamsa's great love and Vivekananda's strong arms. They have carried the great message of fraternity to all believers, to all visionaries, to all who have neither belief nor vision, but who seek for them in all sincerity, to all men of goodwill, rationalists and religious men, to those who believe in great Books or in images, to those with the simple trust of the charcoal-burner, to agnostics and inspired persons, to intellectuals and illiterates. And not merely the fraternity of the first-born, whose right as the eldest dispossesses and subjects his younger brethren, but equality of rights and of privileges.

I have said above that even the word "tolerance",

is further encouraged by the belligerence provoked by the hostile or disdainful attitude of theists and rationalists. Man is always a creature of extremes. When the boat tips too far to one side, he flings himself onto the other. We want equilibrium. Let us recall the real meaning of religious synthesis, as sought by Vivekananda. Its spirit was definitely progressive:

"I disagree with all those who are giving their superstitions back to my people. Like the Egyptologist's interest in Egypt, it is easy to feel an interest in India that is purely selfish. One may desire to see again the India of one's books, one's studies, one's dreams. My hope is to see again the strong points of that India, reinforced by the strong points of this age, only in a natural way. The new state of things must be a *growth* from within." (Interviews with Sister Nivedita during the last journey from India to Europe, 1899).

There is here no thought of return to the past. And if some blind and exaggerated followers of the Master have been self-deceived on the subject, the authorised representatives of the Ramakrishna Mission, who are the real heirs of Vivekananda's spirit, contrive to steer a course between the two reefs of orthodox reaction, which tries to galvanise the skeletons of ideas into fresh life, and rationalist pseudo-progress which is only a form of imperialistic colonisation by races of different mentality. Real progress is like the sap rising from the bottom of the roots throughout the whole tree.

which is the most magnificent generosity in the eyes of
the West (such an old, miserly peasant!), wounded
the sense of justice and the proud delicacy of Vivekananda; for it seemed to him an insulting and protective concession, such as a superior might make to
weaker brethren whom he had the right to censure.
He wished people to "accept" on the basis of equality
and not to "tolerate". Whatever shape the vase might
be that contained the water, the water was always the
same, the same God. One drop is as holy as the ocean.
In fact this declaration of equality between the
humblest and the highest carries all the more weight
because it comes from the highest—from an intellectual
aristocrat, who believed that the peak he had scaled,
the Advaitic faith, was the summit of all the mountains in the world. He could speak as one having
authority, for, like his master Ramakrishna, he had
traversed all the stages of the way. But, while Ramakrishna by his own powers had climbed all the steps
from the bottom to the top, Vivekananda with Ramakrishna's help learnt how to come down them again
from the top to the bottom and to know them and
to recognise them all as the eyes of the One, who is
reflected in their pupils like a rainbow.

But you must not suppose that this immense diversity spells anarchy and confusion. If you have fully
digested Vivekananda's teaching on the Yogas, you will
have been impressed on all sides by the order of the
superimposed designs, the beautiful perspective, the
hierarchy—not in the sense of the relation between a
master and his subjects, but of the architecture of stone
masses or of music rising tier on tier: the great concord
that steals from the keyboard under the hand of the

Master Organist. Each note has its own part in the harmony. No series of notes must be suppressed, and polyphony reduced to unison with the excuse that your own part is the most beautiful! Play your own part, perfectly and in time, but follow with your ear the concert of the other instruments united to your own! The player who is so weak that instead of reading his own part, he doubles that of his neighbour, wrongs himself, the work, and the orchestra. What should we say of a double-bass if he insisted on playing the part of the first violin? Or of the instrument that announced "Silence the rest! Those who have learnt my part, follow me!"?—A symphony is not a class of babies taught in a primary school to spell out a word all on the same tone!

And this teaching condemns all spirit of propaganda, whether clerical or lay, that wishes to mould other brains on its own model (the model of its own God or of its own non-God, who is merely God in disguise). It is a theory which upsets all our preconceived and deep-seated ideas, all our age-long heritage. We can always find a good reason, Churchmen or Sorbonnes alike, for serving those who do not invite us to do so, by uprooting the tares (together with the grain) from the patch of ground that provides them with food! Is it not the most sacred duty of man to root out the tares and briars of error from his own heart and from that of his neighbour—especially from that of his neighbour? And error surely is nothing but that which is not truth to us? Very few men are great enough to rise above this naively egocentric philanthropy. I have hardly met a single one among my masters and companions of the rationalist and scientific secular army—however virile, strong, and generous they appeared to be: for with their hands full of the harvest they had gleaned, their one idea was to shower it willy-nilly on humanity.... "Take, eat, either voluntarily or forcibly! What is good for me must be good for you. And if you perish by following my prescription, it will be your fault and not the fault of the prescription, as in the case of Molière's doctors. The Faculty[1] is always right." And the opposite camp of the Churches is still worse, for there it is a question of saving souls for eternity. Every kind of holy violence is legitimate for a man's real good.

That is why I was glad to hear Gandhi's voice quite recently—in spite of the fact that his temperament is the antithesis of Ramakrishna's or Vivekananda's—remind his brethren of the International Fellowships, whose pious zeal disposed them to evangelise, of the great universal principle of religious "Acceptation", the same preached by Vivekananda.[2] *"After long study and experience,"* he said, *"I have come to these conclusions, that:*

1. *All religions*—(and by that, I, the Author, personally understand those of reason as well as of faith) —*are true;*

2. *All religions have some error in them;*

3. *All religions are almost as dear to me as my own Hinduism.* My veneration for other faiths is the same as for my own faith. Consequently, the thought of conversion is impossible. The object of the Fellowships ought to be to help a Hindu to be a better Hindu, a Mussulman

---

[1] The Faculty=the Faculty of Medicine (this passage is an imitation of the style of Molière).

[2] Notes taken at the annual meeting of the Council of the Federation of International Fellowships at the Satyagraha Ashram, Sabarmati, January 13-15, 1928.

to become a better Mussulman, a Christian to become
a better Christian. An attitude of protective tolerance
is opposed to the spirit of the International Fellowships. If in my innermost heart I have the suspicion
that my religion is the truest, and that other religions
are less true, then, although I may have a certain kind
of fellowship with the others, it is an extremely different
kind from that required in the International Fellowships. Our attitude towards the others ought to be
absolutely frank and sincere. Our prayer for others
ought never to be: 'God! give them the light Thou
hast given to me!' But: 'Give them all the light and
truth they need for their highest development!' "

And when the inferiority of animist and polytheistic
superstitions, which seemed to the aristocracy of the
great theistic religions to be the lowest step on the
human ladder, was urged against him, Gandhi replied
softly, "In what concerns them I ought to be humble
and beware lest arrogance should sometimes speak
through the humblest language. It takes a man all
his time to become a good Hindu, a good Christian,
or a good Mussulman. It takes me all my time to
be a good Hindu, and I have none left over for evangelising the animist; I cannot really believe that he
is my inferior."[1]

[1] To a colleague who asked him, "Can I not hope to give my
religious experience of God to my friend?" Gandhi replied, "Can
an ant desire his own knowledge and experience to be given to an
elephant? And vice versa? Pray rather that God may give your
friend the fullest light and knowledge—not necessarily the same that
He has given to you."
    Another asked, "Can we not share our experience?"
    Gandhi replied, "Our spiritual experiences are necessarily shared
(or communicated) whether we suspect it or not—but by our lives
(by our example), not by our words which are a very faulty medium.
Spiritual experiences are deeper than thought itself.... (From

At bottom Gandhi not only condemns all religious propaganda either open or covert, but all conversion, even voluntary, from one faith to another is displeasing to him: "If some persons think that they ought to change their religious 'etiquette', I cannot deny that they are free to do so—but I am sorry to see it."

Nothing more contrary to our Western way of both religious and secular thought can be imagined. At the same time there is nothing from which the West and the rest of the modern world can derive more useful teaching. At this stage of human evolution, wherein both blind and conscious forces are driving all natures to draw together for "co-operation or death", it is absolutely essential that the human consciousness should be impregnated with it, until this indispensable principle becomes an axiom: that every faith has an equal right to live, and that there is an equal duty incumbent upon every man to respect that which his neighbour respects. In my opinion Gandhi, when he stated it so frankly, showed himself to be the heir of Ramakrishna.[1]

the one fact that we live) our spiritual experience will overflow. But where there is a consciousness of sharing (the will to work spiritually), there is selfishness. If you Christians wish another to share your Christian experience, you will raise an intellectual barrier. Pray simply that your friends may become better men, whatever their religion."

[1] The proper mission of Ramakrishna's disciples seems to me to be precisely this—to watch that his vast heart, which was open to all sincere hearts in the world and to all forms of their love and their faith, should never, like other "Sacred Hearts", be shut up upon an altar, in a Church where access is only permitted after giving the password of a *Credo*. Ramakrishna ought to be for all. All are his. He ought not to *take*. He should *give*. For he who *takes* will suffer the fate of those who have taken in the past, the Alexanders, the conquerors: their conquests vanish with them into the grave. He alone is victorious in space and time who *gives*, who gives the whole of himself, without any thought of return.

There is no single one of us who cannot take this lesson to heart. The writer of these lines—he has vaguely aspired to this wide comprehension all through his life—feels only too deeply at this moment how many are his shortcomings in spite of his aspirations; and he is grateful for Gandhi's great lesson—the same lesson that was preached by Vivekananda, and still more by Ramakrishna—to help him to achieve it.

# CONCLUSION

BUT this difference will always remain between the thought of Gandhi and that of Vivekananda, that the latter, being a great intellectual—which Gandhi is not in the slightest degree—could not detach himself as Gandhi has done from systems of thought. While both recognised the validity of all religions, Vivekananda made this recognition an article of doctrine and a subject of instruction. And that was one of the reasons for the existence of the Order he founded. He meant in all sincerity to abstain from any kind of spiritual domination whatsoever.[1] But the sun cannot moderate his rays. His burning thought was operative from the very fact that it existed. And although Vivekananda's Advaitism might revolt from the annexationist propaganda of faith, it was sufficient for him to appear

---

[1] All those who knew him bear witness to his absolute respect for the intellectual freedom of those near him—at least so long as they had not subscribed to any formal engagement towards his monastic order and himself by initiation of a sacred character. The beautiful text which follows breathes his ideal of harmonious freedom:

"Nisthâ (devotion to one ideal) is the beginning of realisation. Take the honey out of all flowers; sit and be friendly with all; pay reverence to all; say to all: 'Yes, brother, yes brother'; but keep firm in your own way. A higher stage is actually to take the position of the other. If I am all, why can I not really and actively sympathise with my brother and see with his eyes? While I am weak I must stick to one course (Nistha), but when I am strong, I can feel with every other, and perfectly sympathise with his ideas. The old idea was: 'Develop one idea at the expense of the rest'. The modern way is 'harmonious development'. A third way is 'to develop the mind and control it', then put it where you will; the result will come quickly. That is developing yourself in the truest way. Learn concentration and use it in one direction. Thus you lose nothing. He who gets the whole must have the parts too." (*Cf. Prabuddha Bharata*, March, 1929.)

as a great flaming fire for other wandering souls to
gather round it. It is not given to all to renounce
command. Even when they speak to themselves, the
Vivekanandas speak to humanity. They cannot whisper
if they would, and he did not attempt to do so. A great
voice is made to fill the sky. The whole earth is its
sounding-box.[1] That is why, unlike Gandhi whose
natural ideal is in proportion to his nature, free, equi-
table, average, and measured, tending in the realm
of faith as in politics to a Federation of men of goodwill—Vivekananda appeared in spite of himself as an
emperor, whose aim was to discipline the independent
but co-ordinate kingdoms of the spirit under the
sceptre of the One. And the work which he founded
has proceeded according to this plan.

His dream was to make the great monastery, the
mother house of Belur, a human "Temple of Knowledge." And since with him "to know" and "to do"
were synonymous,[2] the ministry of Knowledge was
subdivided into three departments: 1. Charity (Anna-
dâna, that is, the gift of food and other physical
necessities); 2. Learning (Vidyâ-dâna, that is intellectual knowledge); 3. Meditation (Jnâna-dâna, that is
spiritual knowledge)—the synthesis of all three teachings being indispensable to the constitution of a man.
There was to be gradual purification, necessary pro-

---

[1] "Knowledge of the Advaita was hidden for a long time in forests
and caves. It was given to me to make it come forth from its
seclusion and to carry it into the heart of family life and of society,
until they are interpenetrated with it. We shall make the drum of
the Advaita sound in all places, in the markets, on the hills, and
through the plains...." (Book of Vivekananda's Dialogues, collected
by his disciple, Sharat Chandra Chakravarti, Part I).

[2] "What good is the reading of the Vedanta to me? We have to
realise it in practical life," (Ibid.).

gression—starting from the imperious necessities of the
body of humanity which needs nourishment and succour[1]—up to the supreme conquest of the detached
spirit absorbed in Unity.

For a Vivekananda the light is not to be hidden
under a bushel; hence every kind of means for self-
development should be at everybody's door. No man
ought to keep anything for himself alone.

"Of what consequence is it to the world if you or I
attain to Mukti (Liberation)? We have to take the
whole universe with us to Mukti.... Unparalleled
Bliss! The Self realised in all living beings and in every
atom of the universe!"[2]

The first statutes drawn up by him in May, 1897,
for the foundation of the Ramakrishna Mission established expressly that "The aim of the Association is
to preach those truths, which Shri Ramakrishna has,
for the good of humanity, given out and demonstrated
by practical application in his own life, and to help
those truths being made practical in the lives of
others for their temporal, mental, and spiritual
advancement."

Hence the spirit of propaganda was established in
the doctrine whose essence is "the establishment of
fellowship among the followers of different religions,
knowing them all to be so many forms only of one
undying Eternal Religion."

It is so difficult to extirpate from the human spirit

[1] Vivekananda wished to impose five years of novitiate in the
department of social service (homes, dispensaries, free and popular
kitchens, etc.) before entering the temple of science—and five years
of intellectual apprenticeship before access to spiritual initiation
properly so-called.
[2] *Book of Vivekananda's Dialogues.*

the need to affirm to others that its own truth and its
own good must also be their truth and their good!
And it may be asked whether, if it were extirpated, it
would still be "human". Gandhi's spiritual detachment is almost disincarnate, as was the universal attachment of Ramakrishna, the lover, to all minds, although
he arrived at it by the reverse process. Vivekananda
never achieved it.* He remained flesh and bones.
Even from his appearance it was possible to infer that
although absolute detachment bathed the heights of
his mind, the rest of his body remained immersed in
life and action. His whole edifice bears this double
impress: the basement is a nursery of apostles of truth
and social service who mix in the life of the people and
the movement of the times. But the summit is the
*Ara Maxima*, the lantern of the dome, the spire of the
cathedral, the Ashrama of all Ashramas, the Advaita
built on the Himalayas, where the two hemispheres,
the West and the East, meet at the confluence of all
mankind in absolute Unity.

The architect had accomplished his work. Brief
though his life, he saw before he died, as he said,
his "machine in strong working order!" He had
inserted in the massive block of India "a lever for the

* It is not correct, we think, to consider Shri Ramakrishna's attitude
to religious preaching as "disincarnate" and passive. Shri Ramakrishna
clearly believed in the preaching of religion by qualified persons,
and he repeatedly asked his disciples, especially his chief disciple,
to do Mother's work which was mainly the imparting of spiritual
instruction, and we know how well they have done and are doing it.
There are numerous passages in the recorded teachings and conversations of the Master to corroborate our statement. We are bound to
infer, therefore, that in this, Mahatma Gandhi's attitude, as mentioned by M. Rolland, is quite different from Shri Ramakrishna's.
There is no conflict between the acceptance of the truth of all religions
and religious preaching (*vide* "*Expansion of Hinduism: a Defence.*"
*Prabuddha Bharata*, April, 1929).—*Publisher*.

good of humanity which no power can drive back".[1]

Together with our Indian brethren it is our task to bear upon it. And if we cannot flatter ourselves that the crushing mass of human inertia, the first and last cause of crime and sin, will be raised for centuries to come, what matters a century? We shake it nevertheless.... *"E pur si muove"*...[2] And new gangs will always arise to replace the worn out gangs. The work begun by the two Indian Masters, will be carried on resolutely by other workmen of the spirit in other parts of the world. In whatever tunnel a man may be digging, he is never out of sound of the sap being dug on the other side of the mountain....

My European companions, I have made you listen through the Wall, to the blows of the coming one, Asia.... Go to meet her! She is working for us. We are working for her. Europe and Asia are the two halves of the Soul. Man *is not* yet. He *will be*. God is resting and has left to us His most beautiful creation[3] —that of the Seventh Day: to free the sleeping forces of the enslaved Spirit; to reawaken God in man; to re-create the Being itself.

R. R.

October 9, 1928.

[1] Letter of July 9, 1897.
[2] "And still it moves." The words of Galileo when he was forced to deny the movement of the earth.
[3] Allusion to the six days' creation in Genesis.

# APPENDICES

# NOTE I

## THE RAMAKRISHNA MATH AND MISSION

THE spiritual harvest of Ramakrishna and Vivekananda was not scattered broadcast to the winds. It was garnered by Vivekananda's own hands and placed under the protection of wise and laborious farmers, who knew how to keep it pure and to bring it to fruition.

In *The Life of Vivekananda* I have described his foundation in May, 1897, of a great religious Order to whose trust he confided the storing and administration of his Master's spirit—the Ramakrishna Mission. And there we have also traced the first steps of the Order with its twofold activity of preaching and social work from its inception up to Vivekananda's death.

His death did not destroy the edifice. The Ramakrishna Mission has established itself and grown.[1] Its first director, Brahmananda, busied himself to secure it a regular constitution. By an act of donation prepared by Vivekananda the Order of Sannyasins of Ramakrishna, domiciled in the Belur Math, near Calcutta, became possessed in 1899 of a legal statute. But in order that the Order might be empowered to receive gifts for its charitable work the necessity arose for a legal fiction to double the original foundation into a Math (monastery) and a Mission. The latter was duly registered on May 4, 1909, "under Act XXI of 1860 of the Governor-General of India in Council." The Math and

[1] We can follow its development in detail in the General Reports of the Mission, published by the Governing Body of the Ramakrishna Mission from 1913 to 1926.

the Mission are really the two aspects, the monastic and the philanthropic, of the same organisation, both controlled by the General Council of the Order. But the popular name, wrongly applied to the whole, is that of the Ramakrishna Mission.

The aims of the Mission, as defined in the Memorandum annexed to the act of registration of 1909, are divided into three classes:

1. Charitable works.
2. Missionary works (organisation and publications).
3. Educational works.

Each is subdivided into permanent institutions (Maths, Ashramas, Societies, Homes of Service, Orphanages, Schools, etc.)—and transient enterprises, activities of casual help called into being by urgent but temporary necessity.[1]

In the Maths or monasteries there are regular monks, who have renounced the world and have received initiation after a period of novitiate. They are constantly moved from one centre to another according to the exigencies of the work, but they remain under the control of the General Council of the Order at Belur. There are some five hundred of them.

A second army is composed of laymen (householders), forming a kind of Third Estate. They are intimate disciples who come for spiritual instruction to the Maths where they sometimes spend short periods of retreat. They number no less than twenty-five thousand.

The other class of the reserve, rising to some millions, is composed of those who have partly or wholly adopted the ideals of the Mission, and serve it from outside without labelling themselves its disciples.

[1] The first General Report of 1913 enumerated twenty:—for famine in ten districts (1897, 1899, 1900, 1906, 1907, 1908)—for flood in three districts (1899, 1900, 1909)—for epidemics in three districts (1899, 1900, 1904, 1905, 1912, 1913)—for fire (1910)—for earthquakes (1899, 1905).

During the first part of April, 1926, the Mission held an extraordinary general Reunion at the Math of Belur in order to form some idea of its full scope. About 120 institutions were represented; of which half were in Bengal, a dozen in Bihar and Orissa, fourteen in the United Provinces, thirteen in the Province of Madras, one in Bombay. Outside the Peninsula there were three centres in Ceylon directing nine schools, where fifteen hundred children were being educated, a student centre at Jaffna, not to mention the Vivekananda Society at Colombo. In Burma there was a monastic centre with a large free hospital. Another centre was at Singapore; there were six in the United States: at San Francisco, La Crescenta near Los Angeles, San Antone Valley, Portland, Boston, New York—without reckoning the Vedanta Societies of St. Louis, Cincinnati, Philadelphia, Tacoma, etc. At Sao Paulo in Brazil a group of men have busied themselves since 1900 with Vivekananda's teaching. *The Gospel of Sri Ramakrishna*, and *Raja-Yoga* of Vivekananda have been translated into Portuguese. *Circulo Esoterico da Communhao do Pensamento* which has 43,000 members publishes Vedantic studies in its organ: *O Pensamento*.

The Order possesses a dozen Reviews: three monthly Reviews at Calcutta (two in Bengali: *Udbodhan* and *Visvavani*, and one in Hindi: *Samanvaya*): one in Tamil at Madras: *Shri Ramakrishna Vijayam;* one in Malayalam in Travancore: *Probuddha Keralam;* two monthlies and one weekly in English: *Prabuddha Bharata* at Mayavati in the Himalayas, *Vedanta Kesari* at Madras, *The Morning Star* at Patna—without counting one in Canarese, and one in Gujarati run by the disciples of the Mission; in the Federated Malay States a monthly Review in English: *Voice of Truth;**

---

* *Visvavani* does not actually belong to the Order though it is conducted by one who belongs to the Order. *Samanvaya* and *Voice of Truth*

21

in the United States a monthly review in English: *The Message of the East*, published by the La Crescenta centre.[1]

The education given within the monasteries follows the principles laid down by Vivekananda.[2] "The aim of the monastery," he had said, "is to create man"—the complete man, who "would combine in his life an immense idealism with perfect common sense." Hence in turn with hardly a break, the initiates practise spiritual exercises, intense meditation, reading and study of the sacred and philosophical texts, and manual work: household duties, baking, gardening and sewage-farming, bridges and roads, farms and agriculture, the care of animals as well as the double ministry of religion and medicine.

"Equal importance should be given to the triple culture

have since been discontinued and *The Morning Star* has been converted to a monthly—*Publisher* (1931).

[1] I owe these particulars to Swami Ashokananda, the chief editor of *Prabuddha Bharata* at Mayavati, Advaita Ashrama.

[2] Vivekananda's spirit was essentially realistic both in education and religion. He said, "The real teacher is he who can infuse all his power into the bent of his pupil...who will take someone as he stands, and help him forward..." (1896, in America). And in his interviews with the Maharaja of Khetri (before his first journey to America) he laid down this curious definition: "What is education? Education is the nervous association of certain ideas." He then explained that it was a question of developing ideas into instincts. Until they had reached that stage they could not be considered to be real and vital possessions of knowledge. And he gave as an example "the perfect educator", Ramakrishna, whose renunciation of gold had been so vital that his body could not bear to come into physical contact with the metal.

He said that it was the same with religion. "Religion is neither word nor doctrine....It is deed. It is to be and to become: not to hear and accept. It is the whole soul changed into that which it believes. That is what religion is." (*A Study of Religion*).

And I will permit myself to add that although I recognise the effectiveness of such an education, my free spirit is opposed to the dominion of certain ideas over the whole nature of an individual. I would rather use the same contagious energy to fill his being with the inextinguishable thirst for liberty: a freedom from control ever keenly aware of its own thoughts.

of the head, the heart, and the hands," said the great Abbot, the present head of the direction of the Order, Swami Shivananda.[1] "Each one if practised to the exclusion of the rest is bad and harmful."

The necessities of organisation called for a hierarchy within the Order. But all are equal in their allegiance to the common Rule. The Abbot Shivananda reminded them that "the chiefs ought to be the servants of all." And his presidential address of 1926 ended with an admirable declaration of universal happiness, accorded in equal measure to each one who serves, whatever his rank:

"Be like the arrow that darts from the bow. Be like the hammer that falls on the anvil. Be like the sword that pierces its object. The arrow does not murmur if it misses the target. The hammer does not fret if it falls in the wrong place. And the sword does not lament if it breaks in the hands of the wielder. Yet there is joy in being made, used, and broken; and an equal joy in being finally set aside...."

\*

It would be interesting to discover how this powerful organisation affects the diverse political and social currents that have been flowing for the past twenty years through the body of the awakened India.

It repudiates politics. In this it is faithful to the spirit of its Master, Vivekananda, who could not find sufficiently strong terms of disgust wherewith to spurn all collusion with politics. And perhaps this has been the wisest course for the Mission to pursue. For its religious, intellectual, and social action, eminently pro-Indian as it is, is exercised in the profound and silent depths of the nation, without giving any provocation to the British power to fetter it.

[1] Presidential Address of the first Convention of the Ramakrishna Math and Mission, April 1, 1926.

But even so it has been obliged to lull the suspicions of the ever vigilant watch dogs by continual prudence. On more than one occasion Indian revolutionaries, by using the words and name of Vivekananda, have placed it in a very embarrassing position. On the other hand its formal declarations of abstention from politics during hours of national crisis, have laid it open more than once to the accusation of patriots that it is indifferent to the liberties of India. The second General Report of the Mission, which appeared in May, 1919, testified to these difficulties and laid down precisely the non-political line the Math was to follow. It is not necessary to give a summary of it here.

1905, the year of the division of the Province of Bengal, marked the beginning of the Swadeshi movement and political unrest. The Mission refused to take any part in them. It even thought it prudent to suspend its work of preaching in Calcutta, Dacca, and Western Bengal, although it still carried on its charitable activities. In 1908 it was obliged to make a rule not to receive strangers at night in its establishments, because it feared that some were abusing its hospitality in order to prepare their political offensives. It transpired from the answers of political prisoners that more than one, disguised under the robe of a Sannyasin, had cloaked their designs under the name of its work and religion. Copies of the Gita and Vivekananda's writings were found on several of them. The Government kept a strict watch over the Mission, but it continued to preach its ideal of social service; it publicly reproved all sectarian and vengeful spirit, and even condemned selfish patriotism, pointing out that eventually it led to degradation and ruin. It replied alike to the accusations of the patriots and the suspicions of the Government by these words of Vivekananda, which were inscribed on the covers of its publications:

"The national ideals of India are Renunciation and Service. Intensify her in those channels and the rest will take care of itself."

Nevertheless, the struggle grew more bitter. According to their usual tactics of compromising all independent spirits, the revolutionary agitators used in a twisted form portions of the religious and philosophical publications of the Mission. In spite of its public declaration in April, 1914, the Government of Bengal in its Administration Report of 1915 accused the Mission and its founders of having been the first instigators of Indian nationalism.

And in 1916 the first Governor of Bengal, Lord Carmichael, although he sympathised with the Ramakrishna Mission's work, announced publicly that terrorists were becoming its members in order to achieve their ends with more ease: nothing more was needed for the dissolution of the Mission. Fortunately devoted English and American friends in high places came forward and warmly supported its defence in a long Memorial of January 22, 1917, so that the danger was averted.

\*

It has been seen that, like Gandhi, the Ramakrishna Mission absolutely repudiates violence in politics. But it is remarkable that the violent have more than once invoked it, despite its protestations: a thing that I believe they have never dreamed of doing in the case of Gandhi. And yet Ramakrishna's followers, more absolutely than Gandhi, reject all compromise, not only with certain forms of politics, but with them all.

This seeming paradox comes from the individual character —I might almost say—from the temperament of Vivekananda, their Master. His fighting and ardent Kshatriya nature appears even in his renunciation and Ahimsa (Non-Resistance).

"He used to say that the Vedanta may be professed by a coward, but it could be put into practice only by the most stout-hearted. The Vedanta was strong meat for weak stomachs. One of his favourite illustrations used to be that the doctrine of non-resistance necessarily involved the capacity and ability to resist and a conscious refraining from having recourse to resistance. If a strong man, he used to say, deliberately refrained from making use of his strength against either a rash or weak opponent, then he could legitimately claim higher motives for his action. If, on the other hand, there was no obvious superiority of strength or the strength really lay on the side of his opponent, then the absence of the use of strength naturally raised the suspicion of cowardice. He used to say that that was the real essence of the advice of Shri Krishna to Arjuna."[1]

And talking to Sister Nivedita in 1898 he said, "I preach only the Upanishads. And of the Upanishads, it is only that one idea—*strength*. The quintessence of Vedas and Vedanta and all, lies in that one word. Buddha's teaching was Non-resistance or Non-injury. But I think this a better way of teaching the same thing. For behind that Non-injury lay a dreadful weakness. It is weakness that conceives the idea of resistance. I do not think of punishing or escaping from a drop of sea-spray. It is nothing to me. Yet to the mosquito it would be serious. Now I would make all injury like that. Strength and fearlessness. My own ideal is that giant of a saint whom they killed in the Mutiny, and who broke his silence, when stabbed to the heart, to say— 'And thou also art He!' "

Here we can recognise Gandhi's conception: a Non-

[1] Reminiscences of Prof. G. S. Bhate, M.A. (*Prabuddha Bharata*).

Resistance in name, that is in reality the most potent of Resistances—a *Non-Acceptation*, only fit for spiritual heroes. There is no place in it for cowards....[1] But if, in practice, Gandhi's ideal is akin to that of Vivekananda, to what passionate heights did Vivekananda carry it! With Gandhi all things are moderated, calm, and constant. With Vivekananda everything is a paroxysm of pride, of faith, or of love. Under each of his words can be felt the brazier of the burning Atman—the Soul-God. It is then easy to understand that exalted revolutionary individualism has wished to use these flames in social incendiarism, and this is a danger that the wise successors of the great Swami, who have charge of his heritage, have often had to avoid.

Further, the tenacious and unwavering moderation of Gandhi's action is mixed up with politics, and sometimes becomes their leader, but Vivekananda's heroic passion (that of Krishna was battle) rejects politics of all kinds, so that the followers of Ramakrishna have kept themselves aloof from the campaigns of Gandhi.

It is regrettable that the name, the example, and the words of Vivekananda have not been invoked as often as I could

[1] The temperament of a born fighter like Vivekananda could only have arrived at this heroic ideal of Non-Acceptation without violence, by violating his own nature. And he did not attain to it without a long struggle.

Even in 1898 before the pilgrimage to the temple of Kshirbhavani, which produced a moral revolution in him, when he was asked, "What should we do when we see the strong oppress the weak?" he replied, "Why, thrash the strong, of course."

On another occasion he said, "Even forgiveness, if weak and passive, is not good: fight is better. *Forgive* when you can bring (if you wished) legions of angels to an easy victory." (That is to say, forgive when you are the stronger).

Another asked him, "Swamiji, ought one to seek an opportunity of death in defence of right, or ought to learn never to react?"

"I am for no reaction," replied the Swami slowly, and after a long pause added, "—for Sannyasins. Self-defence for the householder." (Cf. *The Life of Swami Vivekananda*, p. 594.)

have wished in the innumerable writings of Gandhi and his disciples.[1] The two movements, although independent of each other and each going its own way, have none the less the same object. They may be found side by side in service that is devoted to public well-being; and both of them—though with different tactics—follow the great design, the national unity of the whole of India. The one advances to the great day by his patent Non-Co-operation struggles (it has been crowned with victory during the past year, 1928)—the other by peaceful but irresistible universal Co-operation. Take for example the tragic question of Untouchability. The Ramakrishna Mission does not conduct a crusade against it like Gandhi, but better still, denies it according to those words of Vivekananda that I have just quoted: "It is weakness which conceives the idea of resistance."

"We think," Swami Ashokananda wrote to me, "that a rear attack is better than a frontal one. We invite people of all classes, beliefs, and races to all our festivals and we

[1] But on January 30, 1921, Gandhi went on pilgrimage with his wife and several of his lieutenants (Pandit Motilal Nehru, Maulana Muhammad Ali, etc.) to the sanctuary of Belur for the anniversary festival of Vivekananda's birth; and from the balcony of his room declared to the people his veneration for the great Hindu, whose word had lighted in him the flame of love for India.

In this very year (March 14, 1929) Gandhi presided at Rangoon over the festival of the Ramakrishna Sevashrama, in honour of the ninety-fourth anniversary of Ramakrishna. And while the followers of Ramakrishna saluted in him the realisation of Ramakrishna's ideal of a life of action, Gandhi paid a beautiful tribute to the Ramakrishna Mission:

"Wherever I go," he said, "the followers of Ramakrishna invite me to meet with them; I feel that their blessings go with me. Their relief works are spread over India. There is no point where they are not established on a large or a small scale. I pray God that they will grow, and that to them will be united all who are pure and who love India."

After him his Mohammedan lieutenant, Maulana Muhammad Ali, extolled Vivekananda.

sit and eat together, even Christians. In our Ashramas we do not keep any distinction of caste, either among the permanent residents or among visitors. Quite recently at Trivandrum, the capital of the Hindu state of Travancore, notorious for its extreme orthodoxy and its obstinate maintenance of untouchability, all the Brahmin and non-Brahmin castes sat together to take their meals on the occasion of the opening of our new monastery in that town; and no social objection was raised. It is by indirect methods that we try to put an end to the evil, and we think that thus we can avoid a great deal of irritation and opposition."

And so, while the great liberal Hindu sects like the Brahmo Samaj, the Prarthana Samaj, etc., storm orthodoxy from the front with the result that having broken their bridges behind them, they find themselves separated from the mass of their people, and partially rejected by the mother Church, so that their reforms are lost upon it—the Ramakrishna Mission believes in never losing contact with the Hindu rank and file; it remains within the bosom of the Church and of society, and from thence carries out reforms for the benefit of the whole community. There is nothing aggressive or iconoclastic, nothing that can wound, such as that attitude of Protestant rigidity, which, although armed with reason, has too often torn the universe by schism. Keep within the Catholic fold, but maintain a patient and humanised reason, so that you carry out reform from within, and never from without.

"Our idea," Swami Ashokananda wrote in another place, "is to awaken the higher conscience of Hinduism. That done, all necessary reforms will follow automatically."

The results already achieved speak volumes for these tactics. For example, amelioration of the condition of women has been vigorously pursued by the Brahmo Samaj, their self-constituted and chivalrous champion. But the suggested reforms have often been too radical and their means too heterodox. "Vivekananda said that the new ought to be a development rather than a condemnation and rejection of the old....The female institutions of the Ramakrishna Mission combining all that is best in Hinduism and the West, are today considered models of what ought to be the education of women." It is the same with regard to service of the lower classes, but I have already emphasised this point sufficiently and need not return to it. The excellent effect of a spirit that weds the new to the old has been also felt in the renaissance of Indian culture, to which other powerful elements have contributed, such as the glorious influence of the Tagores and their school at Santiniketan. But it must never be forgotten that Vivekananda and his devoted Western disciple, Sister Nivedita, were their predecessors; and that the great current of popular Hindu education began with Vivekananda's return to Colombo. Vivekananda was indignant that the Indian Scriptures, the Upanishads, Gita, Vedanta, etc., were practically unknown to the people, and reserved for the learned. Today Bengal is flooded with translations of the Holy Writings in the vernacular and with commentaries upon them. The Ramakrishna schools have spread a knowledge of them throughout India.

Nevertheless—(and this is the most beautiful characteristic of the movement)—the Indian national renaissance is not accompanied, as is the general rule, by a sentiment of hostility or superiority towards the alien. On the contrary, it holds out the hand of fellowship to the West. The followers of Shri Ramakrishna admit Westerners, not only into their sanctuaries but into their ranks (an unheard-of thing in India)—into their holy order of Sannyasins, and have insisted on their reception on equal footing by all, even by the orthodox monks. Moreover, the latter, the orthodox Sannyasins who in their hundreds of thousands exercise a constant influence on the Hindu masses, are gradually adopting the ways and the ideas of Ramakrishna's followers, to whom they were at first opposed, and whom they accused of heresy. Finally, the hereditary Order of Ramakrishna and Vivekananda has made it a rule never to take anything into the world that makes for division, but only what makes for union.

"Its sole object," it was said at the public meeting of the Extraordinary General Convention of the Mission in 1926, "is to bring about harmony and co-operation between the beliefs and doctrines of the whole of humanity"—to reconcile religions among themselves and to free reason—to reconcile classes and nations—to found the brotherhood of all men and all peoples.

And further, because the Ramakrishna Mission is permeated with a belief in the quasi-identity of the Macrocosm and the Microcosm, of the universal Self and the individual self—because it knows that no reform can be deep and lasting in a society unless it is first rooted in an inner reformation of the individual soul—it is on the formation of the universal man that it expends the greatest care. It seeks to create a new human type, wherein the highest powers at present scattered and fragmentary, and the diverse and complementary energies of man shall be combined—the heights of intelligence towering above the clouds, the sacred wood of love, and the rivers of action. The great Rhythm of the soul beats from pole to pole, from intense concentration to *"Seid umschlungen, Millionem!"*[1] with its universal

---

[1] The Ode to Joy of Beethoven's Ninth Symphony.

appeal. As it is possible in spite of difficulties to attain the
ideal in the case of a single man, the Ramakrishna Mission
is trying to realise the same ideal in its Universal Church—
the symbol of its Master—"his Math, which represents the
physical body of Ramakrishna."[1]

Here we can see the rhythm of history repeating itself.
To European Christians such a dream recalls that of the
Church of Christ. The two are sisters. And if a man
wishes to study the dream that is nineteen hundred years
old, he would do better, instead of looking for it in books
that perish, to listen at the breast of the other to its young
heart-beats. There is no question of comparison between
the two figures of the Man-Gods. The elder will always
have the privilege over the younger on account of the crown
of thorns and the spear-thrust upon the Cross, while the
younger will always have an irresistible attraction on
account of his happy smile in the midst of agonising suffering. Neither can yield anything to the other in grace and
power, in divinity of heart and universality. But is it not
true that the scrupulous historian of the Eternal Gospel,
who writes at its dictation, always finds that at each of its
new editions, the Gospel has grown with humanity?

[1] Vivekananda.

# NOTE II

## CONCERNING MYSTIC INTROVERSION AND ITS SCIENTIFIC VALUE FOR THE KNOWLEDGE OF THE REAL

THE intuitive workings of the "religious" spirit—in the wide sense in which I have consistently used the word—have been insufficiently studied by modern psychological science in the West and then too often by observers who are themselves lacking in every kind of "religious" inclination, and so are ill equipped for the study, and involuntarily prone to depreciate an inner sense they do not themselves possess.[1]

One of the best works devoted to this important subject is M. Ferdinand Morel's *Essay on Mystic Introversion*.[2] It is securely based on the principles and methods of pathological psycho-physiology and on the psycho-analysis of Freud, Janet, Jung, Bleuler, etc., and it handles the psychological study of several representative types of Hellenic-Christian mysticism with scrupulous care. His analysis of the Pseudo-Denis[3] is particularly interesting;[4] and his

---

[1] I except from this criticism several beautiful and recent essays rehabilitating intuition on scientific grounds—more or less the offspring of the dynamic *Élan* of Bergson—and the penetrating analysis of Edouard Le Roy—also of the first order.

[2] *Essai sur l'Introversion mystique: étude psychologique de Pseudo-Denys l'Aréopagite et de quelques autres cas de mysticisme*, Geneva, Kunding, 1918.

As far as the author is aware, the term "introversion" was used for the first time in the sense of scientific psychology by Dr. C. G. Jung of Zurich.

[3] Denis (Dionysius) the Areopagite.—*Translator*.

[4] The second part of the work, devoted to "several other cases of mysticism," is unfortunately very inferior—Eastern mysticism ("forty

description of him is on the whole correct, in spite of the fact that in the appreciation wherein he comments upon his work and the conclusions to be deduced from it, the author does not manage to free himself from his preconceived theories drawn from the scientific pathology of the time.

Without being able within the limits of this note to enter into a close discussion such as his theses deserve, I should like briefly to point out their weak points as I see them and the truer interpretation that I should put upon them.

Almost all psychologists are possessed by the theory[1] of Regression, which appears to have been started by Th. Ribot. It is undoubtedly a true one within the limited bounds of his psycho-pathological studies on functional disorganisation, but it has been erroneously extended to the whole realm of the mind, whether abnormal or normal.

Ribot laid down that "the psychological functions most rapidly attacked by disease were the most recently constituted ones, the last in point of time in the development of the individual (ontogenesis), and then reproduced on a general scale in the evolution of the species (phylogenesis)." Janet, Freud, and their followers have applied this state-

centuries of Introversion," as the author says) is studied in a few pages from third-hand information—and Christian mysticism in the West is summarised into a quite arbitrary and inadequate choice of types, including a number of definitely diseased people like Madame Guyon and Antoinette Bourignon, and superior and complete personalities like St. Bernard and Francois de Sales. They are, moreover, all mutilated by a very distorted representation: for the mighty elements of energy and social action, which in the case of these great men were closely bound up with mystic contemplation, are taken out of the picture.

[1] With one notable exception, the fine school of educational psychology at Geneva, grouped round the J. J. Rousseau Institute and the International Bureau of Education. One of the chiefs of this group, Ch. Baudouin, has in these very last months protested against the confusion caused by the term *regression*, attached indiscriminately to all the phenomena of *recoil*, psychologically so varied and sometimes so different. (*Cf. Journal of Psychology*, Paris, November-December, 1928.)

ment to all the nervous affections, and from them to all the activities of the mind. From this it is only a step for them —a false step for us—to the conclusion that the most recently effected operations and the most rapidly worn out are the highest in the hierarchy, and that a return to the others is a retrogression in a backward sense, a fall of the mind.

At the outset let us determine what is meant by "the supreme function" of the mind. It is what Janet calls "the function of the real," and he defines it as awareness of the present, of present action, the enjoyment of the present. He places "disinterested action and thought," which does not keep an exact account of present reality, on a lower level—then imaginary representation at the bottom of the scale, that is to say, the whole world of imagination and fancy. Freud, with his customary energy, asserts that reverie and all that emerges from it, is nothing but the debris of the first stage of evolution. And they all agree in opposing, like Bleuler, a "function of the unreal" akin to pure thought, to the so-called "function of the real", which they would term "the fine point of the soul", (to misuse the famous phrase of Francois de Sales by applying it—what irony!—to the opposite extreme).[1]

Such a classification, which ascribes the highest rank to "interested" action and the lower rank to concentration of thought, seems to me to stand self-convicted in the light of simple practical and moral common sense. And this depreciation of the most indispensable operation of the active mind—the withdrawal into oneself, to dream, to imagine, to reason—is in danger of becoming a pathological

---

[1] With quite unconscious irony a great "introvert" like Plotinus sincerely pities the "extroverts", the "wanderers outside themselves" (*Ennéades* IV, III [17]), for they seem to him to have lost the "function of the real."

aberration. The irreverent observer is tempted to say, "Physician, heal thyself!"

It seems to me that the transcendent value attributed by science to the idea of evolution should be taken with a pinch of salt. The admission of its indestructibility and universality without any exception, is in fact nothing more than the declaration of a continuous series (or sometimes discontinuous) of modifications and of differentiations in living matter. This biological process is not worthy to pose as a dogma, forcing us to see far above and beyond us, suspended to some vague "greasy pole",[1] some equally vague mysterious supreme "Realisation" of the living being—not much less supernatural than the "Realisation" below and behind us (or in the depths) presupposed by religion in its various myths of primitive Eden. Eventually vital evolution would culminate in the inevitable extinction of the species by a process of exhaustion. How can we decide the exact moment when the path begins to go down on the further side instead of going up? There are as many reasons for believing that the most important of the diverse operations and functions of the mind are those which disappear last: for they are the very foundations of Being—and that the part so easily destroyed belongs to a superficial level of existence.

A great aesthete, who is at the same time a scientist and a creative artist—a complete man endowed with both reason and intuition, Edouard Monod-Herzen, has thus expressed it: "The effects of the Cosmos antecedent to a given individual, whose substance still bears their trace, are to be distinguished from the contemporary effects which set their mark

---

[1] The "greasy pole" is a popular game in French country fairs. Competitors try to climb a tall pole covered with slippery soap to obtain a prize fastened to the top of it.

upon him each day. The first are his own inner property, and constitute his heredity. The second are his acquired property and constitute his adaptation."

In what way then are his "acquired properties" superior in hierarchical order to his "innate possessions"? They are only so in point of time. And, continues E. Monod-Herzen, "the actual condition of the individual results from a combination of the two groups of possessions."[1]

Why should they be dissociated? If it is to meet the exigences of scientific investigation, it is not superfluous to remark that by its very definition primitive or "innate possessions" accommodate themselves better to such dissociation than "acquired possessions"—for the simple reason that the latter are posterior and necessarily presuppose what went before them.

As Ch. Baudouin, when he was trying to correct the deprecatory tendencies of psycho-analysis with regard to psychological "phenomena of recoil", wrote on the subject of evolution, "Evolution is not conceived as going from the reflex to instinct, from instinct to the higher psychological life, without appealing to successive inhibitions and their resultant introversions. At each step new inhibitions must intervene to prevent energy from immediately discharging itself in motive channels, together with introversions, inward storings of energy, until little by little thought is substituted for the inhibited action. Thoughts (as John Dewey has shown) may be regarded as the result of suspended action, which the subject does not allow to proceed to its full realisation. Our reasonings are attempts in effigy.... It would therefore be a pity to confound introversion with open retrogression, since the latter marks a

[1] *Science et Esthétique: Principes de morphologie générale*, 1917, Paris, Gauthier-Villars (Vol. II, p. 6, Chap. V, and 42: *Living Matter*).

step backwards in the line of evolution"—(and I would add
that it is a retreat "without any idea of regaining lost
ground and advancing again")—"while introversion is the
indispensable condition of evolution and if it is a recoil,
it is one of those recoils that render a forward thrust
possible."

\*

But let us come frankly to the case of great introversion,
no longer in the mitigated form of normal thought—but
complete, absolute, unmitigated, as we have been studying
it in these volumes in the case of the highest mystics.

To pathological psychology—and M. Ferdinand Morel
accepts these conclusions[1]—it is a return to a primary stage,
to an intra-uterine state. And the symbolic words used
to explain absorption in the Unity by the masters of mysticism, whether of India or of Alexandria, by the Areopagite
or the two fourteenth century whirlwinds of the soul,
Eckhart and Tauler: "*Grund, Urgrund, Boden, Wurzel,
Wesen ohne Wesen, Indéfinité suressentielle...*" etc.—add
weight to this assumption, no less than the curious instinct
which has given birth in Ramakrishna's India to the
passionate worship of the *Mother*, and in Christianity to
that of the *Virgin Mother*.

It must be granted that we are strictly impartial.[2]

Is it then only a similar replunging of conscious thought
into the distant abysses of prenatal life? For the careful

[1] "The deep-seated narcissism of honest introversion is a profound
retrogression into the bosom of the mother; thus the individual epit-
omises the whole development of the race."

[2] As a starting point. But the great analysts of this intuitive "ebbing",
such as Ed. Le Roy, show wherein the final "simplicity", to which
they have already attained, differs from the "simplicity anterior to
the discursive intricacy, belonging solely to the confused pre-intuition
of a child." It is "a rich and luminous simplicity, which achieves
the dispersion of analysis by surpassing and overcoming it. It alone

study of mysticism establishes clearly that consciousness exists undimmed in this gigantic ascent backwards up the ladder of the past, compared to which Wells' "Time Machine" is mere child's play; and M. F. Morel comes back to it on several occasions:

"In the most complete introversion (that of Denis the Areopagite) there is no loss of consciousness, but a displacement of attention.... Ecstatic experiences remain deeply engraven upon those who experience them, and this would not be the case if they were simply empty or void of meaning.... Consciousness is in fact something intensely mobile. When the exterior world has disappeared, the circle of consciousness contracts and seems to withdraw entirely into some unknown and ignored cortical centre. Consciousness seems to gather itself together to confine itself within some unknown psychic pineal gland and to withdraw into a kind of centre wherein all organic functions and all psychic forces meet, and there it enjoys Unity... nothing else."[1]

"Nothing else?"—What more do you want? There, according to your own admission, you have an instrument for penetrating to the depths of functional consciousness, of subliminal life—and yet you do not use it in order to complete your knowledge of the whole activity of the mind. You, doctors of the Unconscious, instead of making yourselves citizens of this boundless empire and possessing yourselves of it, do you ever enter it except as foreigners, imbued with the preconceived idea of the superiority of your own

is the fruit of true intuition, the state of inner freedom, of fusion of the pacified soul with (the Being) non-passive peace, which is action at its highest power...."
("*The Discipline of Intuition*", Review *Vers l'Unité*, 1925, Nos. 35-36.) There is nothing in these sayings to which Vivekananda would not have subscribed.
[1] E. Morel: *op. cit.*, p. 112.

country and incapable of ridding yourselves of the need, which itself deforms your vision, of reducing whatever you catch a glimpse of in this unknown world to the measure of the one already familiar to you?

Think of the extraordinary interest of these striking descriptions—a succession of Indian, Alexandrine, and Christian mystics of all sects without mutual knowledge of each other have all with the same lucidity gone through the same experiences—the triple movement of thought,[1] and especially the "circular movement", which they have tested thoroughly, and "which represents exactly the psychic movement of pure and simple introversion, withdrawing itself from the periphery and collecting itself towards the centre"—the mighty Stygian river that goes seven times round the Being, the round dance with its powerful attraction towards the centre, the centripetal force of the inner soul corresponding to that exercised in the exterior universe by universal gravitation! Is it a slight thing by means of direct inner perception to be able to realise the great cosmic laws and the forces that govern the universe controlled by our senses?

If a scientist maintains that such a knowledge of psychic profundities teaches us nothing about exterior realities, he is really, though perhaps unwittingly, obeying a prejudice of proud incomprehension as one-eyed as that of religious spiritualists who set up an insurmountable barrier between spirit and matter. What is the "function of the real" of which scientific psychology claims to be the standard-bearer? And what is the "real"? Is it what can be observed by extrospection or by introspection like that of

---

[1] The three movements: "circular", when the thought turns entirely towards itself; "spiral", when it reflects and reasons in a discursive fashion; "in a straight line", when it is directed towards the exterior.

the St. John in Raphael's *Discussion*,[1] who gazes into the depths with his closed eyes? Is it "the movement in a straight line" or "in spirals" or "in a circle"? There are not two realities. That which exists in one, exists equally in the other.[2] The laws of the inner psychic substance are of necessity themselves those of outside reality. And if you succeed in reading one properly, the chances are that you will find the confirmation and if not, the presentiment of what you have read or will read in the other. Laotse's deep thought that "a wheel is made up of thirty perceptible spokes, but it is because of the central non-perceptible void of the nave that it turns," leads me to think of the latest hypotheses of astronomical science, which claim to have discovered gulfs of cosmic emptiness to be the homes of the various universes.... Do you suppose that Laotse would ever have been able to imagine such a thought if it had not secretly contained the form of the universal cosmic substance and its forgotten laws? Hypothesis, do you say? Neither more nor less so than your most firmly established and fruitful scientific hypotheses—and quite logically probable: for it satisfies the strict economy of the laws of the universe and partakes of their natural harmony.

(*Cf.* Plotinus, Porphyry, Proclus, Hermias, Denis the Areopagite, etc. and F. Morel's analysis of them).

[1] An allusion to Raphael's fresco in the Vatican known as the Discussion of the Holy Sacrament.

[2] I am glad to find myself here in accord with the thought of one of the masters of the "New Education", Dr. Adolphe Ferrière, the founder-president of the International Bureau of Education, in his monumental work: *Spiritual Progress* (Vol. I of *Constructive Education*, 1927, Geneva):

"If individual reasons are reducible, as to a single common denominator, to Reason conceived as super-individual and impersonal, ...it is because at bottom each mind and what it is convenient to call nature, share the same reality, have the same origin, are the issue of the same cosmic Energy." (p. 45).

If then introspection makes it possible to go back, I do not say to

But if this is true, the judicious use of deep introversion opens to the scientist unexplored resources: for it constitutes a new method of experiment, having the advantage that the observer identifies himself with the object observed —the Plotinian identity of the seer and the thing seen.[1]

The clear intuition of Plotinus, who united in himself the spirit of Greek observation and Eastern introspection, has thus described the operation: "It may happen that the soul possesses a thing without being aware of it;[2] it therefore possesses it better than if it were aware of it; in fact when it is aware of it, it possesses it as a thing that is alien to it; when on the contrary it is not aware of it, it is a real possession."[3]

And that is exactly the idea that one of the greatest thinkers of modern India, Aurobindo Ghose, is trying to incorporate in science: he wishes to reintegrate generative intuition in its legitimate place as advance guard of the

the origin, but nearer to the origin, the vital source that is one of the forms of universal Energy, why ignore it?

(Cf. in the same work of Dr. A. Ferriére, Chap. III, I, "*The Human Microcosm Replies to the Macrocosm*"—its very title and basic idea correspond to the Vedantic conception explained by Vivekananda in several of the most famous lectures of his *Jnana-Yoga*.)

[1] As a matter of fact every great scientific experimenter identifies himself more or less with the object of his experiment. It is an attribute of all passion, whatever its object, whether carnal or intellectual, that it embraces the object, and tends to infuse itself into it. The great biologist, J. C. Bose, has told me that he feels himself becoming one with the plants that he is observing and that now, before he begins an experiment, he preconceives their reactions within himself; and in the case of poets and artists this is still more true. I refer my reader to the chapter in this book on Walt Whitman.

[2] The word "aware" stands here for "discursive intellectual knowledge." It is quite evident that a superior knowledge takes its place: this knowledge may be called "functional," as in M. F. Morel, or "perfect reason" as in Plotinus who adds this comment: "A man only considers discursively that which he does not yet possess.... Perfect reason no longer seeks; it rests upon the evidence of that with which it is filled." (*Enn.* III, VIII, [2] [5]).

[3] *Enn.* IV, IV (4).

Cf. the analysis of intuitive thought by my contemporary French master, Edouard Le Roy:

army of the spirit marching forward to the scientific conquest of the universe.

But if this great effort is rejected with the disdainful gesture of the exclusive rationalists, and particularly of psycho-pathologists, who throw discredit on "the standard of intellectual satisfaction" or—as the great Freud said with austere scorn—on "the principle of pleasure", which in his eyes is that of "the unsuitable", those who reject it are far less the servants of the "real", as they imagine themselves to be, than of a proud and Puritanical faith, whose prejudices they no longer see because those prejudices have become their second nature. There is no normal reason why, on the plausible hypothesis of a unity of substance and cosmic laws, the conquest, the full perception, and the "*fruitio*" by the mind of the logical ordering of the universe should not be accompanied by a feeling of sovereign well-being. And it would be strange if mental joy were a sign of error. The mistrust shown by some masters of psycho-analysis for the free natural play of the mind, rejoicing in

"It is essential that the mind...should free itself from all disuniting egoism, and be led to a state of docility analogous to the purification of the conscience by ascetics, an attitude of generosity resembling the workings of love that divines and understands because it forgets itself, because it accepts the effect of the necessary transformations in order to lose itself in its object and to attain perfect objectivity...." etc.

("*The Discipline of Intuition,*" Review *Vers l'Unité*, 1925, Nos. 35-36). And in conclusion:

"The three stages in the course of intuitive thought are:

1. The 'ascése' preparatory to the renunciation of the usual forms of speech.

2. The final union of the spirit with that which started as a separate object from it.

3. The simplicity of knowledge or rather of perception when it is being rediscovered after passing through the dispersion of analysis and going beyond and below it, but a simplicity which is the result of wealth and not poverty." (Ibid.)

Are there not close analogies here to the Jnana-Yoga of India? (*Cf. Intuitive Thought* by the same author, E. Le Roy, 1925.)

its own possession—the stigma they imprint upon it of "narcissism" and "autoerotism"[1]—betray all unconsciously a kind of perverted asceticism and religious renunciation.

They are, it is true, not wrong to denounce the dangers of introversion, and in so doing no one will contradict them. But every experiment has its own dangers for the mind. Sense and reason itself are dangerous instruments and have to be constantly supervised; and no close scientific observation is carried out on a *tabula rasa*. Whatever it is doing, the eye interprets before it has seen;[2] and in the case of P. Lowell, the astronomer, he has never ceased to see upon the surface of Mars the canals his own eyes have put there. . . . By all means let us continue to doubt, even after having proof! My attitude is always one of profound Doubt, which is to be kept hidden in my cave like a strong, bitter, but health-giving tonic, for the use of the strong.

But in the world of the "real"—that is to say, of the "relative"—where we must needs labour and build our dwellings, I maintain that the principle whereby we ought to attempt to satisfy the operations of the mind is that of proportion, of equilibrium between the diverse forces of the mind. All tendency to exclusiveness is dangerous and defective. Man has different and complementary means of knowledge at his disposal.[3] Even if it is of use to divide

---

[1] That is to say: the state of Narcissus, who was in love with himself.

[2] *Cf.* the definition of scientific hypothesis by one of the intuitive savants of today, J. Perrin, as "a form of intuitive intelligence. . . to divine the existence or the essential faculties of objects which are still beyond our consciousness, to explain the complicated visible by the simple invisible." (*The Atoms*, 1912).

[3] In the study by Charles Baudouin already quoted, see his analysis of complementary instincts (the combative instinct and the instinct of withdrawal; activity, passivity) and their rhythmic connection. In the cases we are considering, the tendencies of recoil and of introversion are complementary to forward impulse and extroversion. Together they form a system in unstable equilibrium which can always be tipped to one side or the other.

them in order to probe with them into the depths of an object of study, synthesis must always be re-established afterwards. Strong personalities accomplish this by instinct. A great "Introvert" will know at the same time how to be a great "Extrovert". Here the example of Vivekananda seems to me to be conclusive.[1] Interiorisation has never led in principle to diminution of action. Arguments drawn from the supposed social passivity of mystic India are entirely erroneous: here what is nothing but *Ersatz* is taken for the cause. The physical and moral devitalisation of India during several centuries is due to quite different factors of climate and social economy. But we shall see with our own eyes that her interiorisation, where the fires of her threatened life have taken refuge, is the principle of her national resurrection. And it will shortly appear what a brazier of action is this Atman, over which she has brooded for several thousand years. I advise the "extrovert" peoples of the West to rediscover in the depths of themselves the same sources of active and creative "introversion". If they fail, there is not much hope for the future. Their gigantic technical knowledge, far from being a source of protection, will bring about their annihilation.

But I am not anxious, the same sources sleep in the depths of the soul of the West. At the last hour but one they will spring up anew.

---

[1] Is it necessary to remind the reader that his example is not in the least unique? The genius for action shown by the greatest of mystic Christian introverts: St. Bernard, St. Theresa, St. Ignatia, is well known.

## NOTE III

## ON THE HELLENIC-CHRISTIAN MYSTICISM OF THE FIRST CENTURIES AND ITS RELATIONSHIP TO HINDU MYSTICISM

### PLOTINUS OF ALEXANDRIA AND DENIS THE AREOPAGITE

IT is one of my chief desires to see Lectureships of Comparative Eastern and Western Metaphysics and Mysticism founded in India and Europe. The two should be mutually complementary; for their work is essential if the human spirit is to learn to know itself in its entirety. Their object would not be a kind of puerile steeplechase seeking to establish the primitive chronology of each group of thought. Such research would be meaningless: religious historians who seek only to discover the intellectual inter-dependence of systems, forget the vital point: the knowledge that religions are not ordinary matter of intellectual dialectic, but facts of experience, and that although reason steps in afterwards to construct systems upon the facts, such systems would not hold good for an hour, if they were not based upon the solid foundation of experience. Hence the facts must first be discovered and studied. I do not know whether any modern psycho-physiologist, armed with all the latest instruments of the new sciences of the soul, will be able to attain to a full knowledge of them one day,[1] but

[1] One of the first to attempt an objective study of them was William James in his famous book on Religious Experience, an Essay of Descriptive Psychology, which appeared in New York in 1902,

I am willing to believe it. In the meanwhile such simple observation as we have at our present disposal, leads us to recognise the existence of *the same religious facts* as the foundations of all the great organised religions, that have spread over the face of the earth throughout the march of the centuries. At the same time it is impossible to attribute to the mutual actions and reactions of the peoples any appreciable effect on their production: for their uprising is spontaneous, it grows from the soil under certain influences in the life of humanity almost "seasonal" in their recurrence like the grain that springs up in natural life with the return of spring.

under the title: *The Varieties of Religious Experience.* It is very remarkable that, owing to the scrupulous honesty of his intellect alone, this man, though not in the least gifted for the attainment of subliminal reality, as he himself frankly declared, "My temperament prohibited me from almost all mystic experience"—should have arrived at the positive statement of the objective existence of these very realities and should have commended them to the respect of scientists. To his efforts were added those of the learned Frederick W. H. Myers, who in 1886, discovered "the subliminal consciousness", a theory propounded in a posthumous work, later than that of William James: *Human Personality.* (Myers like James had known Vivekananda personally). The most interesting part of James' book appears to be the collection of mystic witness coming from his Western contemporaries, chiefly from laymen who were strangers to religious or metaphysical speculation, so that they did not try to attach to it the facts of inner experience, often very striking, which had come to them unawares, like the fall of a thunderbolt (Tennyson, C. Kingsley, J. A. Symonds, Dr. R. M. Bucke, etc.). All unknowing as they were, they realised states identical with the characteristic Samadhis of India. Others, whose natural intelligence cut them off from mysticism, found themselves led, as was James himself, by artificial means (chloroform, ether, etc.) to an astounding intuition of absolute Unity where all contraries are dissolved—a conception quite beyond their ordinary ken. And with the intellectual lucidity of the West, these "amateurs" in ecstasy have given perfect descriptions of it. The hypothetical conclusions to which James arrived testify to a rare mental freedom. Certain of them are the same as Vivekananda's and Gandhi's, for example that religions are necessarily diverse, and that their "complete meaning can only be deciphered by their universal collaboration." Others, curiously enough, admit a "polytheism of the Ego."

The first result of an objective study of Comparative
Metaphysics and Mysticism would be to demonstrate the
universality and perennial occurrence of the great facts of
religious experience, their close resemblance under the
diverse costumes of race and time, attesting to the persistent unity of the human spirit—or rather, for it goes deeper
than the spirit, which is itself obliged to delve for it—to
the identity of the materials constituting humanity.[1] But
before entering into any discussion of the comparative value
of ideological structures erected by religion and metaphysics
in India and Alexandria (the case with which we are dealing
here) it is necessary to establish the fact that at bottom the
illuminations of Philo, the great ecstasies of Plotinus and
Porphyry, so similar to the Samadhis of Indian Yogis,
were identical experiences. Hence we must not use the term
Christianity to the exclusion of the other thousands of
mystic experiences, on whose foundations it was built up—
not in one feverish birth, but by a series of births throughout the centuries, fresh shoots sprouting from the ancient
tree with each spring.

And that is, indeed, the heart of the problem. If these

[1] That is also the conclusion to which one of the exceptionally
religious men of the West has reached after a careful and scientific
study of the comparative mysticism of India and Europe: Professor
Rudolf Otto of Marburg. Having lived for fourteen years in India
and Japan he has devoted a whole series of remarkable works to
Asiatic mysticism. The most important for our purpose is: *West
Oestliche Mystik, Vergleich und Unterscheidung zur Wesensdeutung* (1926,
Gotha, Leopold Koltzverlag), which takes as its types the two mystics,
Shankara and Meister Eckhart.

His main thesis establishes the extraordinary likeness of the
*Urmotiven* (the fundamental motives) of humanity's spiritual
experience, exclusive of race, age, or climate. Mysticism is always and
everywhere the same. And the profound unity of the human spirit
is a fact. Naturally this does not exclude variations between different
mystic personalities. But such variations are not the result of race,
age, or country. They may be found side by side in the same
surroundings.

great experiences have once been established, compared and classified, comparative mysticism would then—and only then—have the right to pass on to a study of systems. Systems exist solely to provide the mind with a means for registering the results of enlightenment and to classify in one complete and co-ordinated whole the claims of the senses, reason, and intuition—(by whatever name we may choose to call the eighth sense or the second reason, which those who have experienced it call the first). Systems then are a continually renewed effort to bring about by all the various instruments at the disposal of knowledge the synthesis of all that a man, a race, or an epoch has experienced. And of necessity the particular temperament of that man, race, or epoch is always reflected in each system.

Moreover, it is intensely interesting that all kinds of minds, morally akin, but scattered through space and time in different countries and different ages, know that the varieties of their own thought, produced by all these different temperaments, are simultaneously the limits and the womb of force. India and Europe are equally concerned to enrich themselves by a knowledge of all the forms developed by this same mental or vital power, a theme upon which each of their diverse races, epochs, and cultures has embroidered its own variations.

Hence, to return to the subject that is occupying us here, I do not believe modern Indian metaphysics can remain any longer in ignorance of Alexandrine and Christian Mysticism —any more than our Western intellectuals can be allowed in future to stop short their study of the "Divine Infinity"[1] at the borders of Greece. When two types of humanity as

[1] This is the title of an excellent Doctorate thesis, written by Henri Guyot: *The Divine Infinity from Philo the Jew to Plotinus with an Introduction on the Same Subject in Greek Philosophy before Plato*, Paris, Alcan, 1906. I have made profitable use of it.

magnificent as India and Greece have dealt with the same subject, it is obvious that each will have enriched it with its own particular splendours, and that the double master-piece will harmonise with the new spirit of universal humanity we are seeking to establish.

In these pages I can do no more than point out the way to the intelligence of my readers. And in this place, where I am addressing myself especially to the Vedantists of India, I want to give them at least a glimpse of the character-istics wherein Mediterranean Mysticism and their own are alike and wherein they differ. I shall particularly insist on the chief monument of early Christian Mysticism— the work of the Pseudo-Denis because, as it came from the East, it possessed already the characteristics that it was to impose upon the metaphysical physiognomy of the West during six centuries of Christianity.

\*

It is generally conceded that the Greek spirit, while eminently endowed for art and science, was almost a closed book to the idea of infinity, and that it only accepted the idea with mistrust. Although the Infinite is included in principle by Anaximander and Anaxagoras, they give it a material character and stamp it with the imprint of scientific instinct. Plato, who in his *Republic* touched in passing on the conception of the Idea of Good superior to being, essence, and intelligence, did not dwell upon it and seemed to regard it merely as an idea of perfection and not of infinity. To Aristotle, the infinite was imperfect: to the Stoics, it was unreal.[1]

It is not until we reach the first century that we find

[1] It must not be forgotten that during the Alexandrine epoch there was an intimate connection between India and the Hellenic West. But the history of thought has not taken it into account and even at the present day is very insufficiently aware of it. Several years

Philo, a Jew of Alexandria who had been brought up in Greek thought, imbuing it with the notion of Infinity derived from his people and attempting to hold the balance between the two currents. The balance, however, remained an unstable one, and all through his life Philo oscillated between the two temperaments. In spite of His Being indeterminate, the God of the Jews kept a very strong personal flavour which Philo's nostrils could not dispense with. On the other hand his Greek education allowed him to analyse with rationalist precision those obscure powers of his prophetic people, that had brought them into contact with God. His theory of ecstasy, first by withdrawal into oneself, then by the flight of the ego and the total negation of the senses, reason, and being itself, so that they might identify themselves with the One, is, in the main, precisely the same as that always practised by the Indian in the East. Philo eventually sketches an attempt to attach the Infinite to the finite by means of intermediary powers, from whence emerges the "second God", the Word, "the only Begotten Son of God." And so, with him, perhaps unwittingly (for he never lost the thumb-mark of his rough modeller: Jehovah), the Infinite of the East entered the Mediterranean world.

A hundred facts testify to how great an extent the East was mingled with Hellenic thought during the second century of our era. Let us recall only three or four of the

---

ago in India a Society was formed to study the radiations of "Greater India" and its forgotten Empire in the past. (*The Greater India Society:* President, Prof. Jadunath Sarkar, the Vice-Chancellor of the University of Calcutta; Honorary Secretary, Dr. Kalidas Nag.) It has published since November, 1926, a regular Bulletin, and the first number included an Essay by Dr. Kalidas Nag, containing a very interesting historical account of the spread of the Indian spirit beyond its own frontiers: *Greater India, a Study in Indian Internationalism.*

most characteristic. Plutarch quoted Zoroaster and devoted a whole treatise to Egyptian mythology. The historian Eusebius was a witness to the interest felt in Asiatic philosophies and religions in his own day. One of the first builders of Alexandrianism, Numenius, who extolled Pythagoras above all other Greeks, sought for the spirit of his age in the past, and believed that Pythagoras had spread in Greece[1] the first wisdom of the Egyptians, the Magi, the Indians, and the Jews. Plotinus, a Greek of Egypt, departed with Gordian's army, in order to study Persian and Indian philosophy. And although Gordian's death, in Mesopotamia, stopped him half way, his intention shows his intellectual kinship with the Indian spirit.[2] But at the same time he was in communion with the Christians. One of his listeners was a Doctor of the New Church—Origen; and they mutually respected each other. Plotinus was not merely a book philosopher. He was, at the same time, a saint and a great Yogi. His pure image, recalling certain of

[1] Numenius, whose influence over Plotinus was of capital importance, "had directed all his efforts," says Eusebius, "towards a fusion of Pythagoras and Plato, while seeking for a confirmation of their philosophical doctrines in the religious dogmas of the Brahmins, the Indians, the Magi, and the Egyptians."

[2] His theory of reincarnation bears the stamp of Indian thought. All actions and thoughts count. The purified and detached are not reborn into the corporeal, they remain in the world of the mind and of bliss, without reason, remembrance, or speech; their liberty is absolute; they are made one with the Perfect, and are absorbed into It without losing themselves in It. Such bliss can be obtained in the present by ecstasy.

His theory of matter and his definitions of it evoke the Hindu Maya.

His vision of the universe as a Divine Game, where "the actors constantly change their costumes," where social revolutions, the crash of empires, are "changes of scene and character, the tears and cries of the actors", is the same as the Indian.

Above all his profound science of "deification", identification with God by the path of Negation, is, as I shall show, one of its most magnificent expressions and might have come from one of the great Indian Yogis.

Ramakrishna's characteristics,[1] deserves to be more piously remembered by both the East and the West.

It would be lacking in the respect his great work deserves, to summarise it here. But I must enumerate its most striking characteristics which are analogous to Indian thought.

\*

Plotinus' First Being, who is "before all things", no less than in all that comes after Him, is the Absolute. "Absolutely infinite, indeterminate, incomprehensible," He can only be defined by negation.

"Let us take all things from Him, let us affirm nothing about Him, let us not lie by saying that there is anything in Him, but let Him simply be."

He is above good and ill, act and knowledge, being and essence. He has neither face nor form, neither movement nor number, neither virtue nor feelings. We cannot even say that He wishes or that He does.... "We say what He is not; we cannot say what He is.".... In brief, Plotinus collects the whole litany of "Noes", so dear to the Indian mystic (and to the Christian), in order to express the Absolute. But without the self-satisfaction mingled with conceit and puerility that most men bring to it, Plotinus impregnates it always with his beautiful modesty, a fact that makes it very touching, and that I should say is more Christlike than are many Christians (such as the author of *Mystic Theology*, which I shall examine later).

"When we say," he wrote, "that He is above being, we do not say that He is this or that. We affirm nothing; we do not give Him any name.... We do not try to understand Him: it would in fact be laughable to try to under-

---

[1] His exquisite kindness and delicate, pure, and rather childlike temperament.

stand that incomprehensible nature. But we being men,
with doubts like the sorrows of childhood, do not know
what to call Him, and so we try to name the Ineffable....
He must have indulgence for our language.... Even the
name of the One expresses no more than the negation of
His plurality.... The problem must be given up, and
research fall into silence. What is the good of seeking when
further progress is impossible?... If we wish to speak of
God, or to conceive Him, let us give up everything! When
this has been done, (let us not add anything to Him but)
let us examine rather whether there is still not something
to be given up...."[1]

In the path of negation has India ever said anything more
perfect or more humble?

Nevertheless, it is not a question of negation. This in-
conceivable Absolute is the supreme and super-abundant
Perfection, whose continual expansion engenders the
universe. He is suspended to it by love and He fills it
entirely: for, without ever coming out of Himself, He is
present everywhere in His entirety. In the effort of the
human spirit to distinguish the successive degrees of this
divine procession of worlds, the mystic Greek in a splendid
outburst of enlightened enthusiasm salutes Intelligence as
the first born of God, the best after Him, itself "a great
God", "the second God", the first Hypostasis, which
engenders the second, the Soul, the one and the multiple,
the mother of all living things. There follows the unfolding of the whole world of the senses, within the bounds
whereof Matter is found, and that is the last degree of
being or rather of non-being, the Infinite negative, the
absolute and unattained limit at the opposite antipodes of
the thrust of Divine Power.

[1] *Enneades*, V. 5. 6; VI. 9. 4; VI. 8. 13, etc.

So, this Absolute, which our minds can only approach through negation, is affirmed in all that is. And it is in ourselves. It is the very basis of ôur being. And we can be rejoined to It by concentration. Yoga, the great path of divine union, as described by Plotinus, is a combination of Jnana-Yoga and Bhakti-Yoga. After a first and long stage of purification, the soul, as it enters the phase of contemplation, must renounce knowledge as a starting point. "The soul withdraws from the One, and is no longer one entity when it acquires knowledge. Knowledge in effect is a discourse, and a discourse is multiplicity. In order to contemplate the first Being a man must be raised above knowledge."[1]

Ecstasy begins. And the door of ecstasy for the Hellenic spirit, always tenacious of its rights, is Beauty. Through it the inflamed soul soars towards the light of the Good, above which there is nothing. And this divine flight of the mystic Alexandrine is precisely the same that Beethoven has translated into the phrase written during the evening of his life:

(1823)

Das      Schö-ne      zum Gu — ten
(The      Beautiful      to the Good).

His description of ecstasy[2] is like the descriptions of both Hindus and Christians: for there is only one form of

[1] *Enneades*, VI. 9. 4; VI. 9. 10.
*Cf.* the analysis of intuitive thought by Ed. Le Roy, quoted in *Note II*.
[2] This admirable conception drawn from the most sacred essence of the West with its passion for Beauty, has its source in our divine Plato:
" In the domain of love," said Socrates to the Stranger of Mantineus, "to do well one must pass from the love of a beautiful form to the

union with the Absolute, by whatever name the mind primarily or eventually seeks to clothe the Absolute. According to Plotinus, the soul ought to empty itself of all form and content, of all evil and good, of all thought of union with that, which is neither form, nor content, nor evil, nor good, nor thought.[1] It should even empty itself of the thought of God in order to become one with Him.[2] When it has reached this point He appears within it. He is it: "it has become God or rather it is God. A centre which

love of all beautiful forms or to physical beauty in general; then from love of beautiful bodies to the love of beautiful souls, beautiful actions, and beautiful thoughts. In this ascension of the spirit through moral beauty, a marvellous beauty will suddenly appear to him, eternal, exempt from all generation, from all corruption, absolutely beautiful: not consisting either in a beautiful face, nor in any body nor any thought nor in any science; not residing anywhere but in itself, whether in heaven or on earth, but existing eternally in itself and for itself in its absolute and perfect unity." (*Banquet: summary*).

Therein is contained a Yoga of Beauty where Bhakti to a certain extent is joined to Jnana. I do not say that it is peculiar to the West for we have traces of it in India, but it is the form which of all others is natural and dear to us.

[1] Not to know but to be, is also taught by the Vedanta: "Knowledge is," said Vivekananda, "as it were, a lower step, a degradation. We are It already. How to know It?" (*Jnana-Yoga: "The Real and the Apparent Man"*).

This is also the famous doctrine of the *Docta Ignorantia*, belonging to Christian mysticism: the knowledge above all knowledge. No man in the world has described it with such power and psychological detail as St. Jean de la Croix in his famous treatise on the *Nuit Obscure*—the double Night: of the senses and of the spirit. "*Primo derelinquere omnia sensibilia, secondo omnia intelligibilia,...*" St. Bonaventura had already said (*Itinerarium mentis ad Deum*).

[2] "The soul ought to be without form, if it wishes no obstacle to stop it from being filled and illuminated by the first Nature. (VI. 9. 7). The first Principle, not having any difference in Him, is always present and we are ourselves present in Him, when we no longer possess anything. (VI. 9. 8). The soul ought to drive out evil, good, and everything else to receive God only in itself....It will not even know that it has been joined to the first Principle. (VI. 9. 7). It is no longer soul, nor intelligence, nor movement.... Resemblance to God ought to be complete. The soul eventually does not even think of God because it no longer thinks....(VI. 7. 3. 5.). When the soul has become like Him, it sees Him appear suddenly;

coincides with another centre...." They are one. There is perfect identity. The soul has returned to itself.[1]

I have said enough to awaken in every Hindu reader the

separation and duality are no more, both are one....This union is imitated on earth by those who love and are loved and who seek to become one flesh. (VI. 7. 34)."

[1] Plotinus often experienced this great ecstasy, according to the definite testimony of Porphyry:

"To him this God appeared, who had neither form nor face, who is above intelligence. I myself, Porphyry, once in my life approached this God and was united to Him. I was seventy-eight. This union formed the sum total of Plotinus' desires. He had this divine joy four times while I was staying with him. What then happened was ineffable."

So it is of the greatest interest to know from the mouth of Plotinus himself what were his impressions during that state. The most striking is the anguish of the soul as it approached Divine Union, for it was unable to sustain the intensity long. "Certainly here below each time that the soul approaches That without form, it shrinks, it trembles as having before it only That which is nothing."

And as I read these lines I think of the mortal terror of young Vivekananda during his first visits to Ramakrishna, when the enlightened Master made him aware for the first time of the dizzy contact with the formless Absolute.

"The soul", continues Plotinus (and the rest of his description would serve for Vivekananda's experience), "returns with joy...it lets itself fall until it meets some sensible object whereon to stop and rest...." (VI. 9. 3; 9. 10).

J. A. Symonds says the same thing: "It (trance) consisted in a gradual but swiftly progressive obliteration of space, time, sensation and the multitudinous factors of experience....But the self persisted, formidable in its vivid keenness, feeling the most poignant doubt about reality, ready, as it seemed, to find existence break as breaks a bubble round about it. And what then? The apprehension of a coming dissolution, the grim conviction that this state was the last state of the conscious self, the sense that I had followed the last thread of being to the verge of the abyss,...stirred or seemed to stir me up again. The return to ordinary conditions of sentient existence began by my first recovering the power of touch.... I was thankful for this return from the abyss...." (One of the many contemporary witnesses quoted by William James, in his chapter on Mysticism in *The Variety of Religious Experience*).

But a great mystic like Plotinus had hardly set foot again on the earth when he longed for that from which he had fled....The deadly vertigo did not cease to attract. The soul that has once tasted the terrible Union yearns to find it again, and it must return to the Infinite.

desire to know more of this great fellow Yogi, who in the last hour of Greece, in her majestic sunset, wedded Plato and India. In this divine marriage the male Hellenic genius, as he embraced the female Kirtana—the inspired Bacchante—imposed upon her thoughts an ordered beauty and intelligent harmony, resulting in one of the most beautiful strains of spiritual music. And the great Christian mysticism of the first centuries was the first born of the union.

In the following pages I shall try to paint, however imperfectly, a portrait of the most beautiful type, in my opinion, of early Christian thought that issued from this marriage of East and West: Denis (Dionysius) the Areopagite.

\*

I have often had occasion in the course of this book to notice analogies and even traces of kinship between the conceptions of Hindu and Christian mysticism at their highest moments. This likeness is the more striking as one approaches the source of Christianity;[1] and I want to demonstrate it to my Eastern readers. They will profit by it more than my Western readers; for as I have already stated they are all too ignorant of the marvellous treasures contained in European Christian metaphysics.[2]

[1] The blind fury of certain neophytes of modern literary Catholicism in the West in their denunciation of the danger of the East, is a fit subject for irony. They make it irrevocably the antithesis of the West, forgetting that the whole faith they proclaim comes to them from the East, and that in the ritual of the first centuries, as decreed by Denis the Areopagite, the West is represented by doctors of the faith, as "the region of shades", making the catechumen "hold up his hands as a sign of anathema" and "blow on Satan three times." (Cf. Book of the Ecclesiastical Hierarchy, II. 2. 6.)

[2] The fault lies partly in the political conditions that interpose between India and Europe the thick screen of the British Empire—with its mind more tightly closed than any other in Europe to suggestions of Catholic (or even Pre-Reformation Christian) mysticism, as

The polemics that have been uttered round the name of the Areopagite whether Denis or Pseudo-Denis[1] matter little to us here, for all accounts agree that his authentic writings fall within the period round about 532 or 533,[2] and that from that date their authority became law in the Christian Church and was invoked by Popes, Patriarchs, and learned Doctors in the Synods and Councils of the seventh and eighth centuries[3] down to the ninth century.

well as to music in the profound sense of the German masters, the other fountain of intuition.

[1] For a thousand years this greatest master of Christian mysticism was supposed to be Denis the Anchorite, a member of the Athenian Areopagus at the time of St. Paul who converted him about 5 A.D., and later Bishop of Athens (he has even been identified with St. Denis of France). First Laurence Valla, then Erasmus, then the Reformation brutally wronging his legend, and being wickedly desirous of discrediting the work, which was sufficiently powerful to lose nothing, they changed the name of the author and tried to make him anonymous. Modern research seems to have agreed that the writer of these books lived about 500 A.D., and that at all events, although he may have been earlier than this date (according to the testimony of some of his learned disciples in the ninth century, when they revived a controversy in existence about 400 A.D. on the subject of the authenticity of his writings), he cannot possibly have been later than Justinian who quoted him as an authority.

*Cf.* Stiglmayr: *Das Aufkommen der Pseudo-Dionysischen Schriften und ihr Eindringen in die christliche Literatur bis zum Lateranconcil* 649— Feldkirch, 1895.

Hugo Kock: *Pseudo-Dionysius Areop. in seinen Beziehungen zum Neoplatonismus und Mysterienwesen*, 1900.

A French translation of the *Works of St. Denis the Areopagite*, by Mgr. Darboy, Archbishop of Paris, shot in the Commune of 1871, appeared in 1845, and was re-edited in 1887. For the benefit of my French readers I have used it in my quotations. [An English translation is also in existence by the Rev. John Parker, 1897, and wherever possible I have referred to it.—*Translator.*]

[2] On the occasion of a religious conference summoned to Constantinople by Justinian. It is also noteworthy that the writings of Denis were invoked by the Severian heretics. A strong argument in their favour is that the orthodox from instincts of defence or resentment made no attempt to throw doubt on their authenticity! And from that time onwards they were invoked and paraphrased until they almost became "holy oracles", in the words of the sacred texts.

[3] Here are some vital facts, showing their uncontested authority

They were then triumphantly installed in Paris by Charles the Bald, who had them translated by Scot Erigene— whence they impregnated the mystic thought of the Western Church. Their power is attested by St. Anselm, by St. Bonaventura, and by St. Thomas, who wrote commentaries upon them; the great doctors of the thirteenth century put them above the writings of the Church Fathers. In the fourteenth century the mystic furnaces of Meister Eckhart and even more those of Ruysbroeck were fed on their fires; again, at the time of the Italian Renaissance, they were the delectation of the great Christian Platonists, Marsilio Ficino, Pico della Mirandola; and they continued to be the substance of our Bérullians, our Salesians,[1] and the greatest mystics of the seventeenth century in France, as the recent works of the Abbé Brémond have shown.

Hence, whatever the name of the architect, they form the monumental substructures of all Christian thought in the West during the ten most important centuries of its development. And they are more than that to the man who has eyes to see—they form one of the most harmonious cathedrals that has grown out of Christian thought and that still remains a living witness to it.

in the Christian Church, both Eastern and Western: In the sixth century Denis was venerated by St. Gregory as "*antiqus videlicet et venerabilis Pater.*" In the seventh century Pope Martin I quoted him textually in the Lateran Council of 649 to prove Catholic dogma against heresy. And his works were again used at the third Council of Constantinople, 692, and at the second Council of Nicea. In the eighth century the great Eastern Father, St. John the Damascene, "the St. Thomas of the Greeks of the Lower Empire", became his disciple. In 824 or 827 the Emperor of Constantinople, Michael the Lame, made a gift of his writings to Louis the Good. Scot Erigene, who translated them for Charles the Bald, was entirely reborn by his spirit. He infused his own ardent breath into it and made of it a leaven of pantheistic mysticism for the West. Since then Denis has been invoked in all mental contests.

[1] I would remind the reader that these names designate the French

Its singular value is that it stands just at the junction of the East and the West, at the precise moment when their teachings were united. Whether its architect has borrowed his art from Alexandrine masters, or whether they borrowed it largely from him,[1] the result is the same for us—a union of the highest Hellenic and the purest Christian thought—a marriage regularly consecrated in the eyes of the Church and acknowledged by her throughout the West.

Before tasting its fruits, I must remove from the minds of my readers the impression of discredit thrown over the old master in advance by the unfortunate word *Pseudo*, which implies a taint of falsehood. There is, for instance, a beautiful picture called a "false Rembrandt" that is still scorned, because the idea of false implies imitation! But if it pleases an artist to hide his work under the name of somebody else who never left any work behind him, is that any argument against his originality? At most the scheme might lead to suspicion of the masked man's honesty. But this is less explicable after a study of Denis' works: for if

religious school of Francois de Sales, or Bérulle, in the seventeenth century.

[1] If the date, 500, generally accepted today, is taken as the central point of Denis' career, he must have seen the end of Alexandria (Proclus 410-485) and of the Neo-Platonic School of Athens in 529. He, therefore, in a sense closed the eyes of Greek Philosophy. It is certain at least that both arise from the common metaphysical depths, wherein the wealth of Platonism, early Christianity, and the ancient East were mingled, and that from this storehouse the first five centuries of our era drew with open hands. It was a period of universalism of thought. According to the tradition (based on one of his extant letters) Denis visited Egypt in his youth with a friend, Appollophanes, who followed the Sophist philosophy, and who had remained a pagan. Appollophanes never forgave him for his conversion to Christianity, and in this letter accuses him of "parricide", "because," as Denis explains, "I lacked filial piety in using against the Greeks what I had learned from the Greeks." The affiliation of Greece and Christianity is here specifically acknowledged.

there is one impression left by them it is that of the highest moral integrity; it is unthinkable that so lofty a mind could have stooped to subterfuge, even in the interest of his faith; and I prefer to think that after his death he was exploited by others. At all events and in spite of quite definite interpolations and retouches in the original text, the text still presents from end to end—both treatise and letters—a unity and harmony, that leave in the memory of those who have read them an indelible impression of the serene face of the old master, more vivid than that left by many living people.[1]

The keystone of the edifice—and the whole edifice itself —the *alpha* and *omega* of the work—is "Super-eminent Unity"—"Unity the mother of all other unity." And the grandeur of his definitions and negations which seek, less to attain than to invoke it,[2] is equal and parallel to Vedantic language.... "Without reason, without understanding,

[1] It is to be regretted on behalf of Christianity that this work should be so difficult of access: for very few religious texts give a higher and at the same time more human, more compassionate or pure representation of Christian thought than these pages. In them no word of intolerance, animosity, and vain and bitter polemic comes to destroy the beautiful concord of intelligence and goodness— whether he is explaining with affectionate and broad understanding the problem of evil, and embracing all, even the worst, in the rays of Divine Good, or whether he is recalling a monk of malicious faith to meekness and telling him the admirable legend (which would have enchanted old Tolstoy) of Christ coming down again from heaven to defend a renegade, about to die, against one of his own sect with this rebuke to the inhuman Christian: "Strike against Me in future, for I am ready even again to suffer for the salvation of men." (Letter VIII).

[2] M. Ferdinand Morel in his *Essai sur l' Introversion mystique* (1918) has submitted Denis the Areopagite to a psycho-analytical examination, and has taken out the words he uses most frequently ὕπερ (always applied to God) and αυτο. They imply the double impetus of returning within the self and the expansion of the inner Being (psycho-analysts would say, "the projection of an introvert"!). M. F. Morel further recognises the powerful activity expended in great intuition, and the acuteness of regard necessary to explore the subconscious world.

without name.... Author of all things, nevertheless It is not because It surpasses all that is."[1] ... "Itself not being," but "the cause of being to all,"[2] and that which is included in the same title as the Non-Being.

Everything is reduced to this unique object, which is at the same time the unique subject. It is an intoxication of unity,[3] wherein intelligence without ever losing its perception gives itself to the torrential flood of immense Love and its "circular" river:

"Divine love (which is the smooth flowing of the ineffable Unity) indicates distinctly its own unending and unbeginning, as it were a sort of everlasting circle, whirling round in unerring combination by reason of the Good... and ever advancing and remaining and returning in the same and throughout the same."[4]

The whole world then is subject to divine gravitation,

[1] *Book of Divine Names*, I. 1.

[2] Ibid., I. 1, p. 2, of the English translation of the Rev. John Parker, 1897.

"The non-being, this transcendental appellation only belongs to that which exists in sovereign good in a super-eminent fashion.... Since the latter (the Sovereign Good) surpasses infinitely the Being, it follows that in a certain way non-being finds a place in Him." (Ibid., IV.)

[3] This intoxication discovers images of Unity to the spirit in all the words that invoke It. Hence the most daring etymologies: the sun, ηλιος, is αολλης, "He who collects and maintains Himself in unity"; beauty, Χαλος, is Χαλεω, "I call, I correct," etc. The spirit is truly haunted with unity.

[4] Ibid., IV. 14.

This conception of the "ring of Love", going and coming, is preserved in the mystic theology of the seventeenth century, which Henri Brémond has analysed for us.

It is the double "Procession" of divine Persons of the Dominican Chardon—generation and grace. "The one is the eternal reason for the production of creatures and for their emergence from their cause. The other is the model of their return.... And both together they form the circle of love, begun by God to come to us, begun by us to end in God. They are one production...." (*The Cross of Jesus*, 1647). And the Bérullian, Claude Séguenot, says the same (1634): "We come out of God through the Creation, which is

and the movement of all beings is a march towards God.
The sole aim of all conscious spirits is to "find their perfection in being carried to the Divine initiation...and
what is more Divine than all, in becoming a fellow-worker
with God."[1]

And the "imitation" may be done in an infinite number
of ways, "for each...find their perfection in being
carried to the Divine imitation in their own proper
degree;"[2] and those become most like Him "who have
participated in it in many forms."[3]

But there are three principal ways of approach to Him.
And each of the three may be followed in two ways, by
*Affirmation* or by *Negation*.

The two affirmative ways are:

(1) By a knowledge of the qualities and attributes of
God, attained by the symbols of the Divine Names, which
"the divine oracles" (that is to say, the Scriptures) have
provided for our infirmity of spirit.

(2) By the method of all that exists—created worlds:
for God is in all creatures, and the imprint of His seal may
be found on all matter, although the mark of the seal varies
according to the different kinds of matter.[4] All the worlds
are united in one river. The laws of the physical world
correspond to the laws of the higher world.[5] It is then
lawful to seek God under the veil of the most humble forms,
for "all the streams" of love (even animal love, which

ascribed to the Father by the Son; we return to Him by grace which
is attributed to the Holy Spirit."

[1] *Book of the Celestial Hierarchy*, III. 2, based upon St. Paul: 1
Corinthians, 3, 9.

[2] *The Celestial Hierarchy*, III. 2.

[3] Ibid., IV. 1.

[4] "Even matter, inasmuch as it is matter, participates in the good."
(*The Book of Divine Names*, II. 6.).

[5] *The Celestial Hierarchy*, XIII. 3.

therein finds its justification)[1] participate in holy Love, their unique source.

But all these means that we possess—thanks to the tenderness of God, who proportions His light to the weak eyes of humanity and places forms and shapes around the formless and shapeless and under the manifold and the complex conceals Unity[2]—the imperfect. And the other path, that of negation, is higher, and more worthy,[3] it is more certain, and goes further.

Few there are "even in the sacred ranks" who attain to the One, and yet some exist. "There are spirits among us called to a like grace, as far as it is possible for man. ...They are those who, by the suspension of all intellectual operation, enter into intimate union with the ineffable light. And they speak of God only through negations...."[4]

The great path of Negation is the object of a special treatise, famous from medieval to modern times: *The Treatise of ·Mystic Theology*. In it Denis instructed an initiate, Timotheus, although he told him to keep the mysteries a strict secret (for their knowledge is dangerous to unprepared minds). He taught him the entry into what

[1] *The Divine Names* (Extracts from pious hymns of the fortunate Hierotheus):
"Love, whether we speak of Divine, or Angelic, or intelligent or psychical, or physical, let us regard as a certain unifying and combining power.... Collecting these again into one, let us say that it is a certain simplex power, which of itself moves to a sort of unifying combination from the Good, to the lowest of things existing and from that again in due order, circling round again, through all the Good from itself, and through itself and by itself, and rolling back to itself always in the same way."
[2] *Divine Names*, 1. 4.
[3] *The Celestial Hierarchy*, II. 3.—"Divine things shall be honoured by the true negations."
Ibid., II. 5. "The negations respecting things Divine are true, but the affirmations are inharmonious."
[4] *Divine Names*, I. 5.

he calls "Divine gloom", and which he explained in his letters[1] as "unapproachable light", and also that "mystic ignorance", which being different from ordinary ignorance, "in its superior sense, is a knowledge of Him, Who is above all known things."

Man must "abandon moderate negations for stronger and stronger ones....And we may venture to deny everything about God in order to penetrate into this sublime ignorance," which is in verity sovereign knowledge. He uses the beautiful simile of the sculptor's chisel removing the covering of stone, and "bringing forth the inner form to view, freeing the hidden beauty by the sole process of curtailment."[2]

The first task is to tear aside the veil of "sensible things."[3]

The second task is to remove the last garments, the wrappings of "intelligible things."[4]

The actual words deserve to be quoted:

"It is neither soul nor mind nor has imagination or opinion, or reason, or conception; neither is expressed nor conceived; neither is number nor order; nor greatness nor littleness; nor equality nor inequality; nor similarity nor dissimilarity; neither is standing nor moving, nor at rest; neither has power, nor is power nor light; neither lives nor is life; neither is essence nor eternity nor time; neither is Its touch intelligible, neither is It science nor truth; nor kingdom nor wisdom; neither one nor oneness; neither Deity nor Goodness; nor is It Spirit according to our

---

[1] Letter I, to Gauis Therapeutes; Letter V, to Deacon Dorotheus.
[2] *Mystic Theology*, II.
[3] *Mystic Theology*. IV: "That the pre-eminent cause of every object of sensible perception is none of the objects of sensible perception."
[4] Ibid., V: "That the pre-eminent cause of every object of intelligible perception is none of the objects of intelligible perception."

understanding; neither Sonship nor Paternity; nor any other thing of those known to us, nor to any other existing being; neither is It any of non-existing nor of existing things nor do things existing know It, as It is; nor does It know existing things *qua* existing; neither is there expression of It, nor name nor knowledge; neither is It darkness nor light; nor error nor truth; neither is there any definition at all of It, nor any abstraction. But when making the predications and abstractions of the things after It, we neither predicate nor abstract from It, since the all-perfect and uniform cause of all is both above every definition, and the pre-eminence of Him, who is absolutely freed from all and beyond the whole, is also above every abstraction."[1]

Is there any religious Hindu who will not recognise in the intellectual intoxication of this total Negation, the Advaitic teaching of absolute Jnana-Yoga, after it has arrived at the fact of realisation?

---

[1] Cf. "*Deus propter excellentiam non immerito Nihil vocatur.*"
(Scot Erigene).
"*L'Amour Primordial n'est rien par rapport à autre chose.*"
(Primordial Love is nothing in relation to anything else.)
(Jacob Boehme).
"*Gott ist lauter Nichts, ihn rührt kein Nun noch Hier.*"
(God is mere nothing, to Him belongs neither Now nor Here.)
(Angelus Silesius).
Negation is not more forcibly emphasised in the famous verses of Shankara, that Vivekananda recited to the dying Ramakrishna in the garden of Cossipore:
"I am neither spirit, nor intelligence, nor the ego, nor the substance of the spirit,
I am neither the senses...nor ether, nor the earth, fire nor air,
I am neither aversion, nor attachment, nor desire....
I am neither sin, nor virtue, nor pleasure, nor pain...etc.
I am Absolute Existence, Absolute Knowledge, Absolute Bliss.
I am He, I am He...."
I would go so far as to say that on this occasion Hindu thought is less daring than Christian thought, since after each strophe of

At this point in the conquest of the Divine, the achievement of the "Unreasonable, the cause of all reason,"[1] the liberated and enlightened soul enters into the Peace and Silence of Unity.[2] It does not see God, it does not know Him; "It rests there."[3] It is deified.[4] It no longer speaks of God: it *is* Himself:

"But you will find that the Word of God calls gods, both the Heavenly Beings above us, and the most beloved of God, and holy men amongst us, although the Divine Hiddenness is transcendentally elevated and established above all, and no created Being can properly and wholly

negation it hastens to find foothold in "Existence, Knowledge, and Bliss", even though it is absolute, and Christian mystics, the descendants of Denis, make a clean sweep of everything, blotting out even Existence and Essence from their conception of God.

[1] "Divine Wisdom, which his excellence renders unreasonable, is the cause of all reason." (*Divine Names*, VII).

[2] *Cf.* in *Divine Names* the beautiful Chapter XI, on the Divine Peace —"that Divine Peace and Repose which the holy Justus calls unutterableness and immobility" marvellously active.

That is the theme of Denis, used again and again after him by all the great Christian mystics for ten centuries in their canticle of "Dark Silence." So Suso:

"Without knowing where, I enter into silence,
And I dwell in ignorance,
Above all knowledge....
A place without light, an effect without a cause."

(Strophes of St. Jean de la Croix on "obscure contemplation")
"The silent desert of the Divinity...who is properly no being,...." said Eckhart.

The French seventeenth century kept pure and unadulterated the great motif of the "darkness" and the "silence" of God, which it drew from the source of the Areopagite (often quoted); but it brought to the description of the Inner Voyage all the psychological resources of its race and time. There is nothing more astounding of its kind— except the *Dark Night* of St. Jean de la Croix—than the pages of the Dominican Chardon (*The Cross of Jesus*, 1647), quoted by Henri Brémond, in his *Métaphysique des Saints*, Vol. II, pp. 59-68.

[3] Letter to Dorotheus.

[4] "(Preservation) cannot otherwise take place, except those who are being saved are being deified. Now the assimilation to and union with God, as far as attainable, is deification."

(*Book of the Ecclesiastical Hierarchy*, I. 3).

be said to be like unto It, except those intellectual, rational Beings, who are entirely and wholly turned to Its oneness as far as possible, and who elevate themselves incessantly to Its Divine illuminations, as far as attainable, by their imitation of God, if I may so speak, according to their power, and are deemed worthy of the same divine name."[1]

From that moment the "deified"—the saint, who is united to God, having drunk from the source of the Divine sun—becomes in his turn a sun to those below. "By ordinance and for Divine imitation, the relatively superior (is source) for each after it, by the fact that the Divine rays are poured through it to that."[2]

And gradually the light spreads through all the ranks of the double Hierarchy of the celestial and the human, in an unbroken chain linking the humblest to the highest. And this hierarchy is reflected in each individual. "Each heavenly and human mind has within itself its own special first, and middle, and last ranks and powers manifested severally in due degree, for the aforesaid particular mystical meanings of the Hierarchical illuminations...for there is nothing that is self-perfect...except the really Self-Perfect and pre-eminently Perfect."[3]

This perfecting is the object of initiation, whereby souls are made to pass through three stages: (1) purification; (2) illumination; (3) consummation in the perfect knowledge of the splendours.[4]

To the first rank of the initiated belong those religious monastics, who, like the Sannyasins of India, are under the vow of complete purification. They "remove their mind from the distraction of multiple things and precipitate

[1] *The Celestial Hierarchy*, XII. 3, and XIII. 2.
[2] Ibid., XIII. 2.
[3] Ibid., X. 3.
[4] *The Ecclesiastical Hierarchy*, V. 3.

24

themselves towards Divine unity and the perfection of holy love."[1] Their perfect philosophy "is trained to the knowledge of the commandments whose aim is the union of man and God."[2]

But it is not necessary to belong to a privileged order to attain this knowledge of the Divine Unity. For it is inscribed in each one. "The Divine Light is always unfolded beneficently to the intellectual visions," even to those who reject it.[3] If it is not seen, it is because a man cannot see it. And the proper business of initiation is to teach him to see it. "Inasmuch as the Divine Being is source of sacred order, within which the holy minds regulate themselves, he who recurs to the proper view of Nature will see his proper self in what he was originally." He has only to contemplate himself with "unbiassed eyes."[4] Purification, symbolised by ritual ablutions, does not only concern the body and the senses, but the spirit as well. The unalterable condition of realising communion (in the sense of the eucharistic sacrifice)[5] is to be "purified to the remotest illusions of the soul."[6]

This word "illusions" used in such a sense is like an echo of the Hindu Maya.[7] I was often reminded of the latter when I was reading the long and beautiful explanation of Evil in the system of the Areopagite. Both use the same terms to deny both being and non-being:

[1] *The Ecclesiastical Hierarchy*, VI. 3.
[2] Ibid., VI. III.
[3] Ibid., II, third part, 3.
[4] Ibid., II, third part, 4.
[5] Denis gives it the mysterious name of *Synaxe*, meaning the act of going back to unity through absolute concentration.
[6] *The Ecclesiastical Hierarchy*, III. 10.
[7] But the reader, being aware to a certain extent of the trend of Hindu Vedantic thought, will have discovered resemblances at each step of my summary between the two mysticisms: The path of Negation, the "deification" of individual souls, Christian Sannyasins

"Evil is neither being, for then it would not be absolutely evil, nor non-being, for this transcendental appellation can only belong to that contained in the sovereign good in a sovereign fashion."[1]

"Evil has neither fixity, nor identity, it is varied, indefinite, as if floating in subjects which do not possess immutability in themselves.... Evil, as evil, is not a reality, it is not a being.... Evil as evil is nowhere...."[2]

Everything exists only of and through the Good, which is the "Super-eminent Unity".

At every moment there is the feeling that the links with the East are still intact, and it is difficult to disentangle them. When he describes the ceremonies to be rendered to the dead, Denis thinks of the "loud laugh" or disdainful smile of some profane persons when brought face to face with rites implying a belief that seems to them absurd. And he alludes to the opposite belief in Reincarnation. But he does not treat it with the pitying scorn that he expects from his opponents. He says with admirable forbearance that in his opinion it is wrong:

"Some of them imagine that the souls depart into other bodies; but this seems to me unjust to the bodies who have shared the works of holy souls, since they are unworthily deprived of the divine rewards awaiting them at the end of the way...."[3]

\*

The Areopagite uses many materials in his religious edifice

freeing themselves from multiplicity and the passionate return to unity, the science of divine unity, etc.

[1] *Divine Names*, IV. 19.

[2] Evil, to Plotinus, is merely a lesser good. And absolute Evil, infinite Matter, symbolised the limit of the less good, the last stage of the "Divine Procession".

[3] *Divine Names*, VII. 1. 2.

that are to be found in the constructions of Indian thought. And if there is nothing to justify the view that the one has borrowed from the other, it must be granted that they both come from a common quarry. I have neither the means nor the desire to find out what it is. My knowledge of the human spirit leads me to discover it in the unity of thought and laws that govern the spirit. The primordial instinct, the desire for mystic union with the Absolute that is embodied in each individual and that urges each man towards It, has very limited means of expression; and its great paths have been traced once and for all by the exigences and limitations of nature itself. Different races merely take with them over the same roads their different temperaments, habits, and preferences.

In my opinion the following is what distinguishes a Christian mystic imbued with the Hellenic spirit and the Indian Vedantist:

It is quite obvious that the former possesses a genius for imperial order which demands good government. A harmonious and strict "Hierarchy" controls the whole edifice of the Areopagite. The associated elements cohere and are ordered with justice, prudence, and lucidity. And in that union each one keeps its own place and its own identity.[1] The vital instinct of the European is to cling to the smallest portions of his individuality and to desire to perpetuate them, and this instinct is curiously wedded to the elementary force of mystic gravitation which tends to lose the multiplicity of beings and forms in the incandescent gulf

---

[1] This desire for order and this majestic Hierarchy are directly inspired by the "*Divine Procession*" of Plotinus:
"There is a procession between the first and the last; and in this procession each keeps his own proper place. The created being is subordinate to the creative being. Nevertheless it remains similar to the Principle to which it is attached—in so far as it is attached."

of Unity. "The Divine Peace", described by Denis in one of his most beautiful hymns,[1] is that perfect peace which ought to reign over the entire universe and in each individual, and which both unites and distinguishes all the elements that constitute the general harmony. It "reconciles" the diverse substances with each other and reunites them without altering them, so that in their alliance there is neither separation nor distance, but they keep the integrity of their own proper sphere and do not lose their own nature by an admixture of contrary elements; nothing disturbs either their unanimous concert or the purity of their own particular essence.[2]

This desire to safeguard the integrity and the continuance of individuals even in the bosom of the absolute Being is so powerful in the case of Denis that he justifies not only natural inequality,[3] but (within Divine Peace itself) the fighting instinct that drives each individual to defend the preservation of its essence,[4] and even the cruelties of nature,

[1] *Divine Names*, XI.
[2] Ibid., pp. 260-261 of the French translation.
[3] He only condemns inequalities "resulting from a lack of proportion. For if by inequality we wish to imply the differences that characterise and distinguish living beings, we should say that it is divine justice that keeps them, to see that disorder and confusion are not re-established in the world." (*Divine Names*).

Goethe's saying is surpassed. Denis does not love "injustice more than disorder"—disorder to him is the supreme injustice.

[4] It was observed to Denis that men and things do not seem to adapt themselves to peace—"that they rejoice in distinction and diversity, and flee from repose above all things." He replied that if this meant that "no being wished to lose its own nature," he saw even in this tendency a desire for peace. "For all things asked nothing but to be at peace and union with themselves and to preserve unshaken and intact their essence and what they derived from it. ... The perfect peace that governs the universe prevents confusion and hostility, protects beings against themselves and others, and confirms them in the firm and invincible power of maintaining peace and stability.... If mobile things, instead of entering into repose, seek to perpetuate their natural movement, this very effort is a desire for peace, which God had set in His creation, for it prevents beings from losing themselves, and keeps constant and unalterable in living

so long as they correspond to the laws of types and elements.[1]

Another dominant characteristic of Christian mysticism is the super-eminent place it gives to Goodness and Beauty. This comes from its double descent—noble on both sides—from Christ and Greece. The word Beauty appears in the very first words of Denis.[2] Beauty is the very quality of the Infinite. It is the source and the end of humanity.[3]

And Goodness to a still higher degree. It is the very

things aptitude to receive it and life to transmit to it; and it is this that allows them to be at peace with themselves and to remain constant and to accomplish their own functions." (*Divine Names*, XI. 3 and 4).

Peace here denotes the Spinozan tendency to persevere in being and cannot be described any more than can Spinozan Peace, as "*belli privatio—sed virtus est, quae ex animi fortitudine oritur.*" ("Peace is not lack of war, but an inner virtue, which has its source in the courage of the soul.")

I think that Vivekananda would have subscribed to this definition.

[1] "Neither is the evil in irrational creatures, for if you should take away anger and lust and the other things which we speak of, and which are not absolutely evil in their own nature, the lion having lost his boldness and fierceness will not be a lion.... So the fact that nature is not destroyed is not an evil, but a destruction of nature, weakness and failure of the natural habitudes and energies and powers."

"And if all things through generation in time have their perfection, the imperfect is not altogether contrary to universal nature."

(*Divine Names*, IV, XXV.)

[2] "All things are very beautiful...."

"Nothing that exists is radically devoid of all beauty."

"Matter,...having had its beginning from the Essentially Beautiful, has throughout the whole range of matter some echoes of the intellectual comeliness."

(*Concerning the Celestial Hierarchy*, II. 3 and 4).

[3] "The Beautiful is the origin of all things, as a creating cause, both by moving the whole, and holding it together by the love of its own peculiar Beauty; and end of all things, and beloved, as final Cause (for all things exist for the sake of the Beautiful) and exemplary (Cause), because all things are determined according to it.... Yea, reason will dare to say even this, that even the non-existing participates in the Beautiful and Good." (*Divine Names*, IV. 7).

All this part of the chapter is a hymn to Beauty.

source of Being. It is the Divine Origin. The Areopagite puts it in the place of the Gaurishankar of the Divine Himalayas, at the zenith of the Attributes of God. It is the sun, but infinitely more powerful.[1] From it issues every thing else that is: light, intelligence, love, union, order, harmony, eternal life. Even Being, "the first of all the gifts of God", is the offspring of Goodness. It is the first born.[2]

This point of view is apparently very different from Hindu Mysticism, where the Absolute reigns supreme above good and evil. But it communicates to the Areopagite's whole thought a serenity, a tranquil and certain joy, without any of the tragic shades of a Vivekananda.[3]

But we must not deceive ourselves: the word Goodness in the mouth of Denis has little in common with Christian sentimentalism. Neither "Divine Peace", nor Divine Goodness, passes over in its scheme of things the mass of weakness, violence, and suffering in the universe: they all go to make up its symphony; and each dissonance, if it is in the right place, adds to the richness of the harmony. It does not even forbid the chastisement of error, if that error violates the laws inherent in human nature; for nature has endowed every man with liberty; "and it is not a function of Providence to destroy nature."[4] On the other hand it

---

[1] Ibid., the whole of Chapter IV.

[2] Ibid., V. 5 and 6. "Absolute and infinite goodness produces the being as its first good action."

[3] And I recall that even Ramakrishna, who lived in a continual state of bliss, loving Maya as a son, was not blind to the tragic face of the universe, and pointed out on occasions the stupidity of characterising God as good. He did not deny the apparent cruelty of nature but he forbade any judgment of the divine will directing it; and his piety bowed down before the inscrutable decrees of the infinite Force.

[4] "We will not admit the vain statement of the multitude that Providence ought to lead us to virtue even against our will. For

must "watch" that the integrity of each individual nature is maintained, and with it the integrity of the whole universe and of each of its parts. And that is what is meant by "universal salvation."[1]

It is clear that all these different terms: Providence, Salvation, Goodness and Peace, express no shallow optimism. Their conception arises from an uncompromising and disillusioned view of nature. They demand an intrepidity of heart and mind,[2] not far removed from the heroism of Vivekananda, but better able to maintain the unshakable serenity of a great soul that is one with the Sovereign Unity and wedded to its eternal designs.

The atmosphere in which Denis' ideas are steeped is less moral, in the ordinary sense, than cosmic, and its temperature is closer to that of Indian Mysticism than to simple Christian thought, which rallies round the Crucified nameless multitudes of the humble and oppressed. The energies are maintained by the impersonal command of nature's laws, which combine and unite the elements in all their multiplicity. But the order of the Areopagite has this advantage over the Indian, that it partakes of the harmony of Greek reason and the Roman genius of Imperial organisation. Denis, so

---

to destroy nature is not a function of Providence. Hence, as Providence is conservative of the nature of each, it provides for the free, as free; and for the whole and individual, according to the wants of all and each. . .distributed proportionately to each." (*Divine Names*, IV. 33).

Even Plotinus' conception of Liberty has traces of it; for he reproved stoic fatalism. Man is the master of his actions. "Liberty is included in the plan of the universe from all eternity." (*Ennéades*, III. 3. 7; 7. 255).

[1] "Divine justice is celebrated also even as preservation of the whole, as preserving and guarding the essence and order of each, distinct and pure from the rest." (*Divine Names*, VIII. 9).

[2] Ibid., VIII. 8.—Compare his quiet reply to those who were astonished and grumbled that "good people are abandoned without redress to the vexations of the wicked." It was one of two things,

we feel strongly, is obliged to satisfy the double exigences of the Hellenic mind, nourished on Eastern thought, and the evangelistic heart filled with the dream of the crucified Saviour. He has encircled the Christ with a rich halo of Alexandrine speculation, and as a result the fascination of the halo has in a measure eclipsed the Christ. The first who approached its circle of light, like John Scott Erigene, was blinded by it. He was the only man of his century to come into contact with it and to live in long and secret communion with this mysterious work; for he was almost the only living man of his age who understood the language in which it was written. He drank of the mystic draught, and from it he imbibed the secret, so dangerous to orthodoxy, of the freedom of the mind that is intoxicated by symbols, where the letter of the Christian faith is little by little drowned in the limitless and unfathomable ocean of the One. By way of Denis, Plotinus, Philo, the Infinite of Asia filtered through him into the religious soul of the West. The Church condemned him in vain during the thirteenth century. He flourished openly in the enchanted philtre of the great mystics of the fourteenth century, the most intoxicated of them, Meister Eckhart, being condemned by the Avignon Papacy.

That is why it is easy to understand the caution wherewith the Church today conceals even though it honours "the Pseudo-Denis"—"that old, equivocal, obscure, un-

he said, either that so-called good people set their affections upon worldly things, which were torn from them; and therefore they were "entirely cut off" from the quality they had usurped and from Divine Love. Or else they really loved eternal things and then they ought to rejoice in all the tribulations whereby they were made worthy to enjoy them.

I have already quoted his conception of Christ as the "chief of the athletes," leading his band into the lists "to fight for liberty." (*The Ecclesiastical Hierarchy*, II, 3rd part, 6). I have compared this passage to words of Vivekananda.

certain, and dangerous master", as he was called by the French historian best qualified to write of Western mysticism.[1] Nobody can deny that the judgment was correct from the orthodox point of view—although ten centuries of orthodoxy has been nourished upon Denis and were none the worse for it! But we, who do not trouble about orthodoxy, who are guided by the attraction of the great sources of intelligence and a common love of humanity, have rejoiced to discover and to show in the work of the Areopagite —(to use again Ramakrishna's ingenious parable)—one of the flights of steps leading to the reservoir with several ghats.[2] There from one of the ghats, Hindus fetch the water they call Brahman. And from another Christians draw the water they call Christ. But it is always the same water.

\*

To sum up: the following, in my opinion, are the three chief lessons that Hindu religious thought should be interested to learn, and to take from European mysticism:

1. The architectural sense of Christian metaphysicians. I have just described it in the work of Denis; and his sovereign art is to be found throughout the Middle Ages. The men who raised the cathedrals carried into the construction of the mind the same genius of intelligent order and harmonious balance that made them the master builders of the arches linking the Infinite to the finite.[3]

---

[1] Henri Brémond: *Histoire littéraire du sentiment religieux en France*— VII. *La Métaphysique des Saints*, Vol. I, p. 148.

[2] *Cf.* our *Life of Ramakrishna*, p. 79.

And in the West on the other side of the Atlantic Emerson's voice was an echo of Ramakrishna's: "All beings proceed from the same spirit, which bears different names, love, justice, or wisdom, in its different manifestations, just as the Ocean receives other names when it bathes other shores." (Lecture at Harvard, 1838).

[3] In this they differ from intellectual logicians who strive to

2. The psychological science of the Christian explorers of the "Dark Night" of the Infinite. In it they expended a genius, at least equal—(sometimes superior)—to that which has since been diverted into profane literature through the theatre and the novel. The psychology of the mystic masters of the sixteenth century in Spain and the seventeenth century in France foreshadowed that of the classical poets; and modern thinkers who imagine that they have discovered the Subconscious, have scarcely reached the same level. It goes without saying that their interpretations differ. But the essential point is not the interpretation, the name given by the mind to what it sees—but *what it sees*. The eyes of Western mysticism reached to the limits of the inaccessible.

3. The formidable energies that Western mysticism uses to achieve Divine Union, in particular the passionate violence of the European accustomed to battle and action. It devoured Ruysbroeck, so that his Bhakti (Love) sometimes took on the guise of the Seven Deadly Sins: "Implacable Desire", the fury of moral "combat", the "torrent of delights", the embrace of carnal possession,[1]

---

separate the mind into compartments. And the difference between St. Jean de la Croix and Calvin, who were almost contemporary, has often been remarked: the latter sacrificed the finite to the Infinite, the former established at the same time the difference and the connection between the two conceptions.

[1] See, in the magnificent French translation by Ernest Hello, (new edition, Perrin, 1912), extracts from *De ornatu spiritalium nuptiarum* ("concerning insatiable hunger," pp. 38-9;—"The combat" between the spirit of God and the soul, a description of unheard-of brutality and crudity, pp. 40-41;—or again "The Meeting on the Mountain", pp. 54-5; and "the Embrace", p. 71 *et seq.*) and from *De Septem Custodiis Libellus* (the description of "the tempest of love," p. 106). A French reader who had been forewarned, would have little difficulty in recognising in this burning torrent the reflected face of more than one illustrious Catholic poet, who borrowed from it, like Claudel.

and the colossal hunger of the Epicurean. Similarly the *"irascibilis"* of Eckhart whose soul being identical with God's, "cannot bear anything above it, even God Himself", and so seizes Him by force.[1]

In these three directions I believe that Indian Mysticism might find sources of enrichment.[2] And, I believe further that it is part of Vivekananda's own spirit to point it out to them. His great Advaitism was continually preoccupied in

---

[1] Eckhart's third proposition was condemned by a Papal Bull. It declared that "man with God has created the heaven and the earth" and that "God can do nothing without man." In a sermon he enumerated the three highest virtues, ascribing *"irascibilis"* to the second place under the definition of "violent upward aspiration." And he added that the lack of it was a sin: *Die Seele kann nicht ertragen, dass irgend etwas über ihr sei. Ich glaube, sie kann nicht einmal das ertragen, dass Gott über ihr sei.*" Thanks to this power, he says, "God is seized (*ergriffen*) by the soul."

[2] We do not claim as do so many Western thinkers—in particular M. Rudolf Otto, in his fine study of *Fichte and the Advaita* (published in *West-Oestliche Mystik*, 1926)—that the superiority of Western Mysticism is in *"Lebendige Tätigkeit,"* in its character of action coupled to divine contemplation. What is the Gita but a heroic exaltation of action?

"... It is not enough to abstain from action to free oneself from the act.... Activity is superior to inaction.... The former carries a man away, who controls his senses by the spirit, and fully detached, imposes on them disciplined effort.... There is not, O son of Prithâ, in the three worlds anything that I am bound to do, nothing in which I am lacking, nothing which I have to acquire, and nevertheless I dwell in action. The worlds would cease to exist, if I did not accomplish My work; I would be the cause of universal confusion and of the end of all creatures. The ignorant work through attachment to the act, while the wise also work, but without attachment and simply for the good of the worlds...." (Bhagavad-Gita, Chapter III)

These famous words which have for so many centuries nourished Indian thought, are still a breviary of action and inspiration to Gandhi and Aurobindo Ghose, as they were to Vivekananda. Aurobindo shows in the God of the Gita not only the God who is unveiled through the consciousness of the spirit, but the God who moves to action, to all our struggle and all our progress, the supreme Master of the work and sacrifice, the friend of the people who toil and struggle, or as Denis the Areopagite would say, "the chief of the athletes in the lists."— (*Cf. Essays on the Gita*, 2 vols., Calcutta.)

enlarging and completing his conceptions of Unity. He sought
to annex all the energies that other races and other religions
had used in the service of this heroic conquest. And his
faith in the "God-Man" was so disinterested that, in order
to serve it, he lowered his high Indian pride and his ardent
patriotism before any people, whoever they might be, if they
seemed to him to be striving more effectively for the common
cause. Without really realising the depths hidden in the
mystic soul of the West, he had an intuition that the East
might find abundant spiritual resources in the West,* and
that together they might realise complete Advaitism—that
is to say the religious Unity of the human family.[1] It

---

* But the Swami always held that in spiritual matters India is and
will be the teacher, and not the West.—*Publisher.*

[1] From a letter of Vivekananda to an Englishman, 9th August,
1895, recently published by *Prabuddha Bharata*, February, 1929, I extract
the following (freely condensed):

"I fully believe that there are periodic ferments of religion in
human society, and that such a period is now sweeping over the
educated world.... The religious ferment which at present is
every day gaining a greater hold over thinking men, has this characteristic that all the little thought-whirlpools into which it has broken
itself, declare one single aim—a vision and a search for the Unity
of Being.... In India, America, and England (the countries I
happen to know about) hundreds of these are struggling at the
present moment.... All these represent Advaita thought more or
less—the noblest philosophy of the unity man ever had.... Now,
if anything is clear to me, it is that one of these must survive,
swallowing up all the rest.... Which is it to be?... Only that
fragment which is fit will survive, and what makes fit to survive
but *character*?... One word more. Doubtless I do love India.
But every day my sight grows clearer. What is India, or England,
or America to us? We are the servants of that God who by the
ignorant is called MAN. He who pours water at the root, does he
not water the whole tree? There is but one basis of well-being,
social, political, or spiritual, to know that I and my brother are *one*.
This is true for all countries and all people. And Westerners, let
me say, will realise it more quickly than Orientals, who have almost
exhausted themselves in formulating the idea and producing a few
cases of individual realisation. Let us work without desire for name
or fame or rule over others...."

is then under his aegis that I present to India this short summary of Christian Advaitism from its Attic cradle in Alexandria. Over that cradle, as over the manger, the Star of the East rested.

*April, 1929.*

# THE COMPLETE WORKS OF
# SWAMI VIVEKANANDA

*In Eight Volumes with Indices*
*(About 530 pages each, Demy 8vo)*

In these volumes we have what is not only a gospel to the world at large, but also to its own children the Charter of the Hindu faith. For the first time in history Hinduism itself forms the subject of generalisation of a Hindu mind of the highest order.

As Sister Nivedita says, "The truths he preaches would have been as true, had he never been born. Nay more, they would have been equally authentic. The difference would have lain in their difficulty of access, in their want of modern clearness and incisiveness of statement, and in their loss of mutual coherence and unity. Had he not lived, texts that today will carry the bread of life to thousands might have remained the obscure disputes of scholars. He taught with authority and not as one of the Pandits. For he himself had plunged to the depths of the realisation which he preached, and he came back, like Ramanuja, only to tell its secrets to the pariah, the outcast, and the foreigner."

PRICE: EACH VOLUME { Board bound Rs. 6.50
Cloth bound Rs. 8.00

ADVAITA ASHRAMA
5 Dehi Entally Road
Calcutta 14

# REMINISCENCES

## OF

# SWAMI VIVEKANANDA

### ( Second Enlarged Edition )

This book presents together for the first time the memoirs of thirty admirers, including disciples of Swami Vivekananda. The articles were previously published in *Prabuddha Bharata* and *Vedanta Kesari*, monthlies of the Ramakrishna order.

Written mostly by persons who were intimately associated with Swamiji, they clearly reveal the intensity of a spiritual life wedded to universal uplift. The impress which his life and character had on those who were about him is discussed from various angles by people who represented different walks of life.

*Excellent get-up*

**Demy 8vo.**          **Pages 440**          **Price: Rs. 7.50**

## ADVAITA ASHRAMA
5 DEHI ENTALLY ROAD
CALCUTTA 14